Hollow Fields

and the Perfect Cog

MADELEINE ROSCA

STORY & ART

SEVEN SEAS ENTERTAINMENT PRESENTS

Hollow Fields
and the Perfect Cog

story and art by **Madeleine Rosca**

TONING
Ludwig Sacramento

LETTERING
Nicky Lim

LAYOUT
Karis Page

PROOFREADER
Shanti Whitesides

PRODUCTION MANAGER
Lissa Pattillo

EDITOR-IN-CHIEF
Adam Arnold

PUBLISHER
Jason DeAngelis

Seven Seas books may be purchased in bulk for educational, business, or promotional use. For information on bulk purchases, please contact Macmillan Corporate & Premium Sales Department at 1-800-221-7945 (ext 5442) or write specialmarkets@macmillan.com.

ISBN: 978-1-626921-02-3

Printed in Canada

First Printing: March 2016

10 9 8 7 6 5 4 3 2 1

FOLLOW US ONLINE: ***www.gomanga.com***

READING DIRECTIONS

This book reads from ***right to left***, Japanese style. If this is your first time reading manga, you start reading from the top right panel on each page and take it from there. If you get lost, just follow the numbered diagram here. It may seem backwards at first, but you'll get the hang of it! Have fun!!

1
2
3
4
5
6
7
8
9

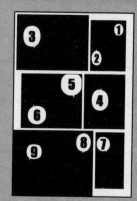

CHAPTER ONE
Back to School, Miss Snow

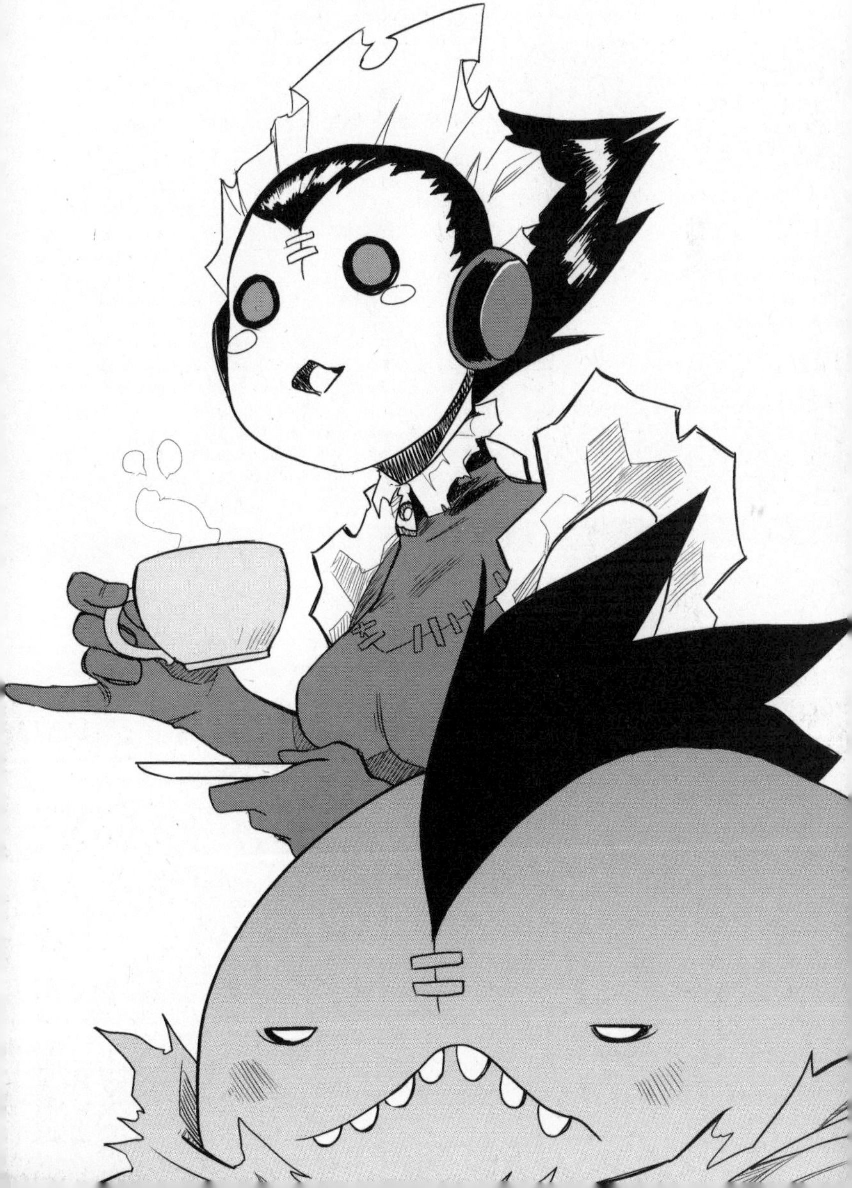

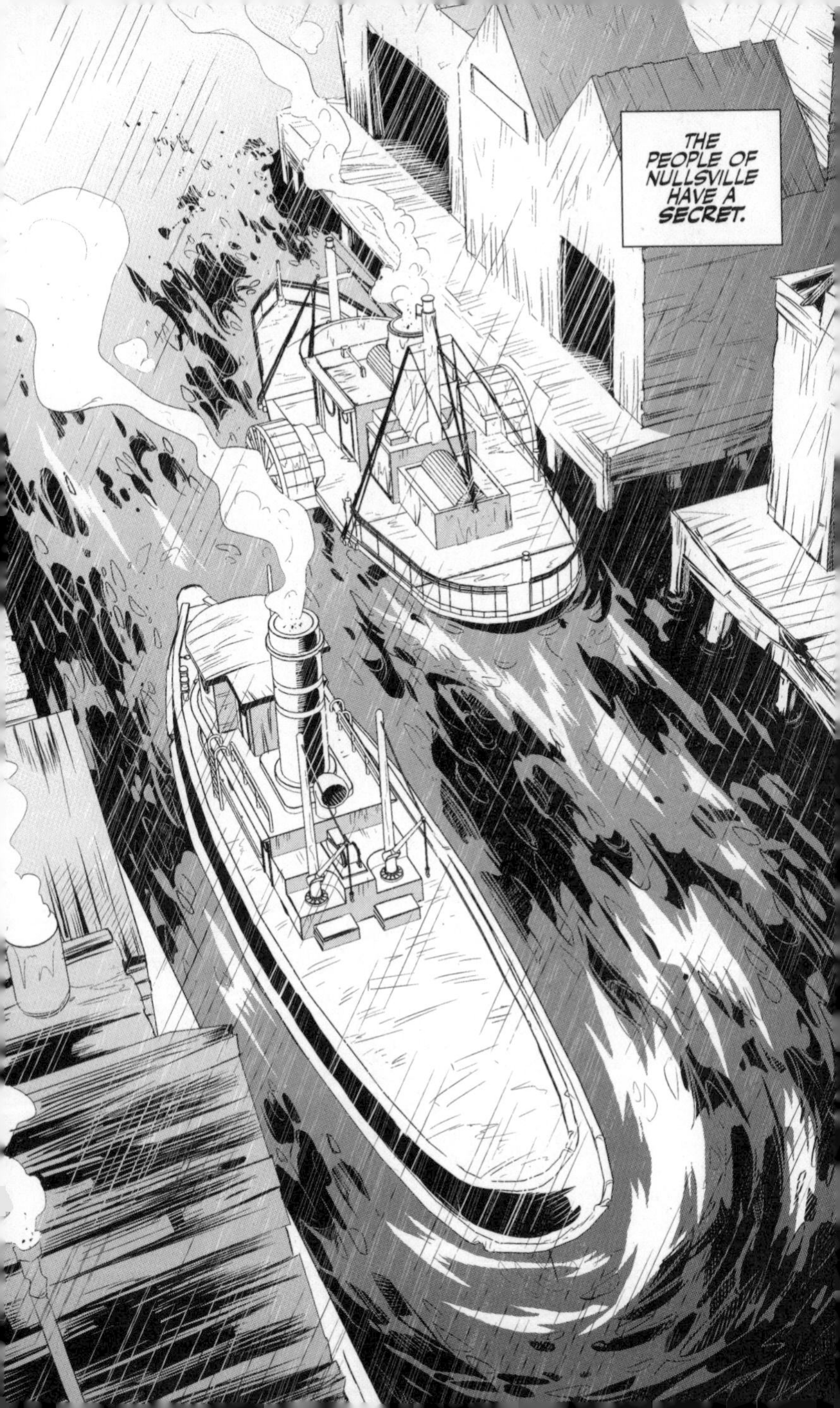
THE PEOPLE OF NULLSVILLE HAVE A SECRET.

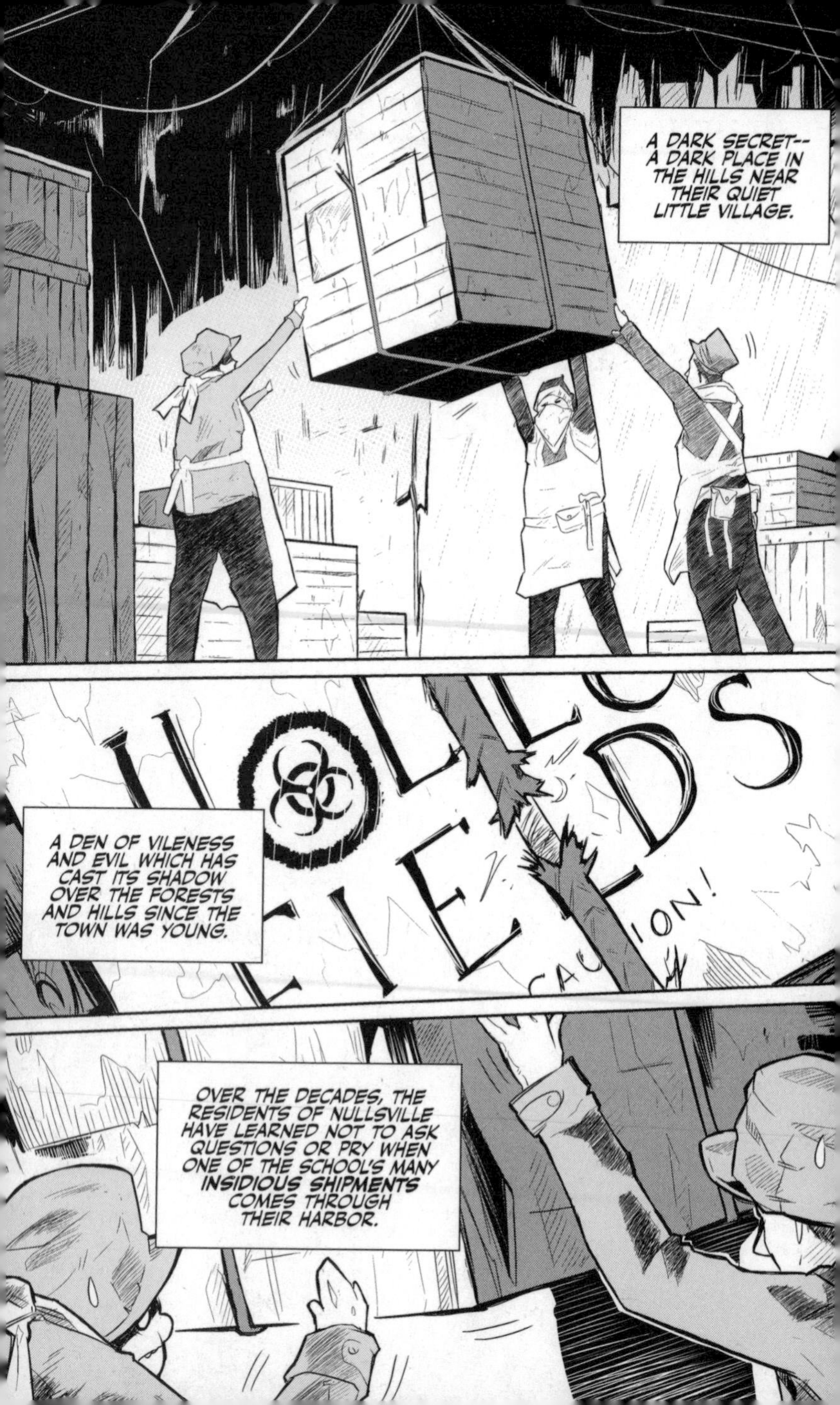
A DARK SECRET--
A DARK PLACE IN THE HILLS NEAR THEIR QUIET LITTLE VILLAGE.
A DEN OF VILENESS AND EVIL WHICH HAS CAST ITS SHADOW OVER THE FORESTS AND HILLS SINCE THE TOWN WAS YOUNG.
OVER THE DECADES, THE RESIDENTS OF NULLSVILLE HAVE LEARNED NOT TO ASK QUESTIONS OR PRY WHEN ONE OF THE SCHOOL'S MANY **INSIDIOUS SHIPMENTS** COMES THROUGH THEIR HARBOR.

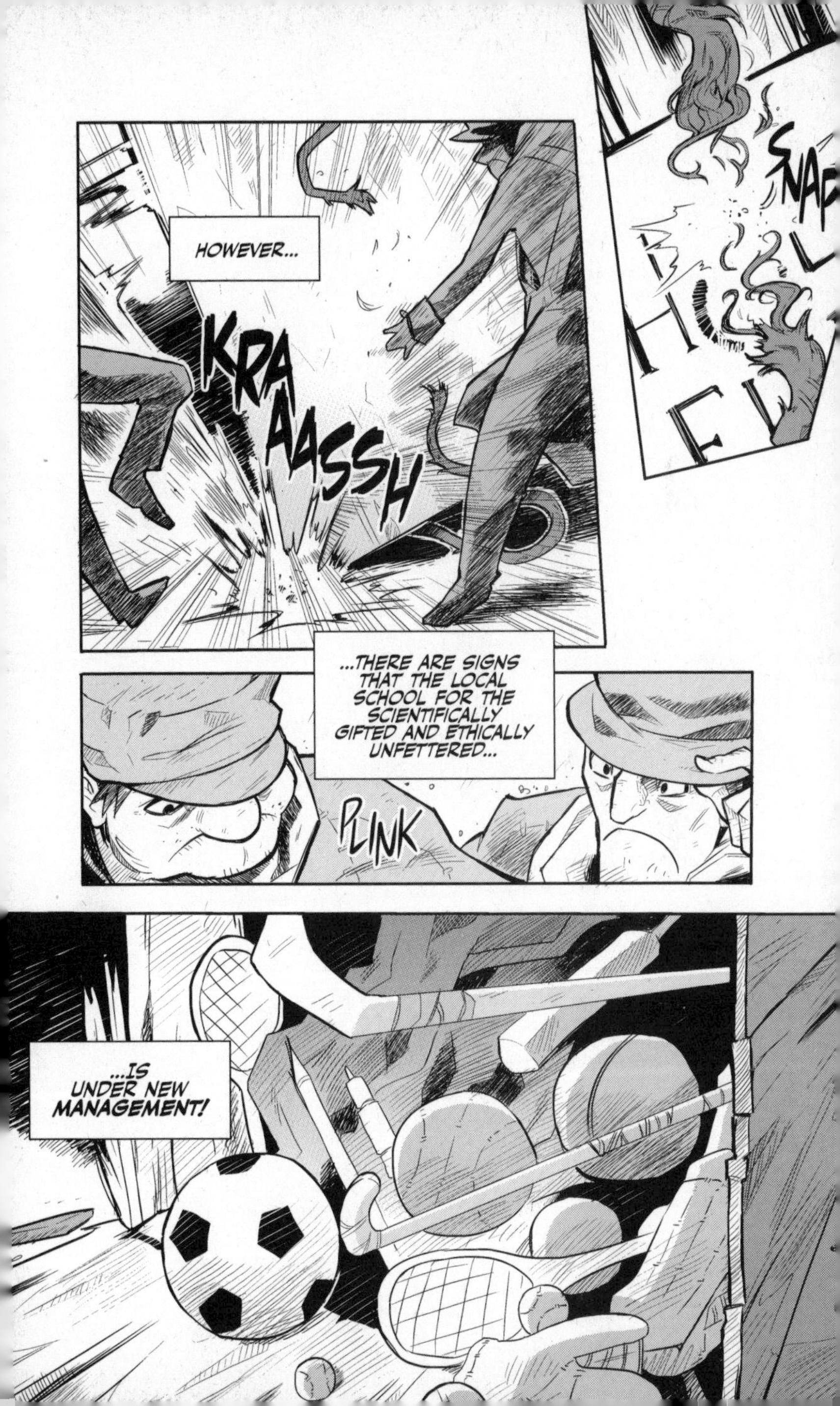
SNAP
HOWEVER...
KRAAASSH
...THERE ARE SIGNS THAT THE LOCAL SCHOOL FOR THE SCIENTIFICALLY GIFTED AND ETHICALLY UNFETTERED...
PLINK
...IS UNDER NEW MANAGEMENT!

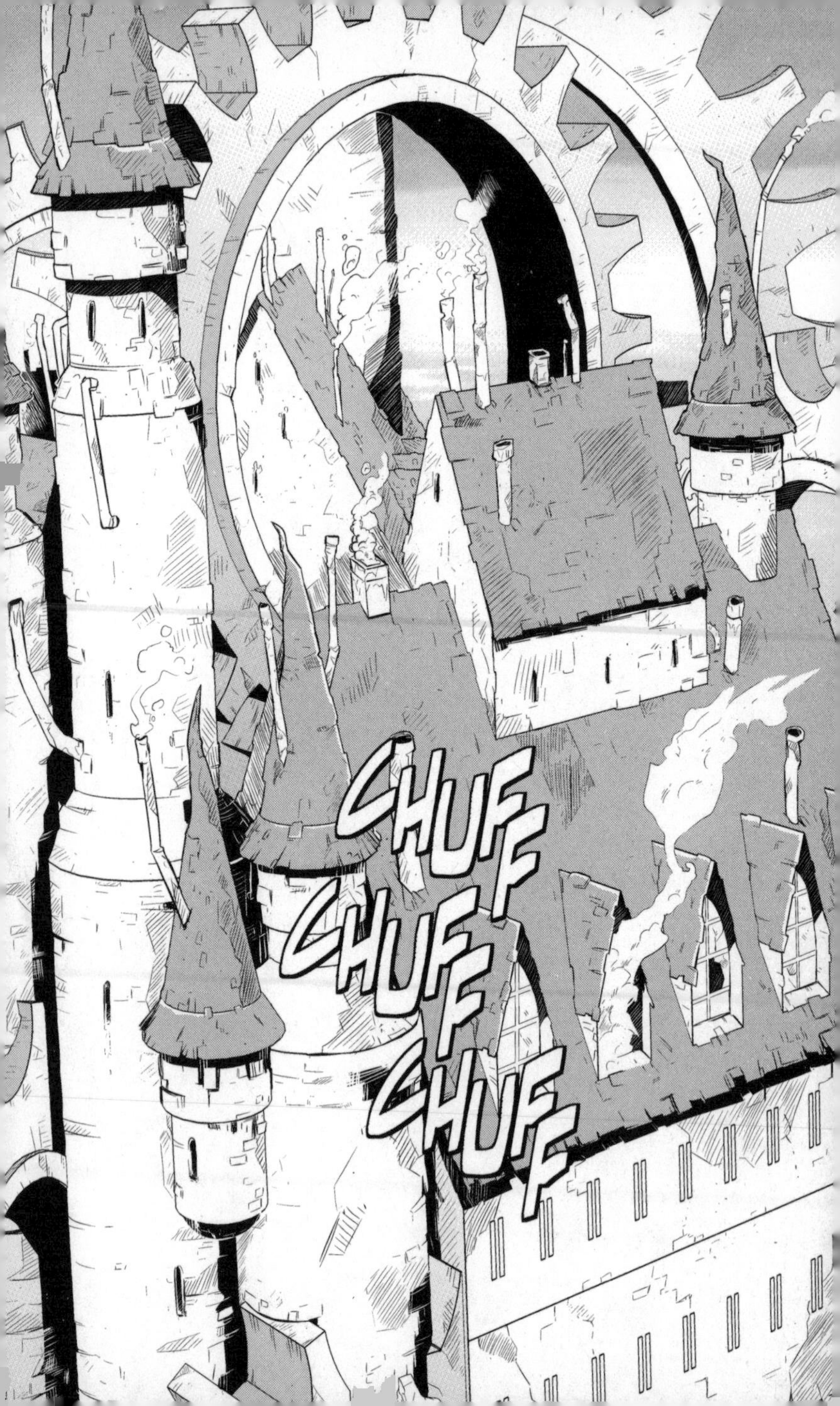
CHUFF
CHUFF
CHUFF

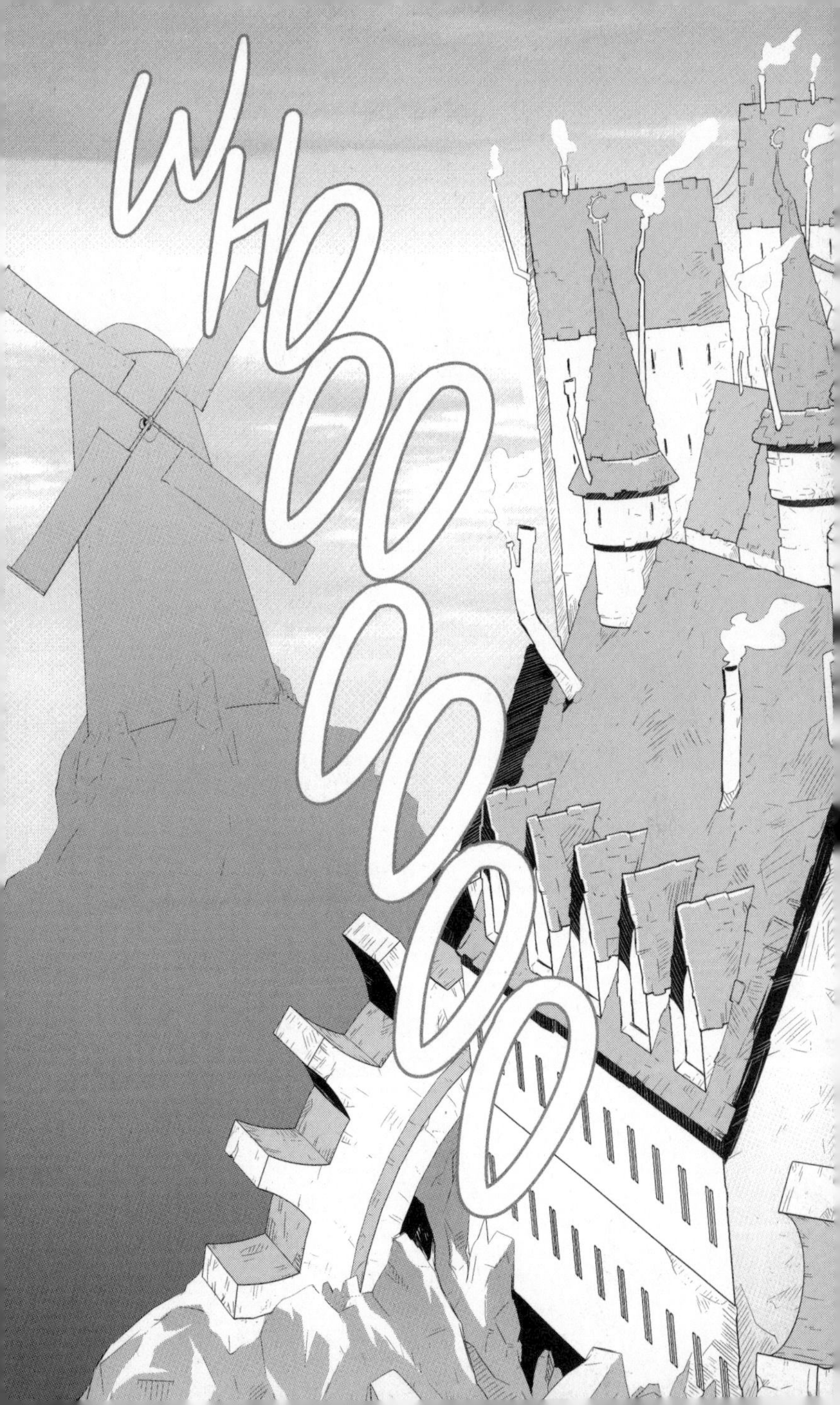
WHOOOOOOOO

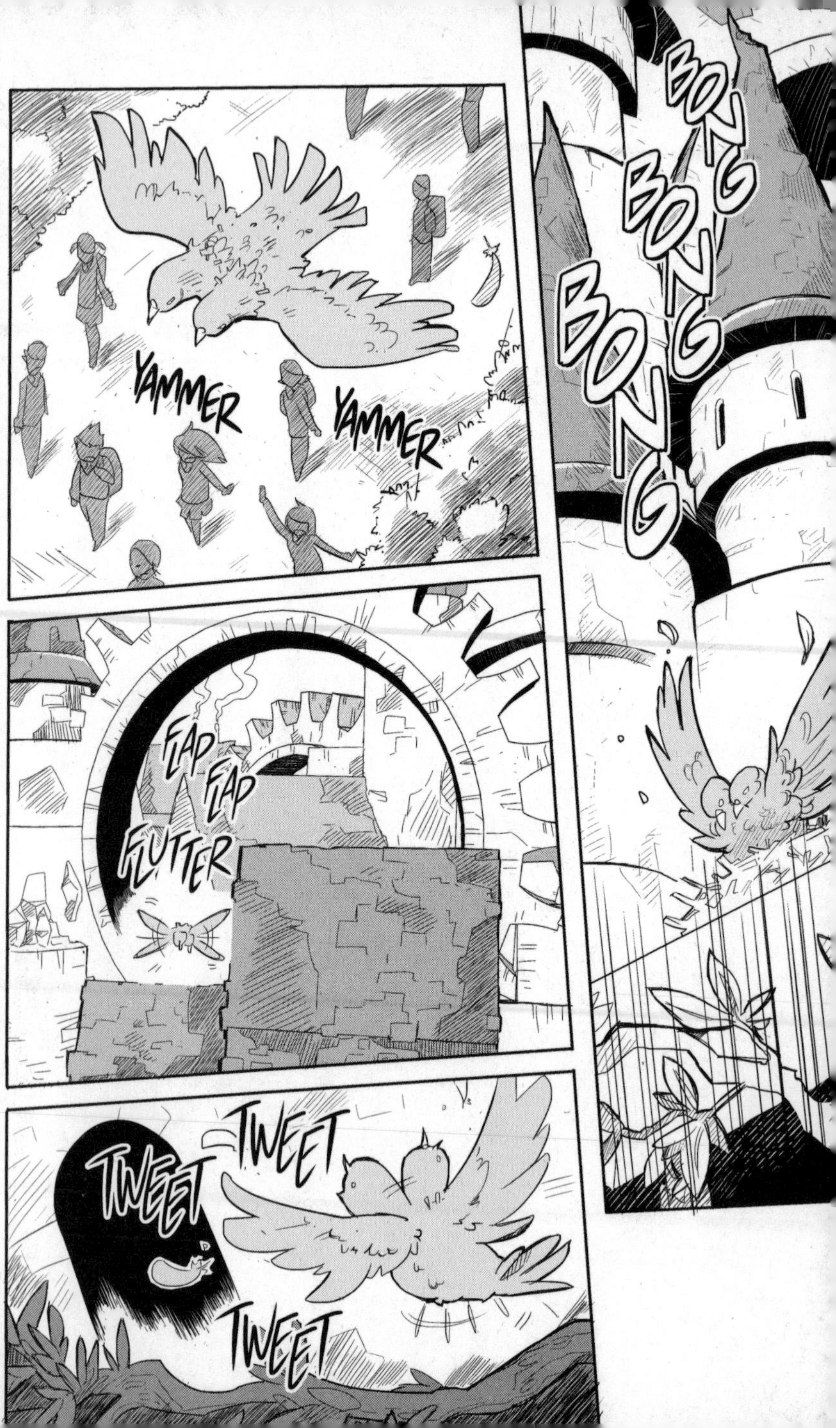
BONG
BONG
BONG
YAMMER
YAMMER
FLAP
FLAP
FLUTTER
TWEET
TWEET
TWEET

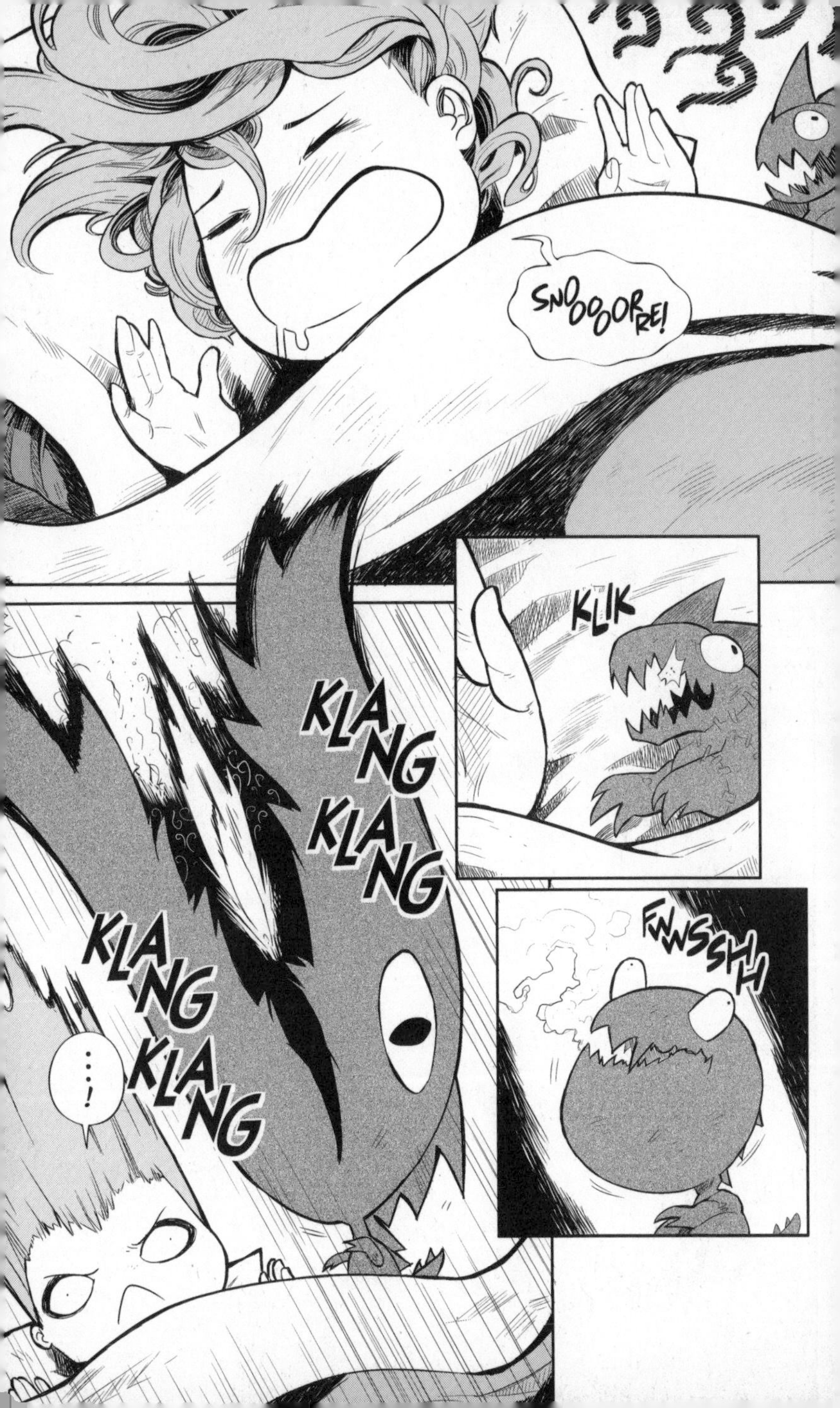
SNOOOOORRE!
KLIK
FWWSSHH
KLANG KLANG
KLANG KLANG
...!

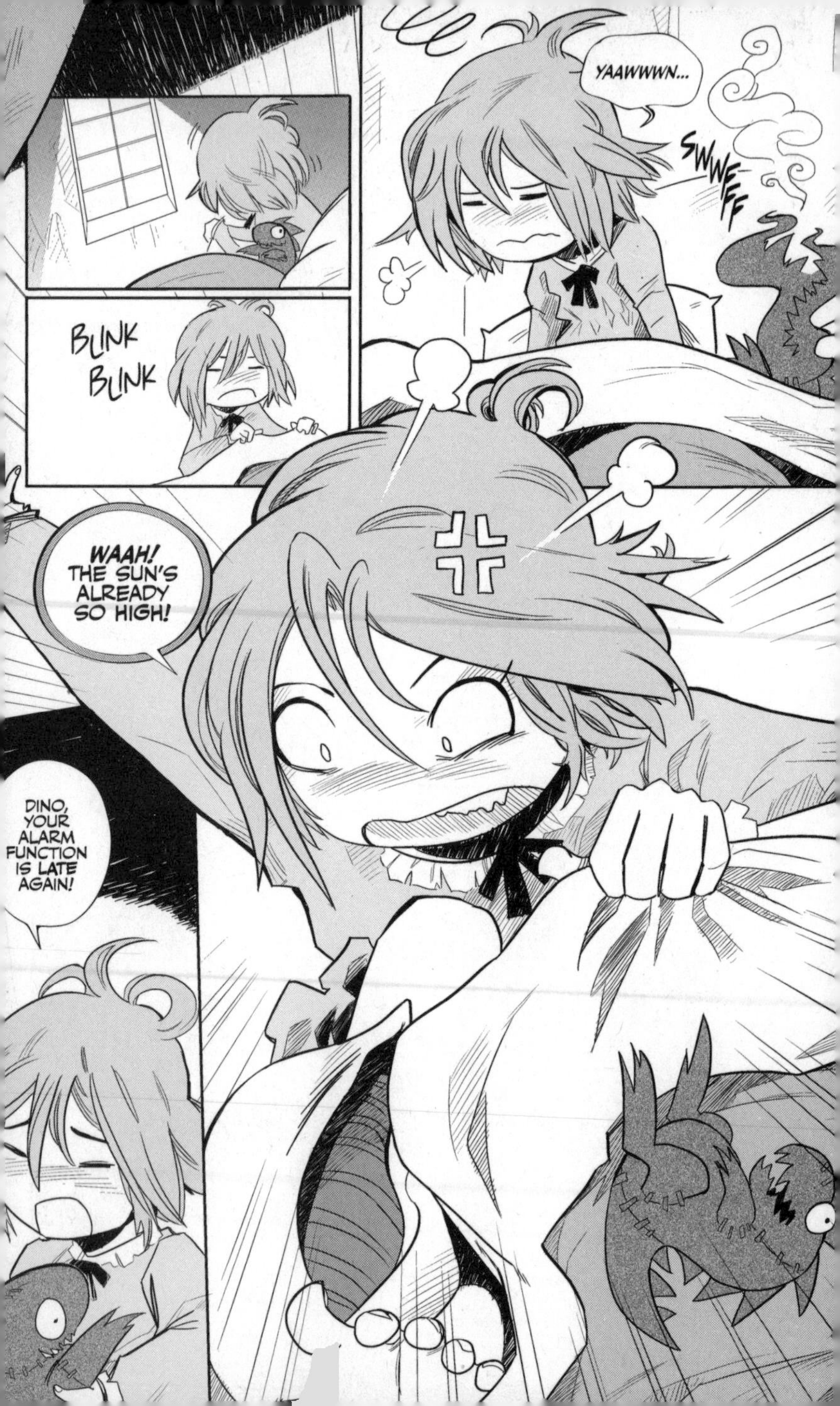
YAAWWWN...
SWNEFF
BLINK BLINK
WAAH! THE SUN'S ALREADY SO HIGH!
DINO, YOUR ALARM FUNCTION IS LATE AGAIN!

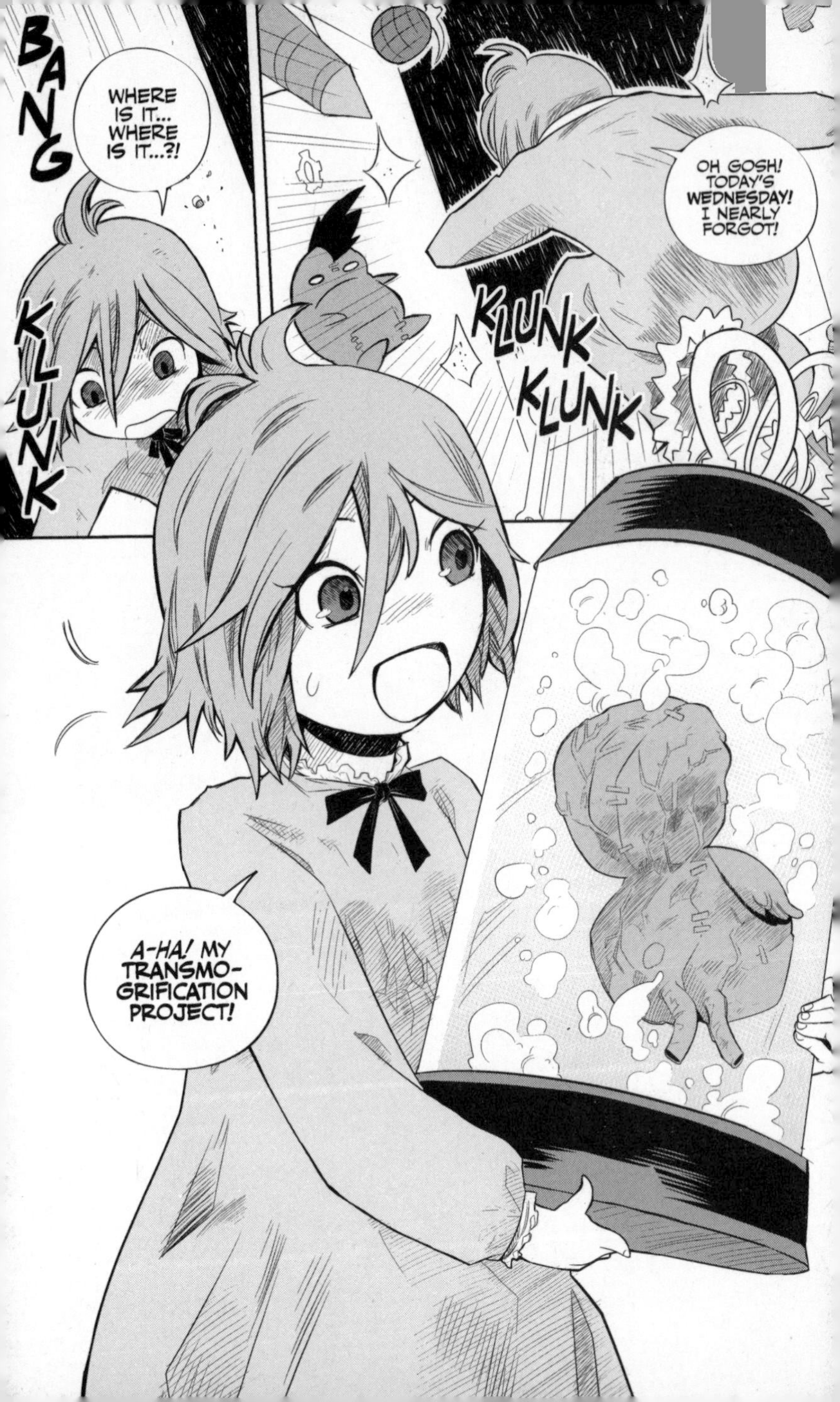
OH GOSH! TODAY'S WEDNESDAY! I NEARLY FORGOT!
KLUNK KLUNK
BANG
WHERE IS IT... WHERE IS IT...?!
KLUNK
A-HA! MY TRANSMO-GRIFICATION PROJECT!

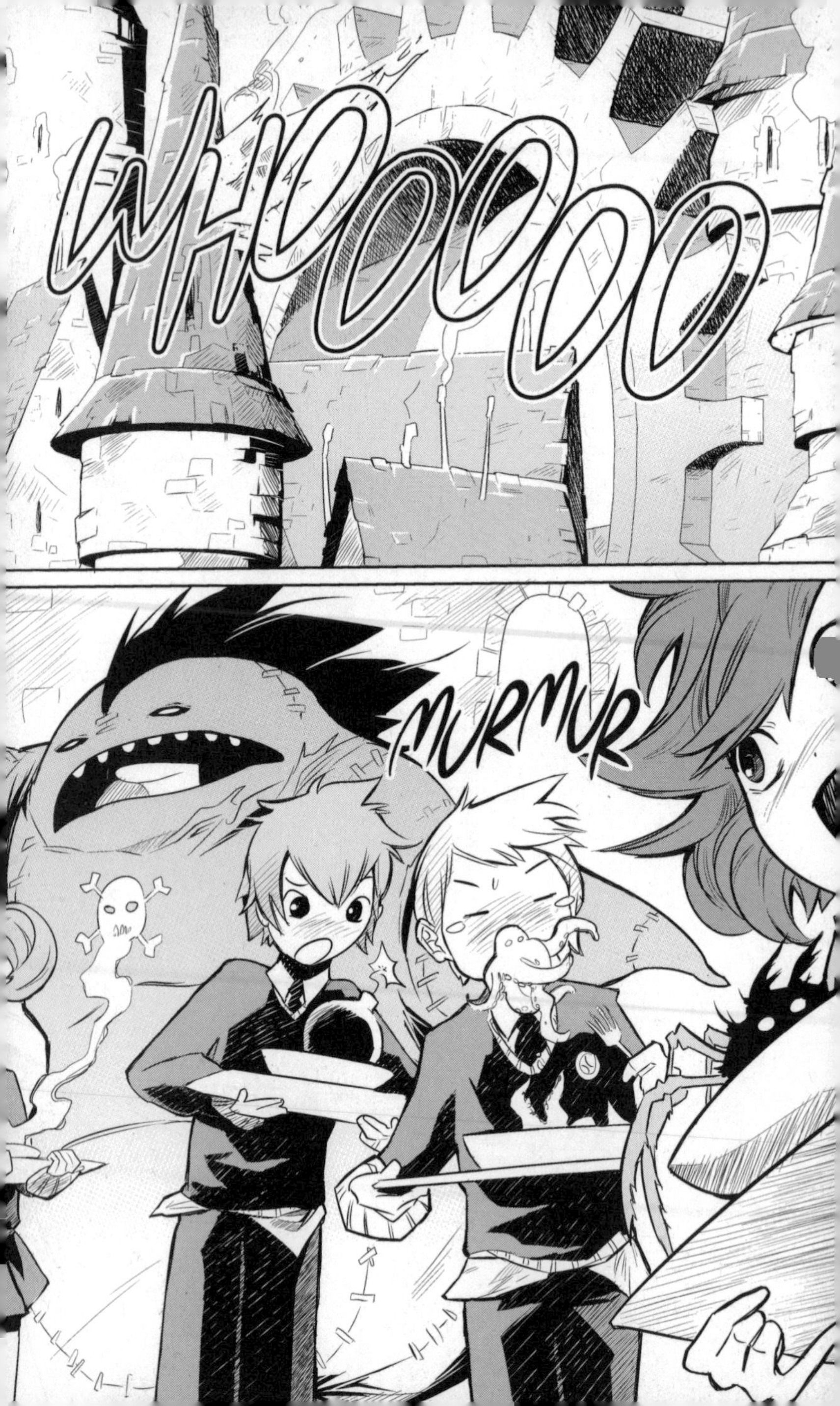
WHOOOOOO
MURMUR

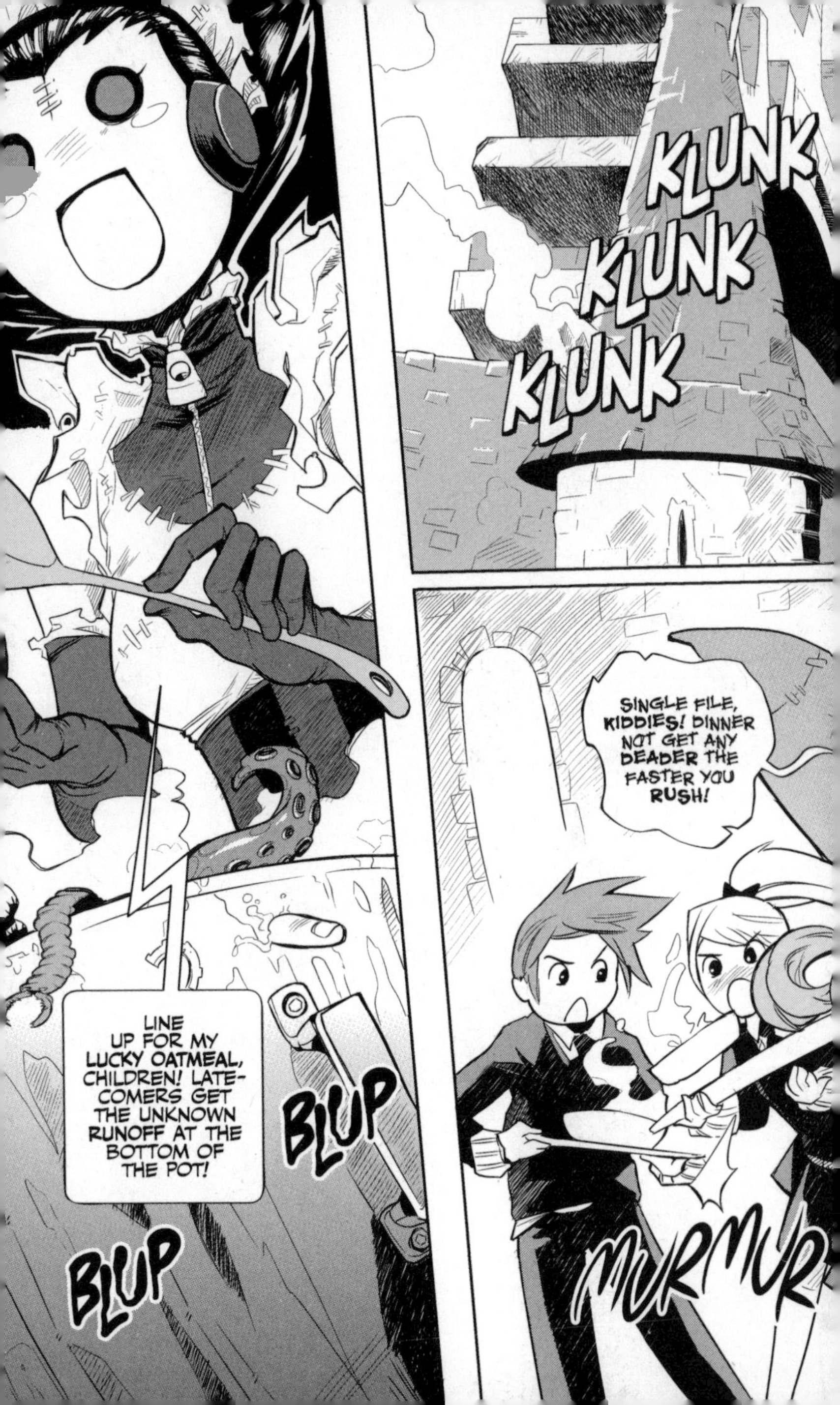
KLUNK
KLUNK
KLUNK
SINGLE FILE, KIDDIES! DINNER NOT GET ANY DEADER THE FASTER YOU RUSH!
MURMUR
LINE UP FOR MY LUCKY OATMEAL, CHILDREN! LATE-COMERS GET THE UNKNOWN RUNOFF AT THE BOTTOM OF THE POT!
BLUP
BLUP

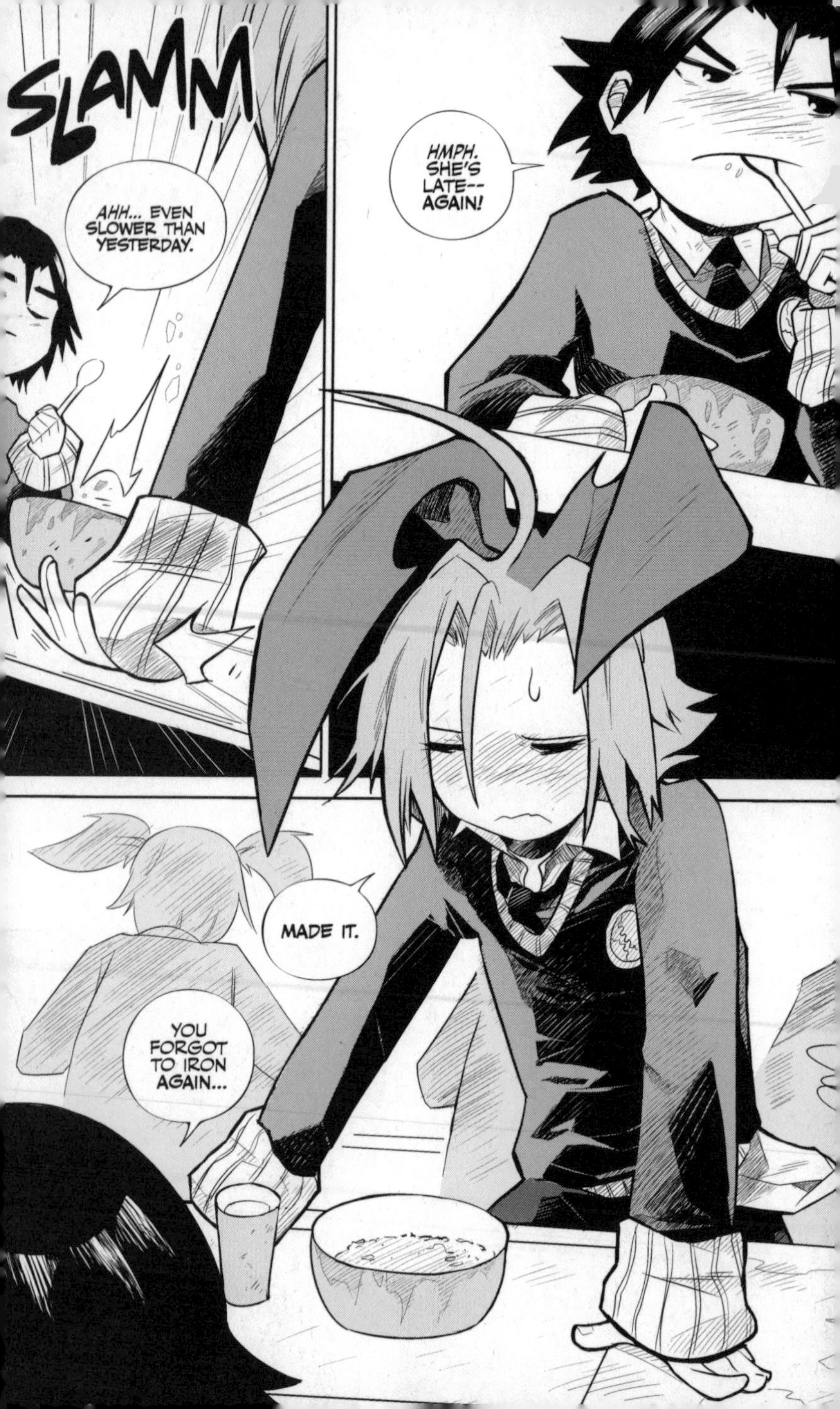
HMPH. SHE'S LATE-- AGAIN!
SLAMM
AHH... EVEN SLOWER THAN YESTERDAY.
MADE IT.
YOU FORGOT TO IRON AGAIN...

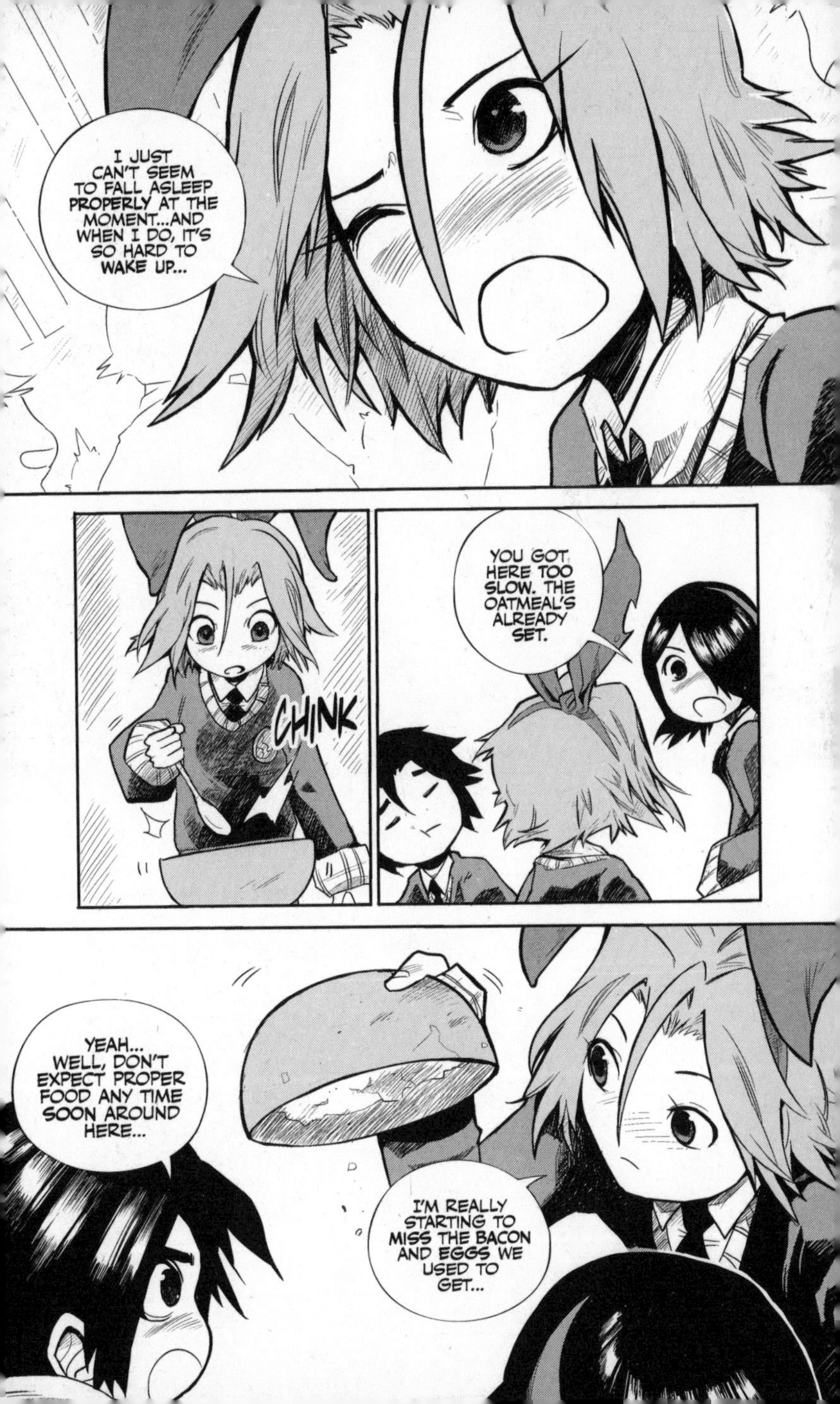
I JUST CAN'T SEEM TO FALL ASLEEP PROPERLY AT THE MOMENT...AND WHEN I DO, IT'S SO HARD TO WAKE UP...
YOU GOT HERE TOO SLOW. THE OATMEAL'S ALREADY SET.
CHINK
I'M REALLY STARTING TO MISS THE BACON AND EGGS WE USED TO GET...
YEAH... WELL, DON'T EXPECT PROPER FOOD ANY TIME SOON AROUND HERE...

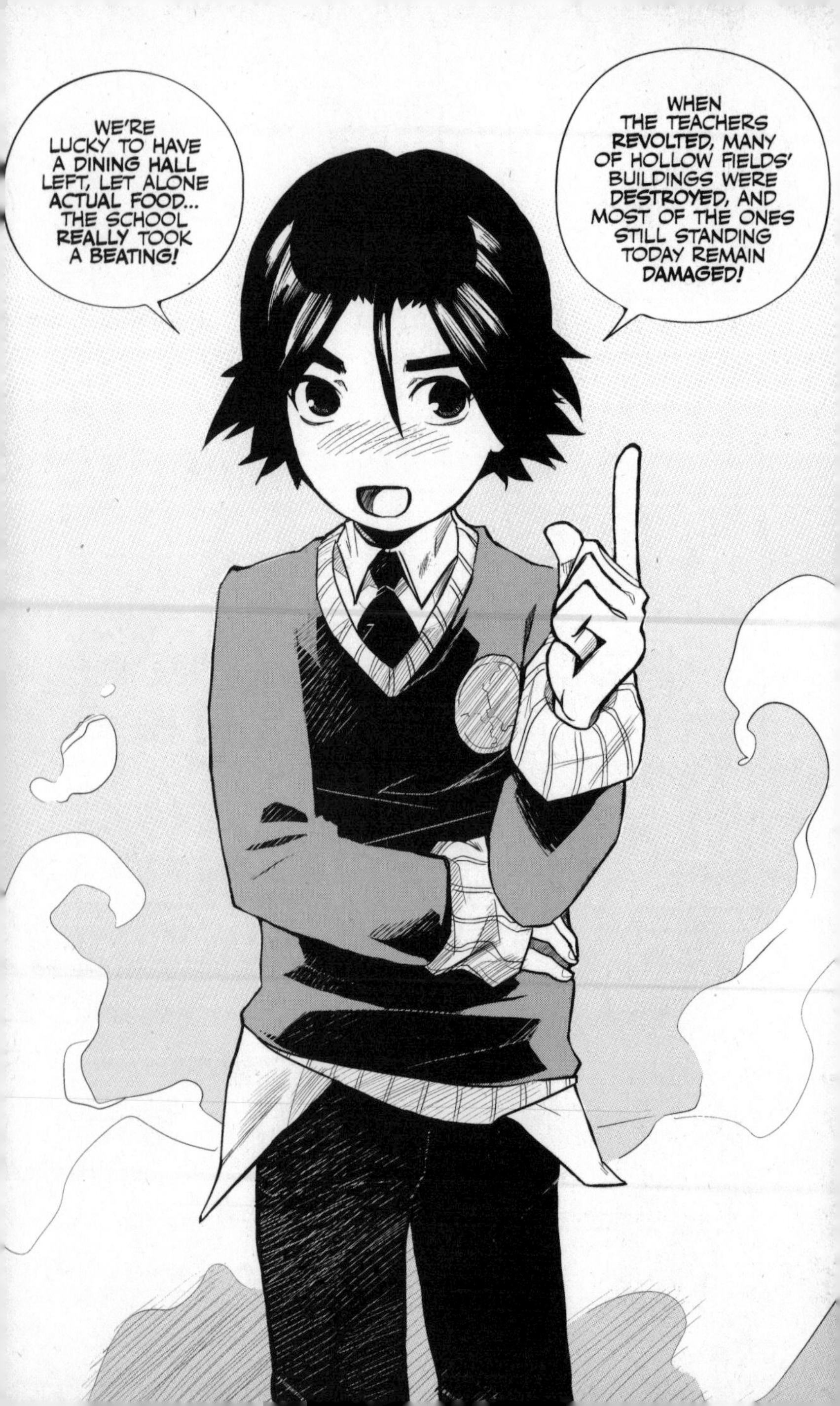
WHEN THE TEACHERS REVOLTED, MANY OF HOLLOW FIELDS' BUILDINGS WERE DESTROYED, AND MOST OF THE ONES STILL STANDING TODAY REMAIN DAMAGED!
WE'RE LUCKY TO HAVE A DINING HALL LEFT, LET ALONE ACTUAL FOOD... THE SCHOOL REALLY TOOK A BEATING!

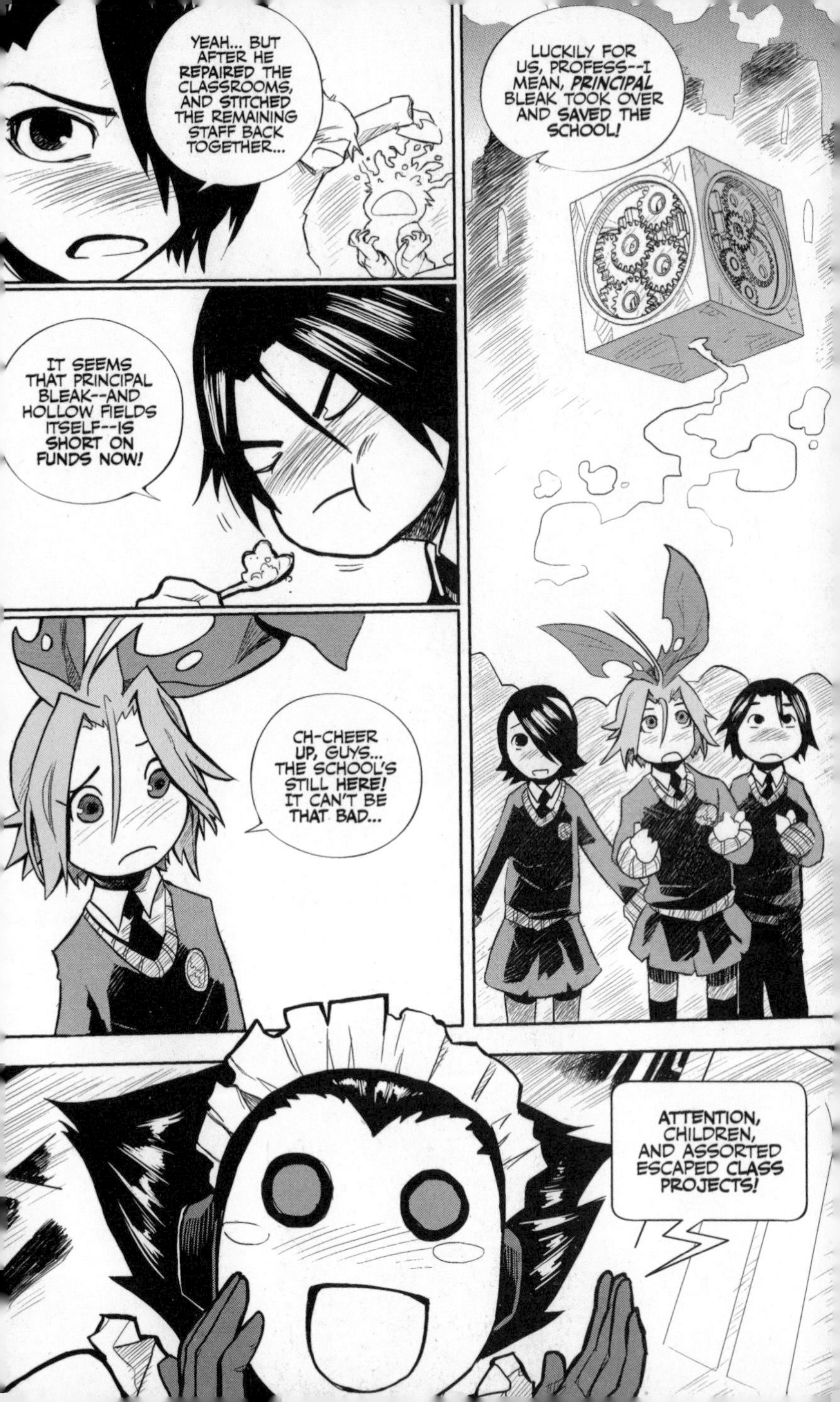
LUCKILY FOR US, PROFESS--I MEAN, *PRINCIPAL* BLEAK TOOK OVER AND SAVED THE SCHOOL!
YEAH... BUT AFTER HE REPAIRED THE CLASSROOMS, AND STITCHED THE REMAINING STAFF BACK TOGETHER...
IT SEEMS THAT PRINCIPAL BLEAK--AND HOLLOW FIELDS ITSELF--IS SHORT ON FUNDS NOW!
CH-CHEER UP, GUYS... THE SCHOOL'S STILL HERE! IT CAN'T BE THAT BAD...
ATTENTION, CHILDREN, AND ASSORTED ESCAPED CLASS PROJECTS!

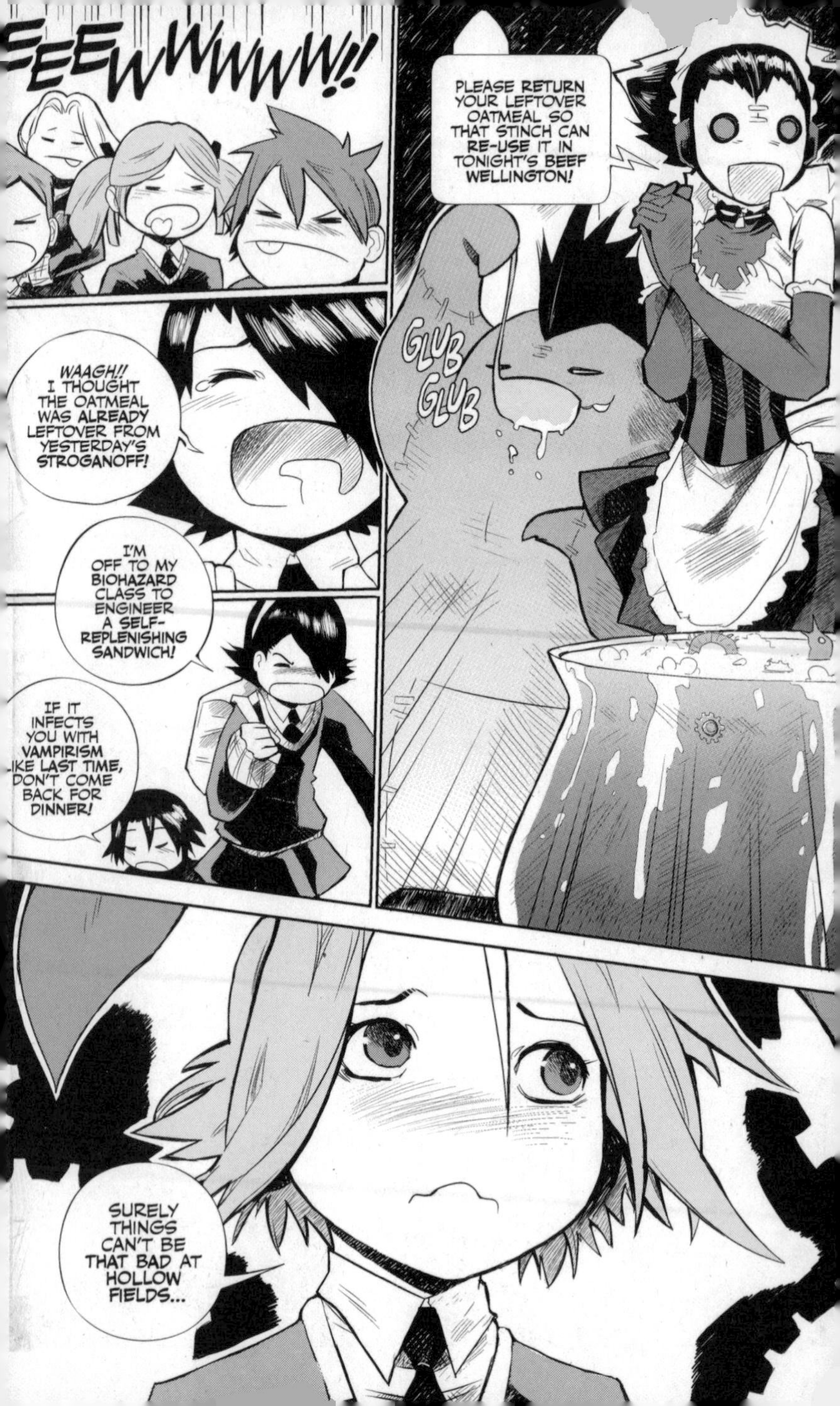
PLEASE RETURN YOUR LEFTOVER OATMEAL SO THAT STINCH CAN RE-USE IT IN TONIGHT'S BEEF WELLINGTON!
GLUB GLUB
EEEWWWWW!!
WAAGH!! I THOUGHT THE OATMEAL WAS ALREADY LEFTOVER FROM YESTERDAY'S STROGANOFF!
I'M OFF TO MY BIOHAZARD CLASS TO ENGINEER A SELF-REPLENISHING SANDWICH!
IF IT INFECTS YOU WITH VAMPIRISM LIKE LAST TIME, DON'T COME BACK FOR DINNER!
SURELY THINGS CAN'T BE THAT BAD AT HOLLOW FIELDS...

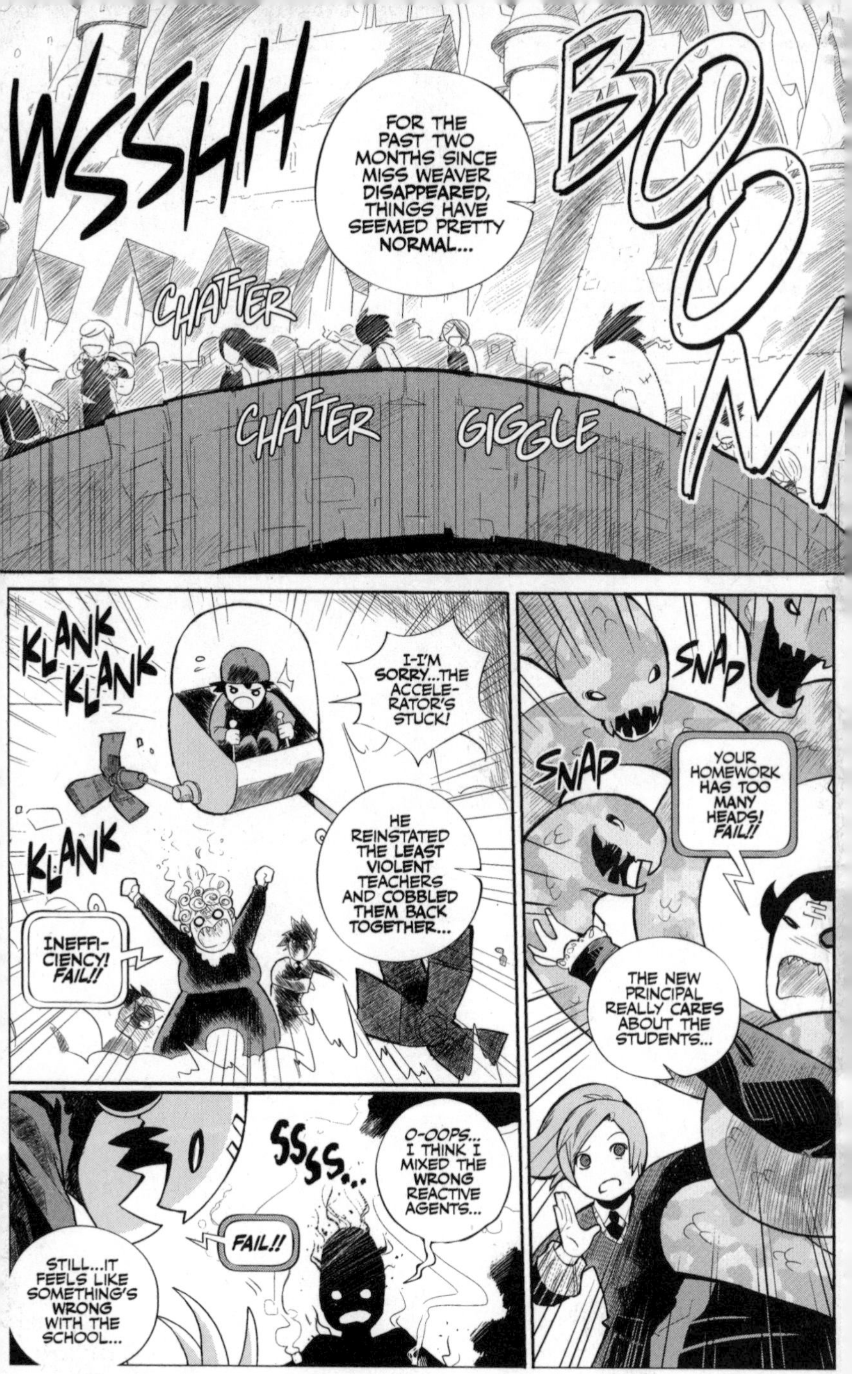
BOOM
FOR THE PAST TWO MONTHS SINCE MISS WEAVER DISAPPEARED, THINGS HAVE SEEMED PRETTY NORMAL...
WSSHH
CHATTER
GIGGLE
CHATTER
SNAP
SNAP
YOUR HOMEWORK HAS TOO MANY HEADS! FAIL!!
THE NEW PRINCIPAL REALLY CARES ABOUT THE STUDENTS...
I-I'M SORRY...THE ACCELE-RATOR'S STUCK!
KLANK KLANK
HE REINSTATED THE LEAST VIOLENT TEACHERS AND COBBLED THEM BACK TOGETHER...
KLANK
INEFFI-CIENCY! FAIL!!
O-OOPS... I THINK I MIXED THE WRONG REACTIVE AGENTS...
SSSS...
FAIL!!
STILL...IT FEELS LIKE SOMETHING'S WRONG WITH THE SCHOOL...

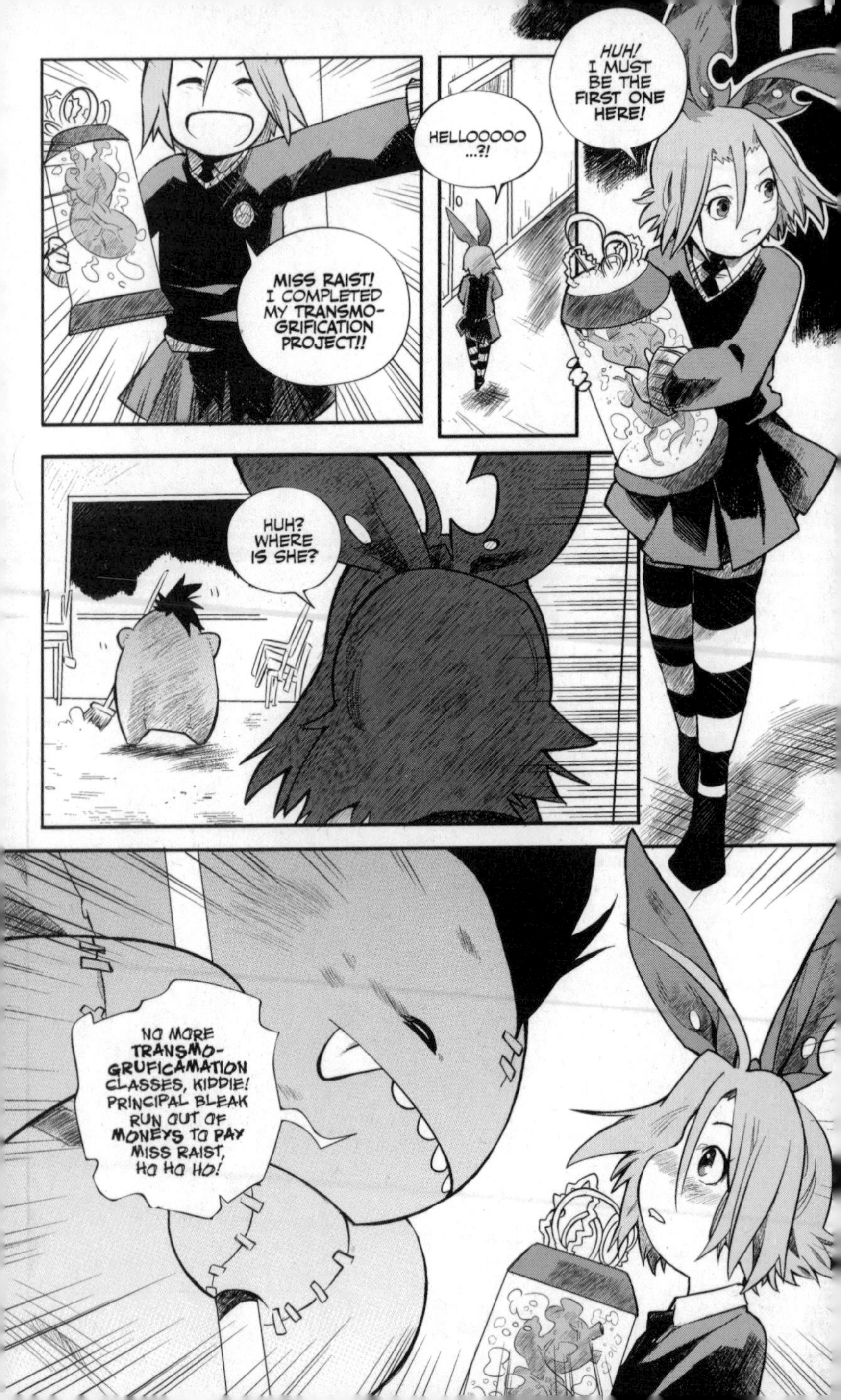
HUH! I MUST BE THE FIRST ONE HERE!
HELLOOOOO ...?!
MISS RAIST! I COMPLETED MY TRANSMO-GRIFICATION PROJECT!!
HUH? WHERE IS SHE?
NO MORE TRANSMO-GRUFICAMATION CLASSES, KIDDIE! PRINCIPAL BLEAK RUN OUT OF MONEYS TO PAY MISS RAIST, HO HO HO!

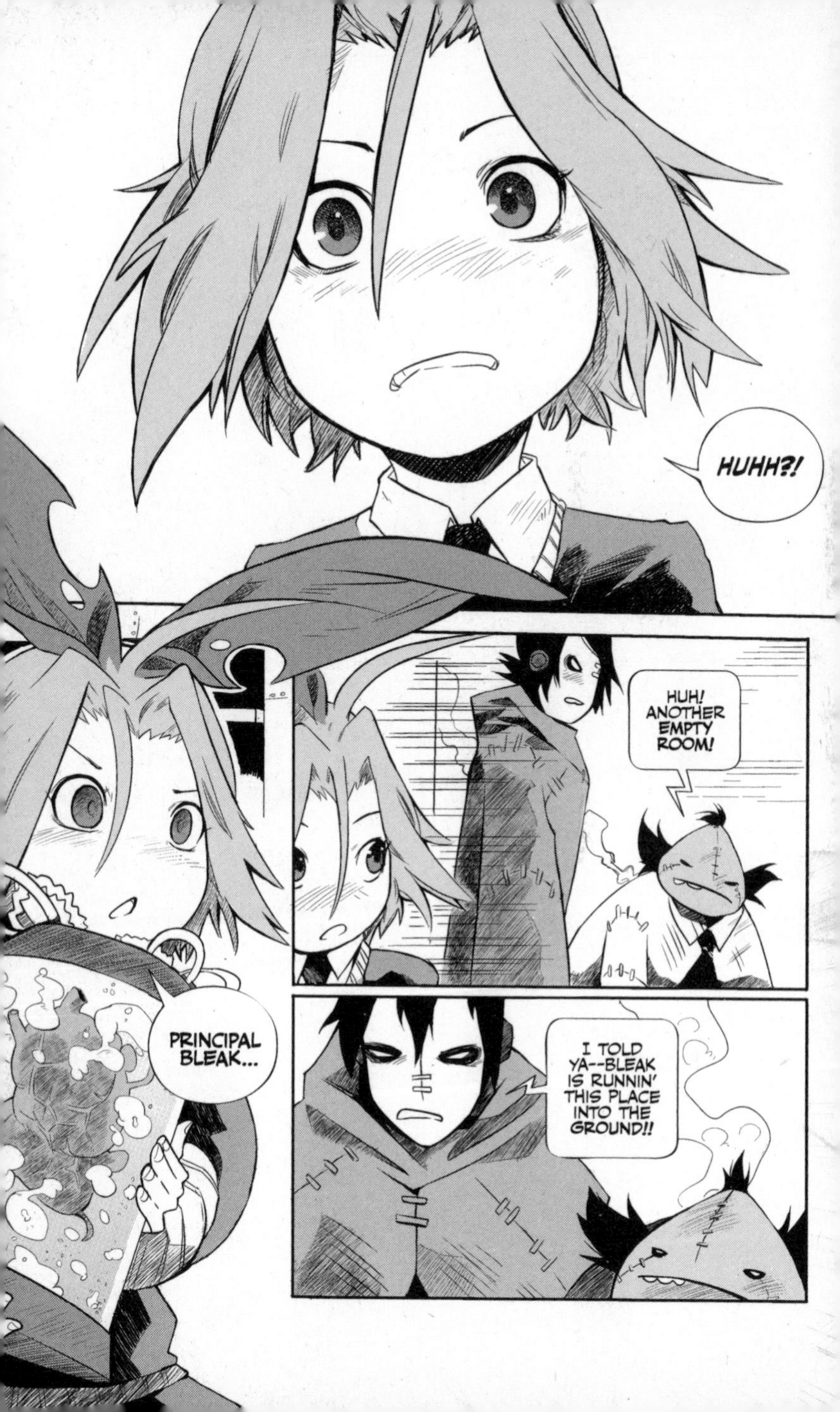
HUHH?!
HUH! ANOTHER EMPTY ROOM!
I TOLD YA--BLEAK IS RUNNIN' THIS PLACE INTO THE GROUND!!
PRINCIPAL BLEAK...

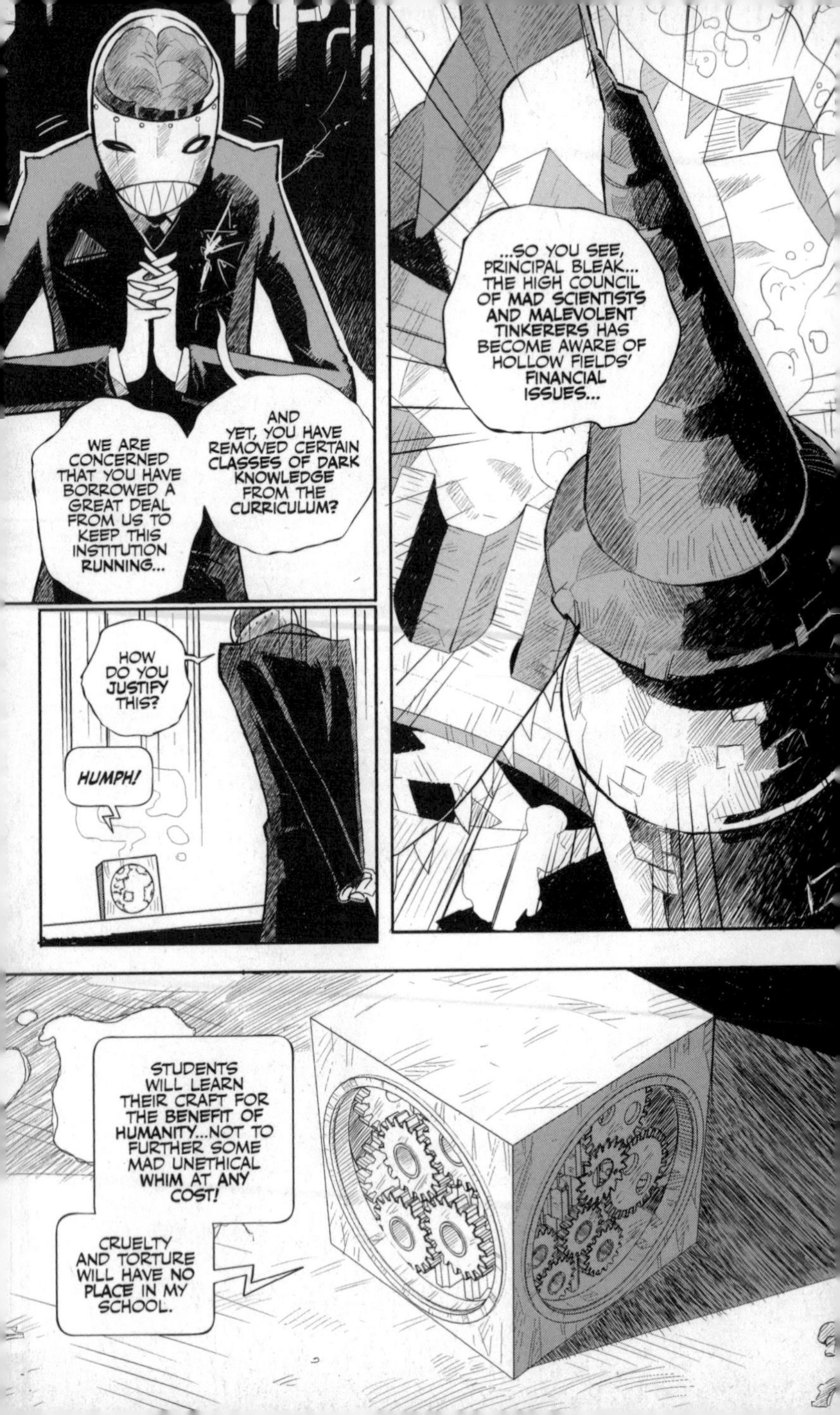
...SO YOU SEE, PRINCIPAL BLEAK... THE HIGH COUNCIL OF MAD SCIENTISTS AND MALEVOLENT TINKERERS HAS BECOME AWARE OF HOLLOW FIELDS' FINANCIAL ISSUES...
WE ARE CONCERNED THAT YOU HAVE BORROWED A GREAT DEAL FROM US TO KEEP THIS INSTITUTION RUNNING...
AND YET, YOU HAVE REMOVED CERTAIN CLASSES OF DARK KNOWLEDGE FROM THE CURRICULUM?
HOW DO YOU JUSTIFY THIS?
HUMPH!
STUDENTS WILL LEARN THEIR CRAFT FOR THE BENEFIT OF HUMANITY...NOT TO FURTHER SOME MAD UNETHICAL WHIM AT ANY COST!
CRUELTY AND TORTURE WILL HAVE NO PLACE IN MY SCHOOL.

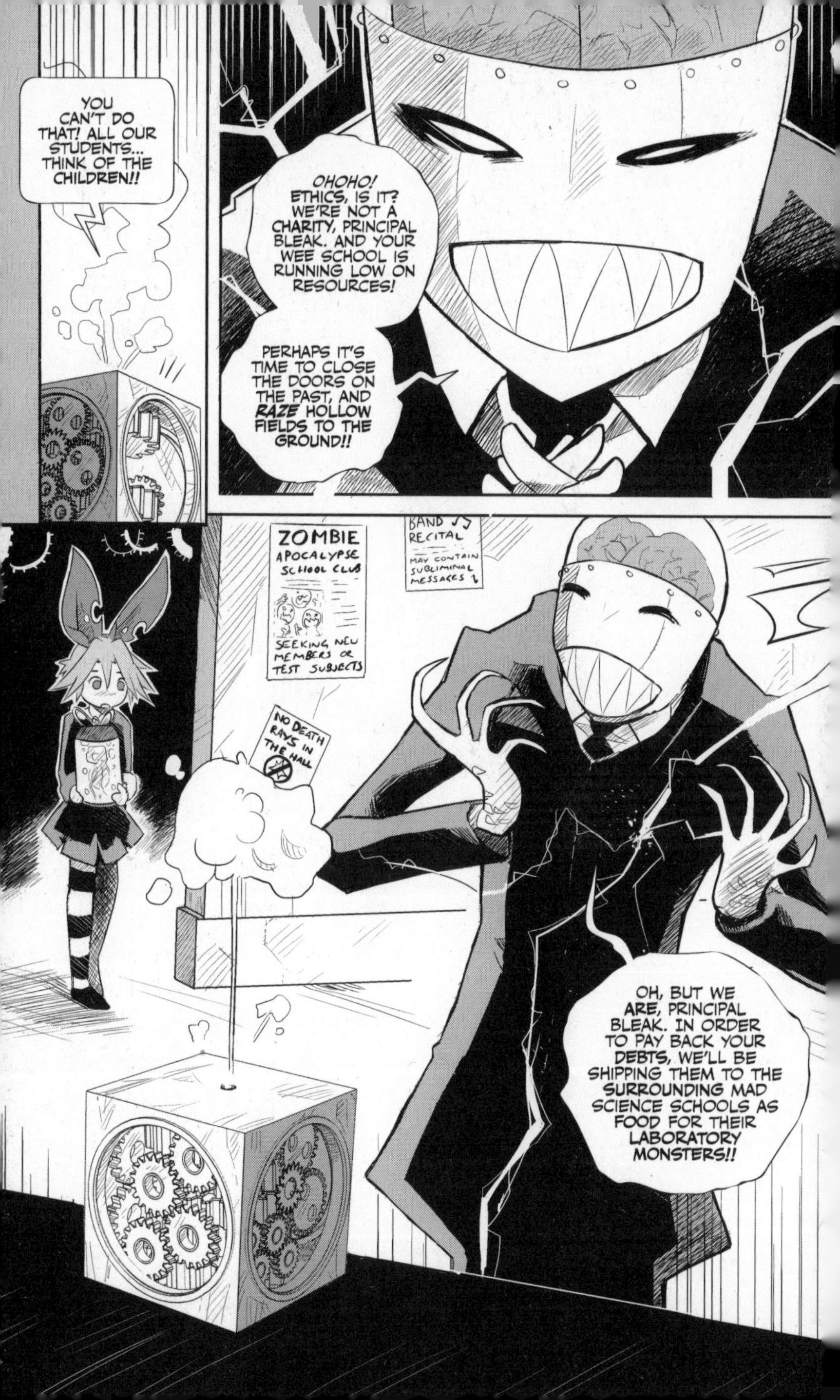
YOU CAN'T DO THAT! ALL OUR STUDENTS... THINK OF THE CHILDREN!!
OHOHO! ETHICS, IS IT? WE'RE NOT A CHARITY, PRINCIPAL BLEAK. AND YOUR WEE SCHOOL IS RUNNING LOW ON RESOURCES!
PERHAPS IT'S TIME TO CLOSE THE DOORS ON THE PAST, AND RAZE HOLLOW FIELDS TO THE GROUND!!
BAND RECITAL
MAY CONTAIN SUBLIMINAL MESSAGES
ZOMBIE APOCALYPSE SCHOOL CLUB
SEEKING NEW MEMBERS OR TEST SUBJECTS
NO DEATH RAYS IN THE HALL
OH, BUT WE ARE, PRINCIPAL BLEAK. IN ORDER TO PAY BACK YOUR DEBTS, WE'LL BE SHIPPING THEM TO THE SURROUNDING MAD SCIENCE SCHOOLS AS FOOD FOR THEIR LABORATORY MONSTERS!!

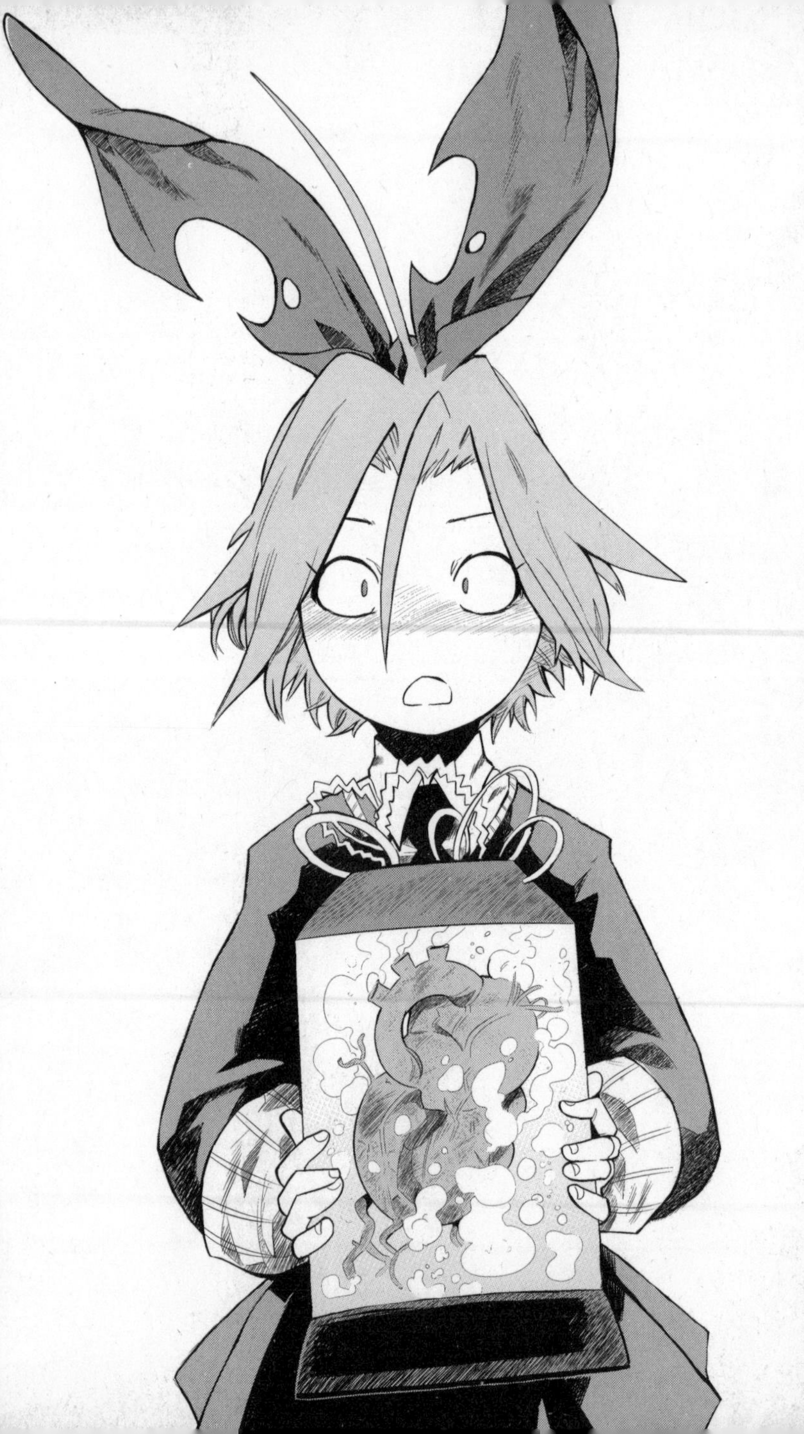

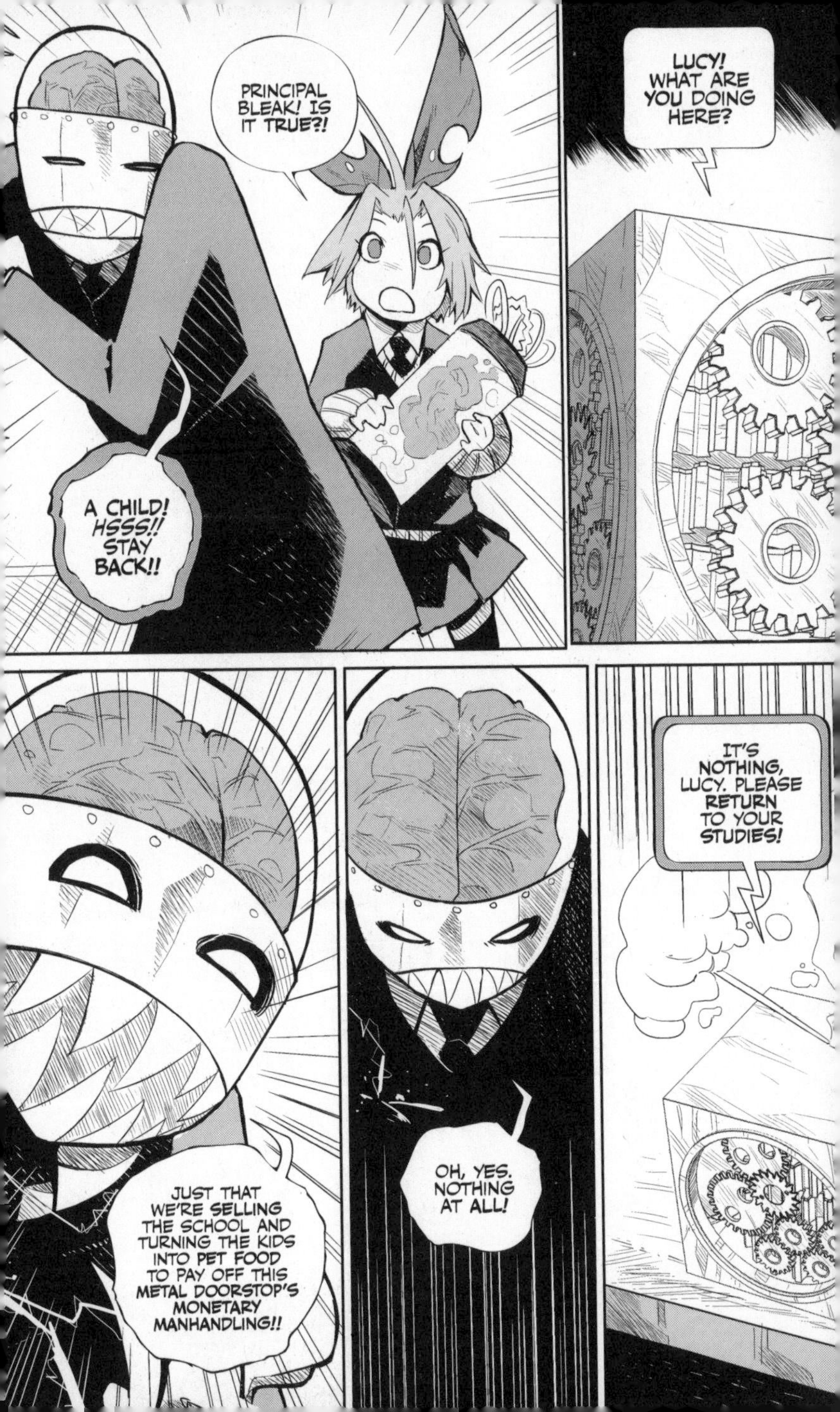
LUCY! WHAT ARE YOU DOING HERE?
PRINCIPAL BLEAK! IS IT TRUE?!
A CHILD! *HSSS!!* STAY BACK!!
IT'S NOTHING, LUCY. PLEASE RETURN TO YOUR STUDIES!
OH, YES. NOTHING AT ALL!
JUST THAT WE'RE SELLING THE SCHOOL AND TURNING THE KIDS INTO PET FOOD TO PAY OFF THIS METAL DOORSTOP'S MONETARY MANHANDLING!!

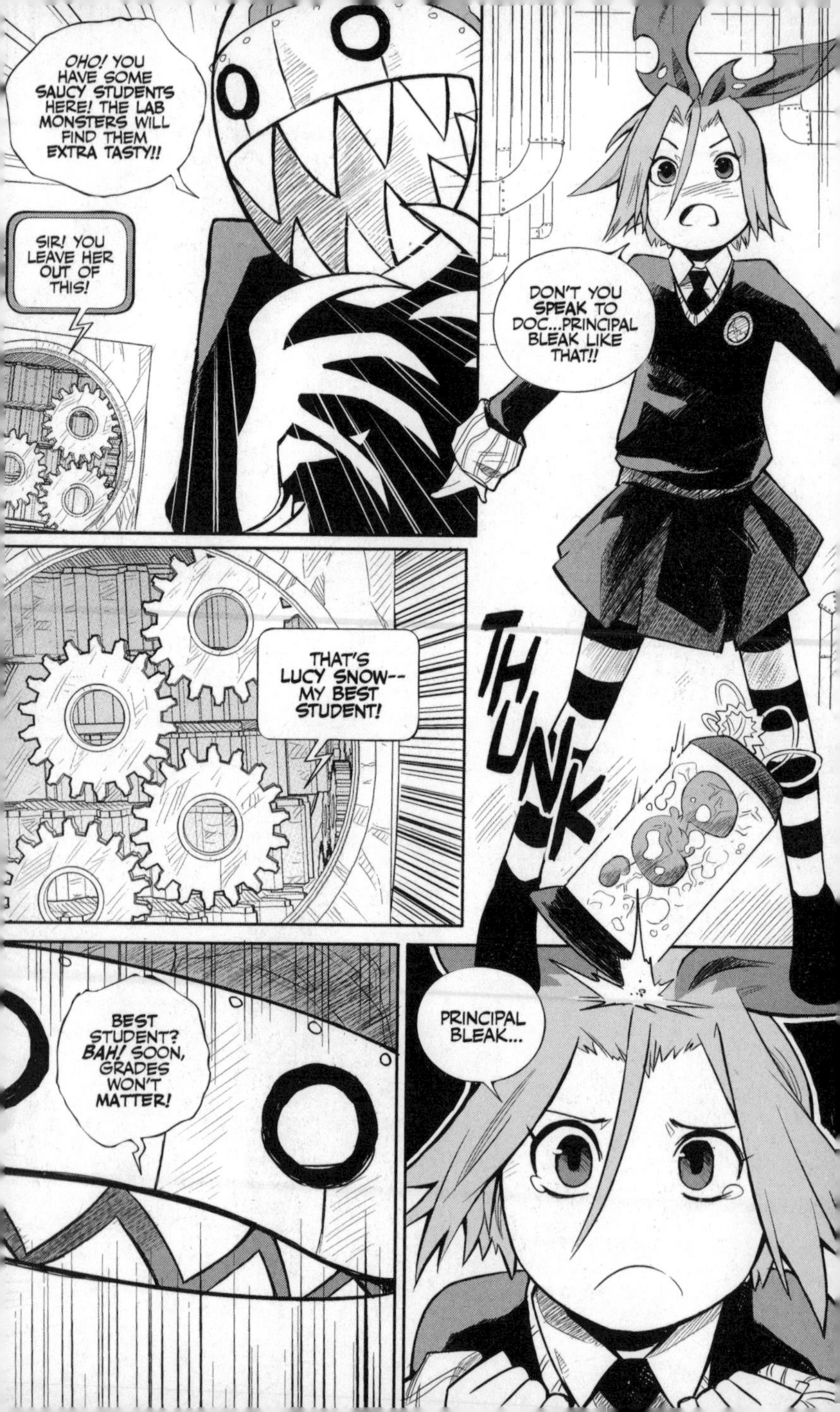

DON'T YOU SPEAK TO DOC...PRINCIPAL BLEAK LIKE THAT!!
THUNK
OHO! YOU HAVE SOME SAUCY STUDENTS HERE! THE LAB MONSTERS WILL FIND THEM EXTRA TASTY!!
SIR! YOU LEAVE HER OUT OF THIS!
THAT'S LUCY SNOW-- MY BEST STUDENT!
PRINCIPAL BLEAK...
BEST STUDENT? BAH! SOON, GRADES WON'T MATTER!

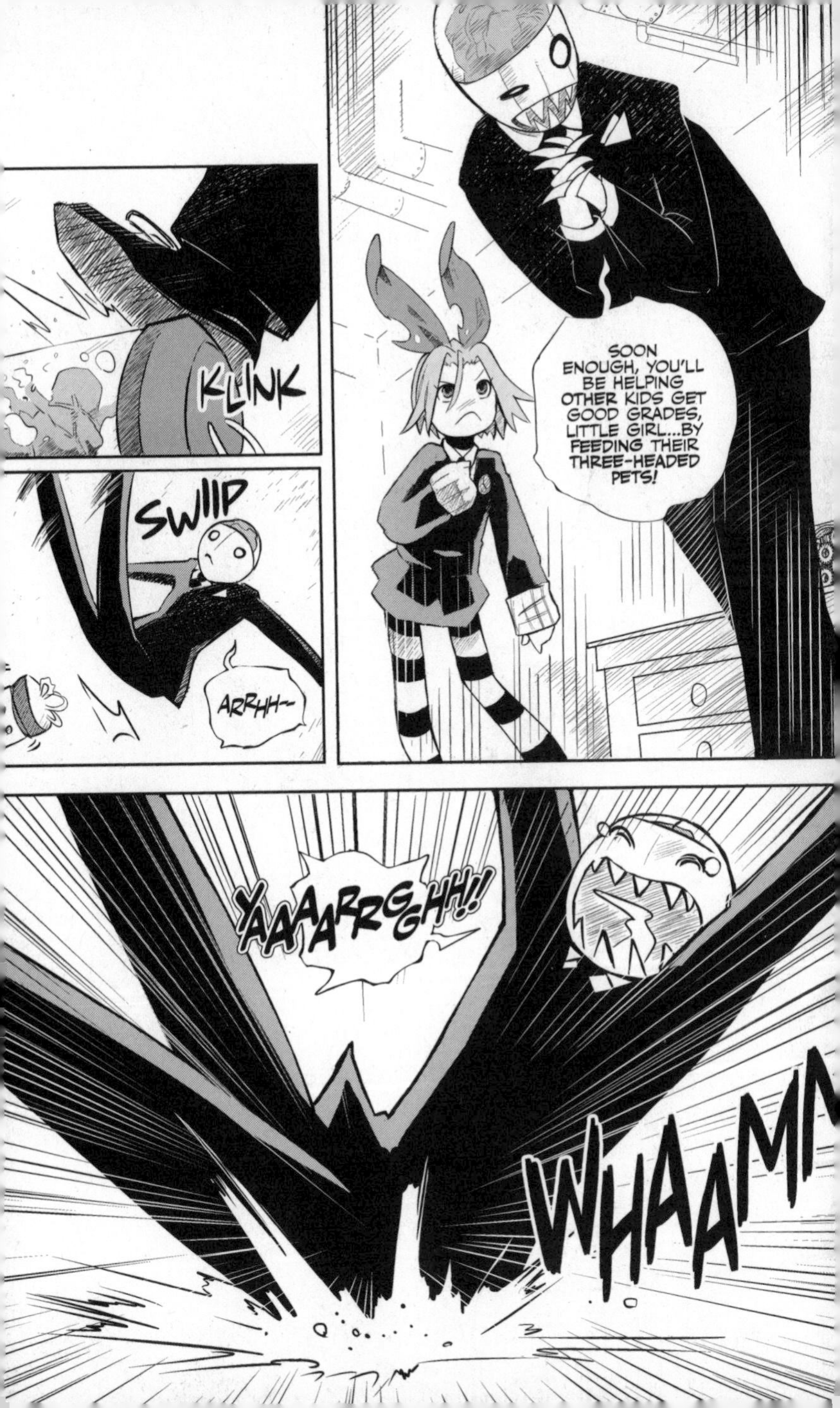
SOON ENOUGH, YOU'LL BE HELPING OTHER KIDS GET GOOD GRADES, LITTLE GIRL...BY FEEDING THEIR THREE-HEADED PETS!
KLINK
SWIIP
ARRHH--
YAAAARRGGHH!!
WHAAM

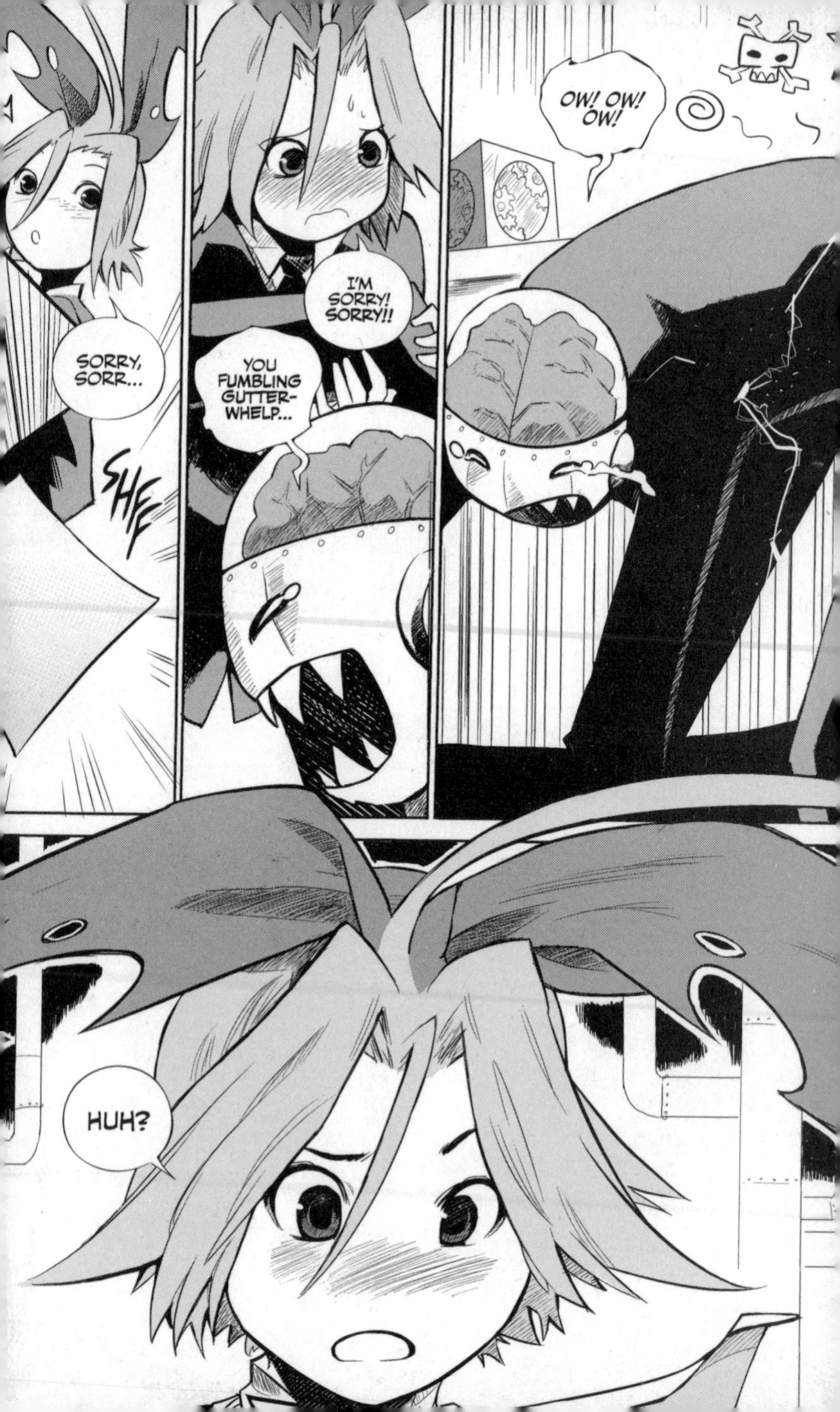
OW! OW! OW!
I'M SORRY! SORRY!!
YOU FUMBLING GUTTER-WHELP...
SORRY, SORR...
HUH?

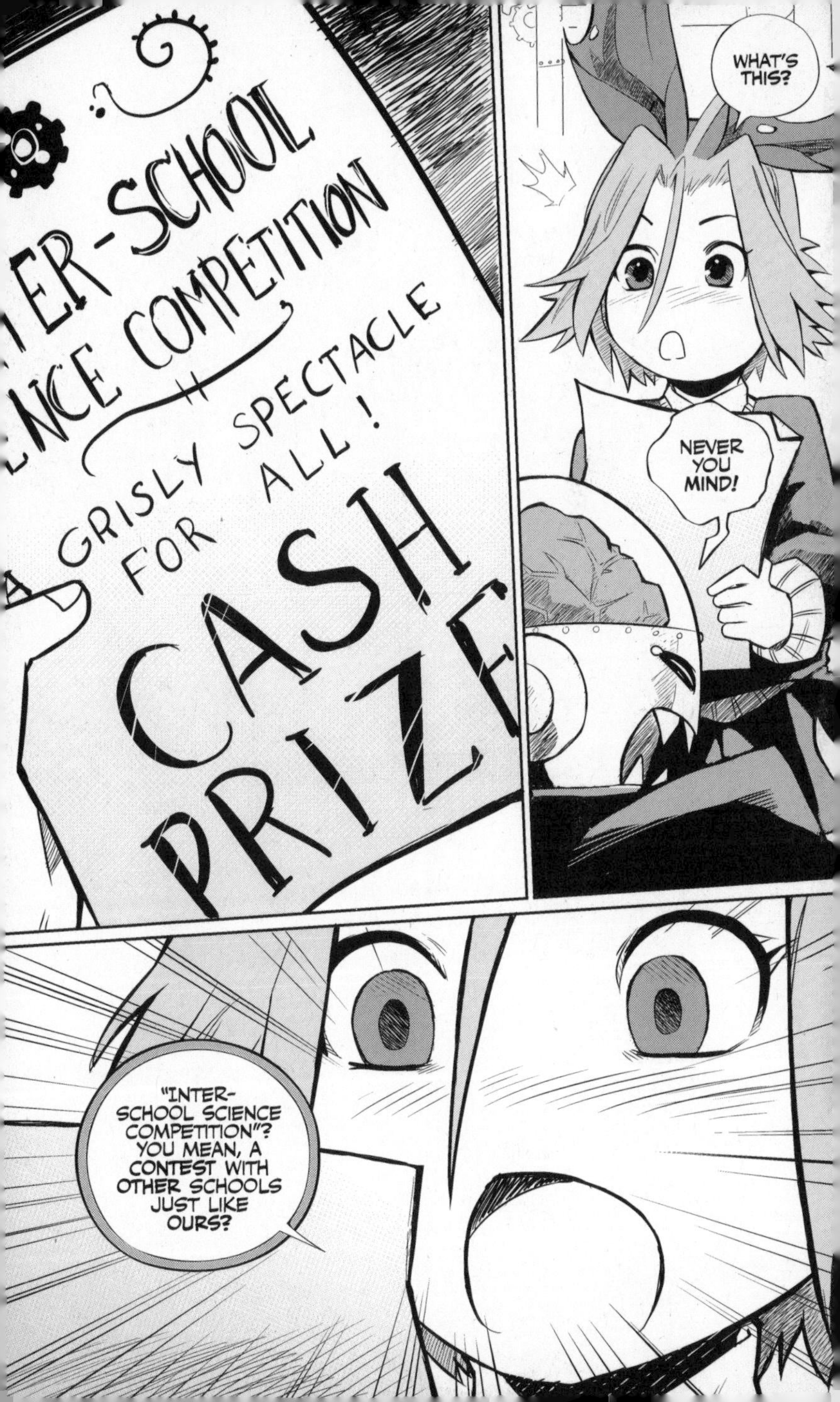
WHAT'S THIS?
NEVER YOU MIND!
ER-SCHOOL
NCE COMPETITION
A GRISLY SPECTACLE FOR ALL!
CASH PRIZE
"INTER-SCHOOL SCIENCE COMPETITION"? YOU MEAN, A CONTEST WITH OTHER SCHOOLS JUST LIKE OURS?

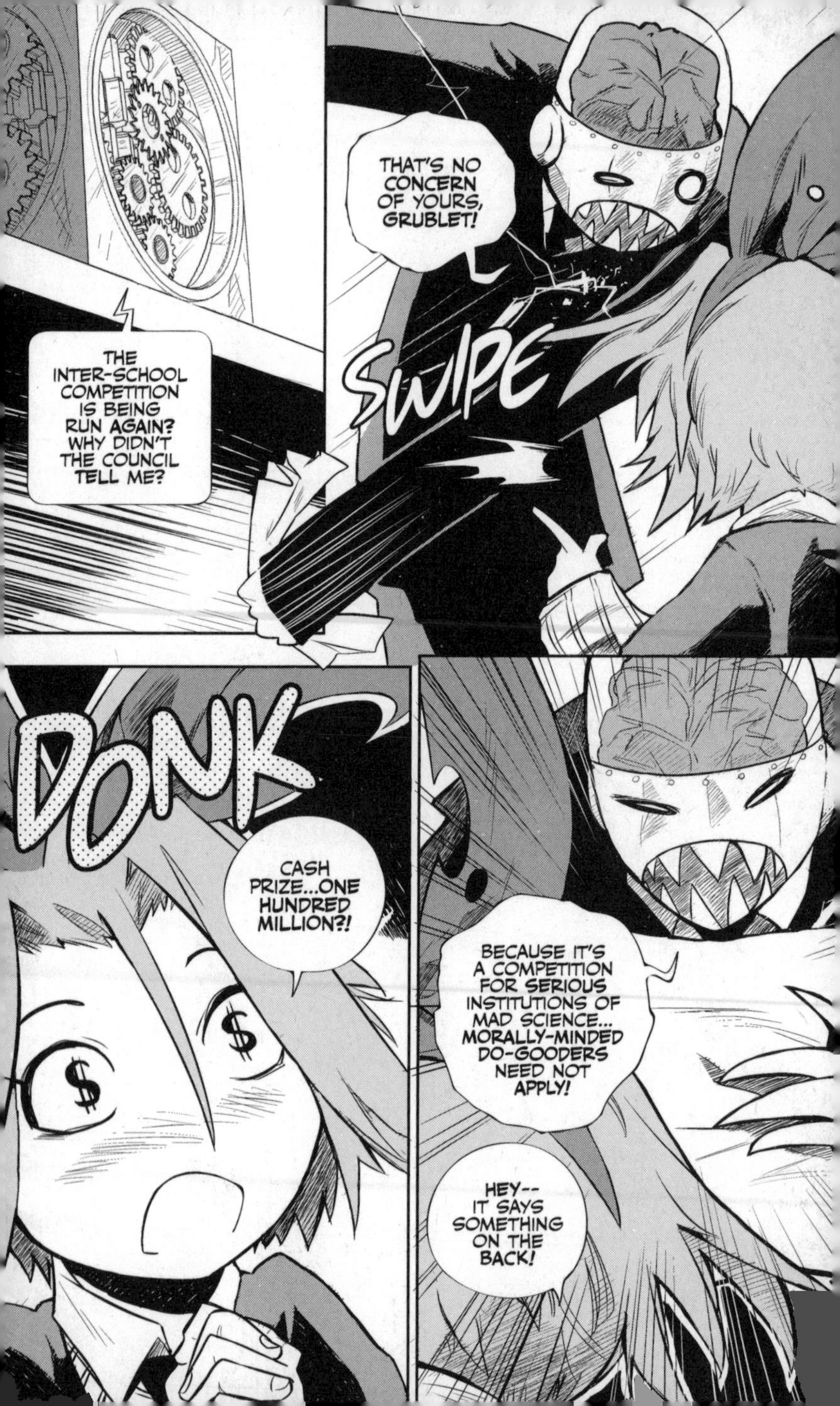
THAT'S NO CONCERN OF YOURS, GRUBLET!
SWIPE
THE INTER-SCHOOL COMPETITION IS BEING RUN AGAIN? WHY DIDN'T THE COUNCIL TELL ME?
BECAUSE IT'S A COMPETITION FOR SERIOUS INSTITUTIONS OF MAD SCIENCE... MORALLY-MINDED DO-GOODERS NEED NOT APPLY!
HEY-- IT SAYS SOMETHING ON THE BACK!
DONK
CASH PRIZE...ONE HUNDRED MILLION?!
$
$

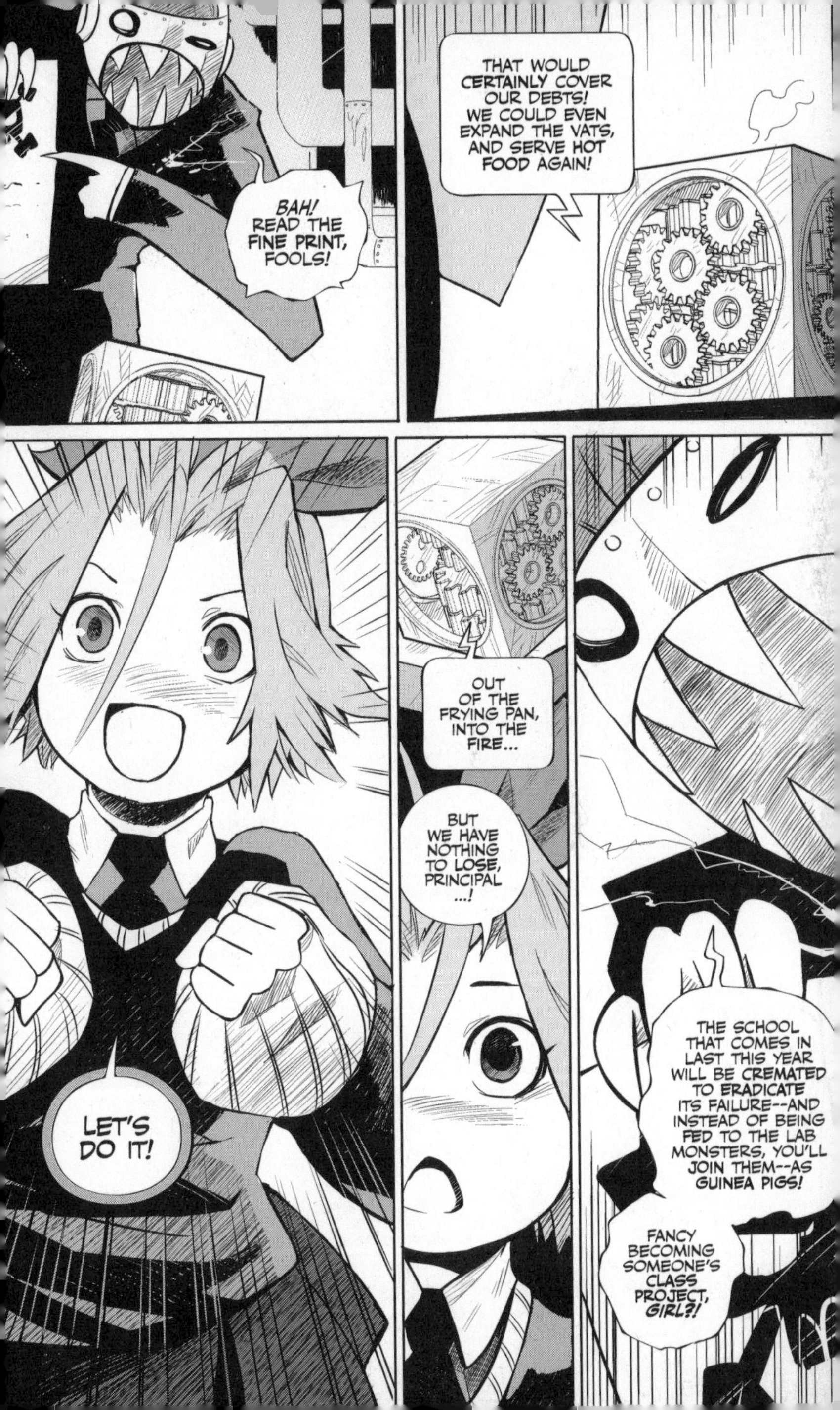
THAT WOULD CERTAINLY COVER OUR DEBTS! WE COULD EVEN EXPAND THE VATS, AND SERVE HOT FOOD AGAIN!
BAH! READ THE FINE PRINT, FOOLS!
THE SCHOOL THAT COMES IN LAST THIS YEAR WILL BE CREMATED TO ERADICATE ITS FAILURE--AND INSTEAD OF BEING FED TO THE LAB MONSTERS, YOU'LL JOIN THEM--AS GUINEA PIGS!
FANCY BECOMING SOMEONE'S CLASS PROJECT, GIRL?!
OUT OF THE FRYING PAN, INTO THE FIRE...
BUT WE HAVE NOTHING TO LOSE, PRINCIPAL ...!
LET'S DO IT!

CHAPTER TWO
TEAMS AND SCHEMES

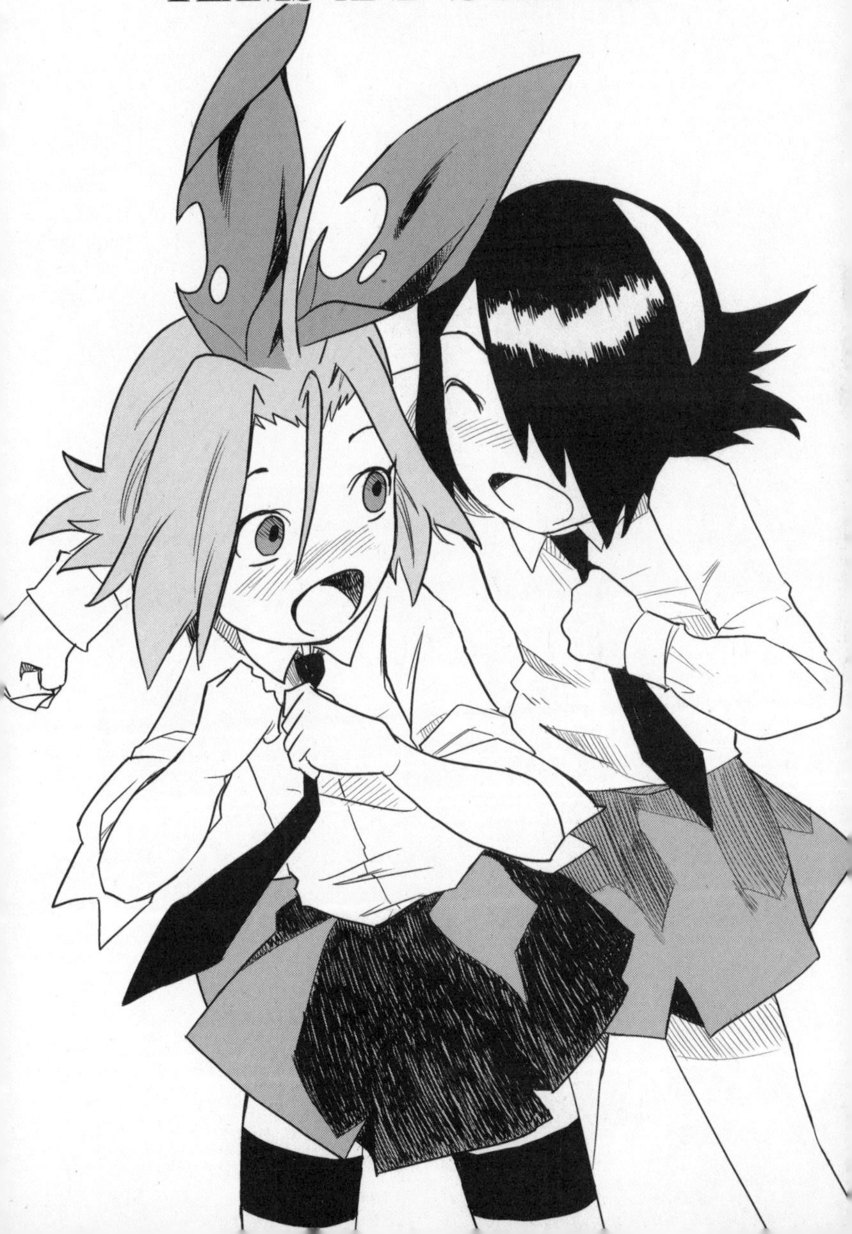

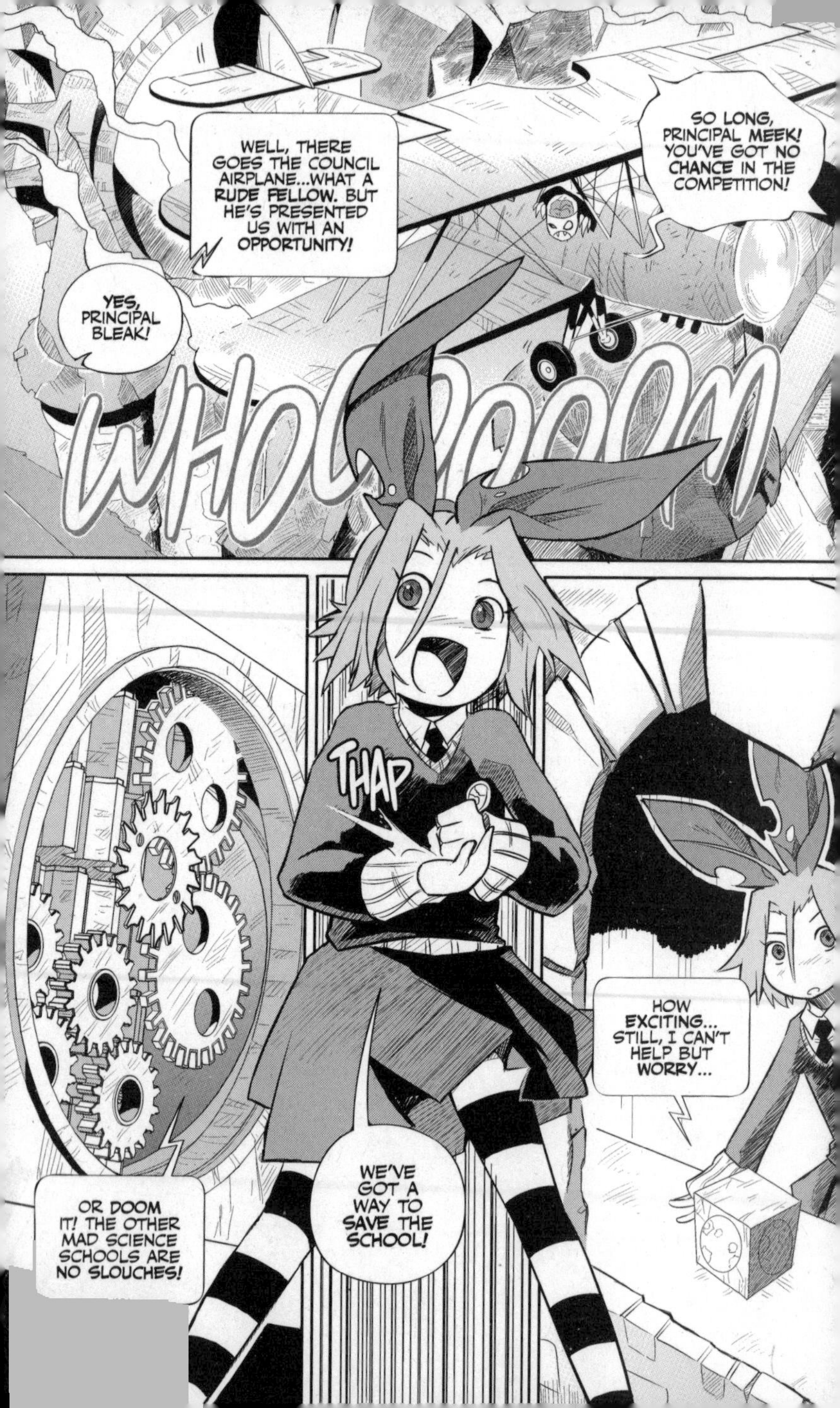
SO LONG, PRINCIPAL MEEK! YOU'VE GOT NO CHANCE IN THE COMPETITION!
WELL, THERE GOES THE COUNCIL AIRPLANE...WHAT A RUDE FELLOW. BUT HE'S PRESENTED US WITH AN OPPORTUNITY!
YES, PRINCIPAL BLEAK!
WHOOOOOM
THAP
WE'VE GOT A WAY TO SAVE THE SCHOOL!
HOW EXCITING... STILL, I CAN'T HELP BUT WORRY...
OR DOOM IT! THE OTHER MAD SCIENCE SCHOOLS ARE NO SLOUCHES!

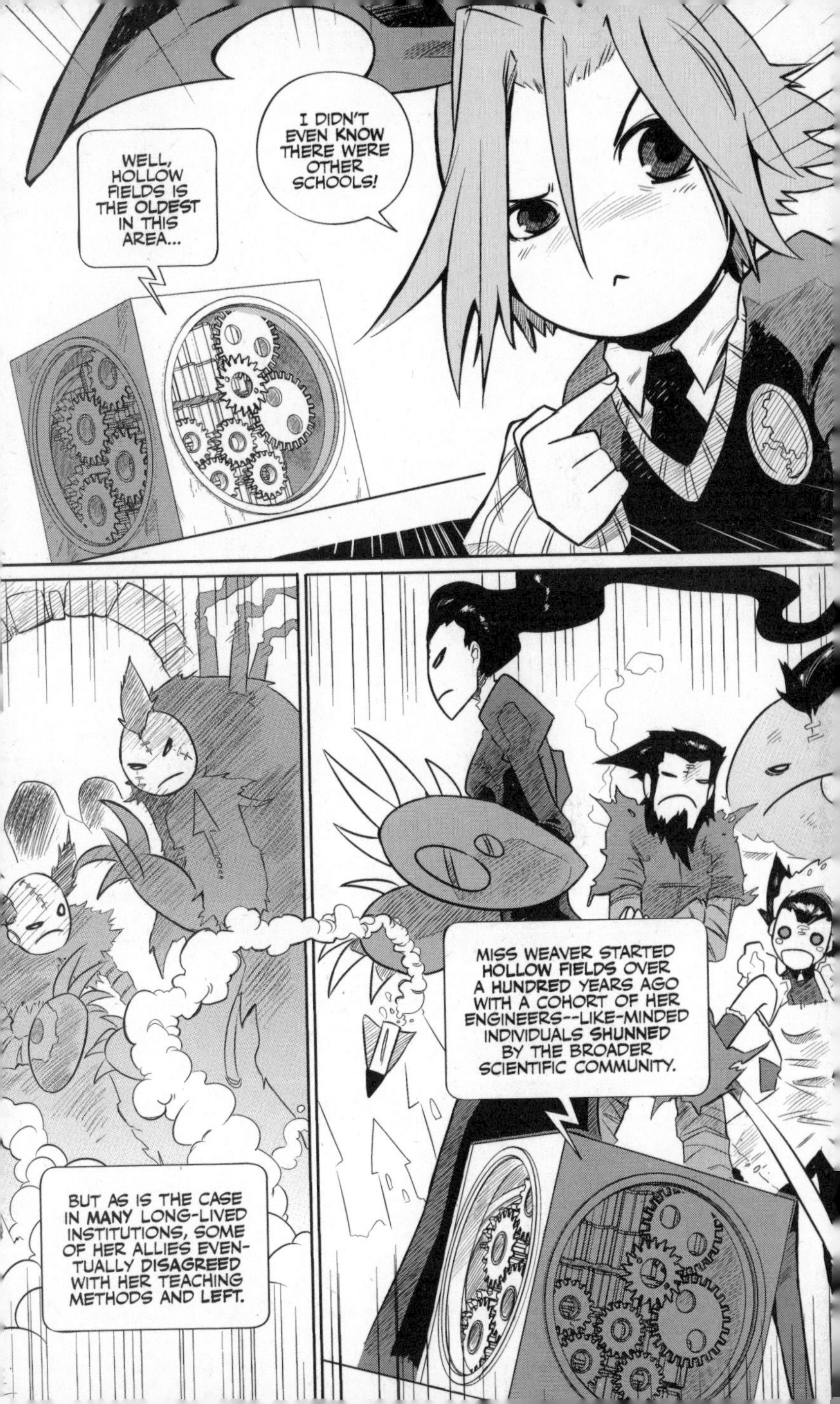

I DIDN'T EVEN KNOW THERE WERE OTHER SCHOOLS!
WELL, HOLLOW FIELDS IS THE OLDEST IN THIS AREA...
MISS WEAVER STARTED HOLLOW FIELDS OVER A HUNDRED YEARS AGO WITH A COHORT OF HER ENGINEERS--LIKE-MINDED INDIVIDUALS SHUNNED BY THE BROADER SCIENTIFIC COMMUNITY.
BUT AS IS THE CASE IN MANY LONG-LIVED INSTITUTIONS, SOME OF HER ALLIES EVEN-TUALLY DISAGREED WITH HER TEACHING METHODS AND LEFT.

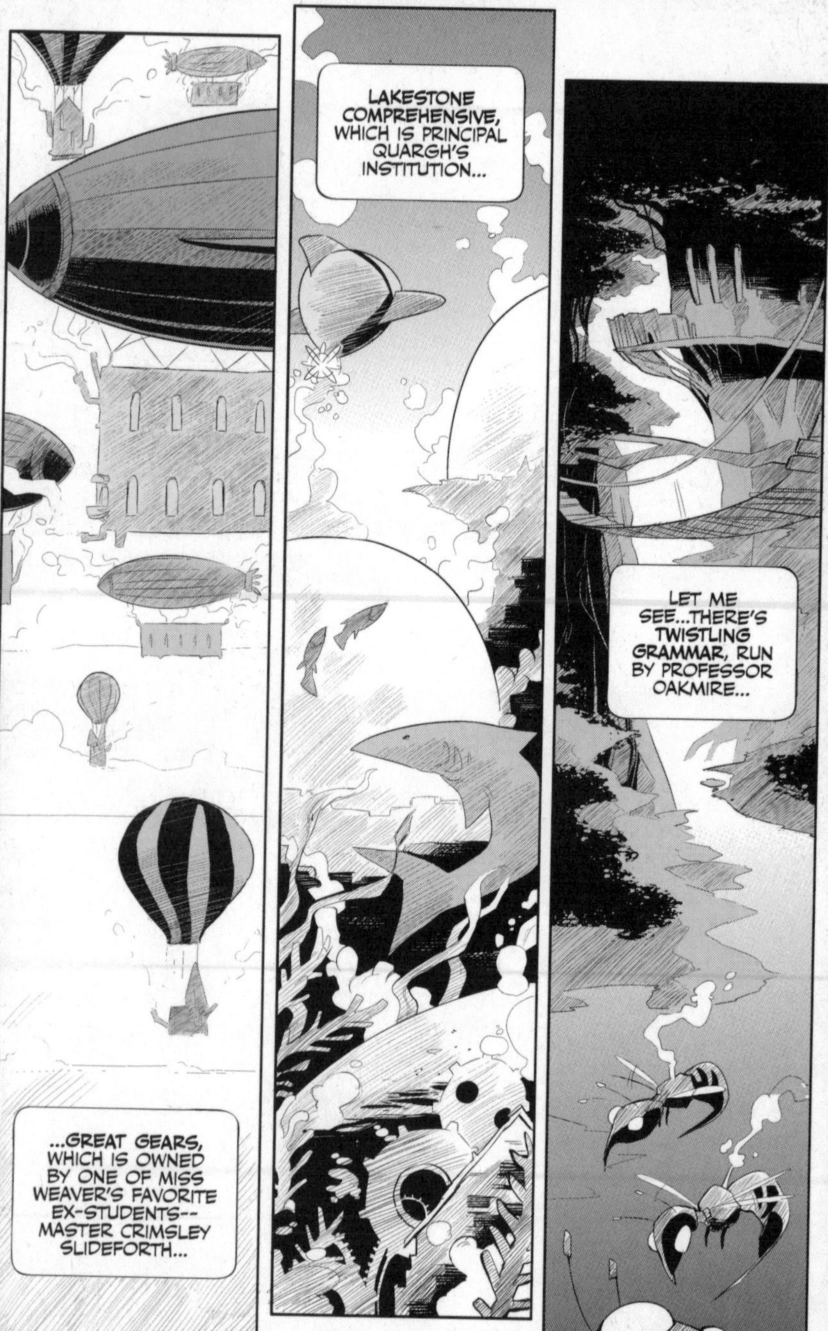
LET ME SEE...THERE'S TWISTLING GRAMMAR, RUN BY PROFESSOR OAKMIRE...
LAKESTONE COMPREHENSIVE, WHICH IS PRINCIPAL QUARGH'S INSTITUTION...
...GREAT GEARS, WHICH IS OWNED BY ONE OF MISS WEAVER'S FAVORITE EX-STUDENTS-- MASTER CRIMSLEY SLIDEFORTH...

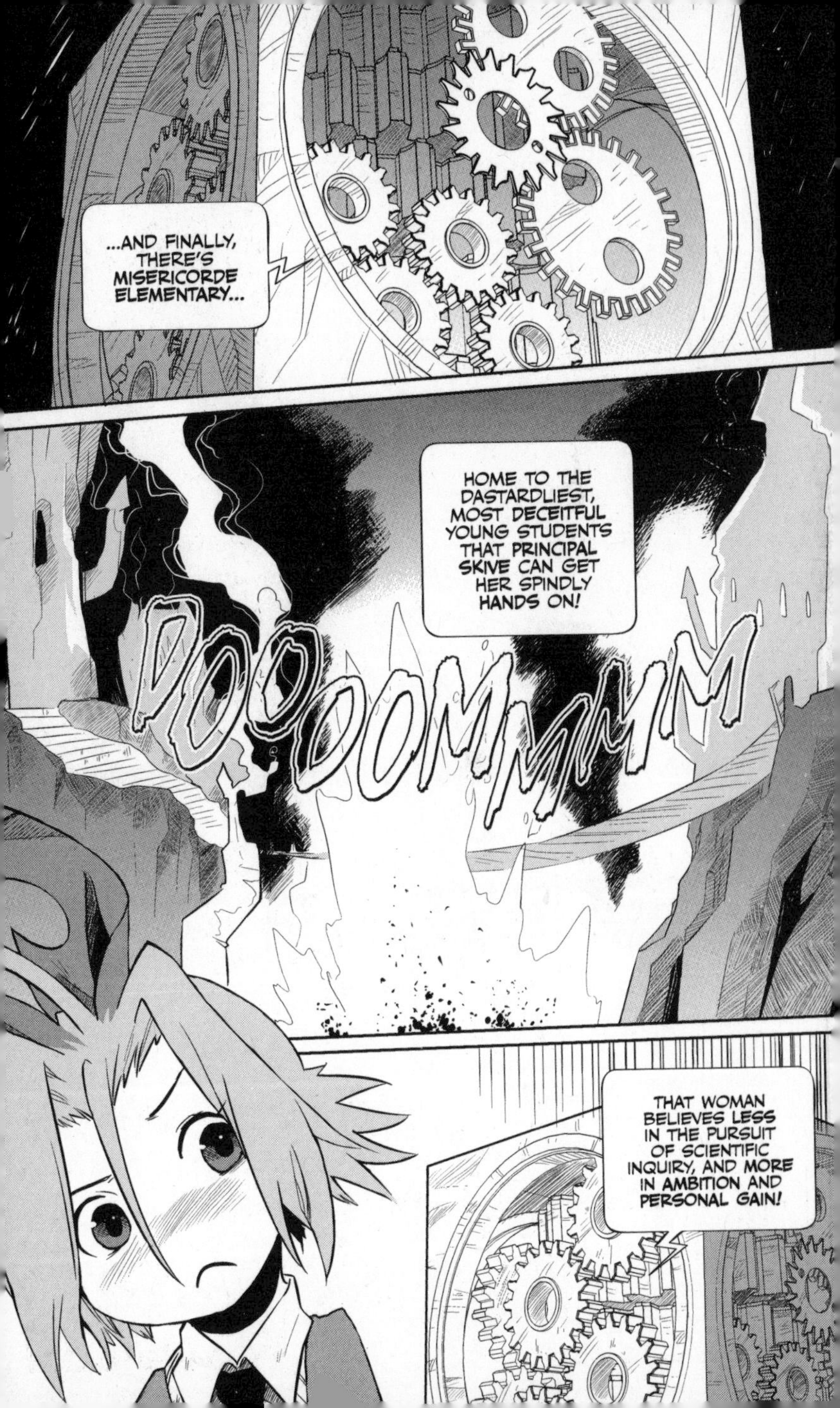
...AND FINALLY, THERE'S MISERICORDE ELEMENTARY...
HOME TO THE DASTARDLIEST, MOST DECEITFUL YOUNG STUDENTS THAT PRINCIPAL SKIVE CAN GET HER SPINDLY HANDS ON!
DOOOOOMMMM
THAT WOMAN BELIEVES LESS IN THE PURSUIT OF SCIENTIFIC INQUIRY, AND MORE IN AMBITION AND PERSONAL GAIN!

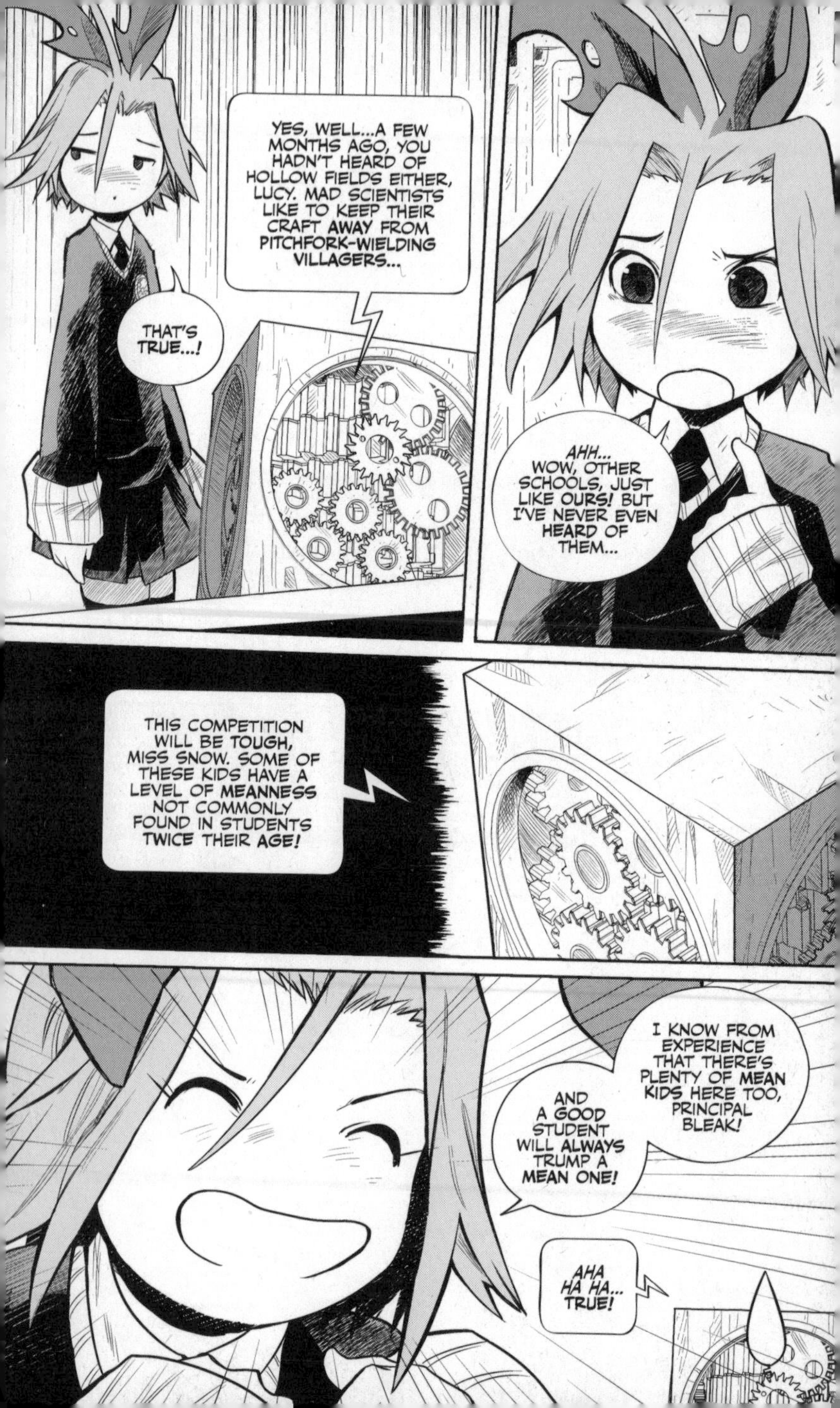
AHH... WOW, OTHER SCHOOLS, JUST LIKE OURS! BUT I'VE NEVER EVEN HEARD OF THEM...
YES, WELL...A FEW MONTHS AGO, YOU HADN'T HEARD OF HOLLOW FIELDS EITHER, LUCY. MAD SCIENTISTS LIKE TO KEEP THEIR CRAFT AWAY FROM PITCHFORK-WIELDING VILLAGERS...
THAT'S TRUE...!
THIS COMPETITION WILL BE TOUGH, MISS SNOW. SOME OF THESE KIDS HAVE A LEVEL OF MEANNESS NOT COMMONLY FOUND IN STUDENTS TWICE THEIR AGE!
I KNOW FROM EXPERIENCE THAT THERE'S PLENTY OF MEAN KIDS HERE TOO, PRINCIPAL BLEAK!
AND A GOOD STUDENT WILL ALWAYS TRUMP A MEAN ONE!
AHA HA HA... TRUE!

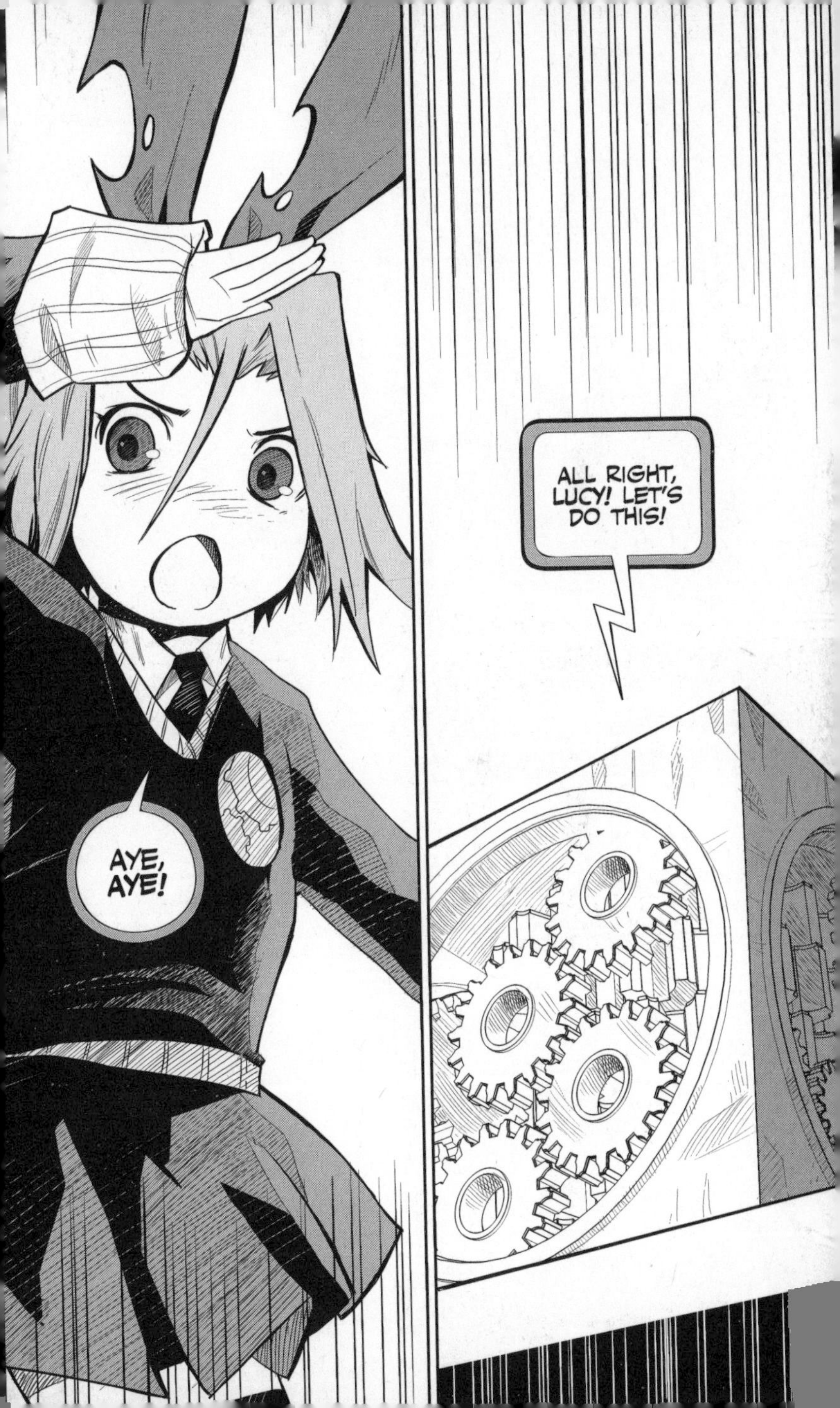
ALL RIGHT, LUCY! LET'S DO THIS!
AYE, AYE!

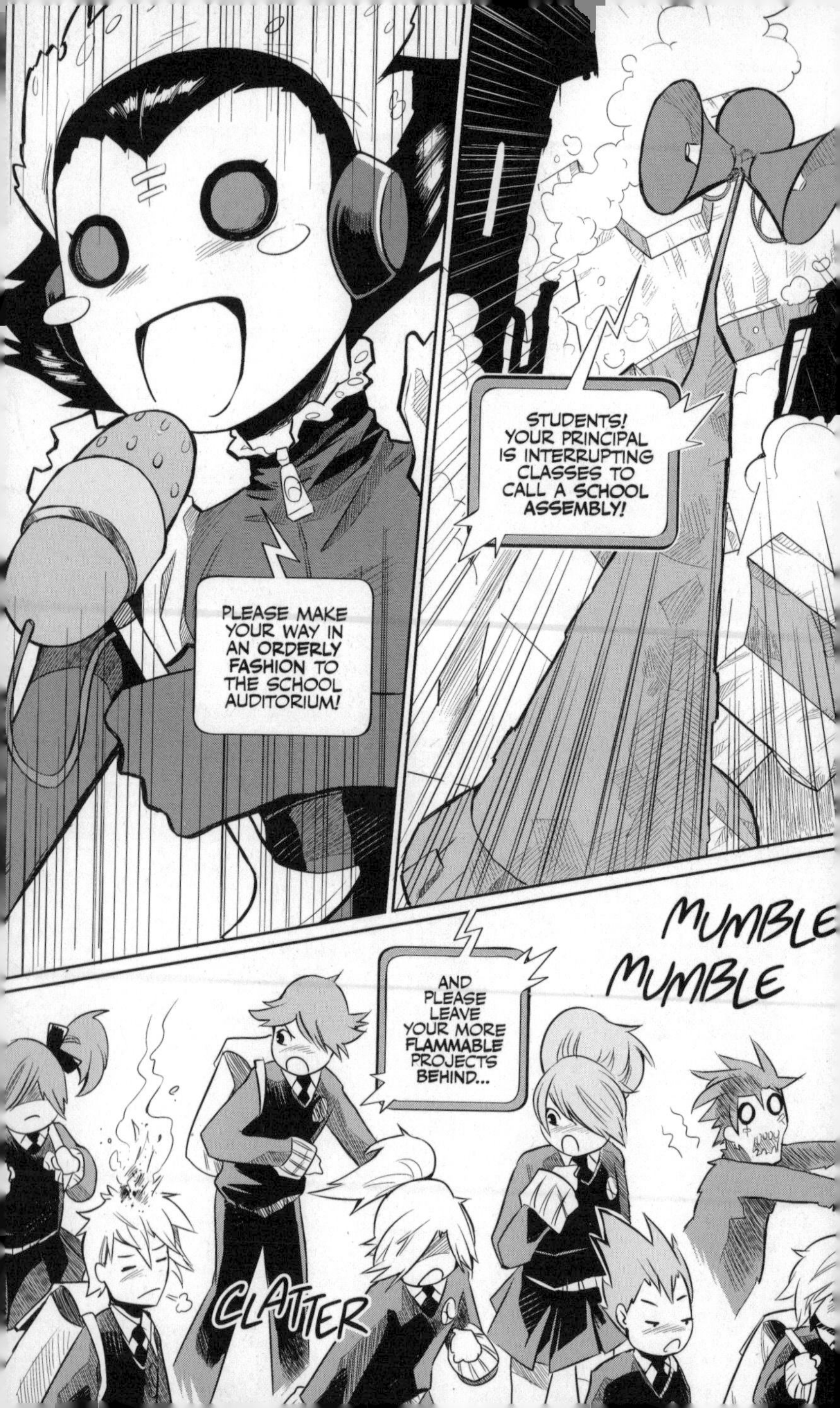
STUDENTS! YOUR PRINCIPAL IS INTERRUPTING CLASSES TO CALL A SCHOOL ASSEMBLY!
PLEASE MAKE YOUR WAY IN AN ORDERLY FASHION TO THE SCHOOL AUDITORIUM!
MUMBLE
MUMBLE
AND PLEASE LEAVE YOUR MORE FLAMMABLE PROJECTS BEHIND...
CLATTER

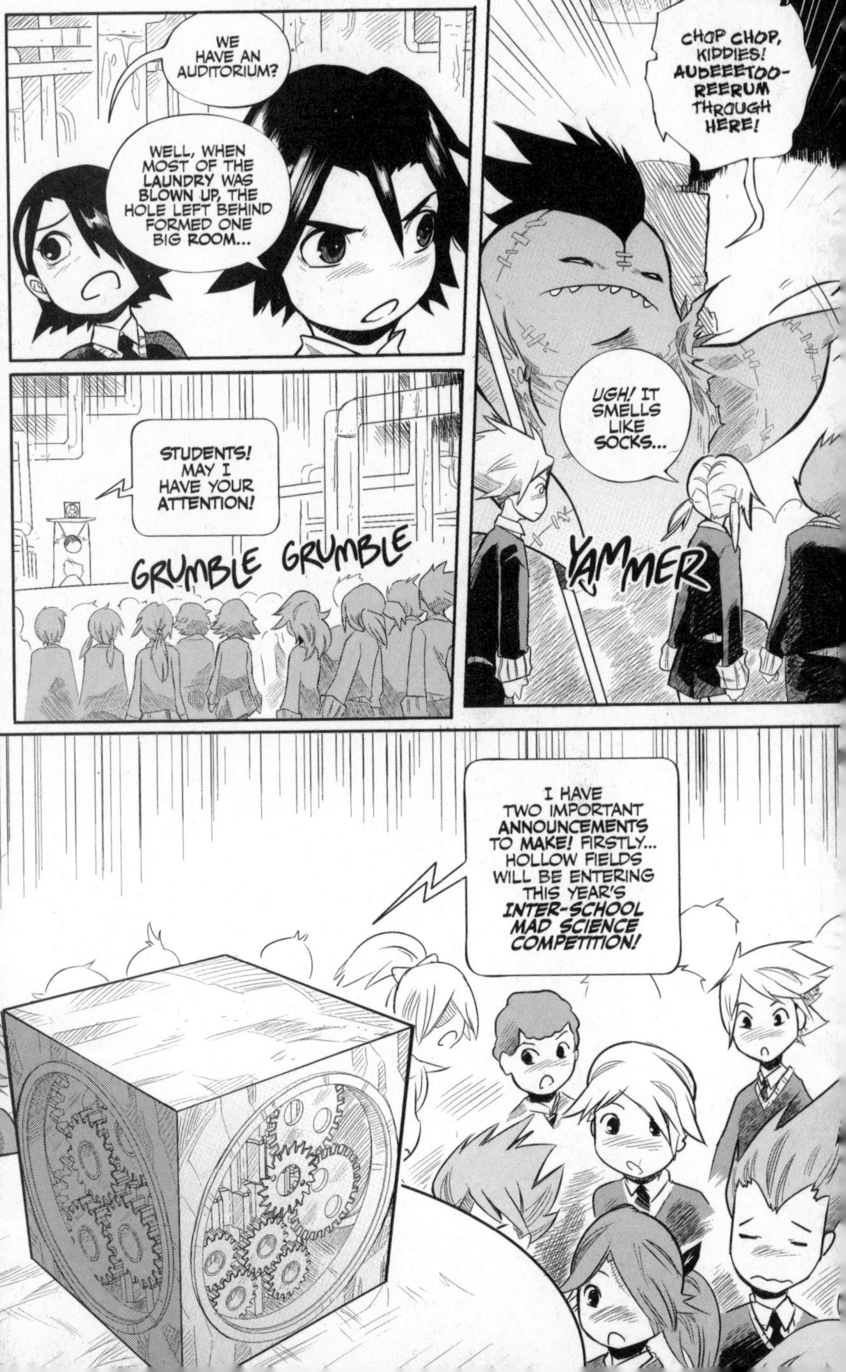
CHOP CHOP, KIDDIES! AUDEEETOO-REERUM THROUGH HERE!
UGH! IT SMELLS LIKE SOCKS...
YAMMER
WE HAVE AN AUDITORIUM?
WELL, WHEN MOST OF THE LAUNDRY WAS BLOWN UP, THE HOLE LEFT BEHIND FORMED ONE BIG ROOM...
STUDENTS! MAY I HAVE YOUR ATTENTION!
GRUMBLE GRUMBLE
I HAVE TWO IMPORTANT ANNOUNCEMENTS TO MAKE! FIRSTLY... HOLLOW FIELDS WILL BE ENTERING THIS YEAR'S *INTER-SCHOOL MAD SCIENCE COMPETITION!*

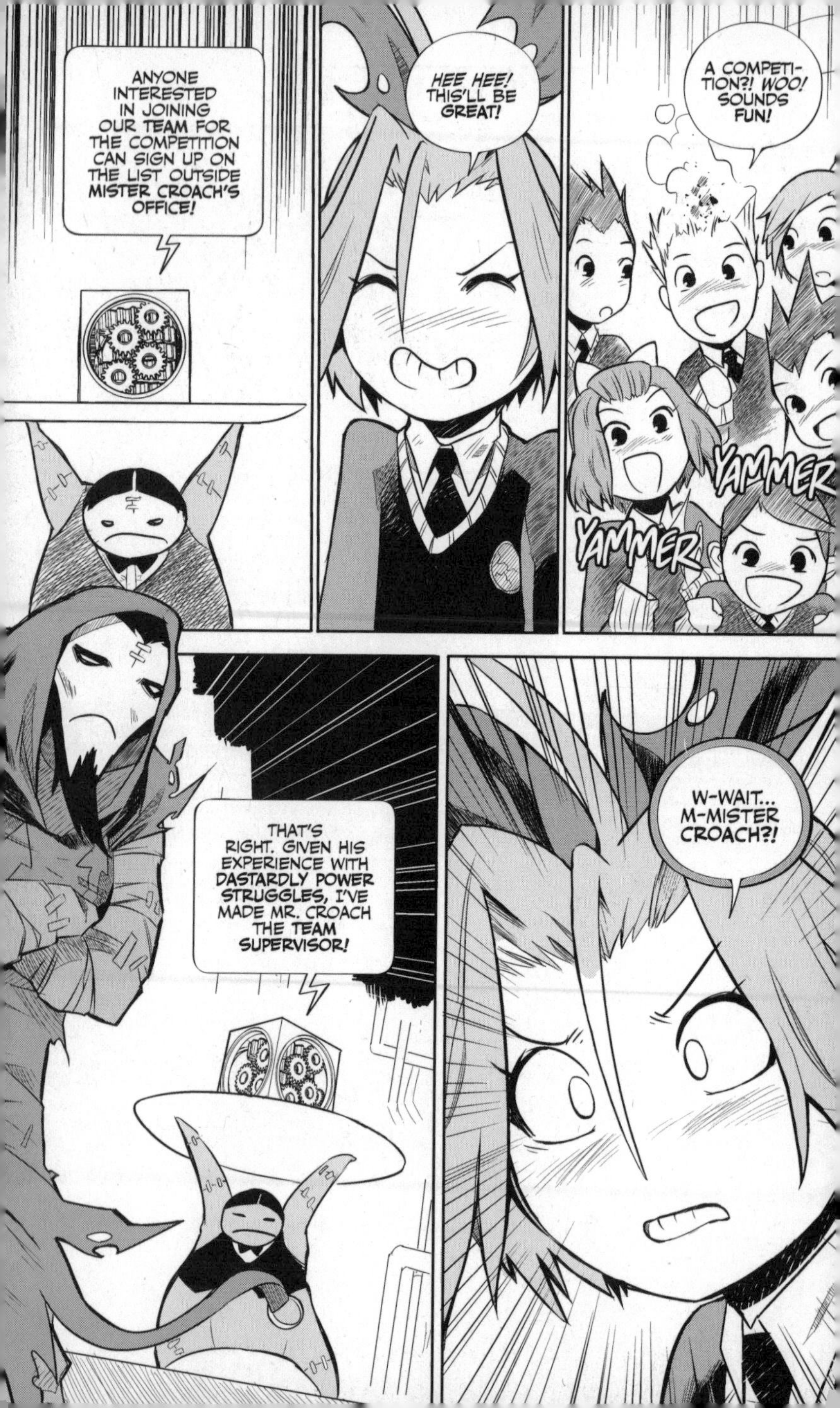

A COMPETITION?! WOO! SOUNDS FUN!
YAMMER
YAMMER
HEE HEE! THIS'LL BE GREAT!
ANYONE INTERESTED IN JOINING OUR TEAM FOR THE COMPETITION CAN SIGN UP ON THE LIST OUTSIDE MISTER CROACH'S OFFICE!
W-WAIT... M-MISTER CROACH?!
THAT'S RIGHT. GIVEN HIS EXPERIENCE WITH DASTARDLY POWER STRUGGLES, I'VE MADE MR. CROACH THE TEAM SUPERVISOR!

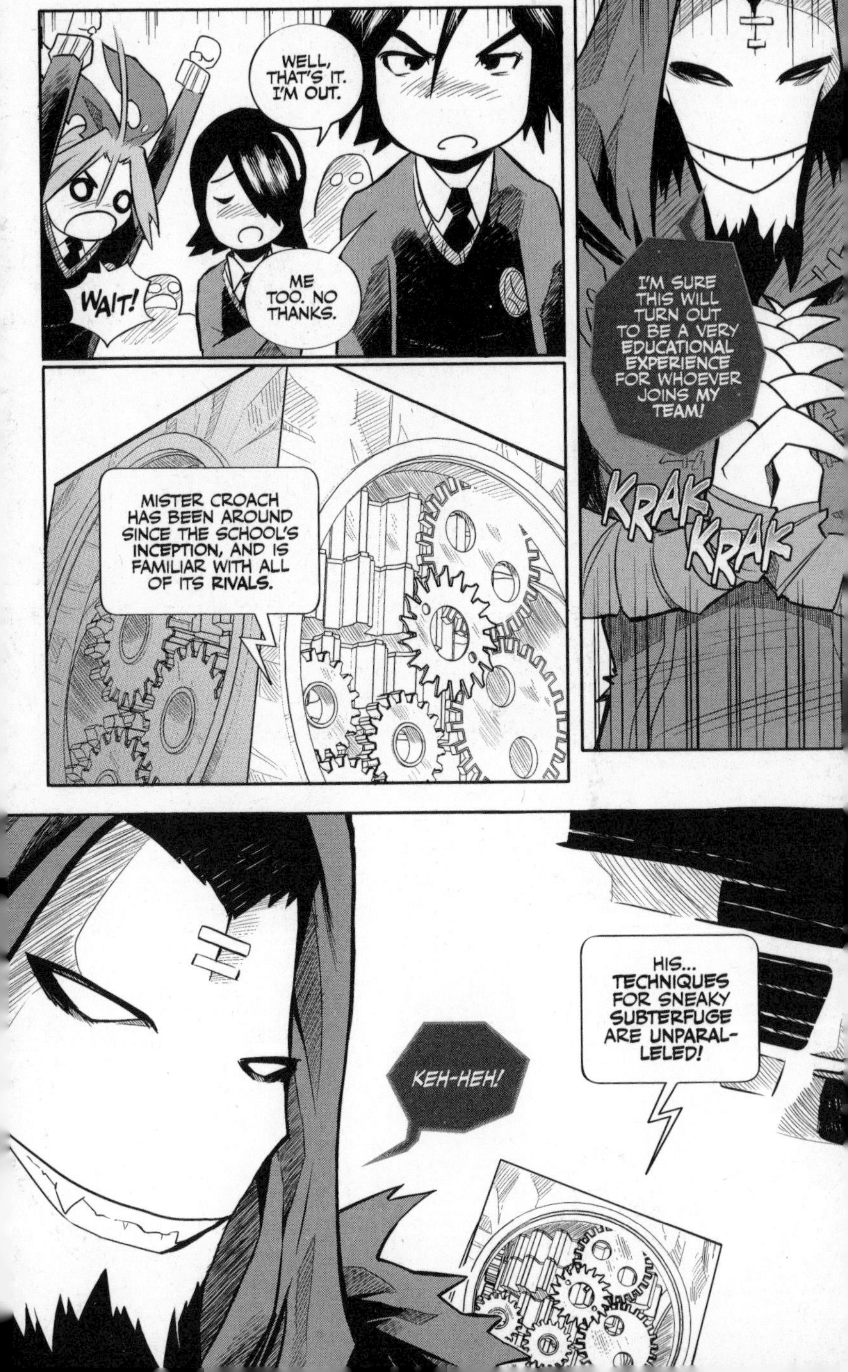
WELL, THAT'S IT. I'M OUT.
ME TOO. NO THANKS.
WAIT!
MISTER CROACH HAS BEEN AROUND SINCE THE SCHOOL'S INCEPTION, AND IS FAMILIAR WITH ALL OF ITS RIVALS.
I'M SURE THIS WILL TURN OUT TO BE A VERY EDUCATIONAL EXPERIENCE FOR WHOEVER JOINS MY TEAM!
KRAK KRAK
HIS... TECHNIQUES FOR SNEAKY SUBTERFUGE ARE UNPARAL-LELED!
KEH-HEH!

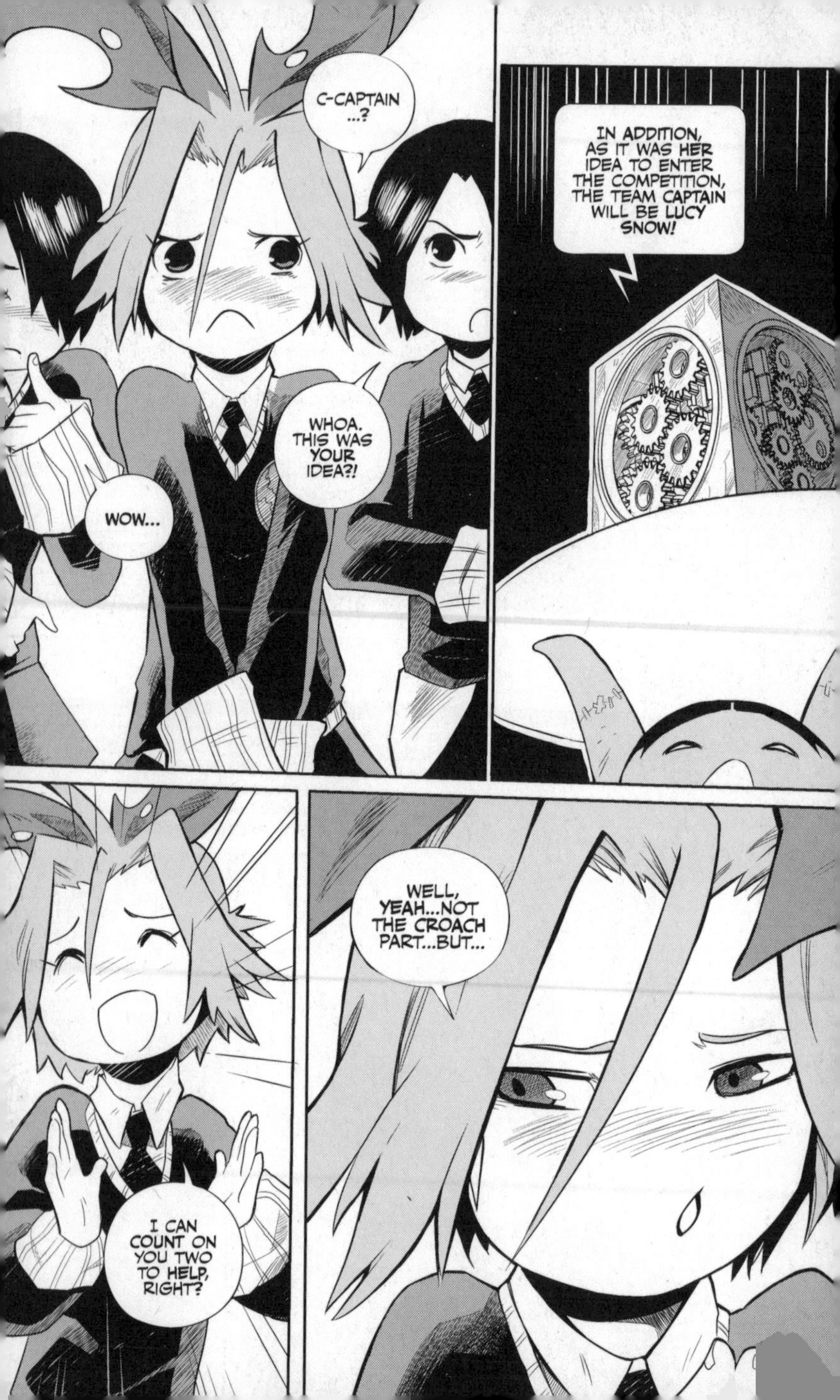
IN ADDITION, AS IT WAS HER IDEA TO ENTER THE COMPETITION, THE TEAM CAPTAIN WILL BE LUCY SNOW!
C-CAPTAIN ...?
WHOA. THIS WAS YOUR IDEA?!
WOW...
WELL, YEAH...NOT THE CROACH PART...BUT...
I CAN COUNT ON YOU TWO TO HELP, RIGHT?

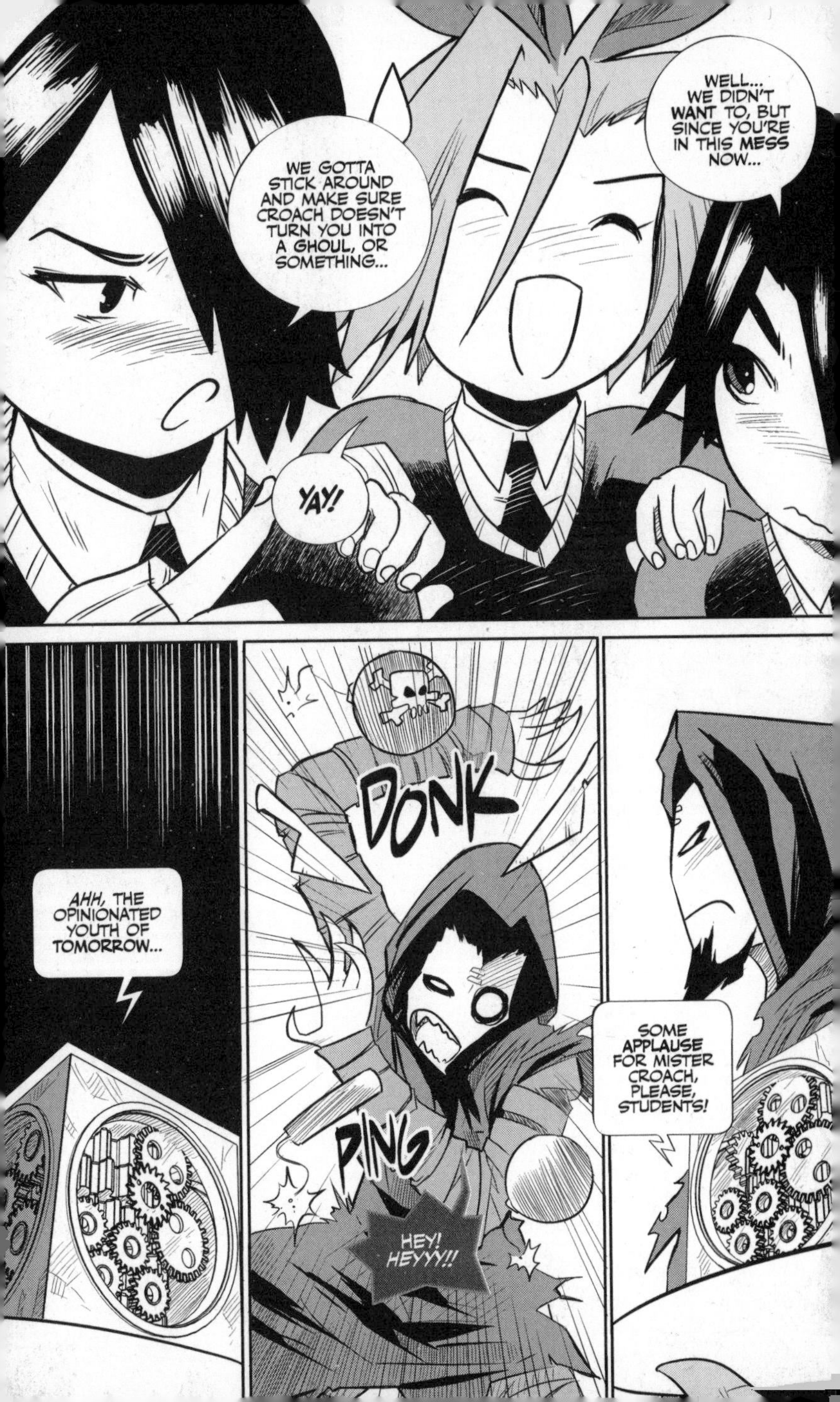
WELL... WE DIDN'T WANT TO, BUT SINCE YOU'RE IN THIS MESS NOW...
WE GOTTA STICK AROUND AND MAKE SURE CROACH DOESN'T TURN YOU INTO A GHOUL, OR SOMETHING...
YAY!
SOME APPLAUSE FOR MISTER CROACH, PLEASE, STUDENTS!
DONK
PING
HEY! HEYYY!!
AHH, THE OPINIONATED YOUTH OF TOMORROW...

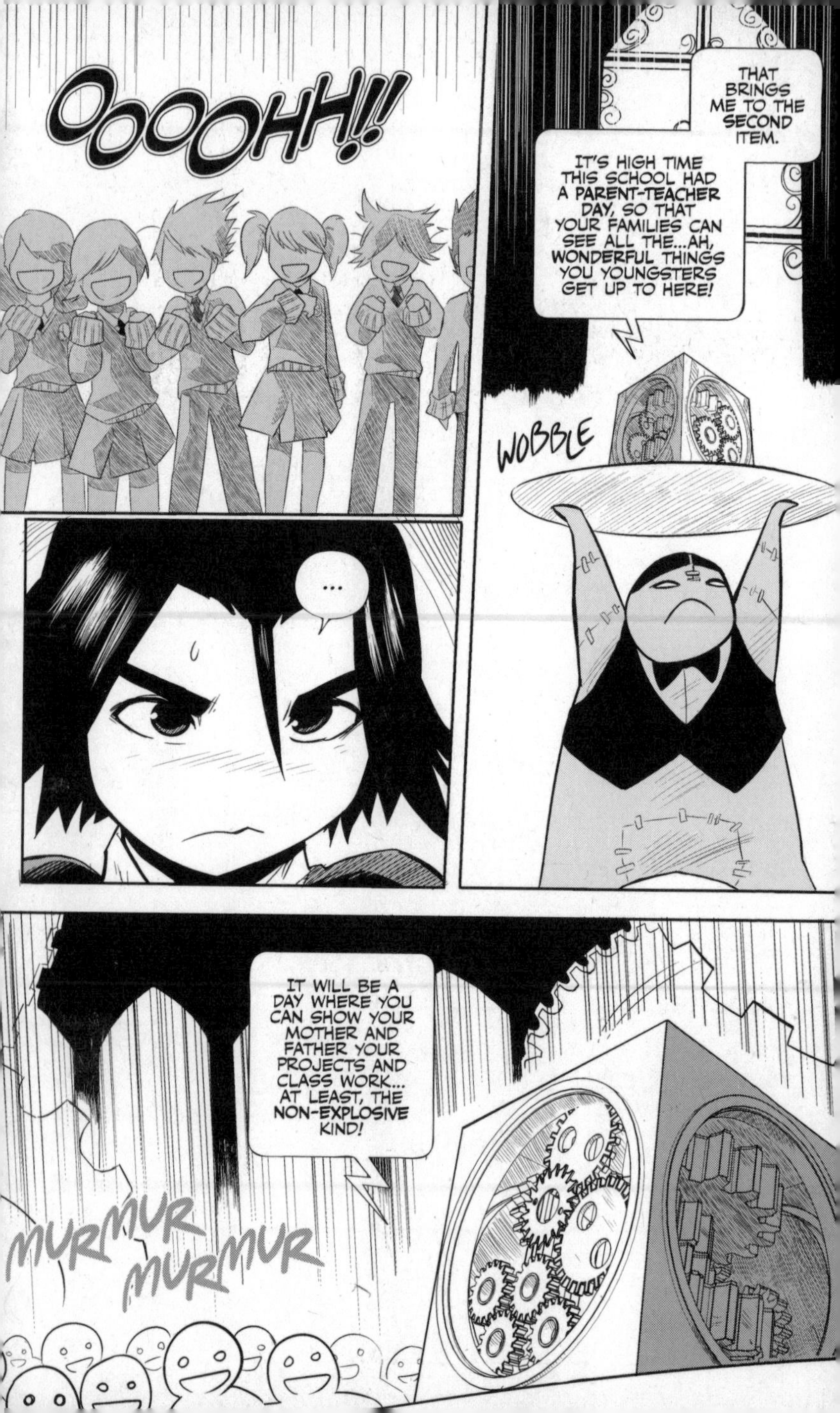
THAT BRINGS ME TO THE SECOND ITEM.
IT'S HIGH TIME THIS SCHOOL HAD A PARENT-TEACHER DAY, SO THAT YOUR FAMILIES CAN SEE ALL THE...AH, WONDERFUL THINGS YOU YOUNGSTERS GET UP TO HERE!
WOBBLE
OOOOHH!!
...
IT WILL BE A DAY WHERE YOU CAN SHOW YOUR MOTHER AND FATHER YOUR PROJECTS AND CLASS WORK... AT LEAST, THE NON-EXPLOSIVE KIND!
MURMUR MURMUR

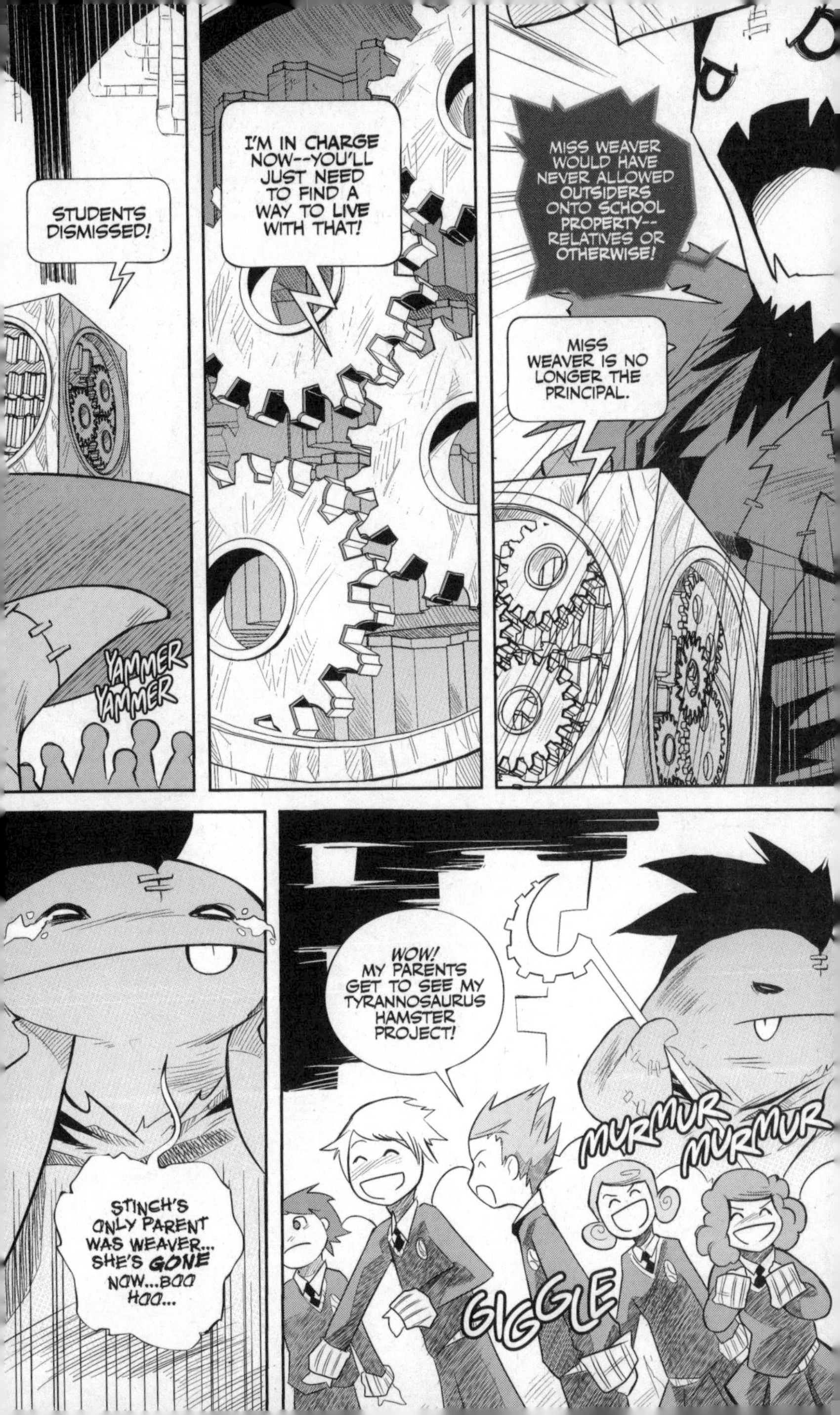
MISS WEAVER WOULD HAVE NEVER ALLOWED OUTSIDERS ONTO SCHOOL PROPERTY--RELATIVES OR OTHERWISE!
MISS WEAVER IS NO LONGER THE PRINCIPAL.
I'M IN CHARGE NOW--YOU'LL JUST NEED TO FIND A WAY TO LIVE WITH THAT!
STUDENTS DISMISSED!
YAMMER YAMMER
WOW! MY PARENTS GET TO SEE MY TYRANNOSAURUS HAMSTER PROJECT!
MURMUR MURMUR
GIGGLE
STINCH'S ONLY PARENT WAS WEAVER... SHE'S GONE NOW...BOO HOO...

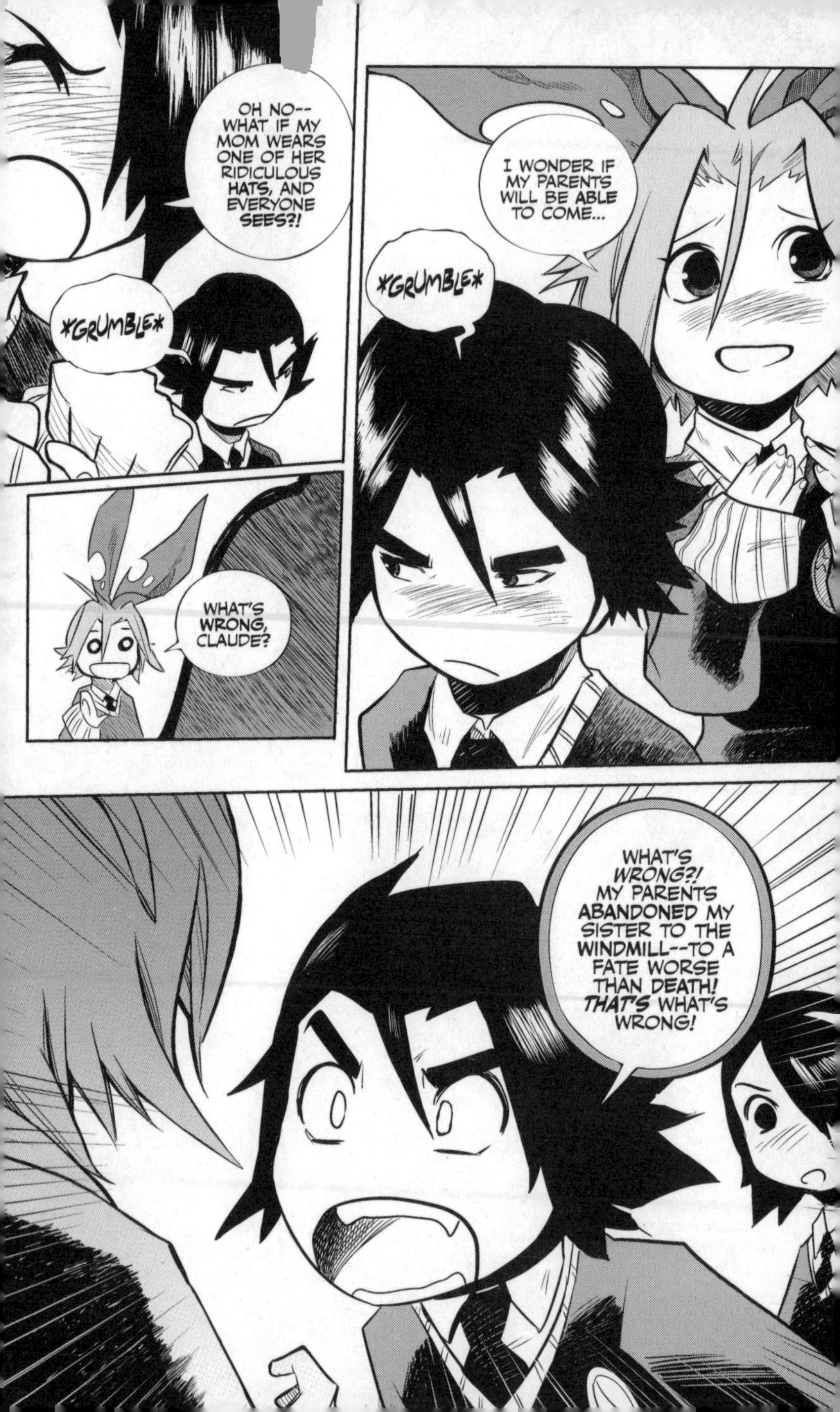
I WONDER IF MY PARENTS WILL BE ABLE TO COME...
GRUMBLE
OH NO--WHAT IF MY MOM WEARS ONE OF HER RIDICULOUS HATS, AND EVERYONE SEES?!
GRUMBLE
WHAT'S WRONG, CLAUDE?
WHAT'S *WRONG?!* MY PARENTS ABANDONED MY SISTER TO THE WINDMILL--TO A FATE WORSE THAN DEATH! ***THAT'S*** WHAT'S WRONG!

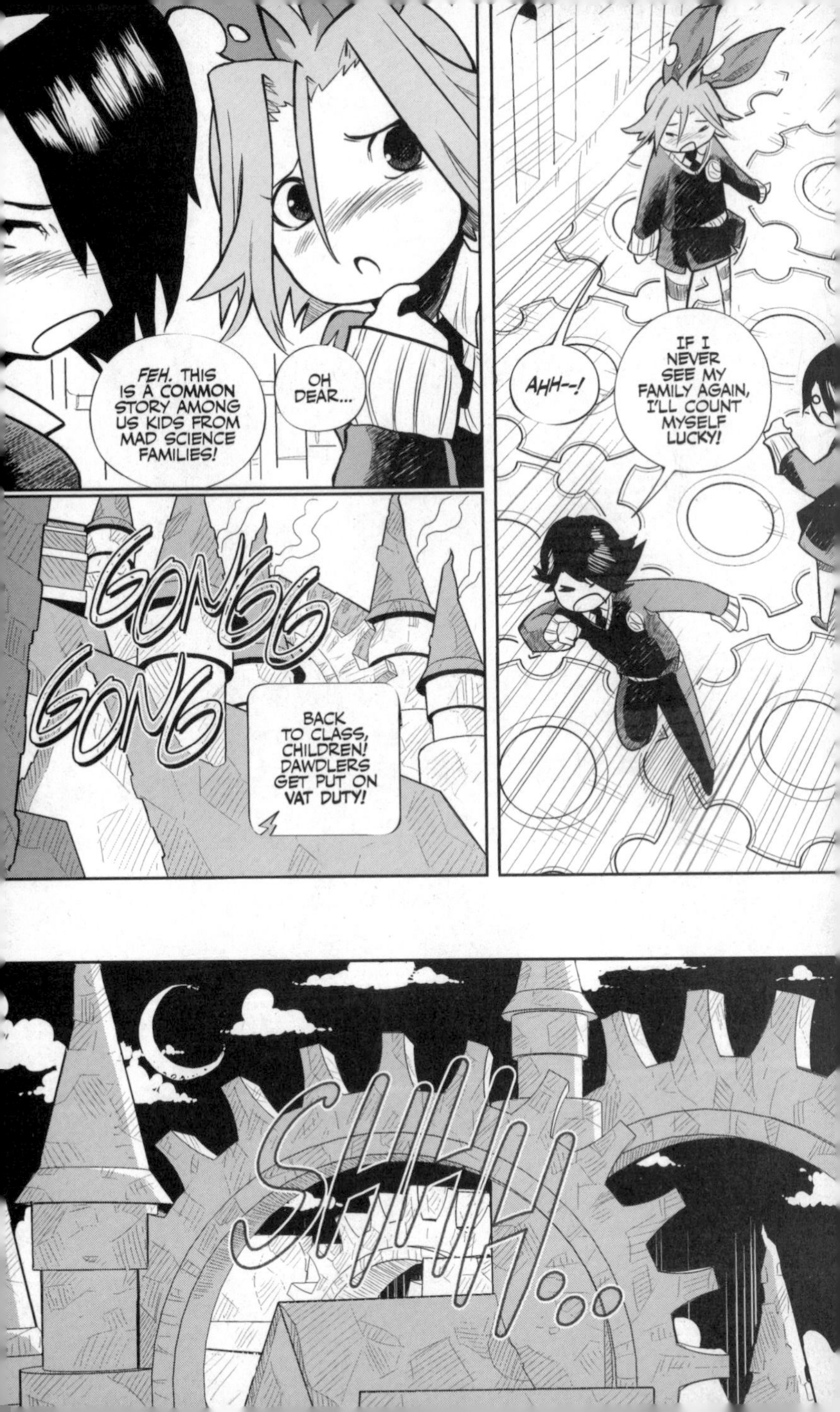
IF I NEVER SEE MY FAMILY AGAIN, I'LL COUNT MYSELF LUCKY!
AHH--!
OH DEAR...
FEH. THIS IS A COMMON STORY AMONG US KIDS FROM MAD SCIENCE FAMILIES!
GONGG GONG
BACK TO CLASS, CHILDREN! DAWDLERS GET PUT ON VAT DUTY!
SHHH...

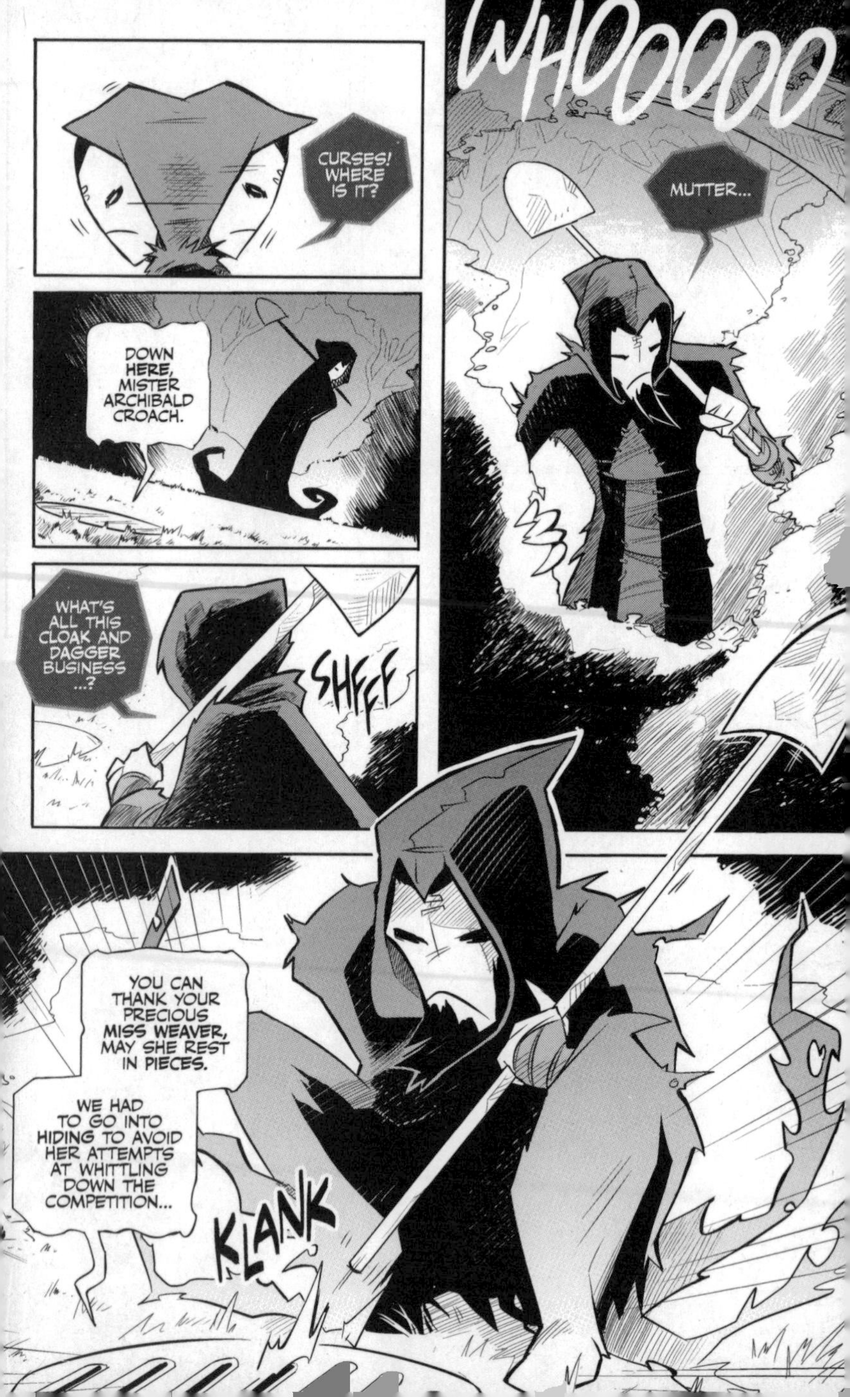
WHOOOOOO
MUTTER...
CURSES! WHERE IS IT?
DOWN HERE, MISTER ARCHIBALD CROACH.
WHAT'S ALL THIS CLOAK AND DAGGER BUSINESS ...?
SHFFF
YOU CAN THANK YOUR PRECIOUS MISS WEAVER, MAY SHE REST IN PIECES.
WE HAD TO GO INTO HIDING TO AVOID HER ATTEMPTS AT WHITTLING DOWN THE COMPETITION...
KLANK

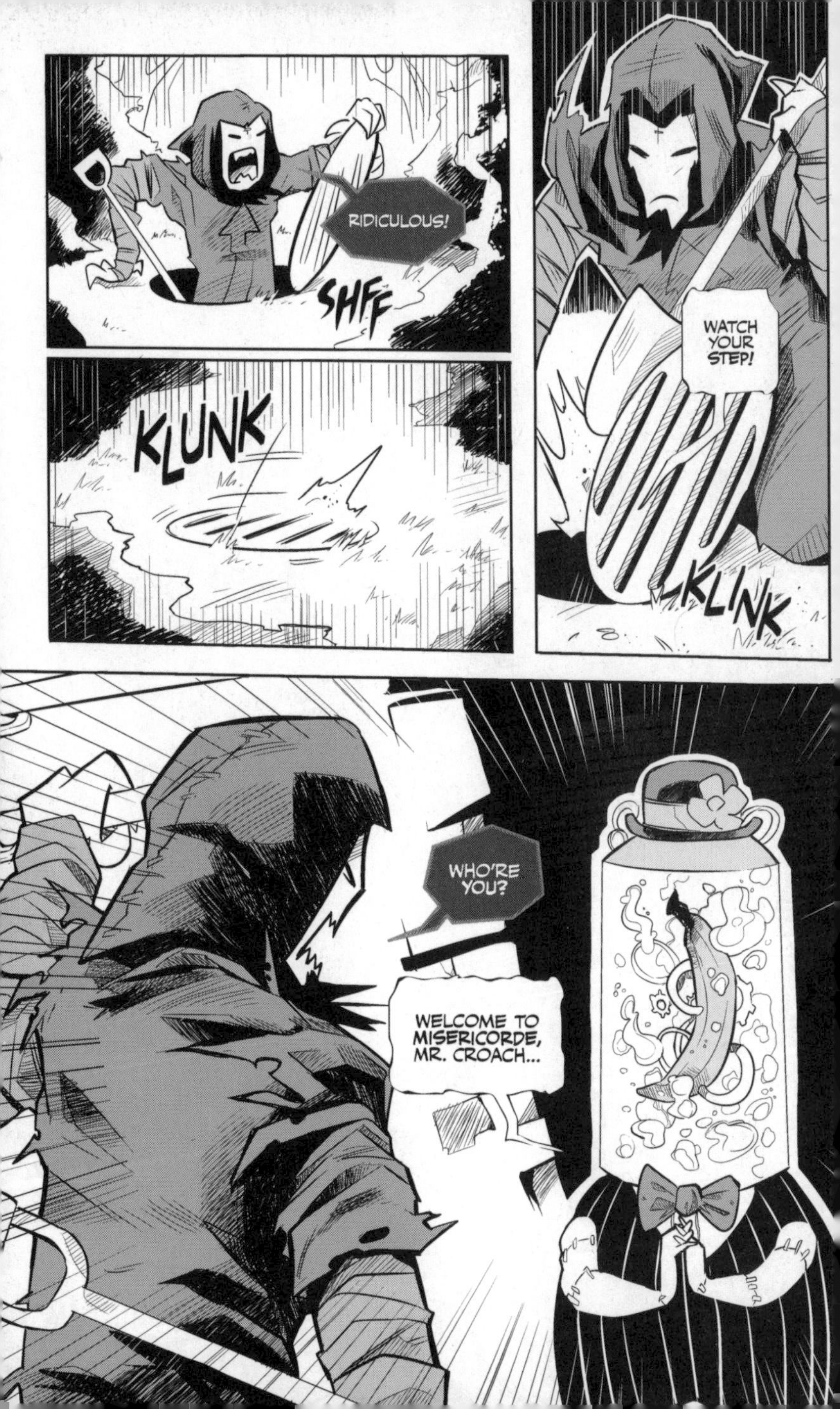
WATCH YOUR STEP!
KLINK
RIDICULOUS!
SHFF
KLUNK
WHO'RE YOU?
WELCOME TO MISERICORDE, MR. CROACH...

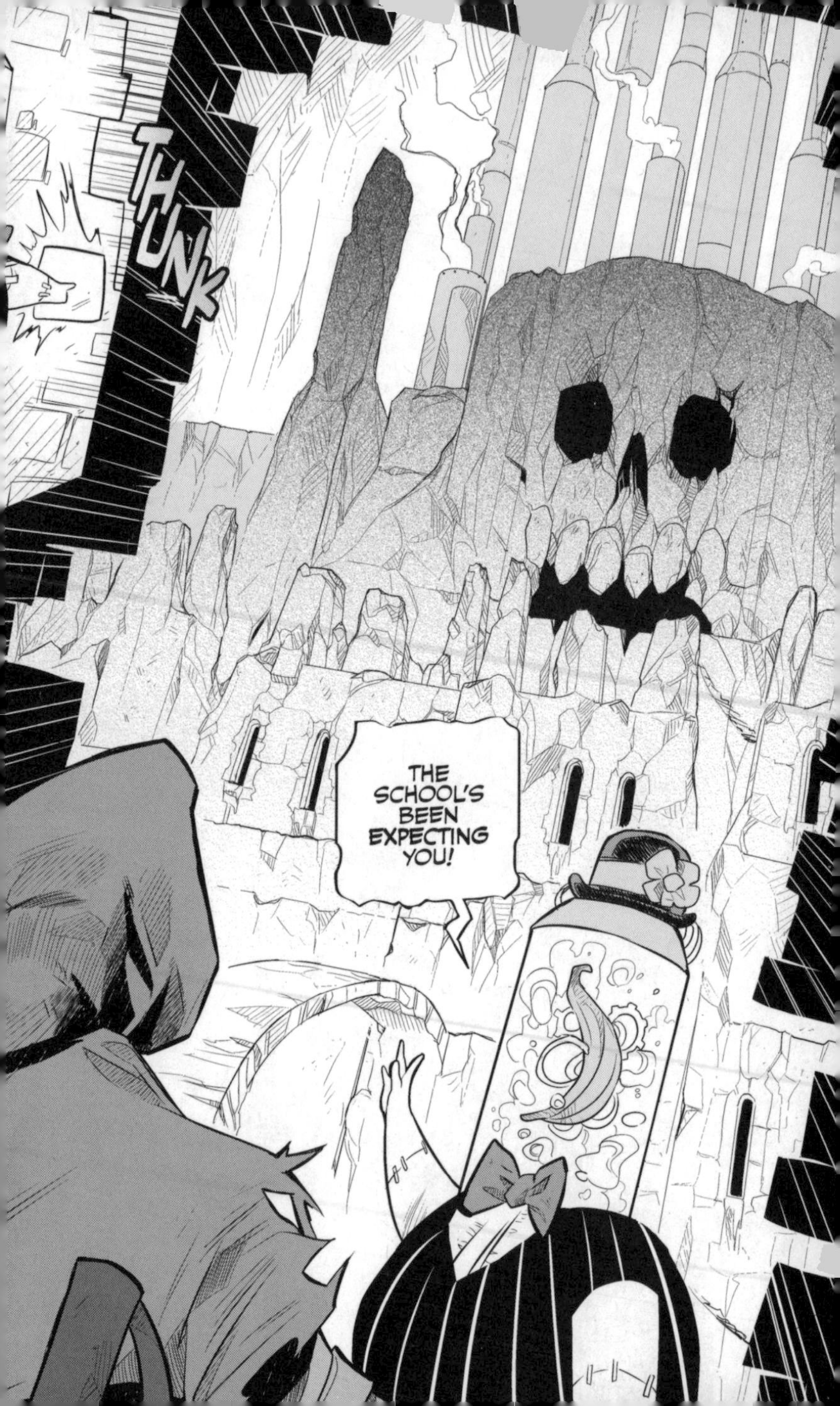
THUNK
THE SCHOOL'S BEEN EXPECTING YOU!

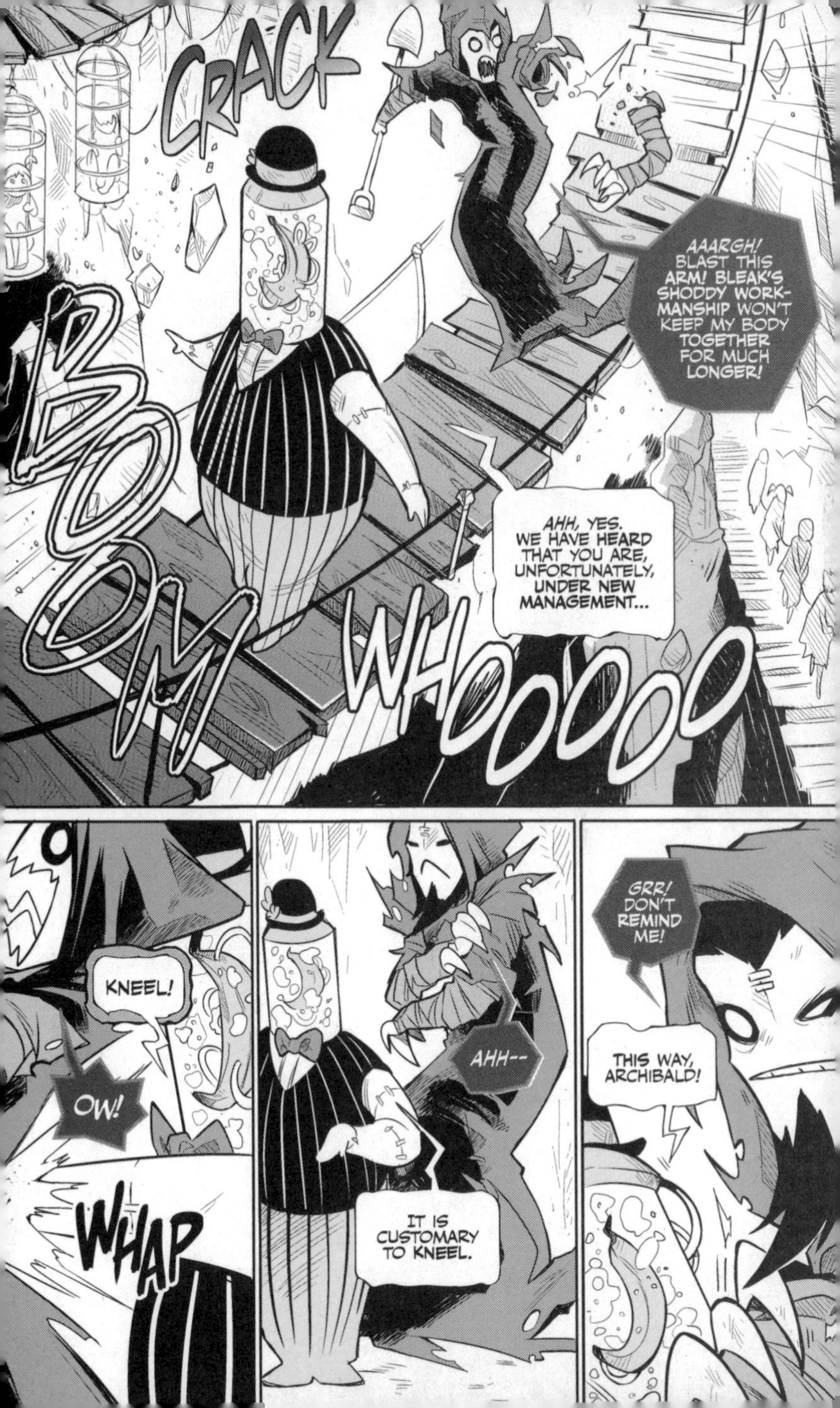
AAARGH! BLAST THIS ARM! BLEAK'S SHODDY WORK-MANSHIP WON'T KEEP MY BODY TOGETHER FOR MUCH LONGER!
CRACK
AHH, YES. WE HAVE HEARD THAT YOU ARE, UNFORTUNATELY, UNDER NEW MANAGEMENT...
BOOM
WHOOOOOO
GRR! DON'T REMIND ME!
THIS WAY, ARCHIBALD!
AHH--
IT IS CUSTOMARY TO KNEEL.
KNEEL!
OW!
WHAP

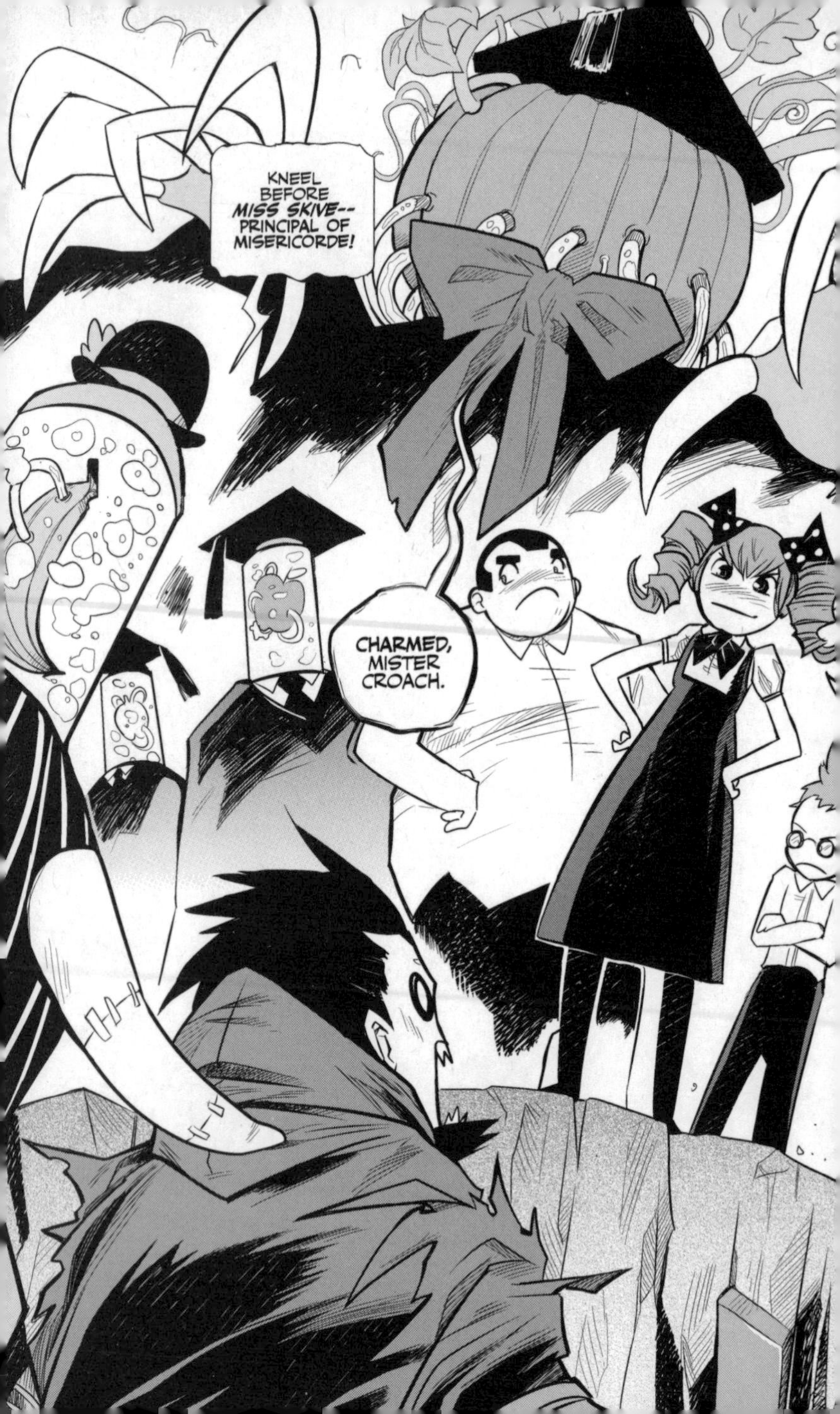
KNEEL BEFORE *MISS SKIVE--* PRINCIPAL OF MISERICORDE!
CHARMED, MISTER CROACH.

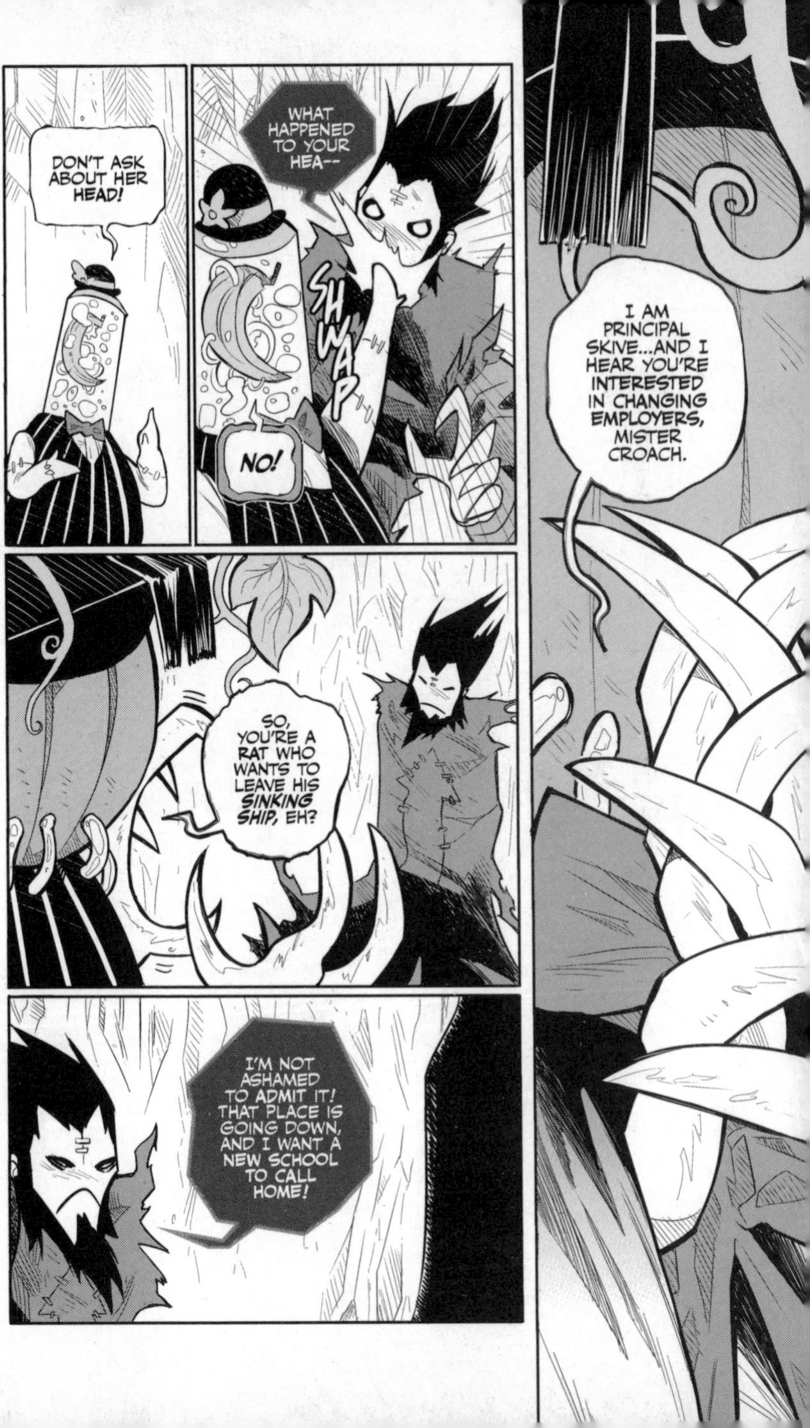
I AM PRINCIPAL SKIVE...AND I HEAR YOU'RE INTERESTED IN CHANGING EMPLOYERS, MISTER CROACH.
WHAT HAPPENED TO YOUR HEA--
SHWAP
NO!
DON'T ASK ABOUT HER HEAD!
SO, YOU'RE A RAT WHO WANTS TO LEAVE HIS *SINKING SHIP*, EH?
I'M NOT ASHAMED TO ADMIT IT! THAT PLACE IS GOING DOWN, AND I WANT A NEW SCHOOL TO CALL HOME!

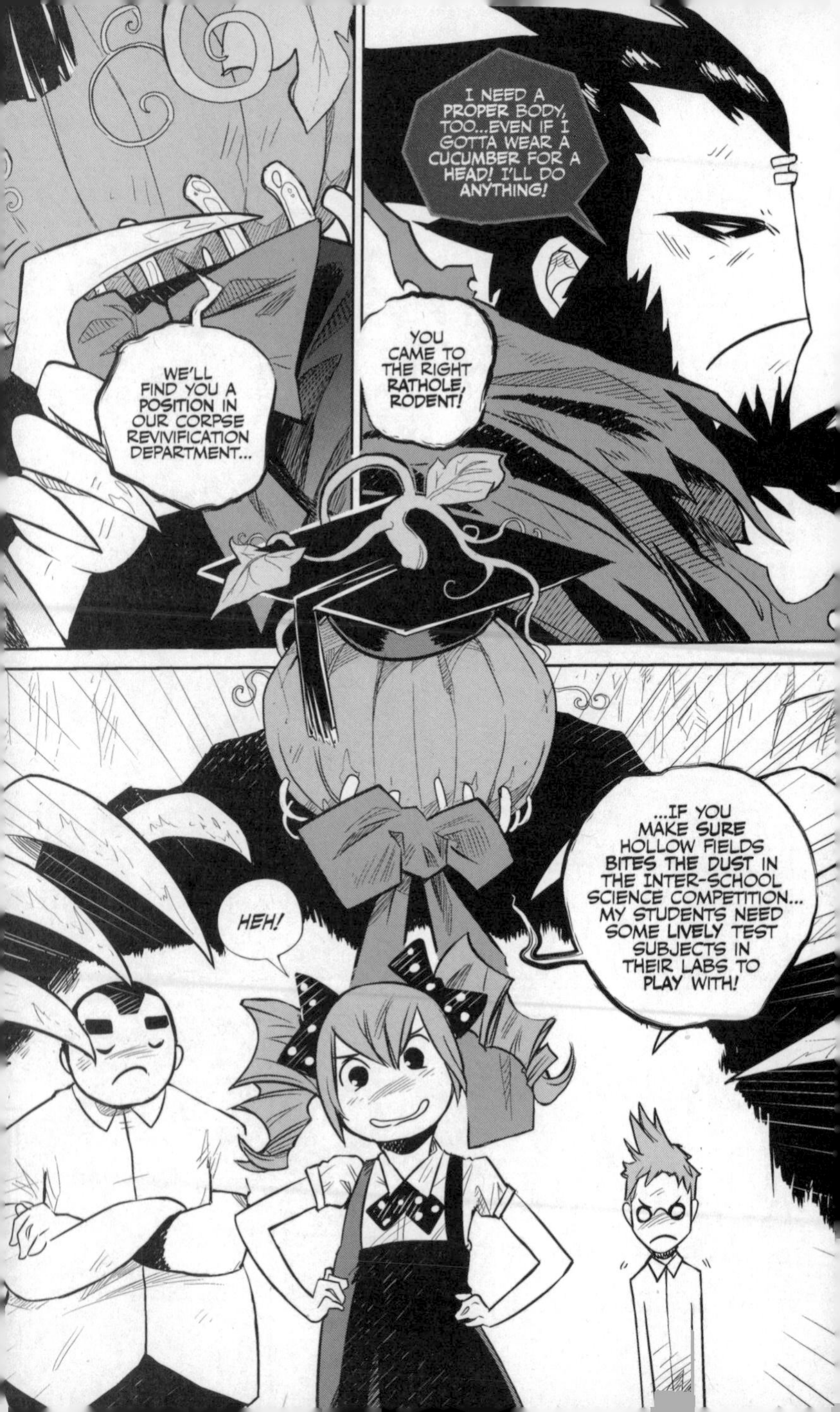
I NEED A PROPER BODY, TOO...EVEN IF I GOTTA WEAR A CUCUMBER FOR A HEAD! I'LL DO ANYTHING!
YOU CAME TO THE RIGHT RATHOLE, RODENT!
WE'LL FIND YOU A POSITION IN OUR CORPSE REVIVIFICATION DEPARTMENT...
...IF YOU MAKE SURE HOLLOW FIELDS BITES THE DUST IN THE INTER-SCHOOL SCIENCE COMPETITION... MY STUDENTS NEED SOME LIVELY TEST SUBJECTS IN THEIR LABS TO PLAY WITH!
HEH!

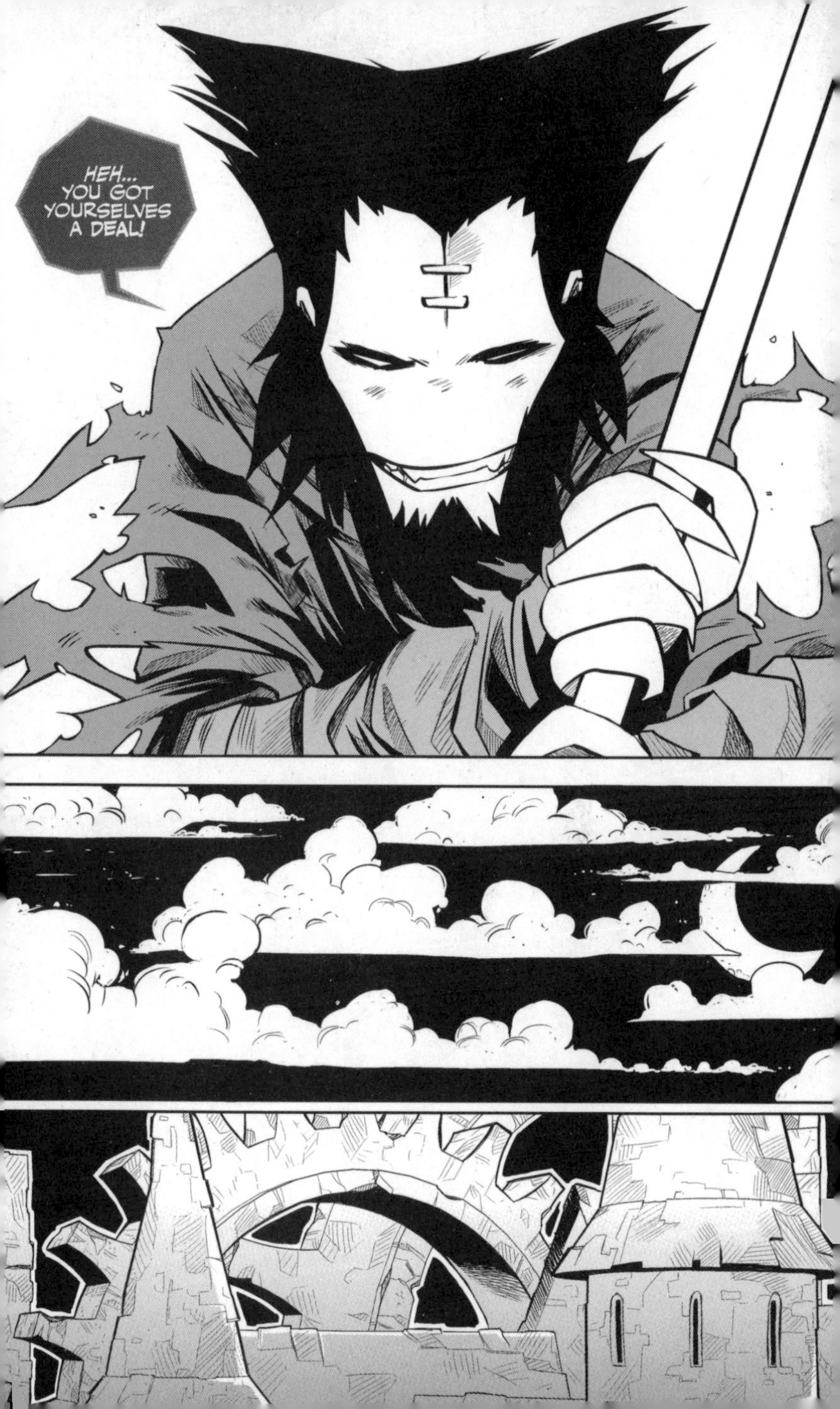
HEH... YOU GOT YOURSELVES A DEAL!

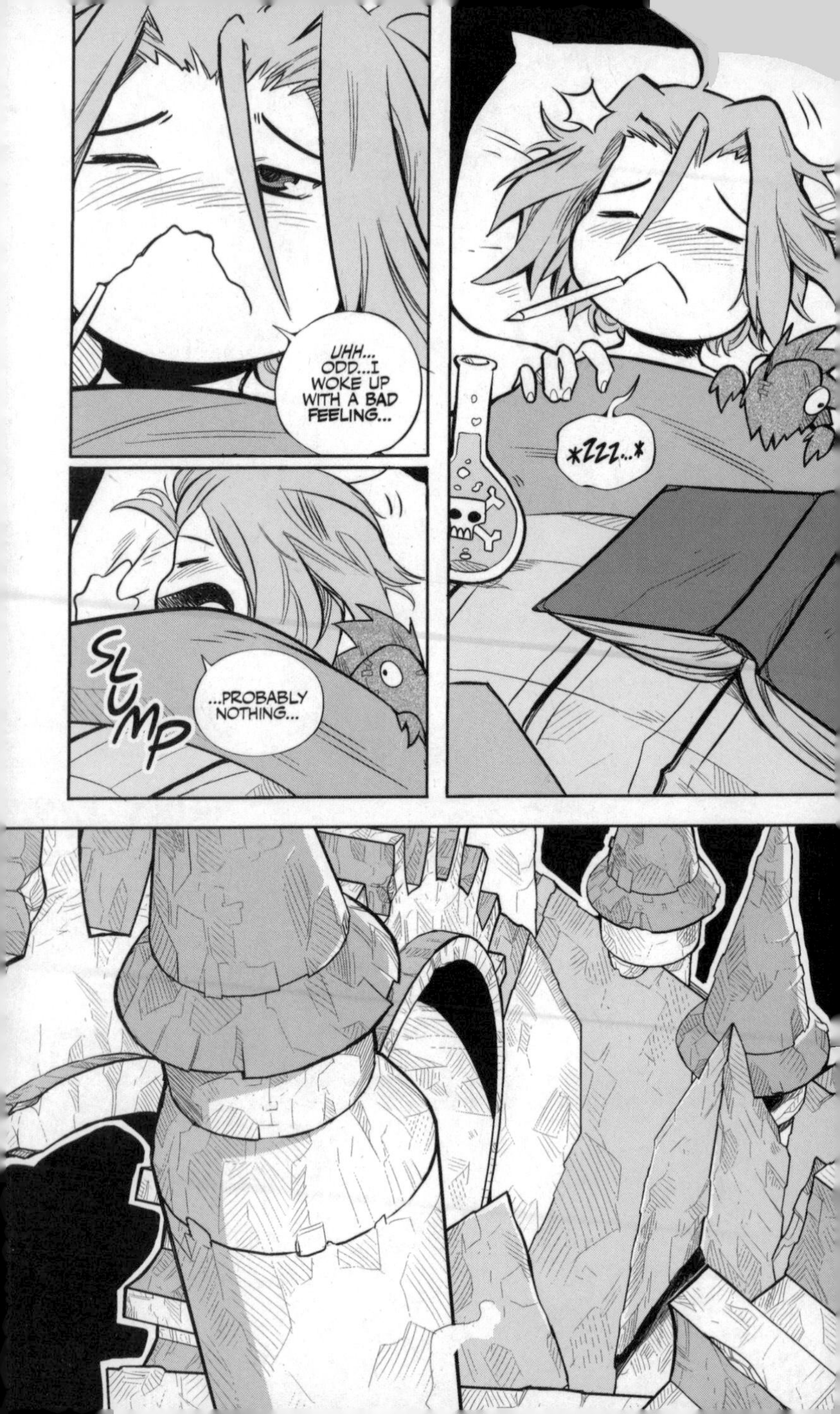
ZZZ...
UHH... ODD...I WOKE UP WITH A BAD FEELING...
...PROBABLY NOTHING...
SLUMP

CHAPTER THREE
MEET THE PARENTS

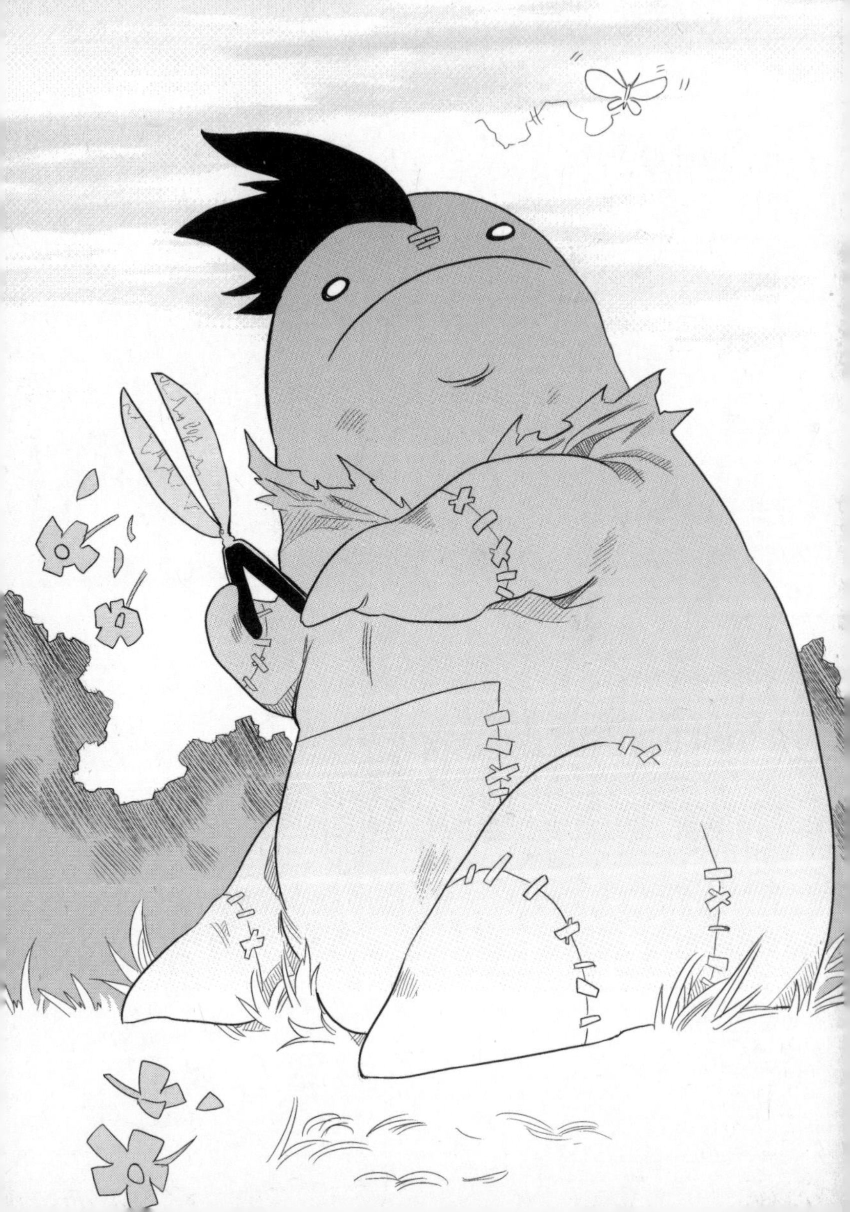

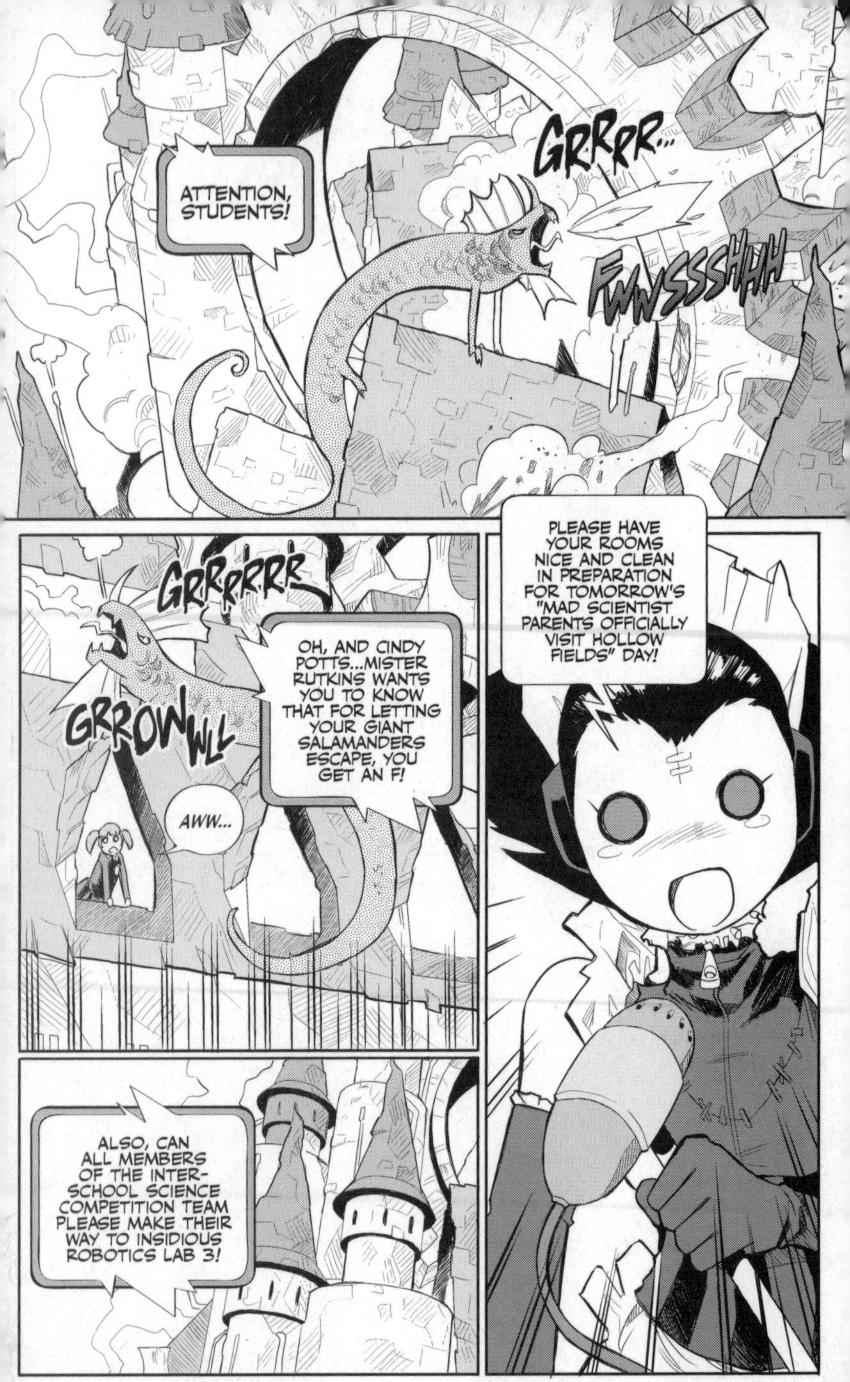
ATTENTION, STUDENTS!
GRRRR...
FWWSSSHHH
PLEASE HAVE YOUR ROOMS NICE AND CLEAN IN PREPARATION FOR TOMORROW'S "MAD SCIENTIST PARENTS OFFICIALLY VISIT HOLLOW FIELDS" DAY!
GRRRRRR
OH, AND CINDY POTTS...MISTER RUTKINS WANTS YOU TO KNOW THAT FOR LETTING YOUR GIANT SALAMANDERS ESCAPE, YOU GET AN F!
GRROWWLL
AWW...
ALSO, CAN ALL MEMBERS OF THE INTER-SCHOOL SCIENCE COMPETITION TEAM PLEASE MAKE THEIR WAY TO INSIDIOUS ROBOTICS LAB 3!

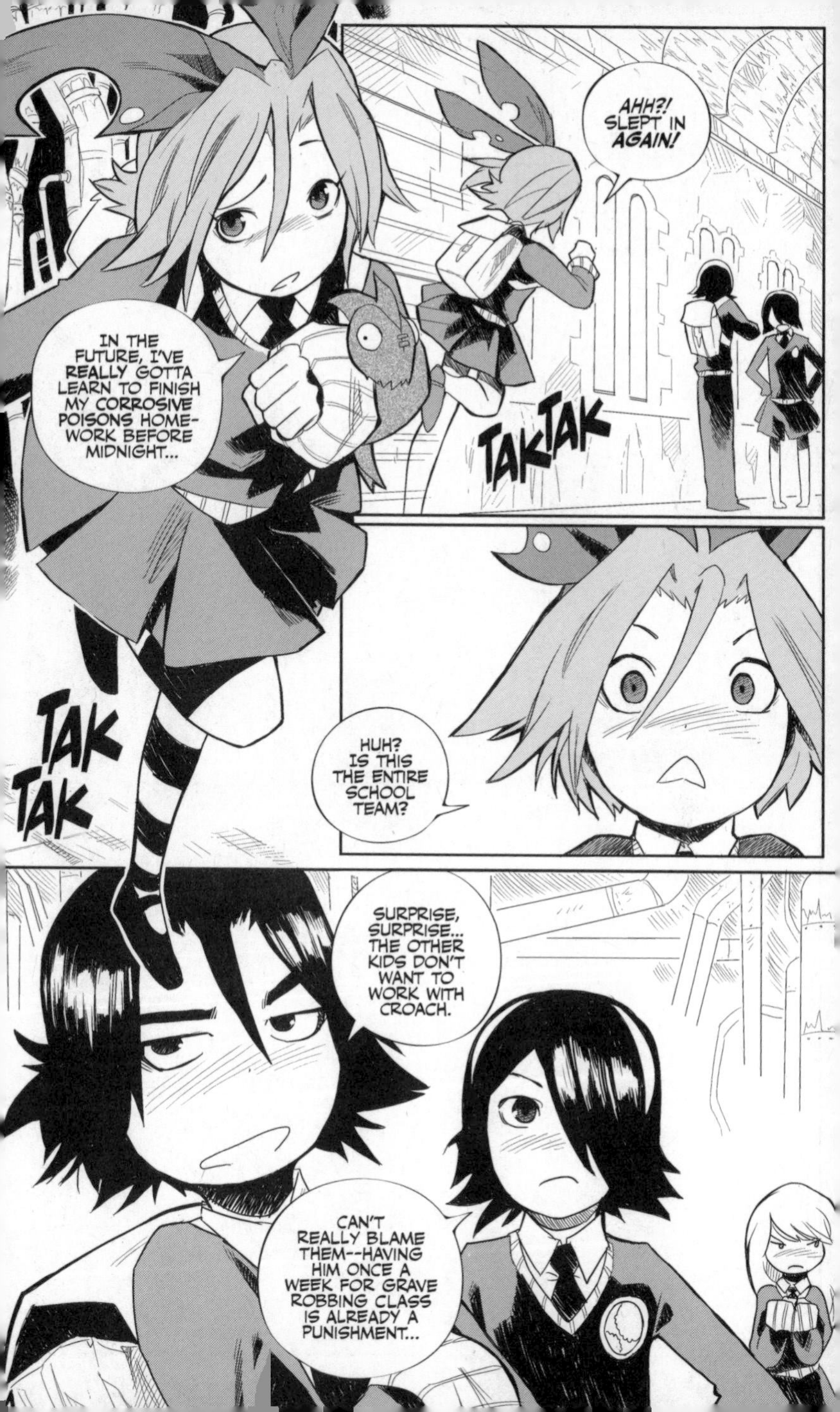
AHH?! SLEPT IN AGAIN!
TAKTAK
HUH? IS THIS THE ENTIRE SCHOOL TEAM?
IN THE FUTURE, I'VE REALLY GOTTA LEARN TO FINISH MY CORROSIVE POISONS HOME-WORK BEFORE MIDNIGHT...
TAK TAK
SURPRISE, SURPRISE... THE OTHER KIDS DON'T WANT TO WORK WITH CROACH.
CAN'T REALLY BLAME THEM--HAVING HIM ONCE A WEEK FOR GRAVE ROBBING CLASS IS ALREADY A PUNISHMENT...

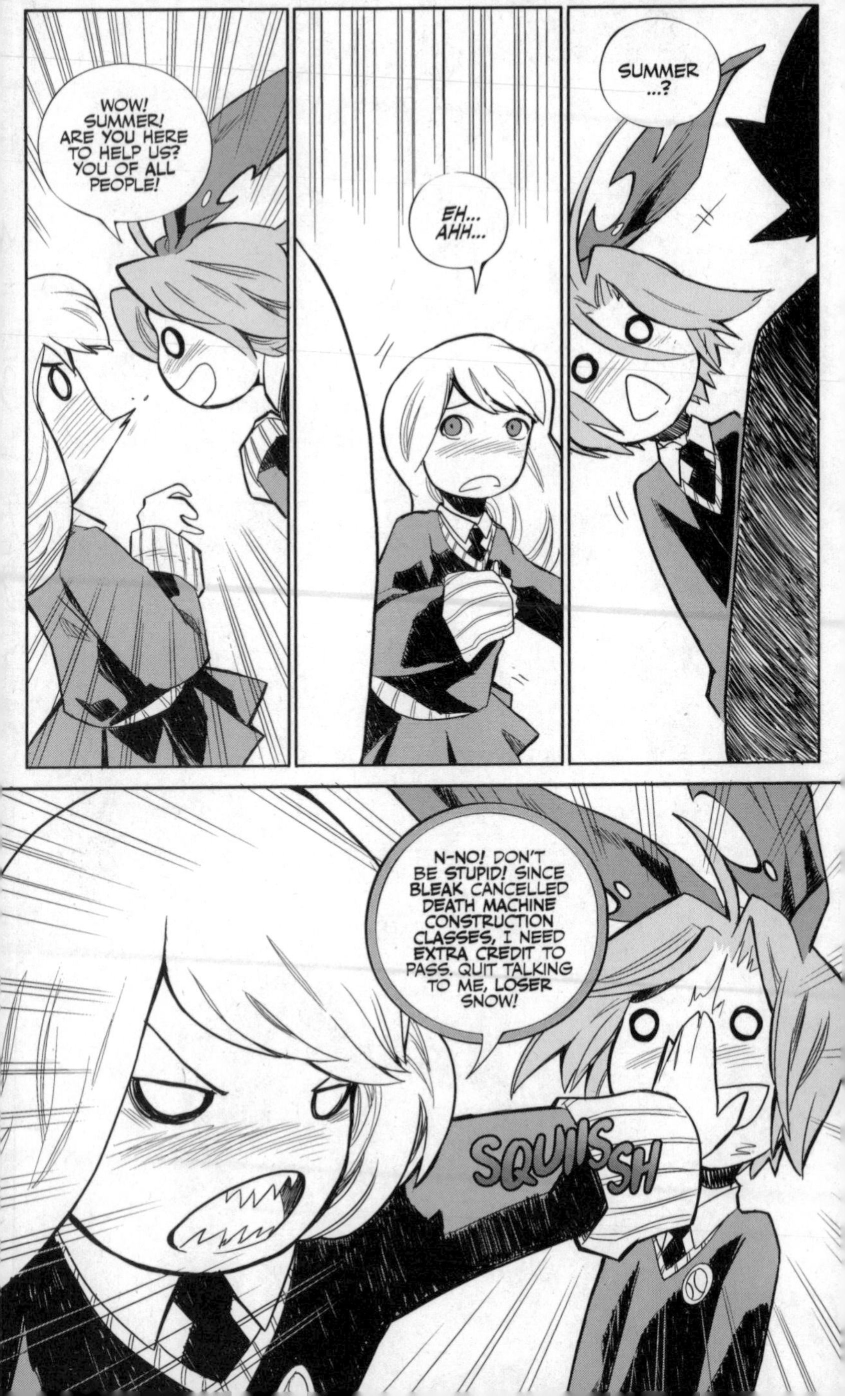
SUMMER ...?
EH... AHH...
WOW! SUMMER! ARE YOU HERE TO HELP US? YOU OF ALL PEOPLE!
N-NO! DON'T BE STUPID! SINCE BLEAK CANCELLED DEATH MACHINE CONSTRUCTION CLASSES, I NEED EXTRA CREDIT TO PASS. QUIT TALKING TO ME, LOSER SNOW!
SQUIISSH

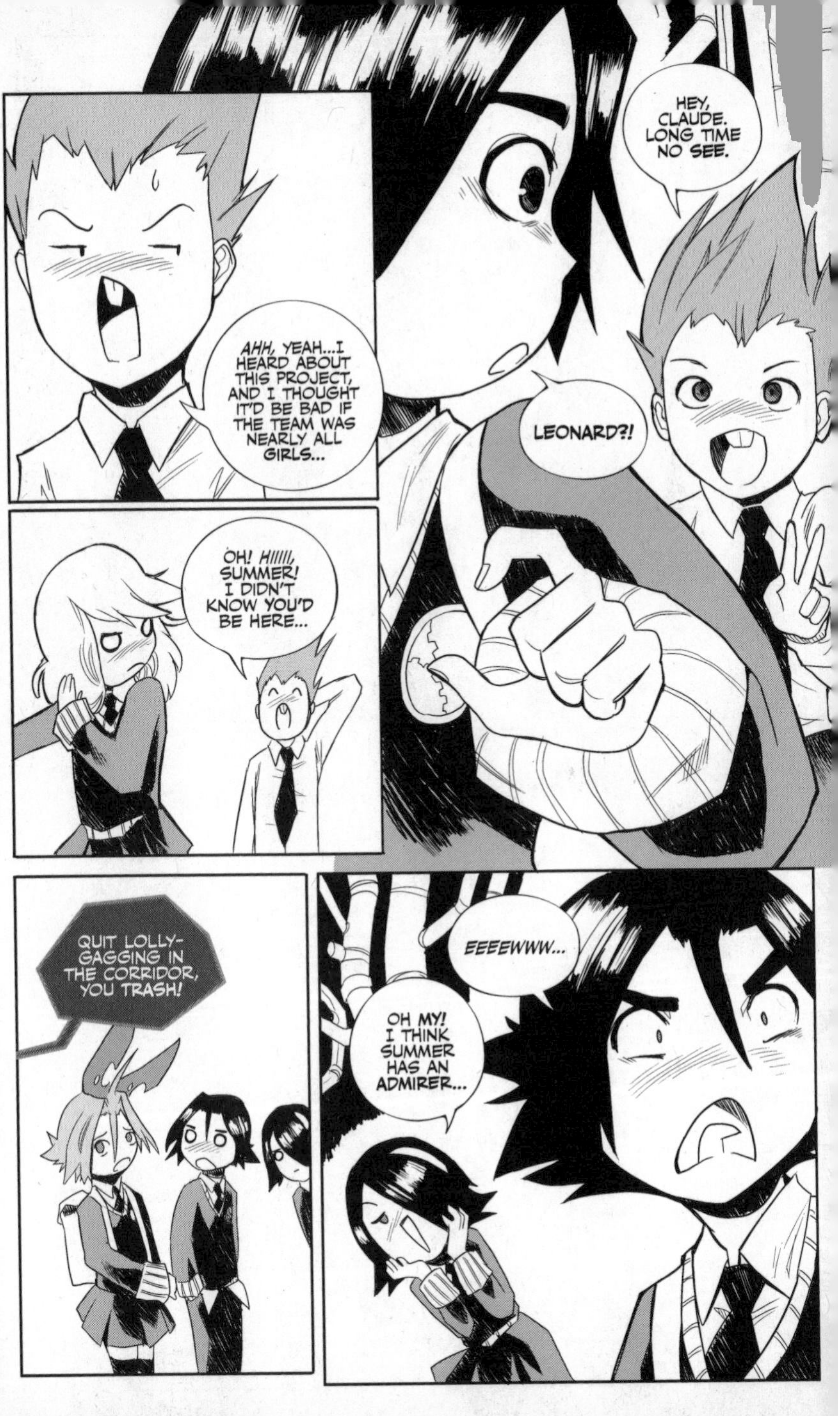
HEY, CLAUDE. LONG TIME NO SEE.
LEONARD?!
AHH, YEAH...I HEARD ABOUT THIS PROJECT, AND I THOUGHT IT'D BE BAD IF THE TEAM WAS NEARLY ALL GIRLS...
OH! HIIIII, SUMMER! I DIDN'T KNOW YOU'D BE HERE...
EEEEWWW...
OH MY! I THINK SUMMER HAS AN ADMIRER...
QUIT LOLLY-GAGGING IN THE CORRIDOR, YOU TRASH!

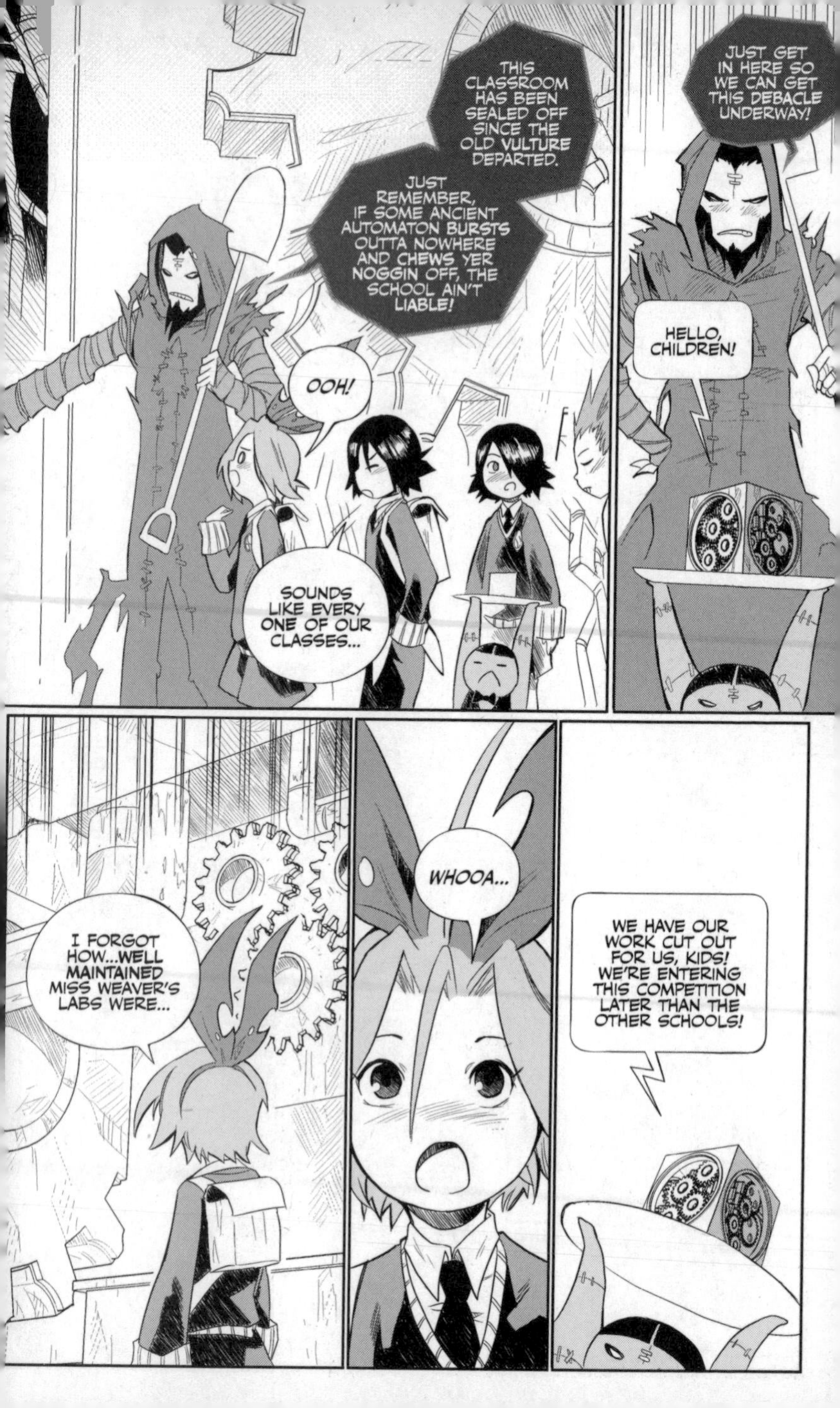
JUST GET IN HERE SO WE CAN GET THIS DEBACLE UNDERWAY!
HELLO, CHILDREN!
THIS CLASSROOM HAS BEEN SEALED OFF SINCE THE OLD VULTURE DEPARTED.
JUST REMEMBER, IF SOME ANCIENT AUTOMATON BURSTS OUTTA NOWHERE AND CHEWS YER NOGGIN OFF, THE SCHOOL AIN'T LIABLE!
OOH!
SOUNDS LIKE EVERY ONE OF OUR CLASSES...
WE HAVE OUR WORK CUT OUT FOR US, KIDS! WE'RE ENTERING THIS COMPETITION LATER THAN THE OTHER SCHOOLS!
WHOOA...
I FORGOT HOW...WELL MAINTAINED MISS WEAVER'S LABS WERE...

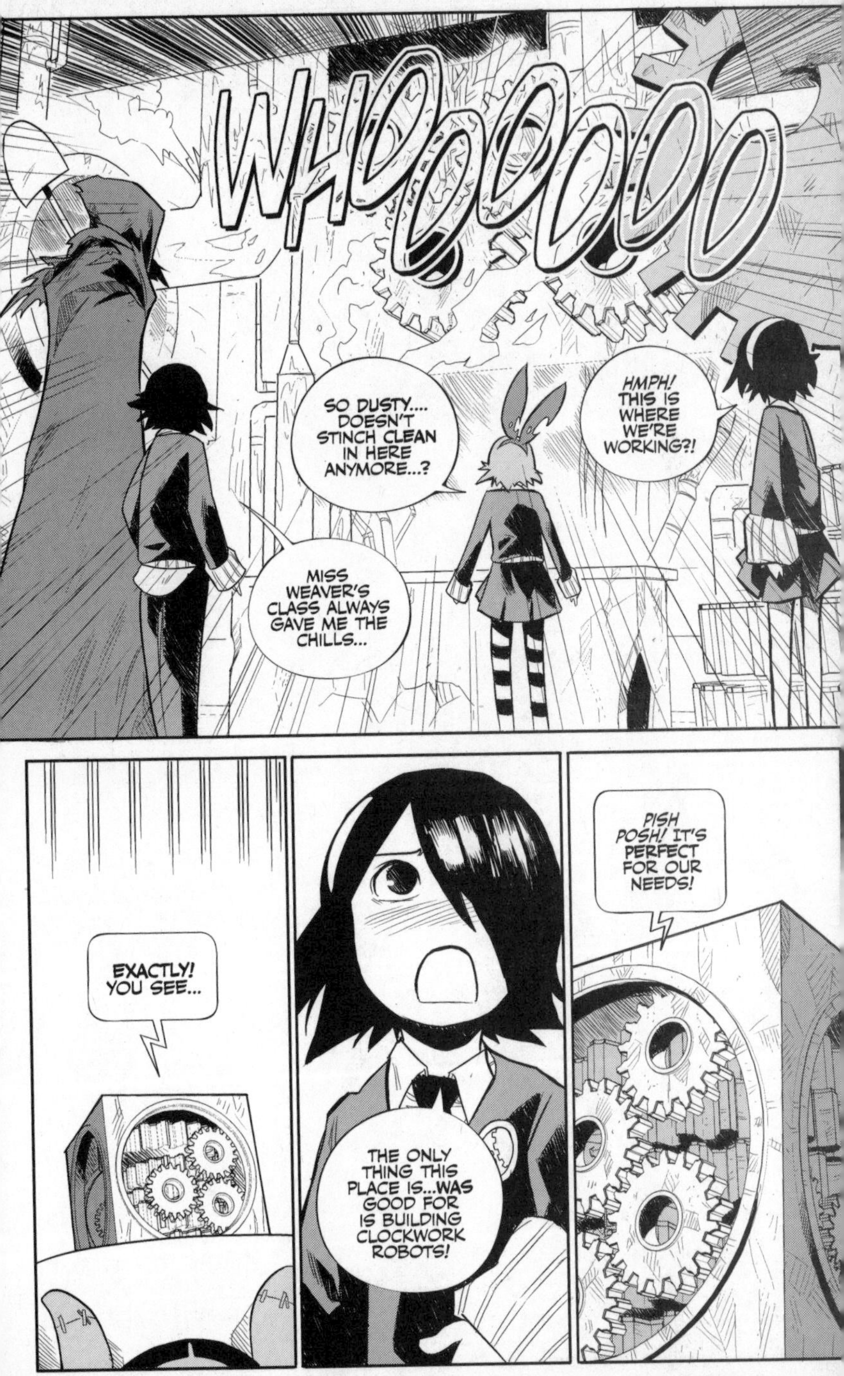
WHOOOOOOOO
HMPH! THIS IS WHERE WE'RE WORKING?!
SO DUSTY.... DOESN'T STINCH CLEAN IN HERE ANYMORE...?
MISS WEAVER'S CLASS ALWAYS GAVE ME THE CHILLS...
PISH POSH! IT'S PERFECT FOR OUR NEEDS!
THE ONLY THING THIS PLACE IS...WAS GOOD FOR IS BUILDING CLOCKWORK ROBOTS!
EXACTLY! YOU SEE...

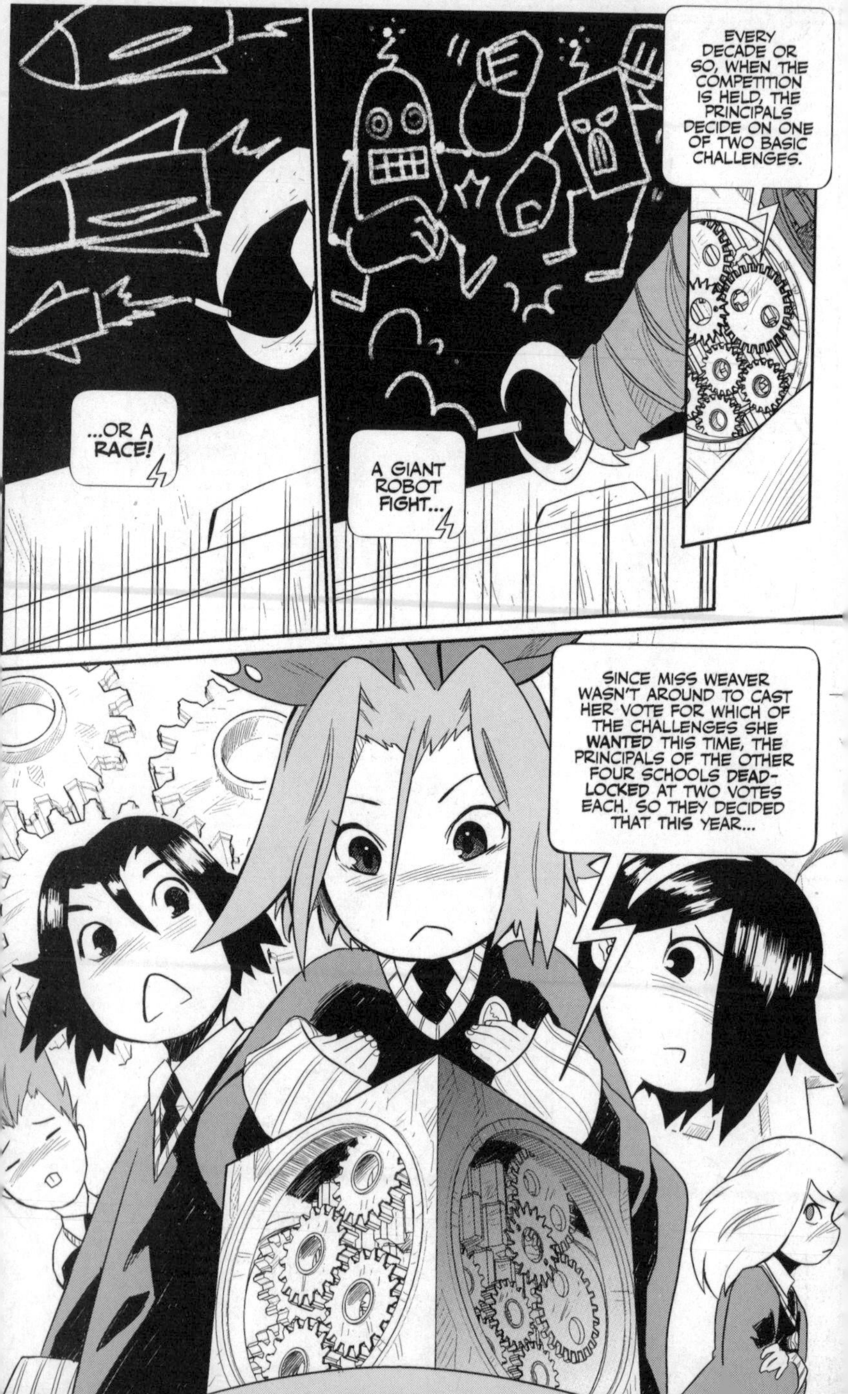

EVERY DECADE OR SO, WHEN THE COMPETITION IS HELD, THE PRINCIPALS DECIDE ON ONE OF TWO BASIC CHALLENGES.
A GIANT ROBOT FIGHT...
...OR A RACE!
SINCE MISS WEAVER WASN'T AROUND TO CAST HER VOTE FOR WHICH OF THE CHALLENGES SHE WANTED THIS TIME, THE PRINCIPALS OF THE OTHER FOUR SCHOOLS DEAD-LOCKED AT TWO VOTES EACH. SO THEY DECIDED THAT THIS YEAR...

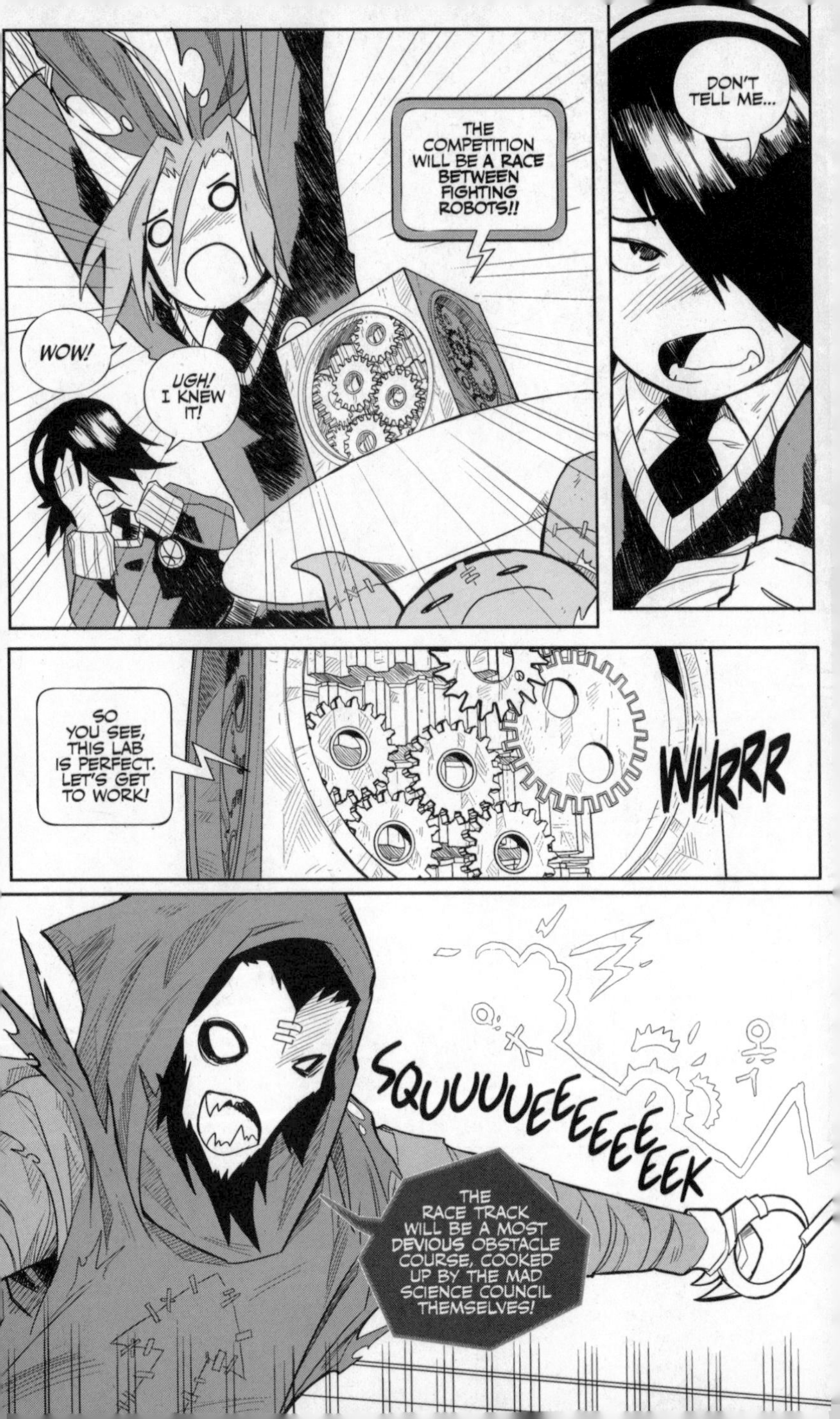

DON'T TELL ME...
THE COMPETITION WILL BE A RACE BETWEEN FIGHTING ROBOTS!!
UGH! I KNEW IT!
WOW!
WHRRR
SO YOU SEE, THIS LAB IS PERFECT. LET'S GET TO WORK!
SQUUUUEEEEEEEEEK
THE RACE TRACK WILL BE A MOST DEVIOUS OBSTACLE COURSE, COOKED UP BY THE MAD SCIENCE COUNCIL THEMSELVES!

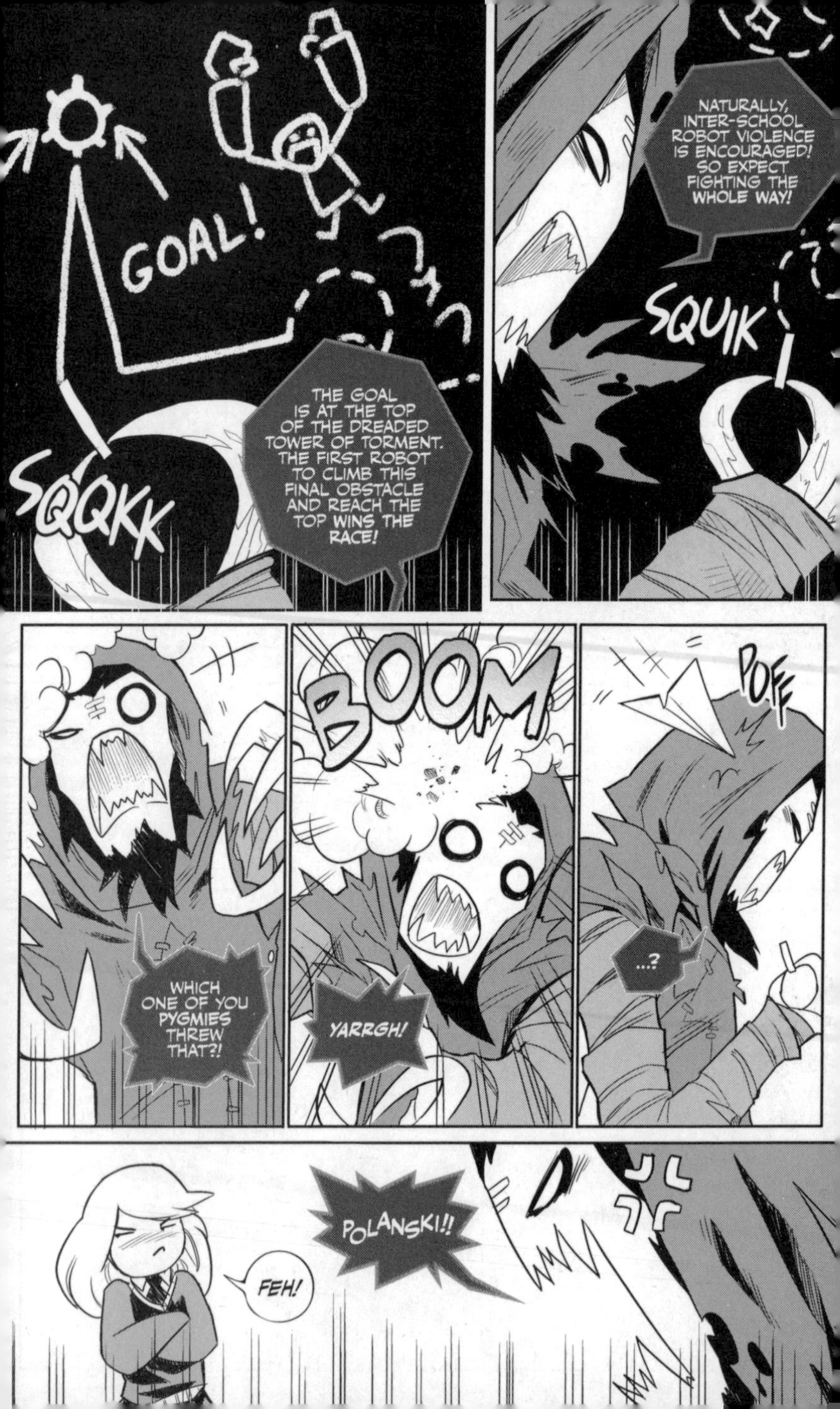
NATURALLY, INTER-SCHOOL ROBOT VIOLENCE IS ENCOURAGED! SO EXPECT FIGHTING THE WHOLE WAY!
SQUIK
GOAL!
SQQKK
THE GOAL IS AT THE TOP OF THE DREADED TOWER OF TORMENT. THE FIRST ROBOT TO CLIMB THIS FINAL OBSTACLE AND REACH THE TOP WINS THE RACE!
POFF
...?
BOOM
YARRGH!
WHICH ONE OF YOU PYGMIES THREW THAT?!
POLANSKI!!
FEH!

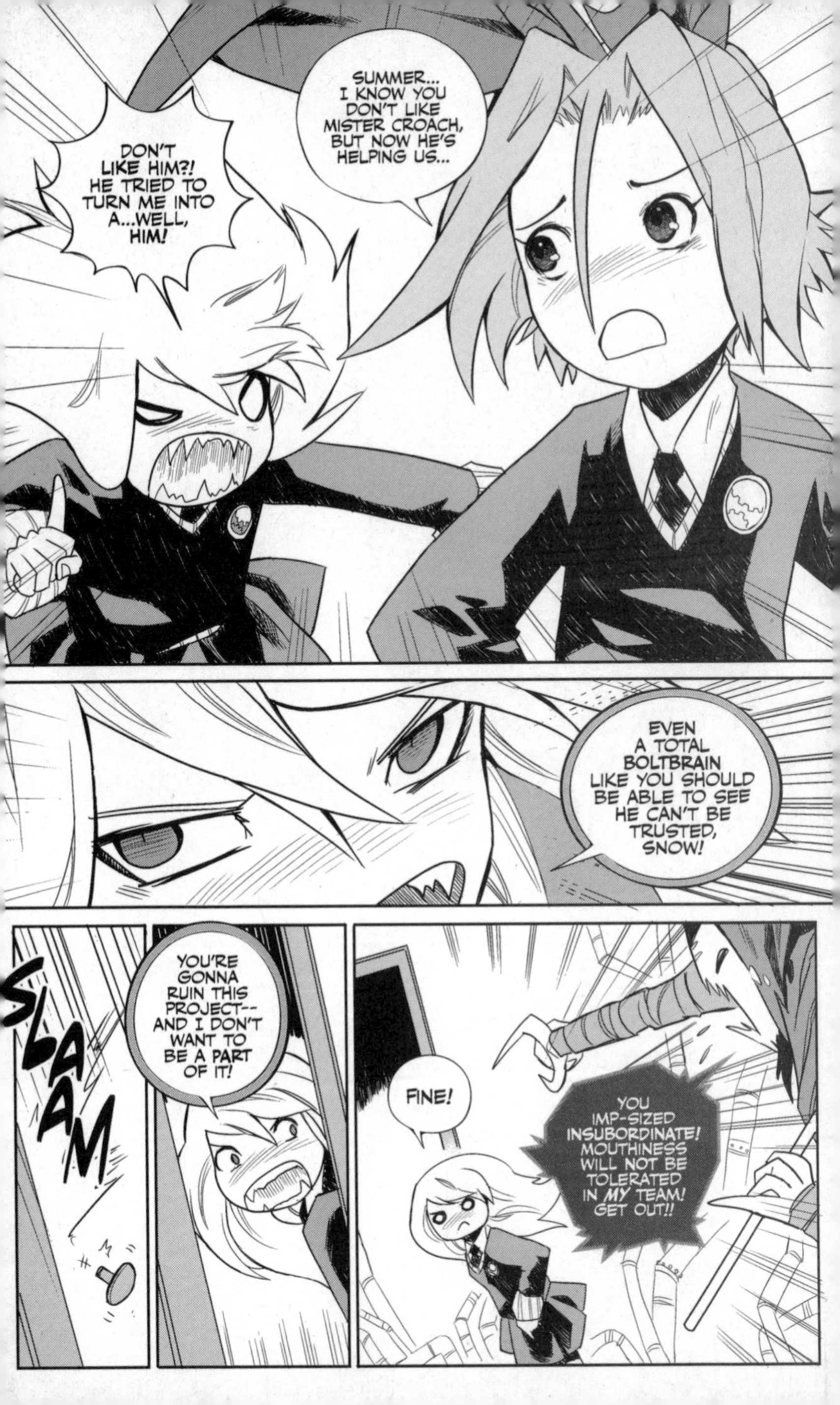
SUMMER... I KNOW YOU DON'T LIKE MISTER CROACH, BUT NOW HE'S HELPING US...
DON'T LIKE HIM?! HE TRIED TO TURN ME INTO A...WELL, HIM!
EVEN A TOTAL BOLTBRAIN LIKE YOU SHOULD BE ABLE TO SEE HE CAN'T BE TRUSTED, SNOW!
YOU IMP-SIZED INSUBORDINATE! MOUTHINESS WILL NOT BE TOLERATED IN *MY* TEAM! GET OUT!!
FINE!
YOU'RE GONNA RUIN THIS PROJECT-- AND I DON'T WANT TO BE A PART OF IT!
SLAM!

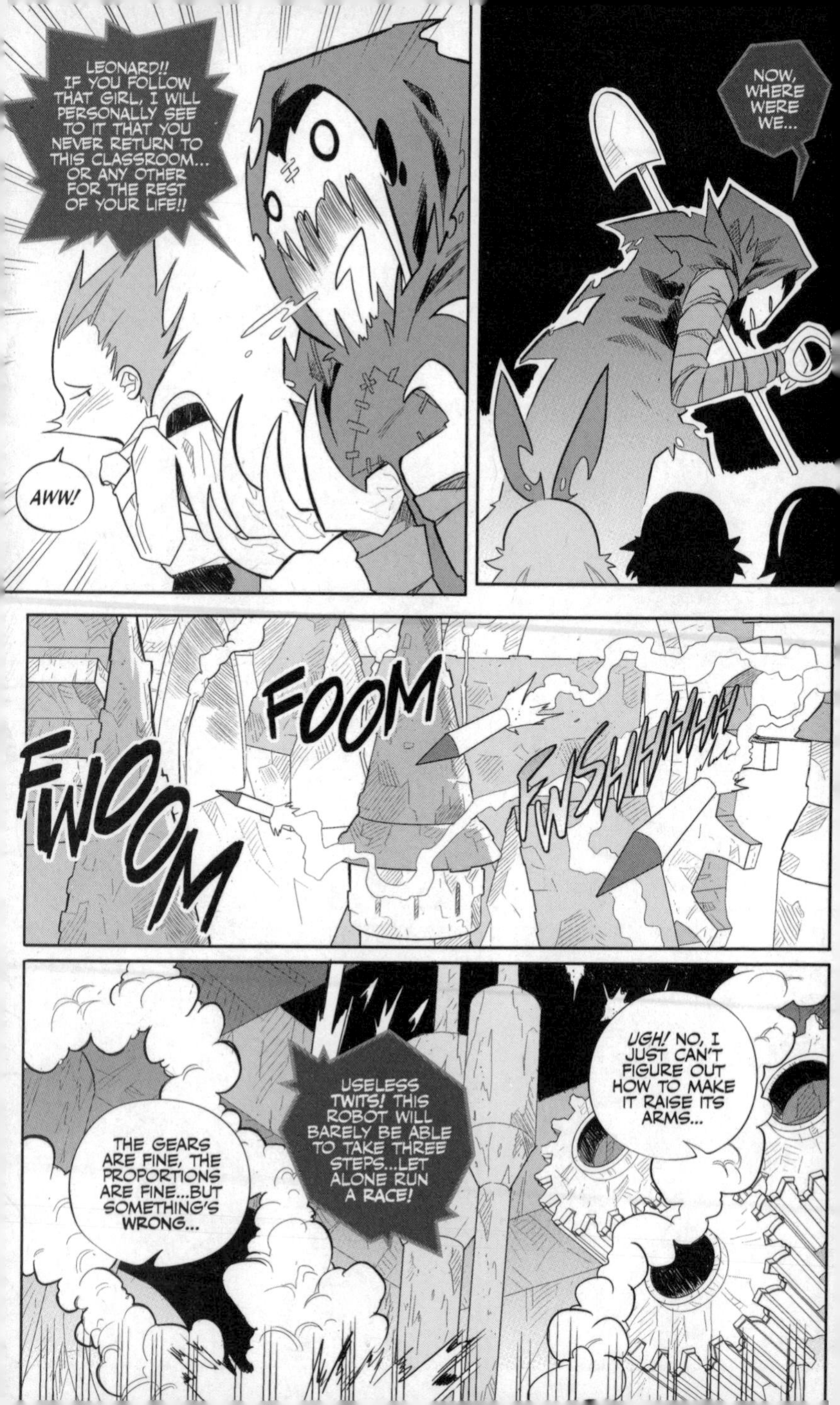
NOW, WHERE WERE WE...
LEONARD!! IF YOU FOLLOW THAT GIRL, I WILL PERSONALLY SEE TO IT THAT YOU NEVER RETURN TO THIS CLASSROOM... OR ANY OTHER FOR THE REST OF YOUR LIFE!!
AWW!
FWSHHHHH
FOOM
FWOOOM
UGH! NO, I JUST CAN'T FIGURE OUT HOW TO MAKE IT RAISE ITS ARMS...
USELESS TWITS! THIS ROBOT WILL BARELY BE ABLE TO TAKE THREE STEPS...LET ALONE RUN A RACE!
THE GEARS ARE FINE, THE PROPORTIONS ARE FINE...BUT SOMETHING'S WRONG...

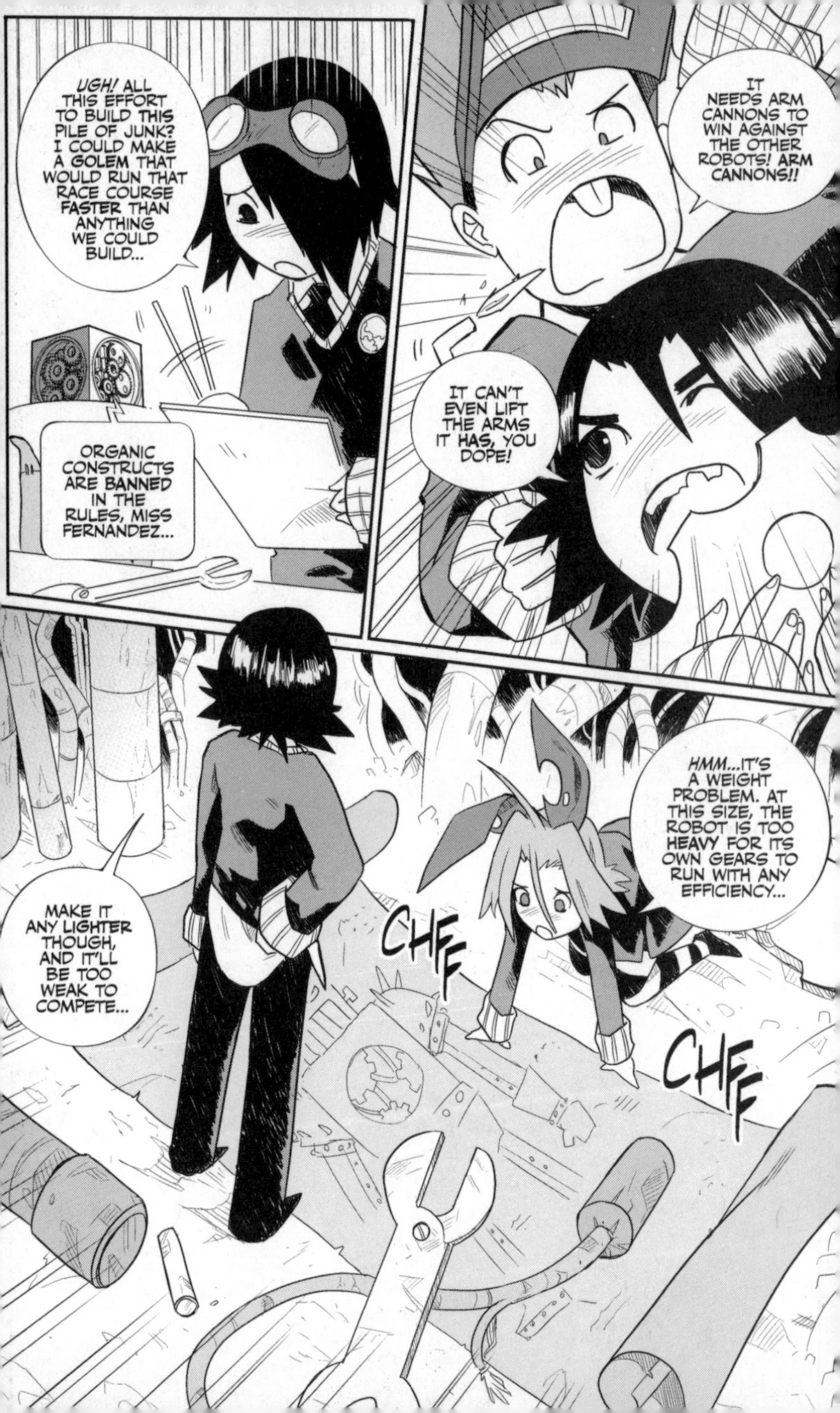
IT NEEDS ARM CANNONS TO WIN AGAINST THE OTHER ROBOTS! ARM CANNONS!!
IT CAN'T EVEN LIFT THE ARMS IT HAS, YOU DOPE!
UGH! ALL THIS EFFORT TO BUILD THIS PILE OF JUNK? I COULD MAKE A GOLEM THAT WOULD RUN THAT RACE COURSE FASTER THAN ANYTHING WE COULD BUILD...
ORGANIC CONSTRUCTS ARE BANNED IN THE RULES, MISS FERNANDEZ...
HMM...IT'S A WEIGHT PROBLEM. AT THIS SIZE, THE ROBOT IS TOO HEAVY FOR ITS OWN GEARS TO RUN WITH ANY EFFICIENCY...
CHFF
CHFF
MAKE IT ANY LIGHTER THOUGH, AND IT'LL BE TOO WEAK TO COMPETE...

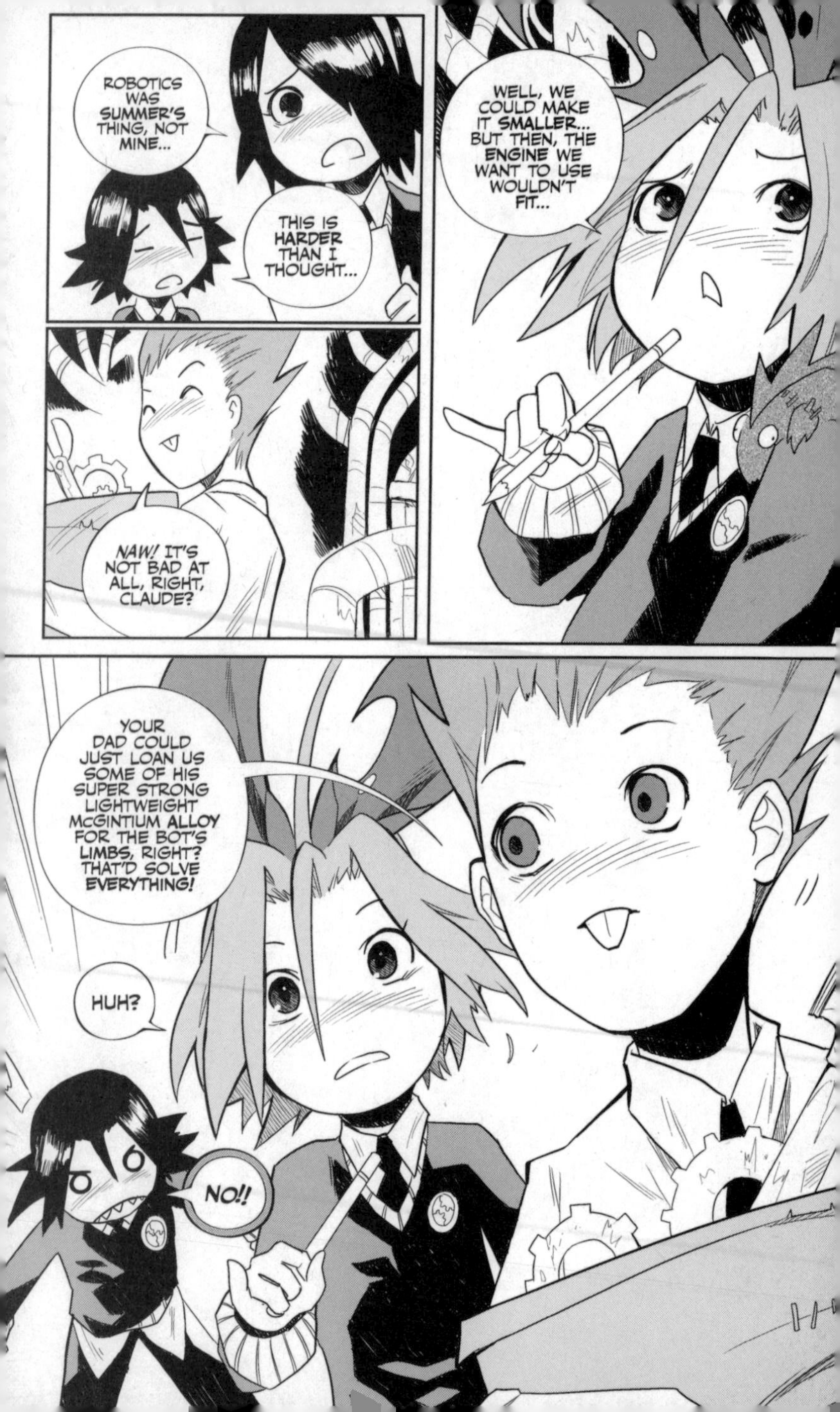
WELL, WE COULD MAKE IT SMALLER... BUT THEN, THE ENGINE WE WANT TO USE WOULDN'T FIT...
ROBOTICS WAS SUMMER'S THING, NOT MINE...
THIS IS HARDER THAN I THOUGHT...
NAW! IT'S NOT BAD AT ALL, RIGHT, CLAUDE?
YOUR DAD COULD JUST LOAN US SOME OF HIS SUPER STRONG LIGHTWEIGHT McGINTIUM ALLOY FOR THE BOT'S LIMBS, RIGHT? THAT'D SOLVE EVERYTHING!
HUH?
NO!!

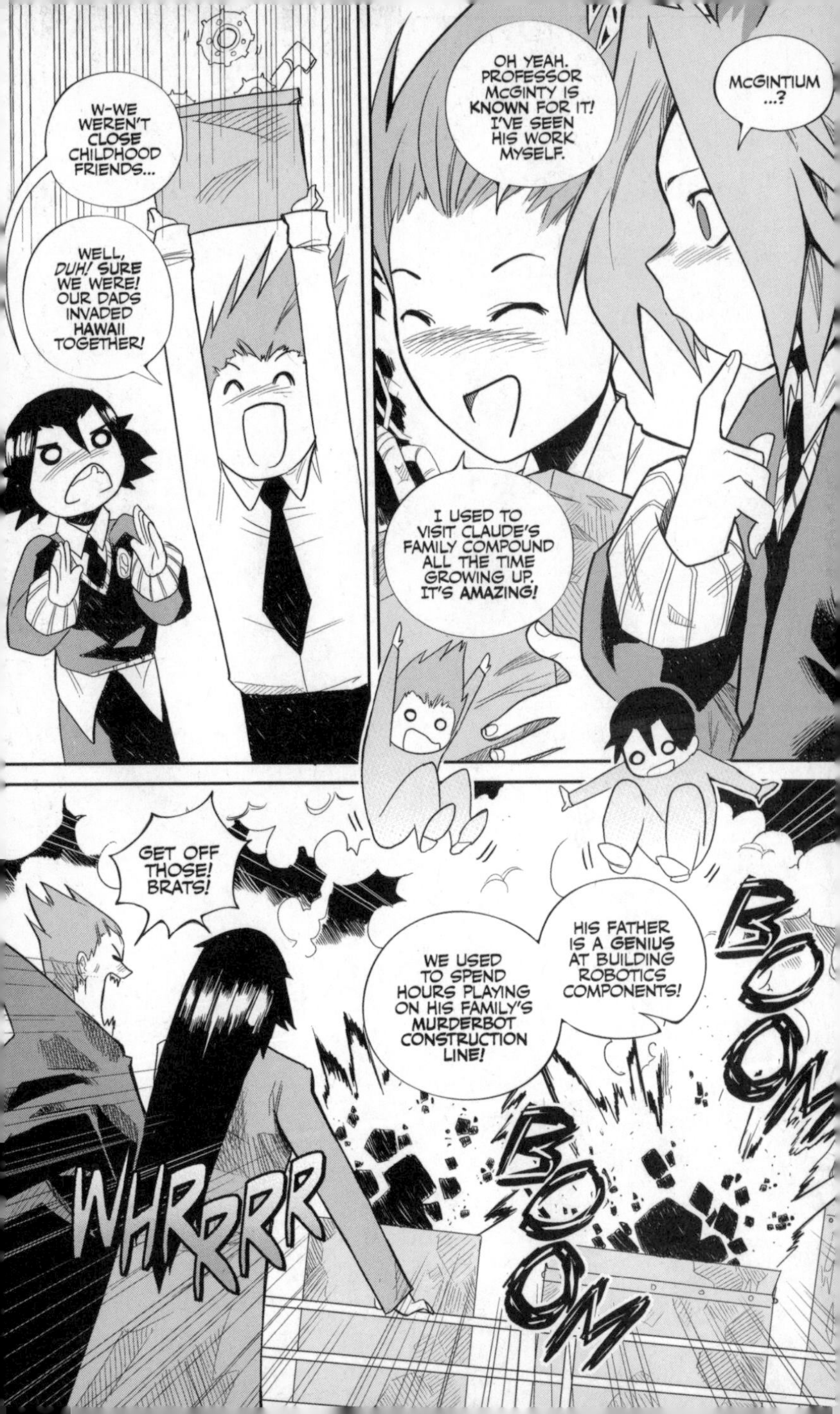
McGINTIUM ...?
OH YEAH. PROFESSOR McGINTY IS KNOWN FOR IT! I'VE SEEN HIS WORK MYSELF.
I USED TO VISIT CLAUDE'S FAMILY COMPOUND ALL THE TIME GROWING UP. IT'S AMAZING!
W-WE WEREN'T CLOSE CHILDHOOD FRIENDS...
WELL, DUH! SURE WE WERE! OUR DADS INVADED HAWAII TOGETHER!
HIS FATHER IS A GENIUS AT BUILDING ROBOTICS COMPONENTS!
WE USED TO SPEND HOURS PLAYING ON HIS FAMILY'S MURDERBOT CONSTRUCTION LINE!
BOOM
BOOM
GET OFF THOSE! BRATS!
WHRRRR

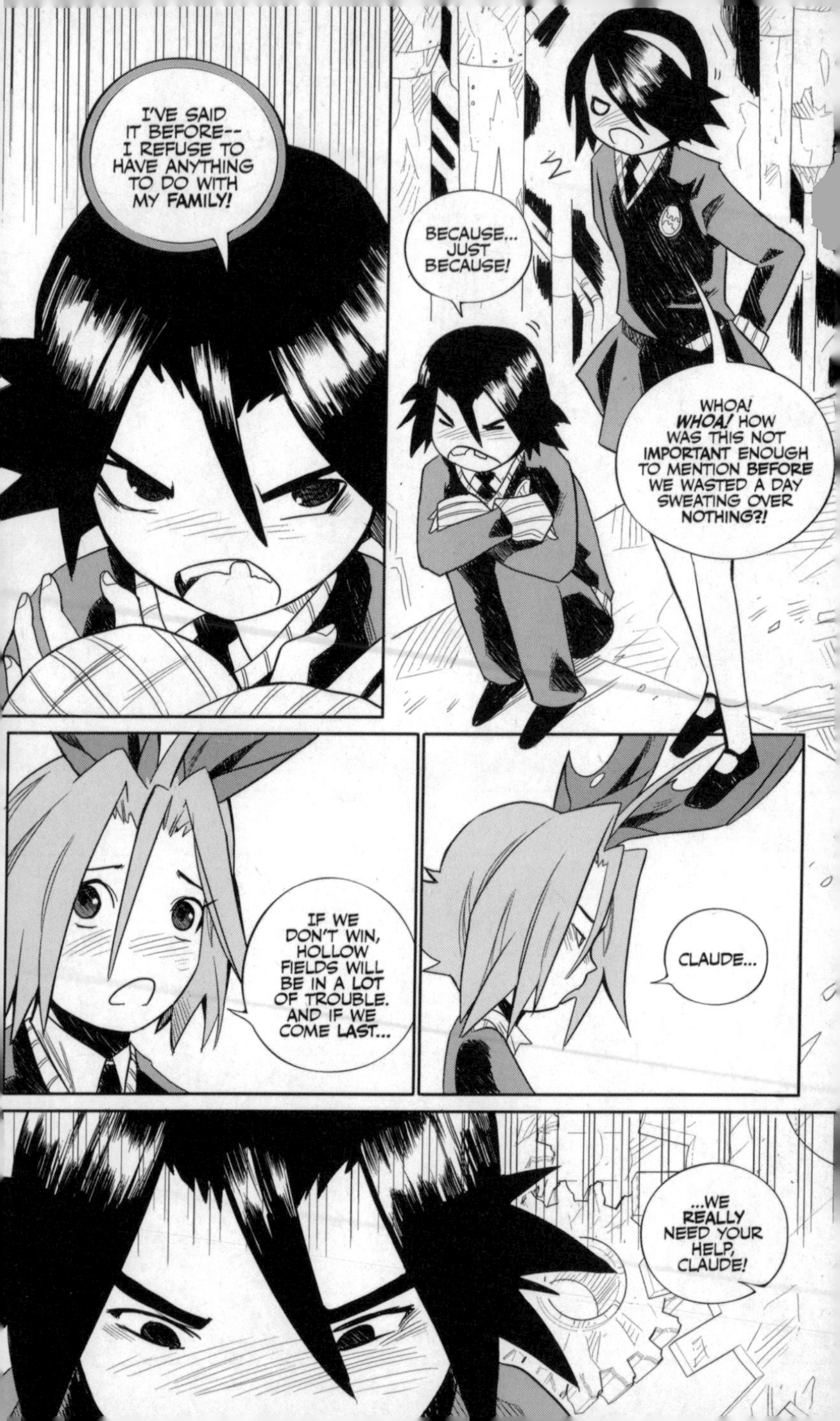
WHOA! *WHOA!* HOW WAS THIS NOT IMPORTANT ENOUGH TO MENTION BEFORE WE WASTED A DAY SWEATING OVER NOTHING?!
BECAUSE... JUST BECAUSE!
I'VE SAID IT BEFORE-- I REFUSE TO HAVE ANYTHING TO DO WITH MY FAMILY!
CLAUDE...
IF WE DON'T WIN, HOLLOW FIELDS WILL BE IN A LOT OF TROUBLE. AND IF WE COME LAST...
...WE REALLY NEED YOUR HELP, CLAUDE!

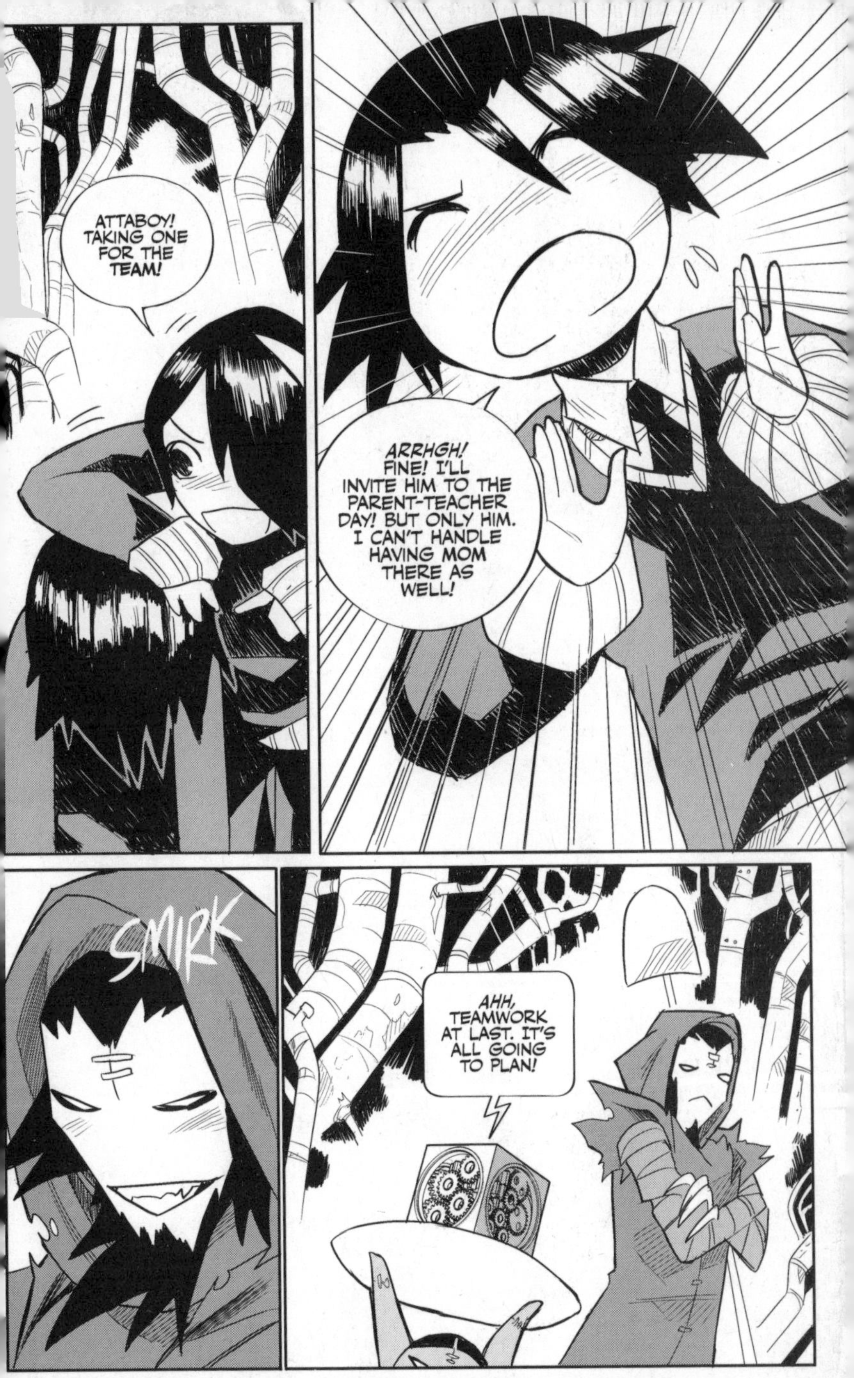
ARRHGH! FINE! I'LL INVITE HIM TO THE PARENT-TEACHER DAY! BUT ONLY HIM. I CAN'T HANDLE HAVING MOM THERE AS WELL!
ATTABOY! TAKING ONE FOR THE TEAM!
AHH, TEAMWORK AT LAST. IT'S ALL GOING TO PLAN!
SMIRK

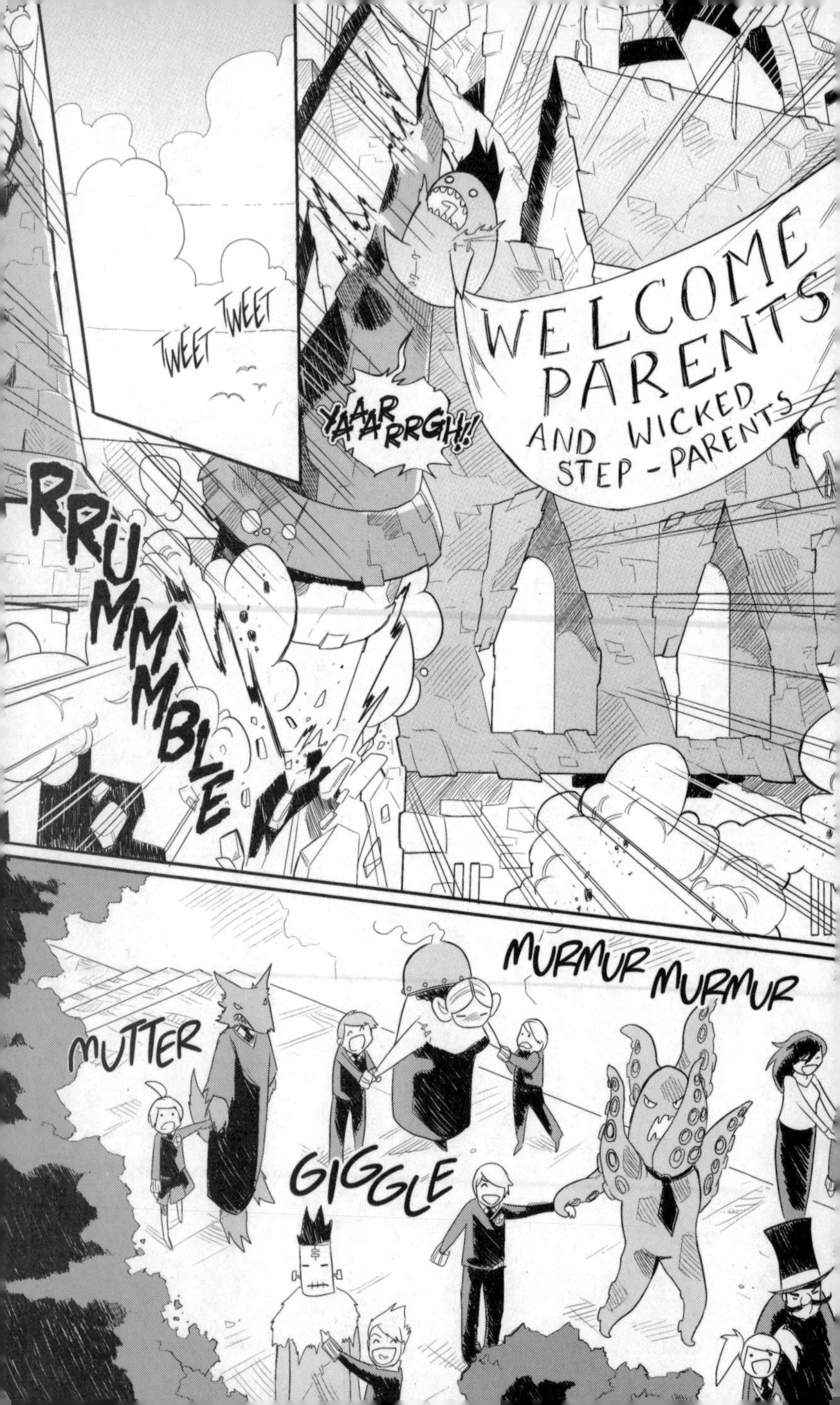
WELCOME PARENTS AND WICKED STEP-PARENTS
TWEET TWEET
YAAARRRGH!!
RRUMMMMBLE
MURMUR MURMUR
MUTTER
GIGGLE

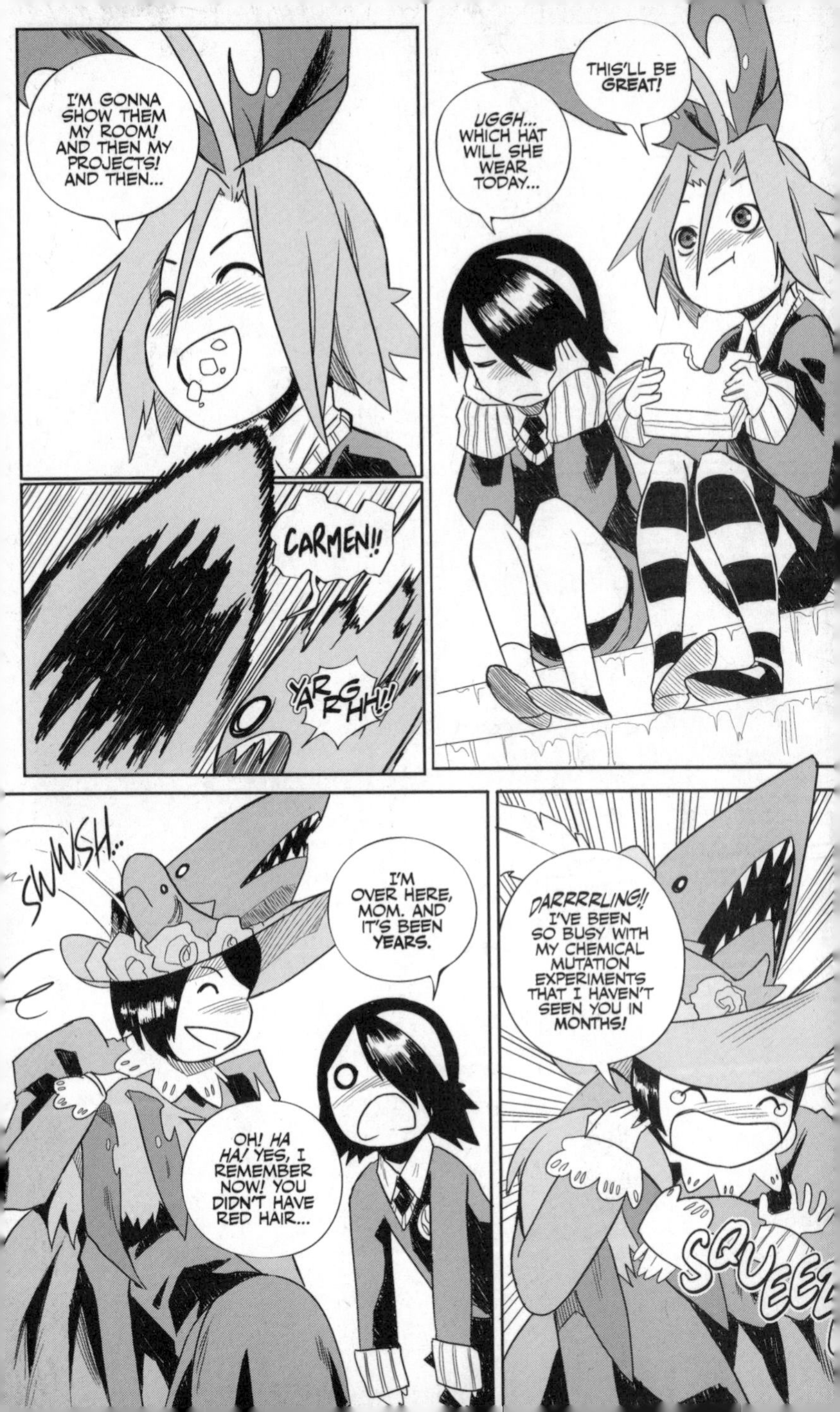
THIS'LL BE GREAT!
UGGH... WHICH HAT WILL SHE WEAR TODAY...
I'M GONNA SHOW THEM MY ROOM! AND THEN MY PROJECTS! AND THEN...
CARMEN!!
YARGHH!!
DARRRRLING!! I'VE BEEN SO BUSY WITH MY CHEMICAL MUTATION EXPERIMENTS THAT I HAVEN'T SEEN YOU IN MONTHS!
SQUEEZ
SWWSH...
I'M OVER HERE, MOM. AND IT'S BEEN **YEARS.**
OH! *HA HA!* YES, I REMEMBER NOW! YOU DIDN'T HAVE RED HAIR...

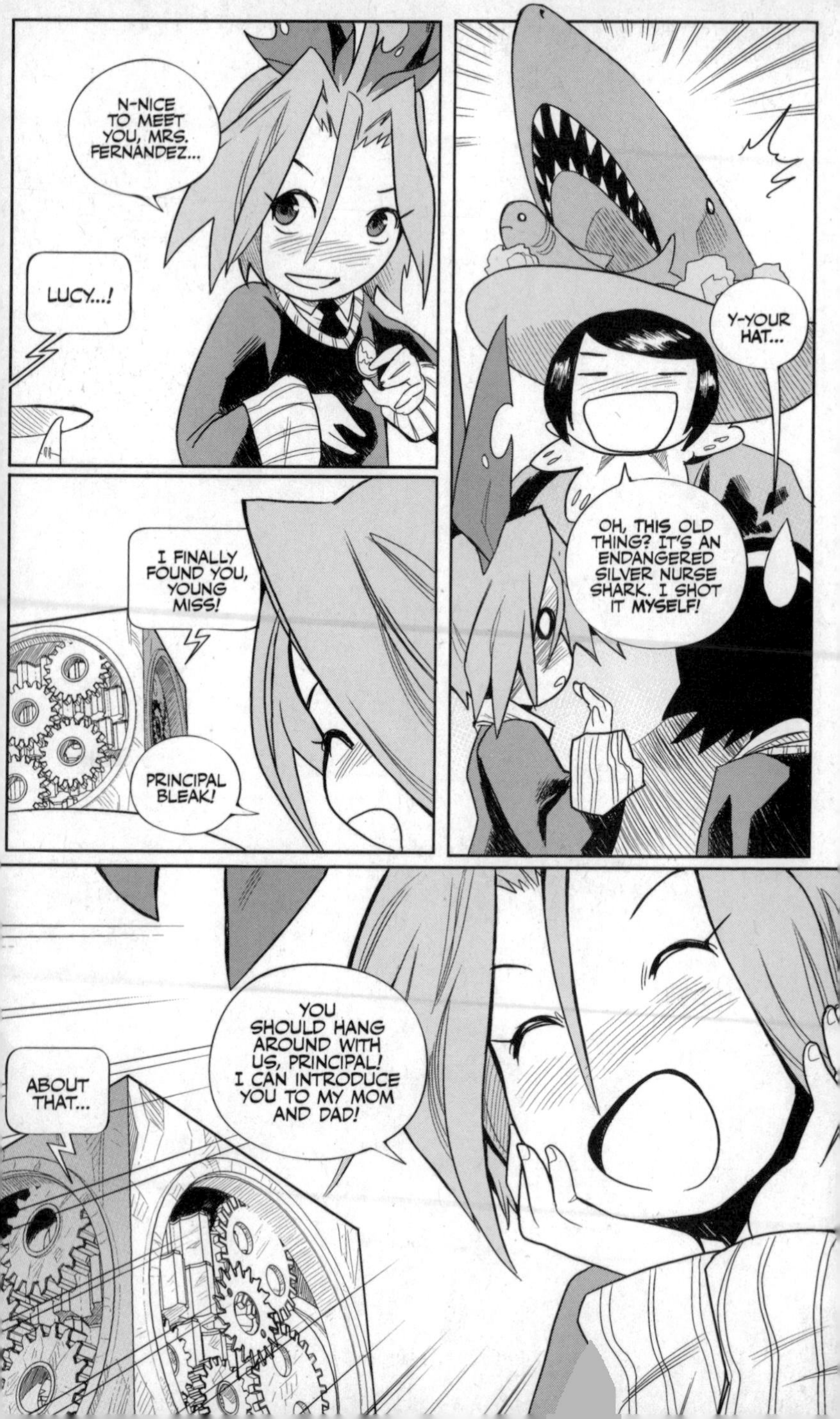
Y-YOUR HAT...
OH, THIS OLD THING? IT'S AN ENDANGERED SILVER NURSE SHARK. I SHOT IT MYSELF!
N-NICE TO MEET YOU, MRS. FERNANDEZ...
LUCY...!
I FINALLY FOUND YOU, YOUNG MISS!
PRINCIPAL BLEAK!
YOU SHOULD HANG AROUND WITH US, PRINCIPAL! I CAN INTRODUCE YOU TO MY MOM AND DAD!
ABOUT THAT...

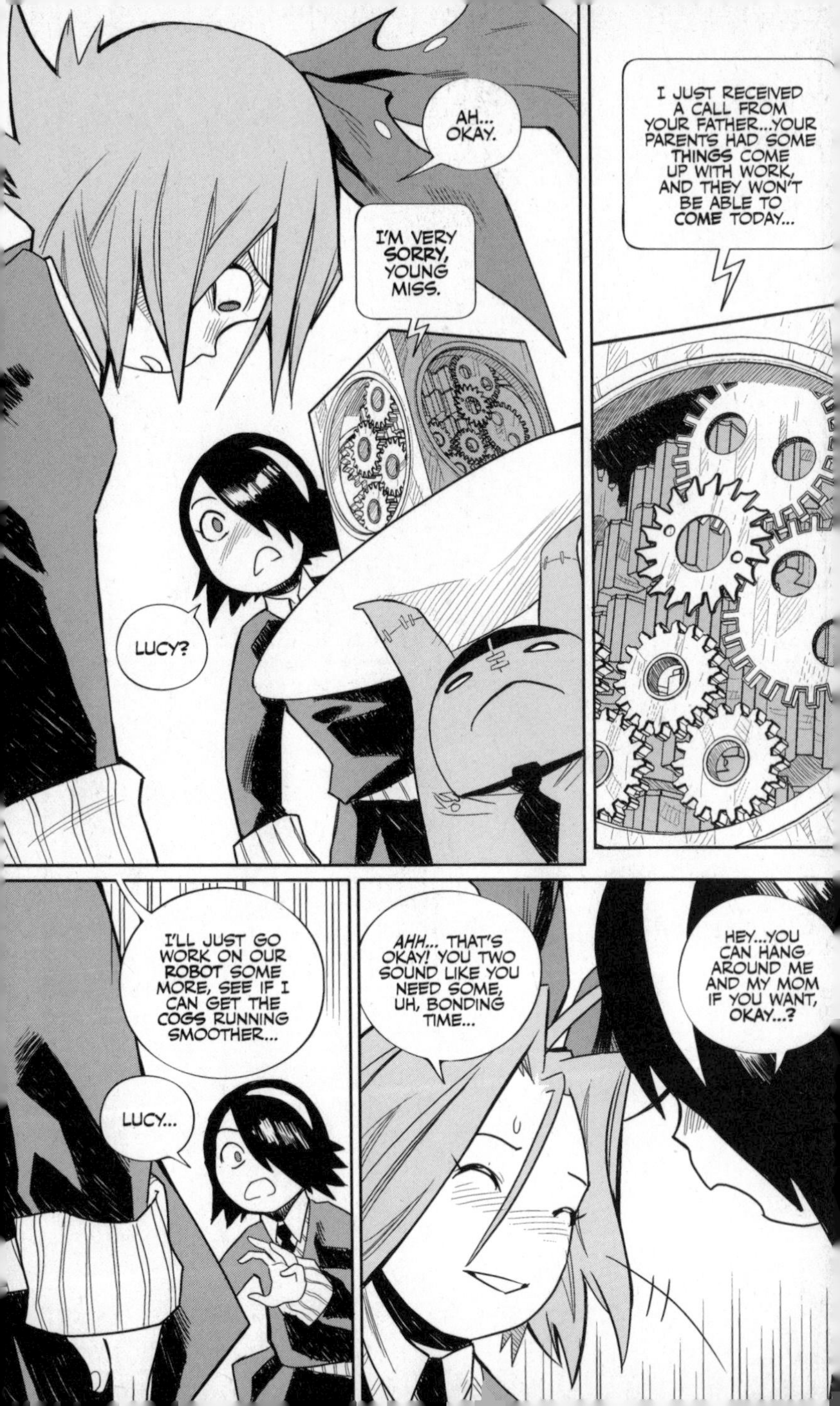
I JUST RECEIVED A CALL FROM YOUR FATHER...YOUR PARENTS HAD SOME THINGS COME UP WITH WORK, AND THEY WON'T BE ABLE TO COME TODAY...
AH... OKAY.
I'M VERY SORRY, YOUNG MISS.
LUCY?
HEY...YOU CAN HANG AROUND ME AND MY MOM IF YOU WANT, OKAY...?
AHH... THAT'S OKAY! YOU TWO SOUND LIKE YOU NEED SOME, UH, BONDING TIME...
I'LL JUST GO WORK ON OUR ROBOT SOME MORE, SEE IF I CAN GET THE COGS RUNNING SMOOTHER...
LUCY...

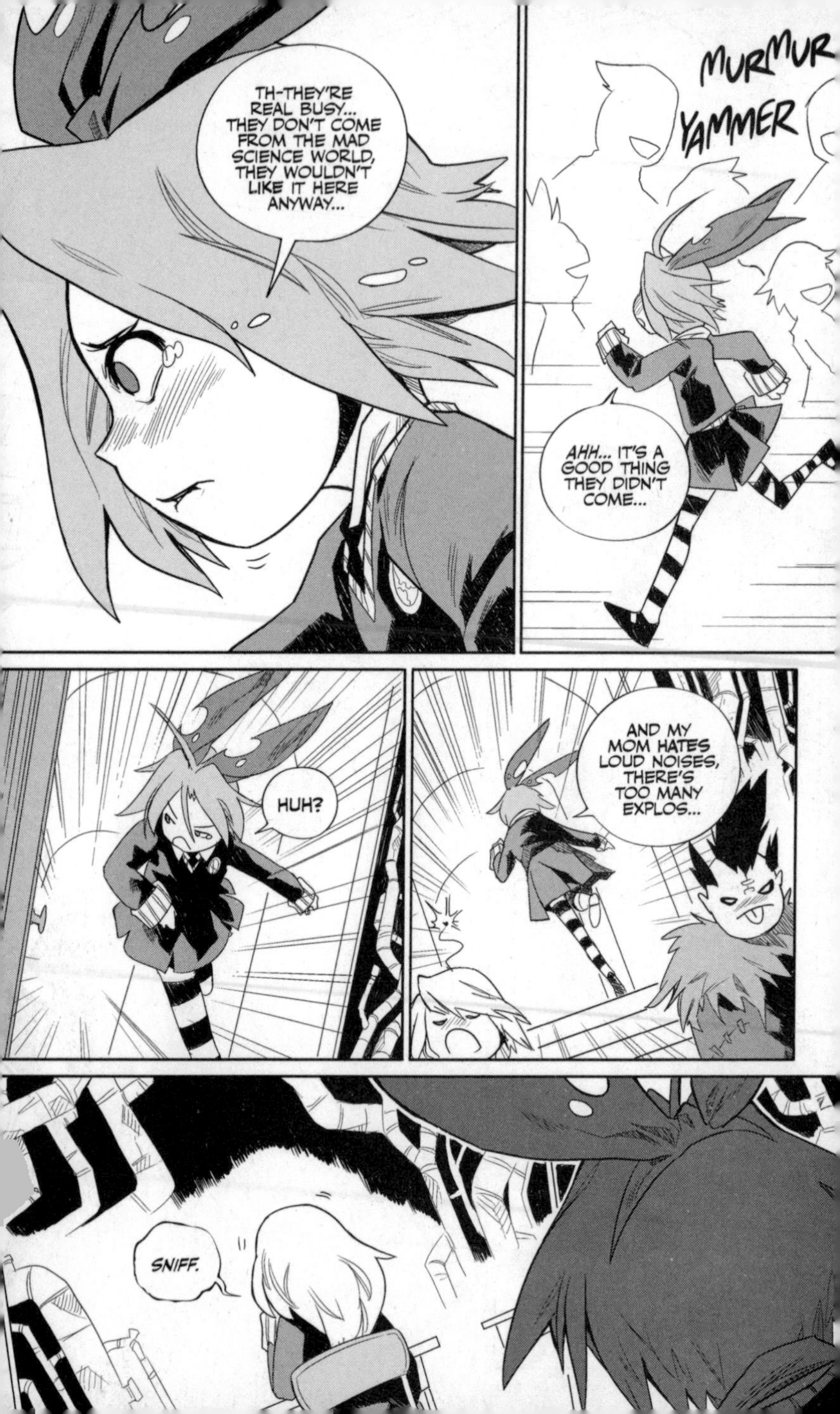
MURMUR
YAMMER
AHH... IT'S A GOOD THING THEY DIDN'T COME...
TH-THEY'RE REAL BUSY... THEY DON'T COME FROM THE MAD SCIENCE WORLD, THEY WOULDN'T LIKE IT HERE ANYWAY...
AND MY MOM HATES LOUD NOISES, THERE'S TOO MANY EXPLOS...
HUH?
SNIFF.

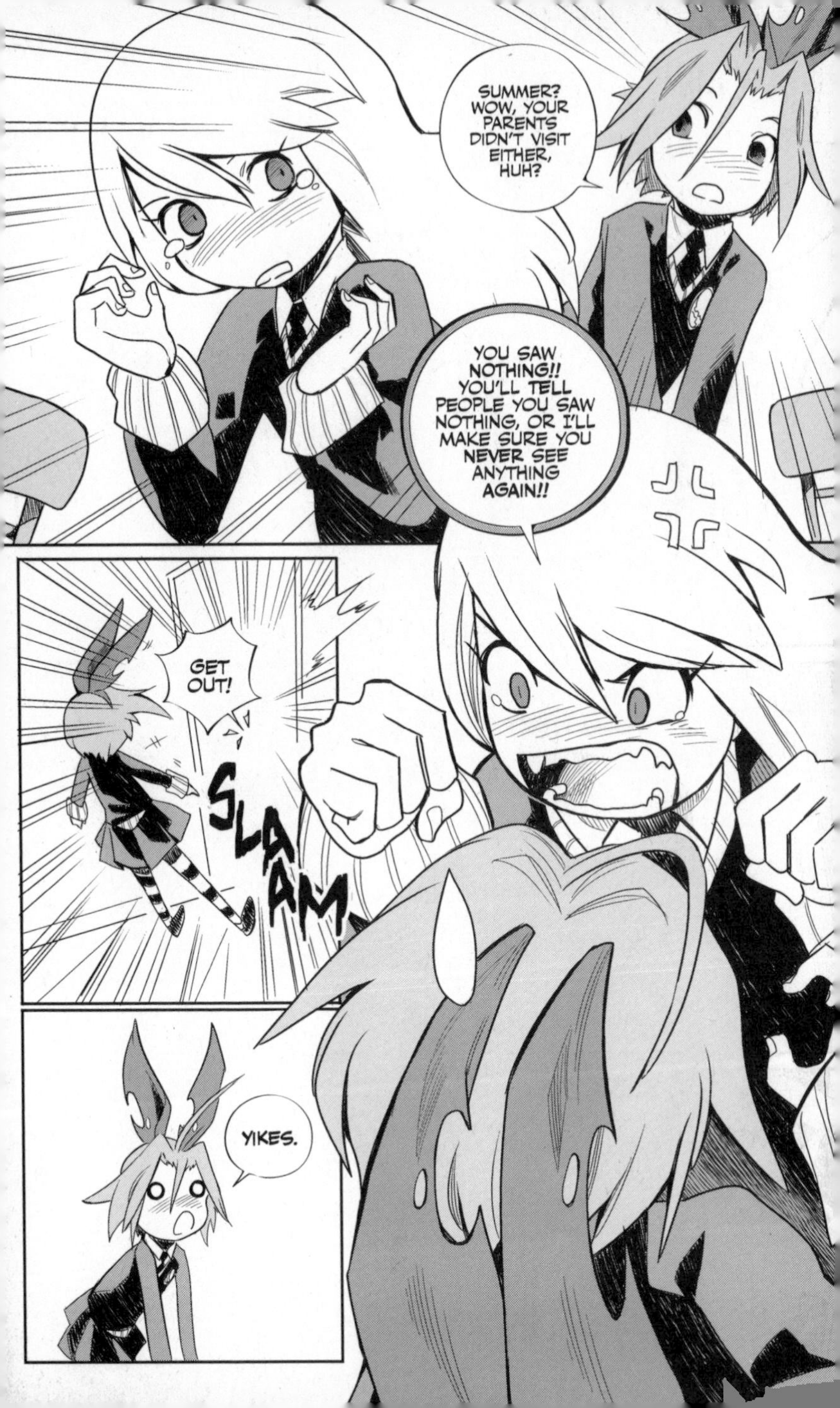
SUMMER? WOW, YOUR PARENTS DIDN'T VISIT EITHER, HUH?
YOU SAW NOTHING!! YOU'LL TELL PEOPLE YOU SAW NOTHING, OR I'LL MAKE SURE YOU NEVER SEE ANYTHING AGAIN!!
GET OUT!
SLAM
YIKES.

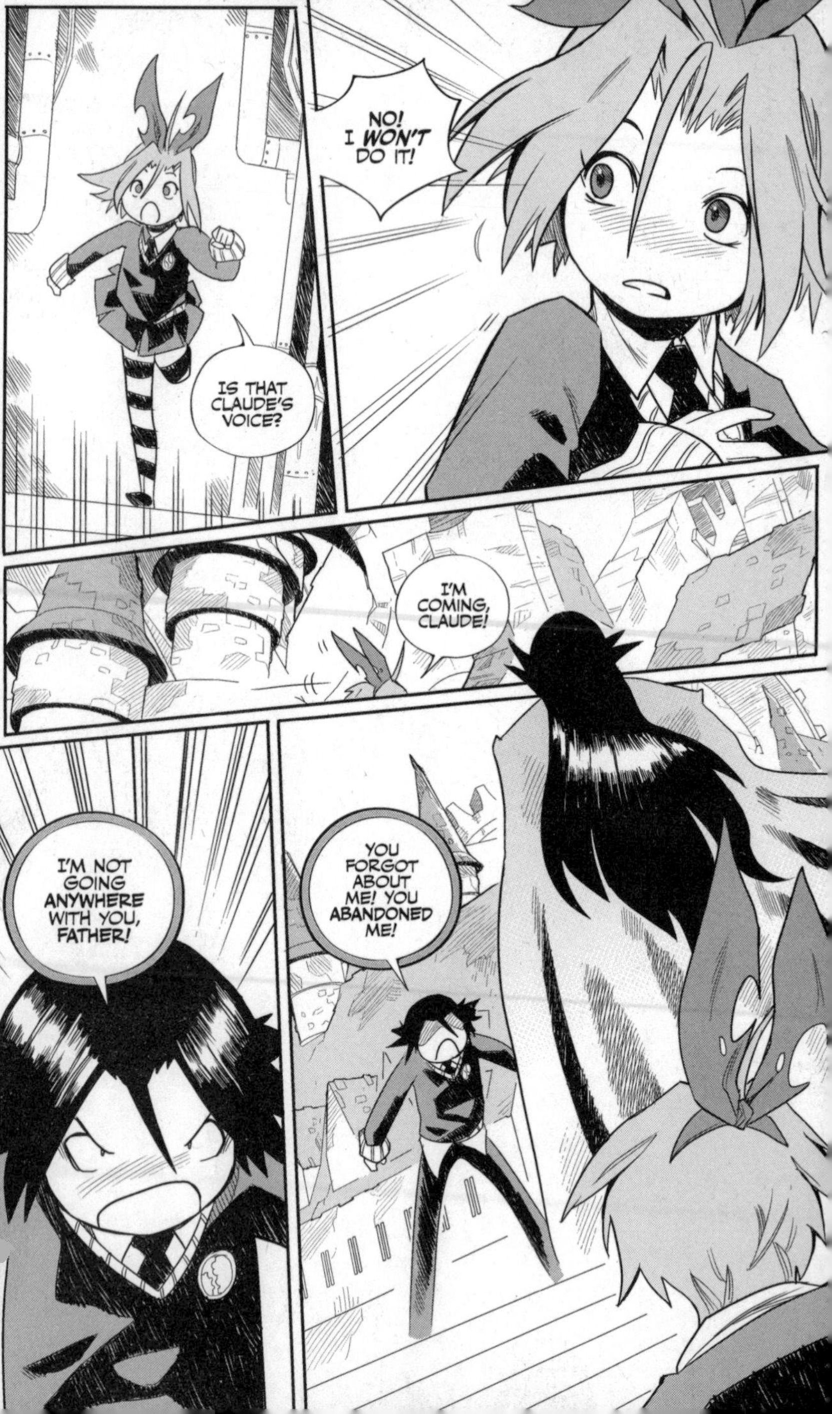
NO! I *WON'T* DO IT!
IS THAT CLAUDE'S VOICE?
I'M COMING, CLAUDE!
YOU FORGOT ABOUT ME! YOU ABANDONED ME!
I'M NOT GOING ANYWHERE WITH YOU, FATHER!

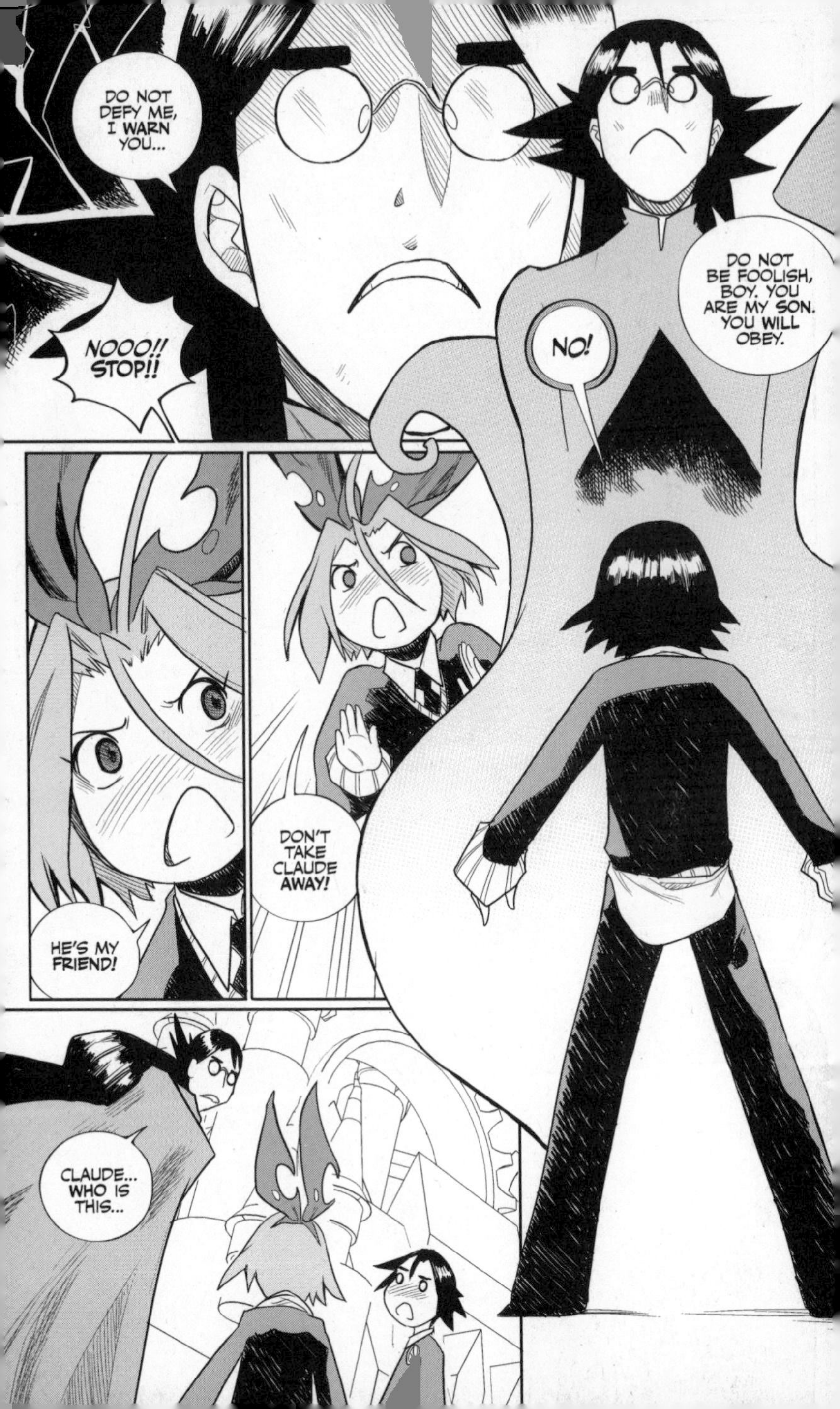
DO NOT BE FOOLISH, BOY. YOU ARE MY SON. YOU WILL OBEY.
NO!
DO NOT DEFY ME, I WARN YOU...
NOOO!! STOP!!
DON'T TAKE CLAUDE AWAY!
HE'S MY FRIEND!
CLAUDE... WHO IS THIS...

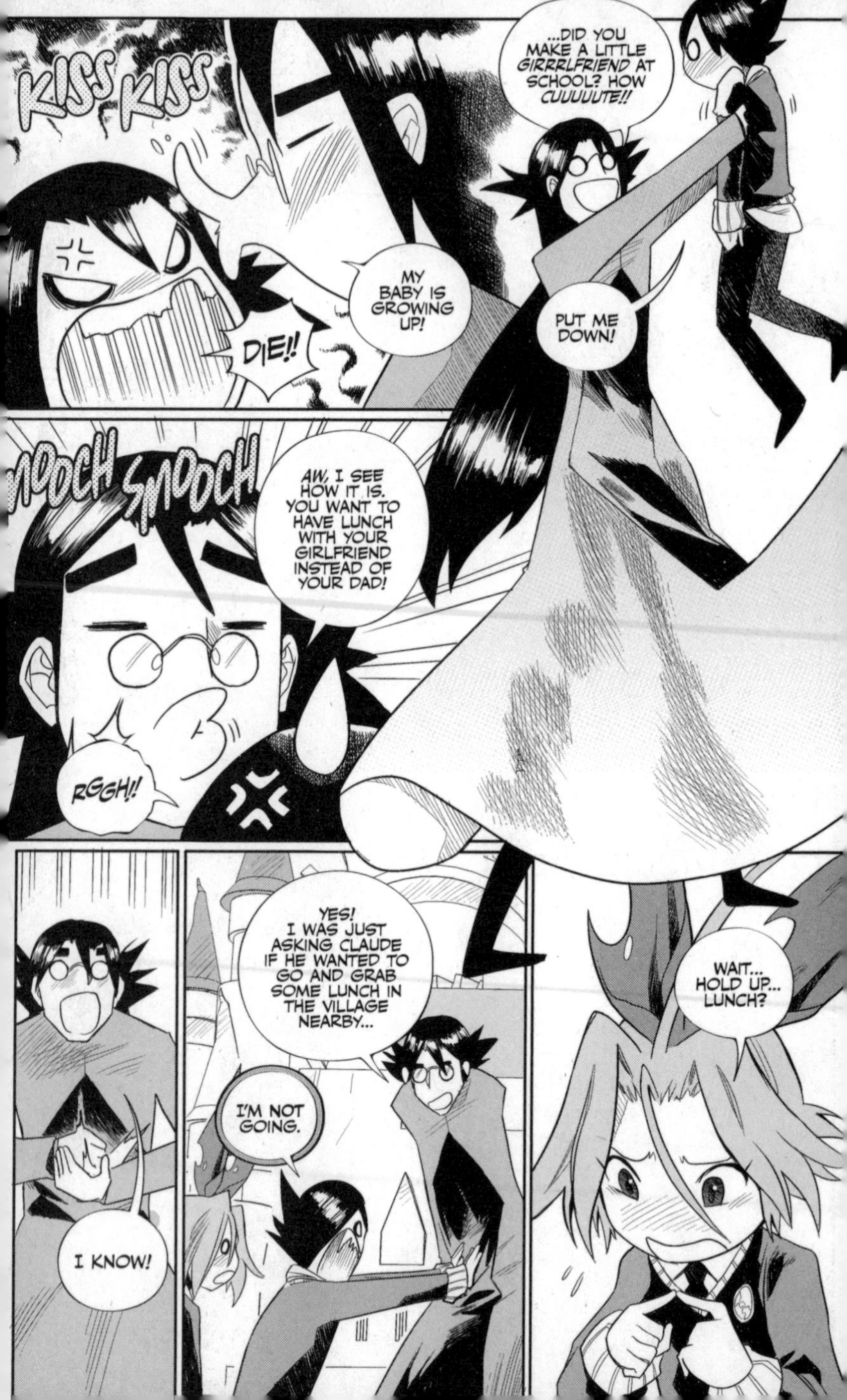
...DID YOU MAKE A LITTLE *GIRRRLFRIEND* AT SCHOOL? HOW *CUUUUUTE!!*
PUT ME DOWN!
KISS KISS
MY BABY IS GROWING UP!
DIE!!
MOOCH SMOOCH
AW, I SEE HOW IT IS. YOU WANT TO HAVE LUNCH WITH YOUR GIRLFRIEND INSTEAD OF YOUR DAD!
RGGH!!
WAIT... HOLD UP... LUNCH?
YES! I WAS JUST ASKING CLAUDE IF HE WANTED TO GO AND GRAB SOME LUNCH IN THE VILLAGE NEARBY...
I'M NOT GOING.
I KNOW!

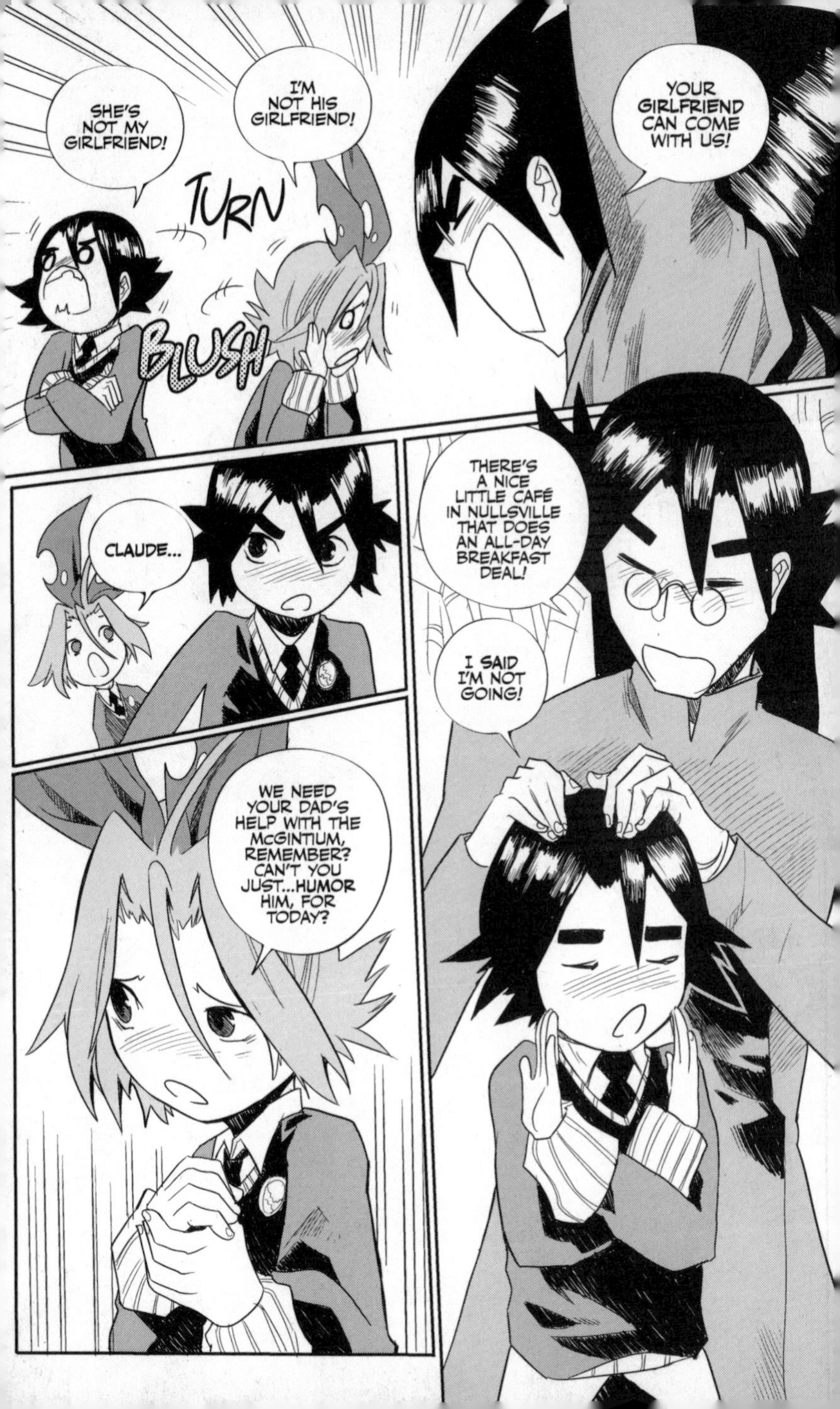
YOUR GIRLFRIEND CAN COME WITH US!
I'M NOT HIS GIRLFRIEND!
SHE'S NOT MY GIRLFRIEND!
TURN
BLUSH
THERE'S A NICE LITTLE CAFÉ IN NULLSVILLE THAT DOES AN ALL-DAY BREAKFAST DEAL!
I SAID I'M NOT GOING!
CLAUDE...
WE NEED YOUR DAD'S HELP WITH THE McGINTIUM, REMEMBER? CAN'T YOU JUST...HUMOR HIM, FOR TODAY?

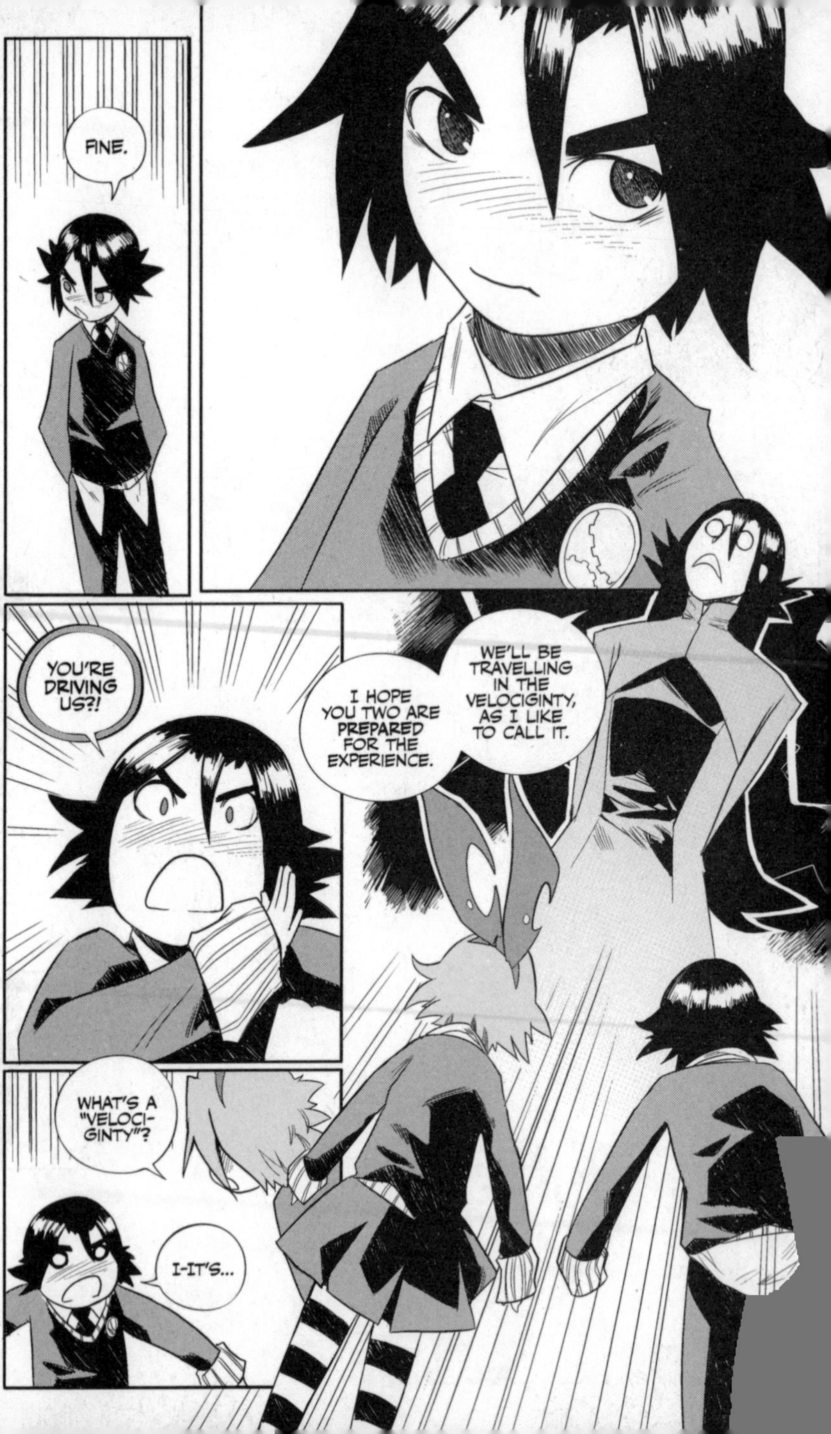
FINE.
WE'LL BE TRAVELLING IN THE VELOCIGINTY, AS I LIKE TO CALL IT.
I HOPE YOU TWO ARE PREPARED FOR THE EXPERIENCE.
YOU'RE DRIVING US?!
WHAT'S A "VELOCI-GINTY"?
I-IT'S...

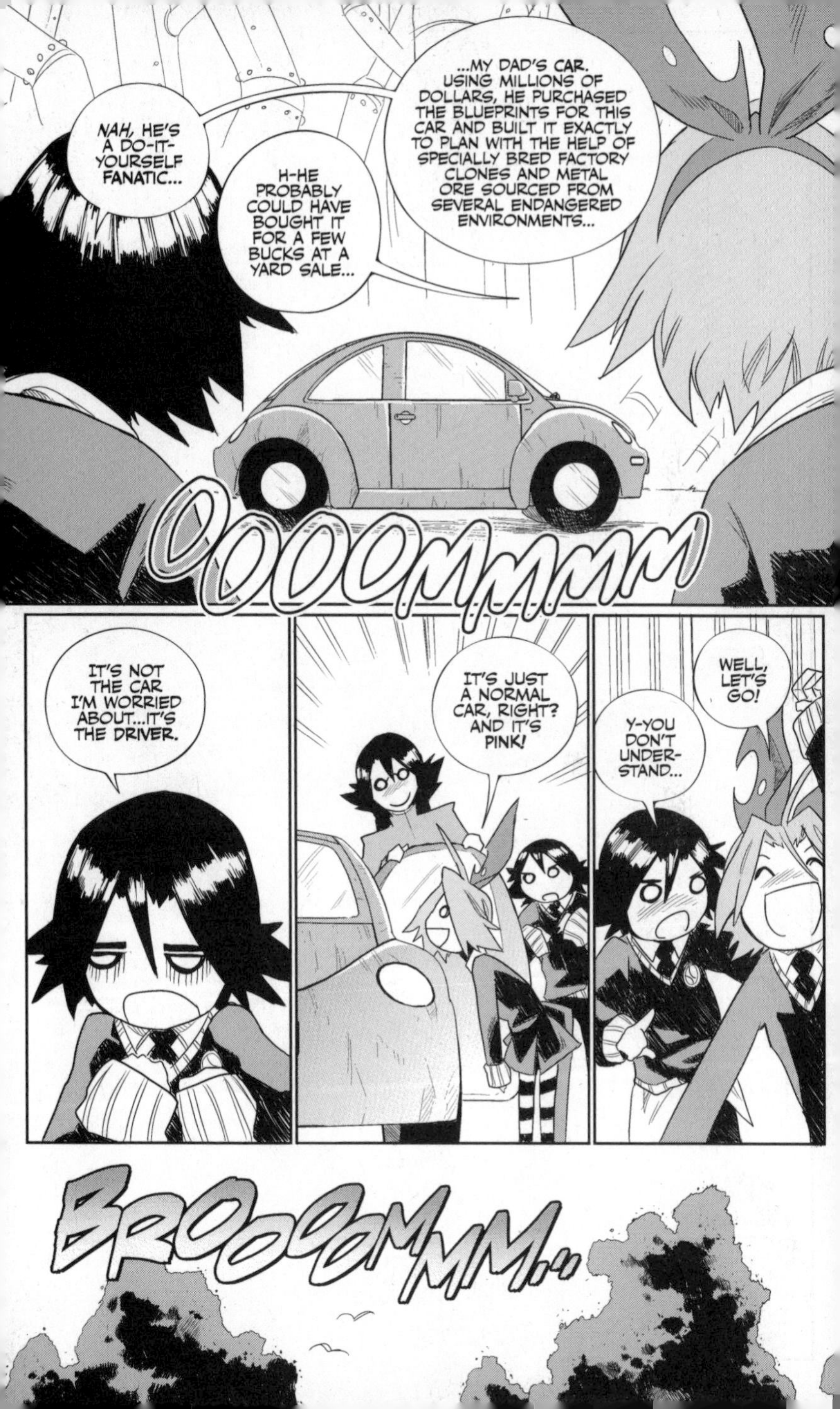
...MY DAD'S CAR. USING MILLIONS OF DOLLARS, HE PURCHASED THE BLUEPRINTS FOR THIS CAR AND BUILT IT EXACTLY TO PLAN WITH THE HELP OF SPECIALLY BRED FACTORY CLONES AND METAL ORE SOURCED FROM SEVERAL ENDANGERED ENVIRONMENTS...
H-HE PROBABLY COULD HAVE BOUGHT IT FOR A FEW BUCKS AT A YARD SALE...
NAH, HE'S A DO-IT-YOURSELF FANATIC...
OOOOMMMM
WELL, LET'S GO!
Y-YOU DON'T UNDER-STAND...
IT'S JUST A NORMAL CAR, RIGHT? AND IT'S PINK!
IT'S NOT THE CAR I'M WORRIED ABOUT...IT'S THE DRIVER.
BROOOOOMMMM...

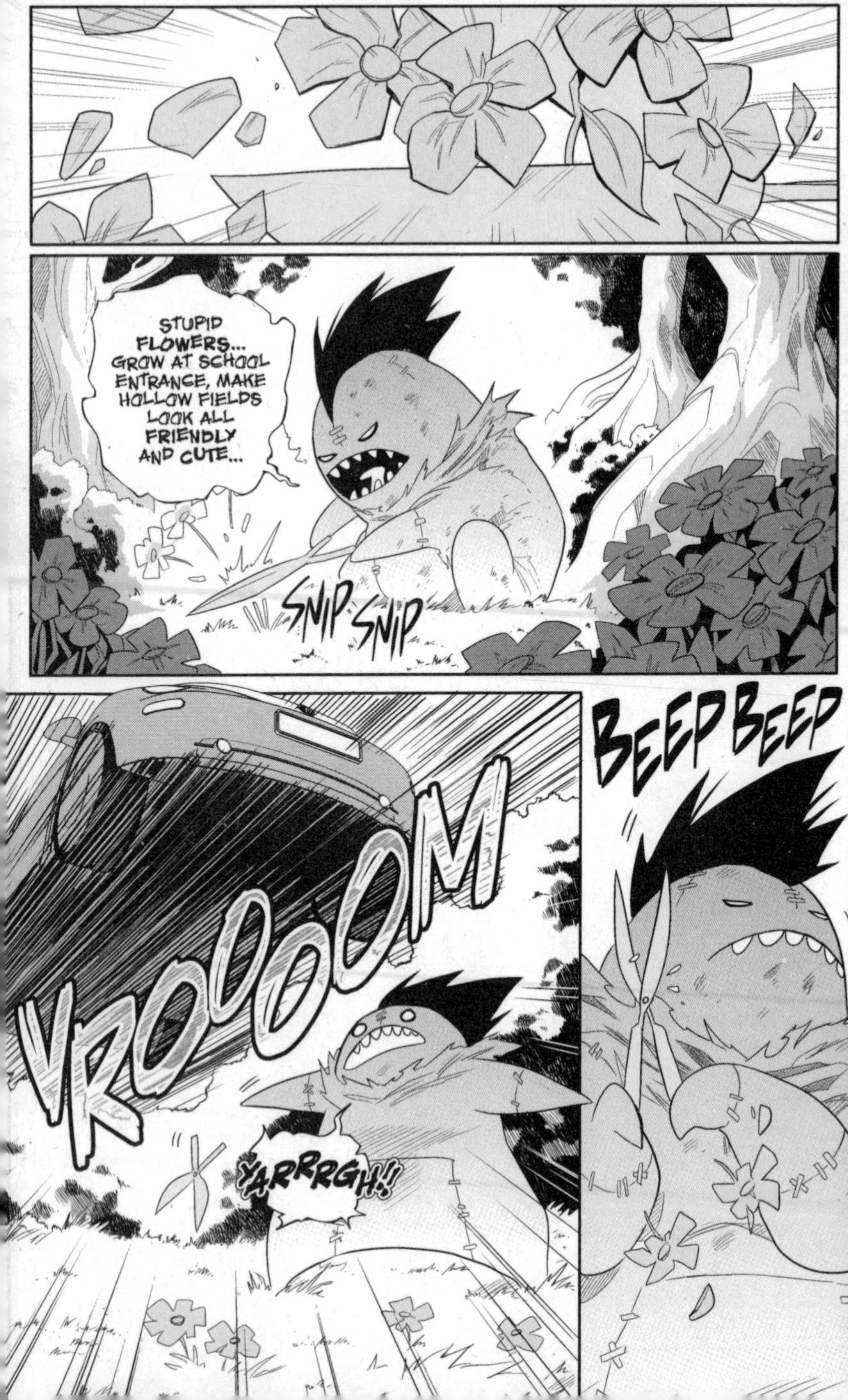
STUPID FLOWERS... GROW AT SCHOOL ENTRANCE, MAKE HOLLOW FIELDS LOOK ALL FRIENDLY AND CUTE...
SNIP SNIP
BEEP BEEP
VROOOOOM
YARRRGH!!

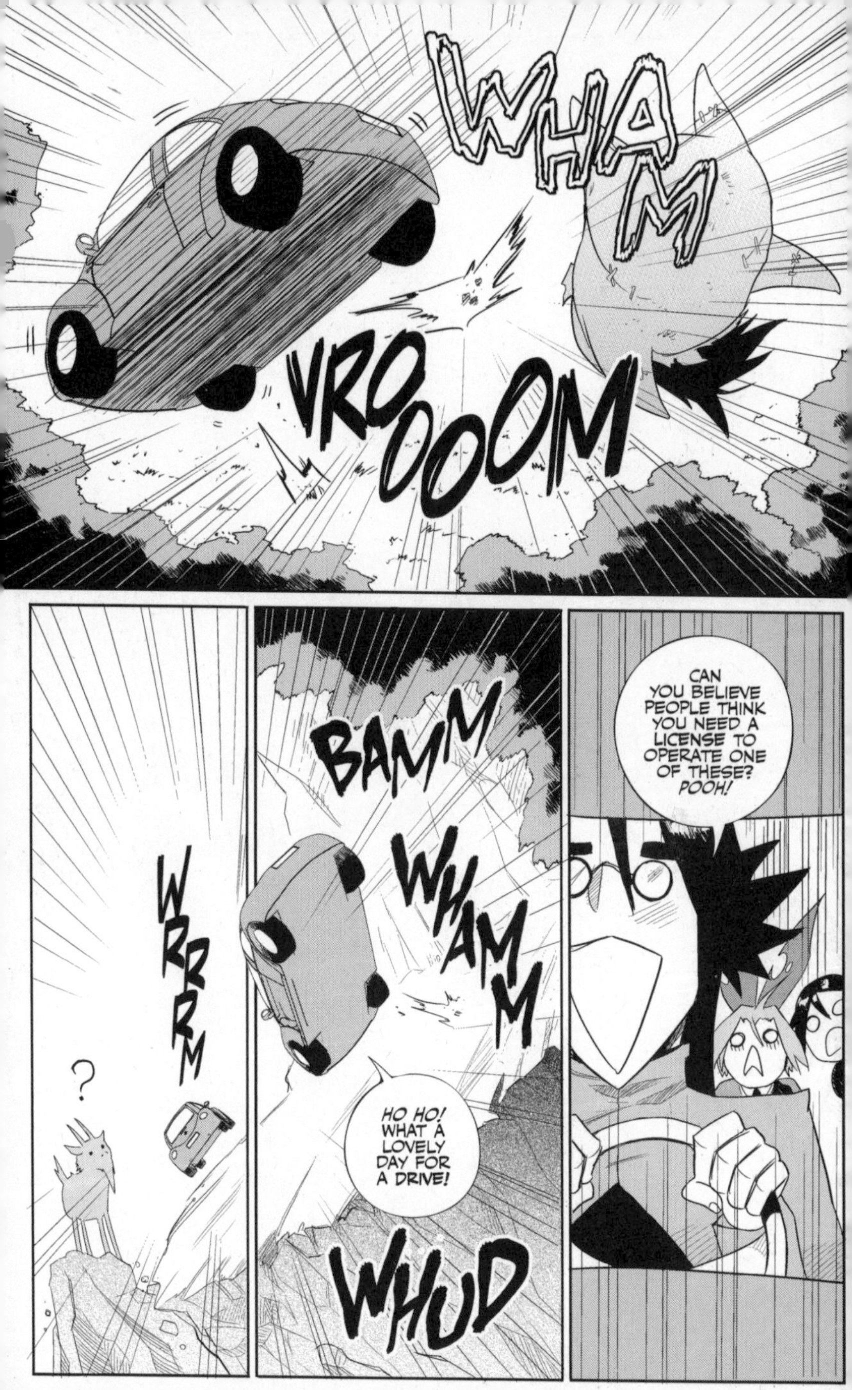
WHAM
VROOOOOM
CAN YOU BELIEVE PEOPLE THINK YOU NEED A LICENSE TO OPERATE ONE OF THESE? *POOH!*
BAMM
WHAMM
HO HO! WHAT A LOVELY DAY FOR A DRIVE!
WHUD
WRRRM
?

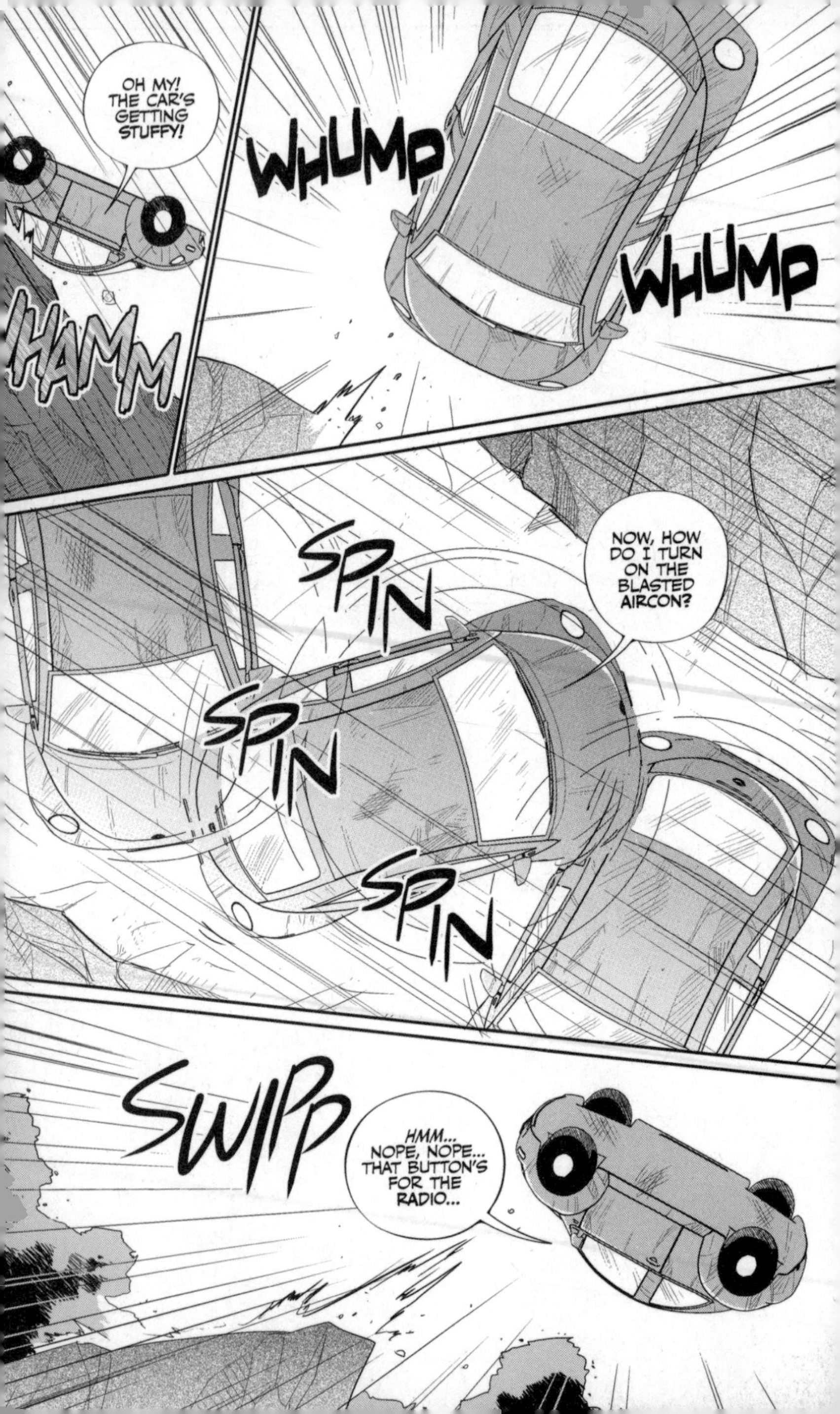
WHUMP
WHUMP
OH MY! THE CAR'S GETTING STUFFY!
HAMM
NOW, HOW DO I TURN ON THE BLASTED AIRCON?
SPIN
SPIN
SPIN
HMM... NOPE, NOPE... THAT BUTTON'S FOR THE RADIO...
SWIPP

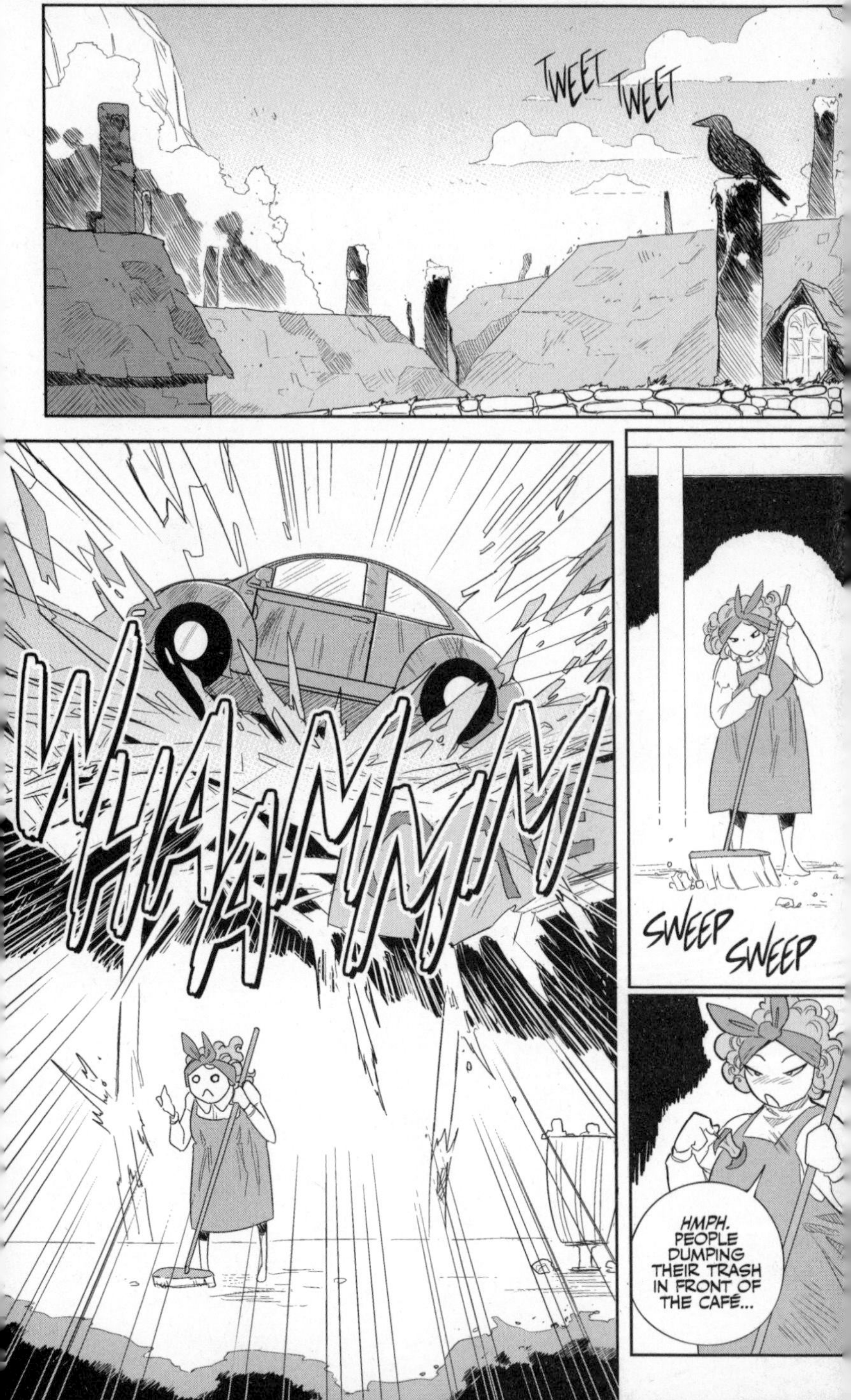
TWEET TWEET
SWEEP SWEEP
HMPH. PEOPLE DUMPING THEIR TRASH IN FRONT OF THE CAFÉ...
WHAMMM

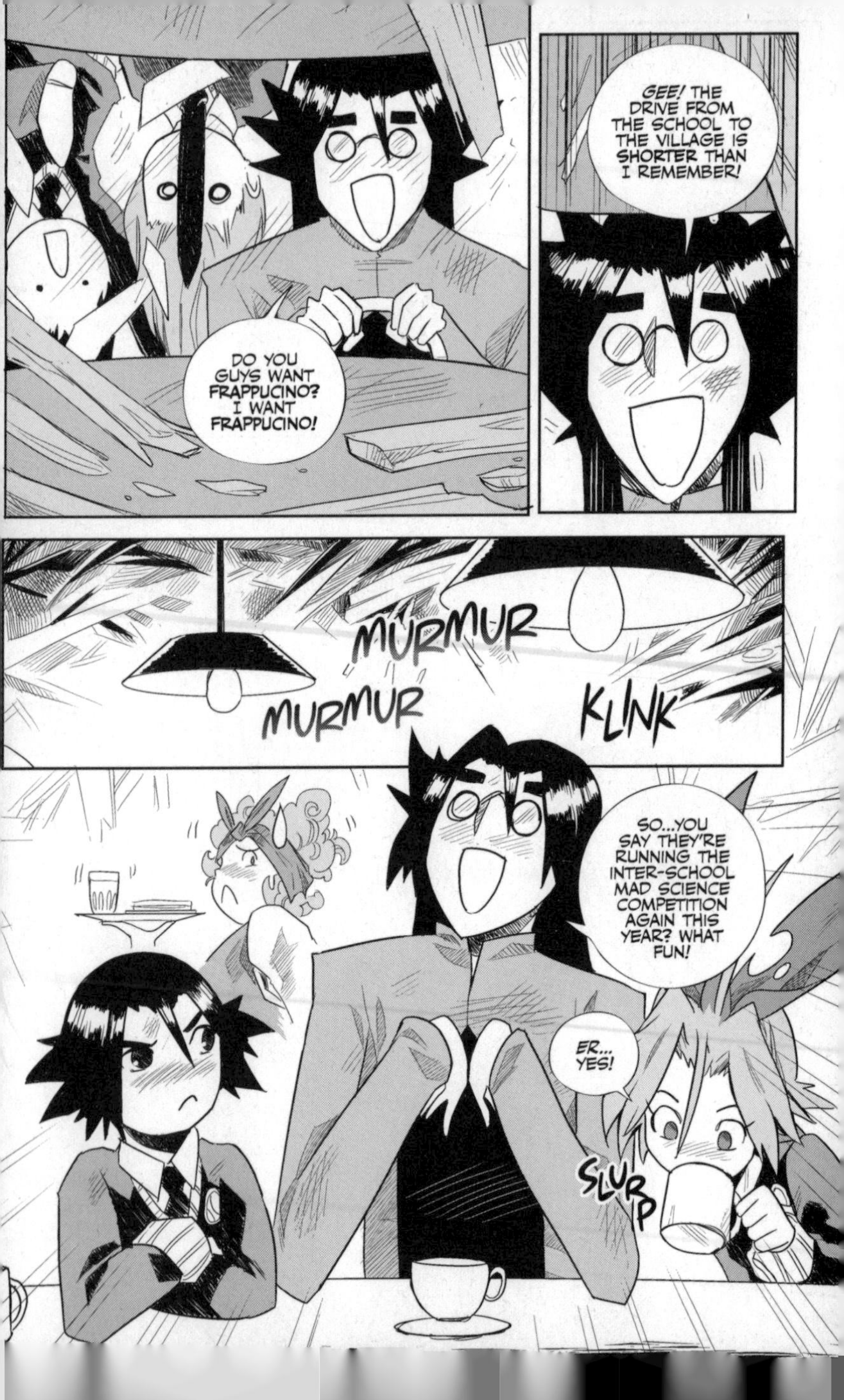
GEE! THE DRIVE FROM THE SCHOOL TO THE VILLAGE IS SHORTER THAN I REMEMBER!
DO YOU GUYS WANT FRAPPUCINO? I WANT FRAPPUCINO!
MURMUR
KLINK
MURMUR
SO...YOU SAY THEY'RE RUNNING THE INTER-SCHOOL MAD SCIENCE COMPETITION AGAIN THIS YEAR? WHAT FUN!
ER... YES!
SLURP

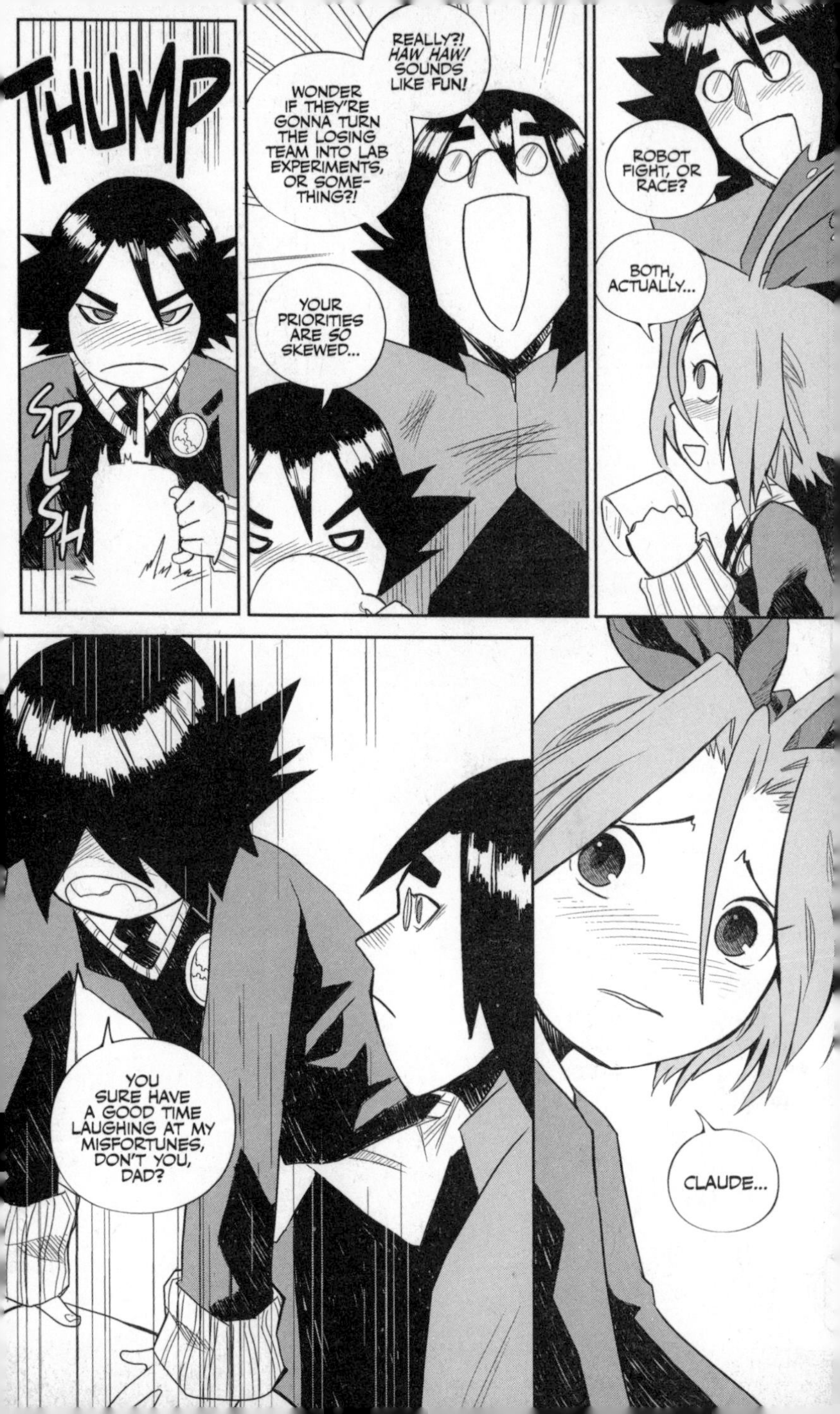
ROBOT FIGHT, OR RACE?
BOTH, ACTUALLY...
REALLY?! *HAW HAW!* SOUNDS LIKE FUN!
WONDER IF THEY'RE GONNA TURN THE LOSING TEAM INTO LAB EXPERIMENTS, OR SOME-THING?!
YOUR PRIORITIES ARE SO SKEWED...
THUMP
SPLSH
CLAUDE...
YOU SURE HAVE A GOOD TIME LAUGHING AT MY MISFORTUNES, DON'T YOU, DAD?

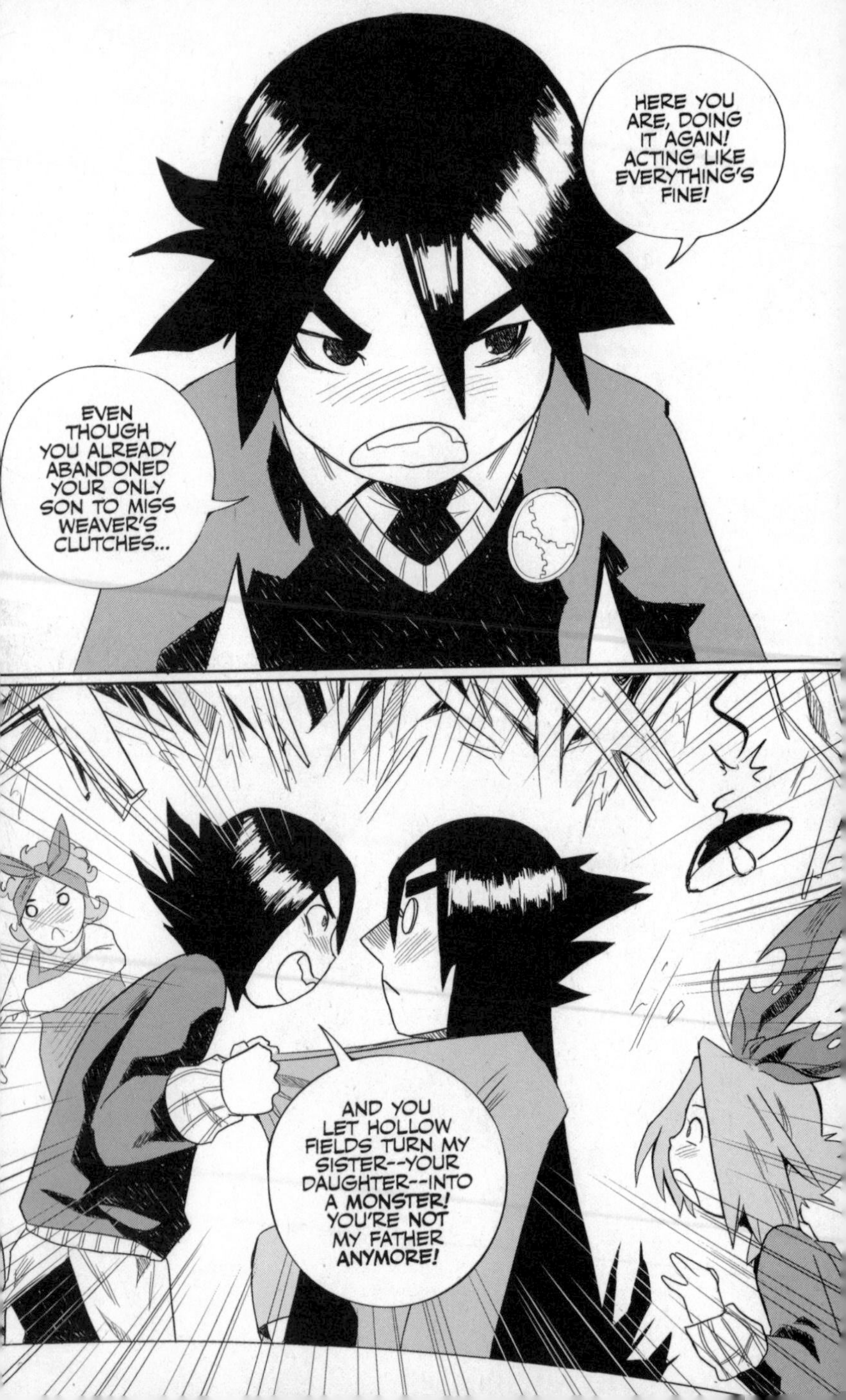
HERE YOU ARE, DOING IT AGAIN! ACTING LIKE EVERYTHING'S FINE!
EVEN THOUGH YOU ALREADY ABANDONED YOUR ONLY SON TO MISS WEAVER'S CLUTCHES...
AND YOU LET HOLLOW FIELDS TURN MY SISTER--YOUR DAUGHTER--INTO A MONSTER! YOU'RE NOT MY FATHER ANYMORE!

CHAPTER FOUR
ALLIES AND ALLOYS

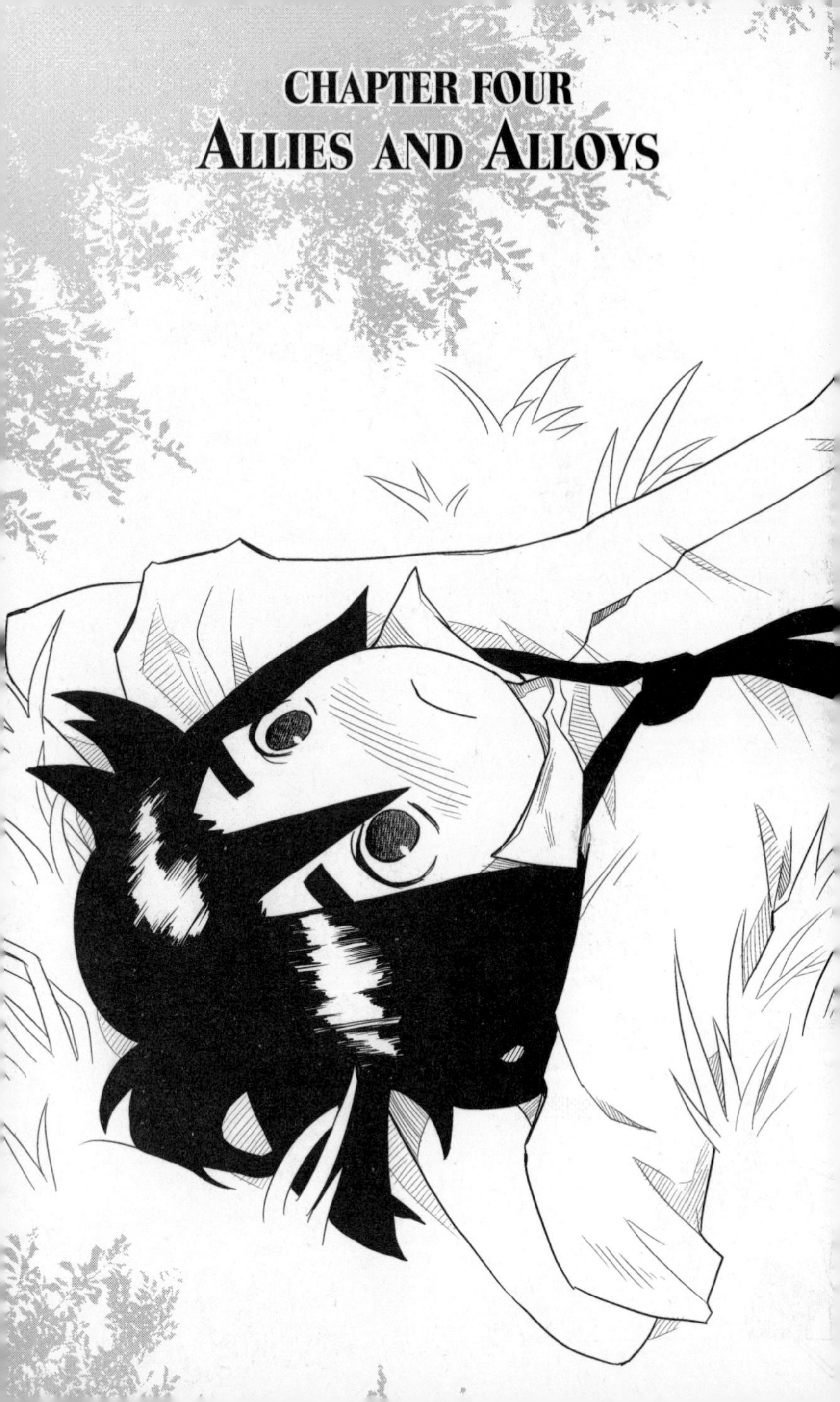

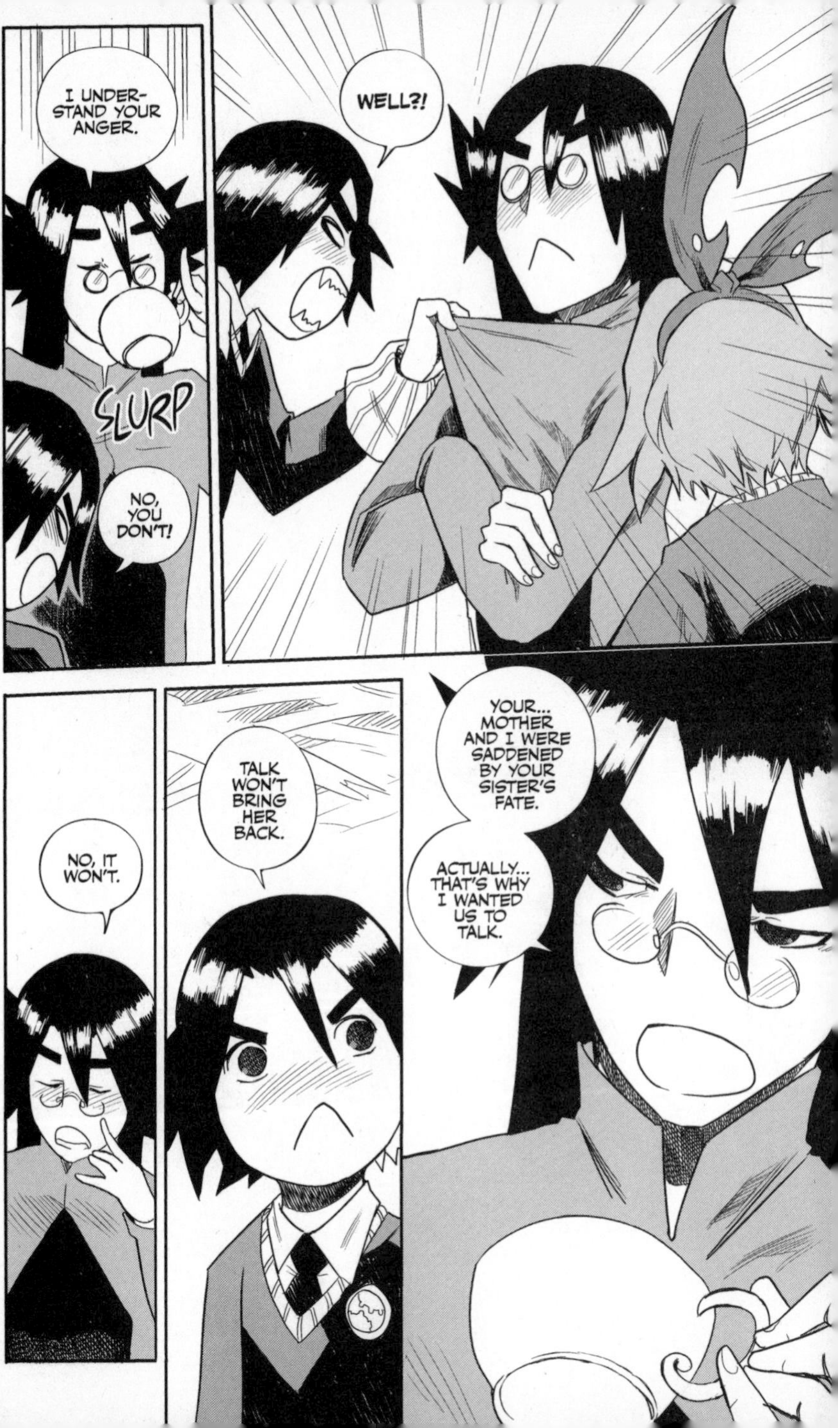
WELL?!
I UNDER-STAND YOUR ANGER.
SLURP
NO, YOU DON'T!
YOUR... MOTHER AND I WERE SADDENED BY YOUR SISTER'S FATE.
ACTUALLY... THAT'S WHY I WANTED US TO TALK.
TALK WON'T BRING HER BACK.
NO, IT WON'T.

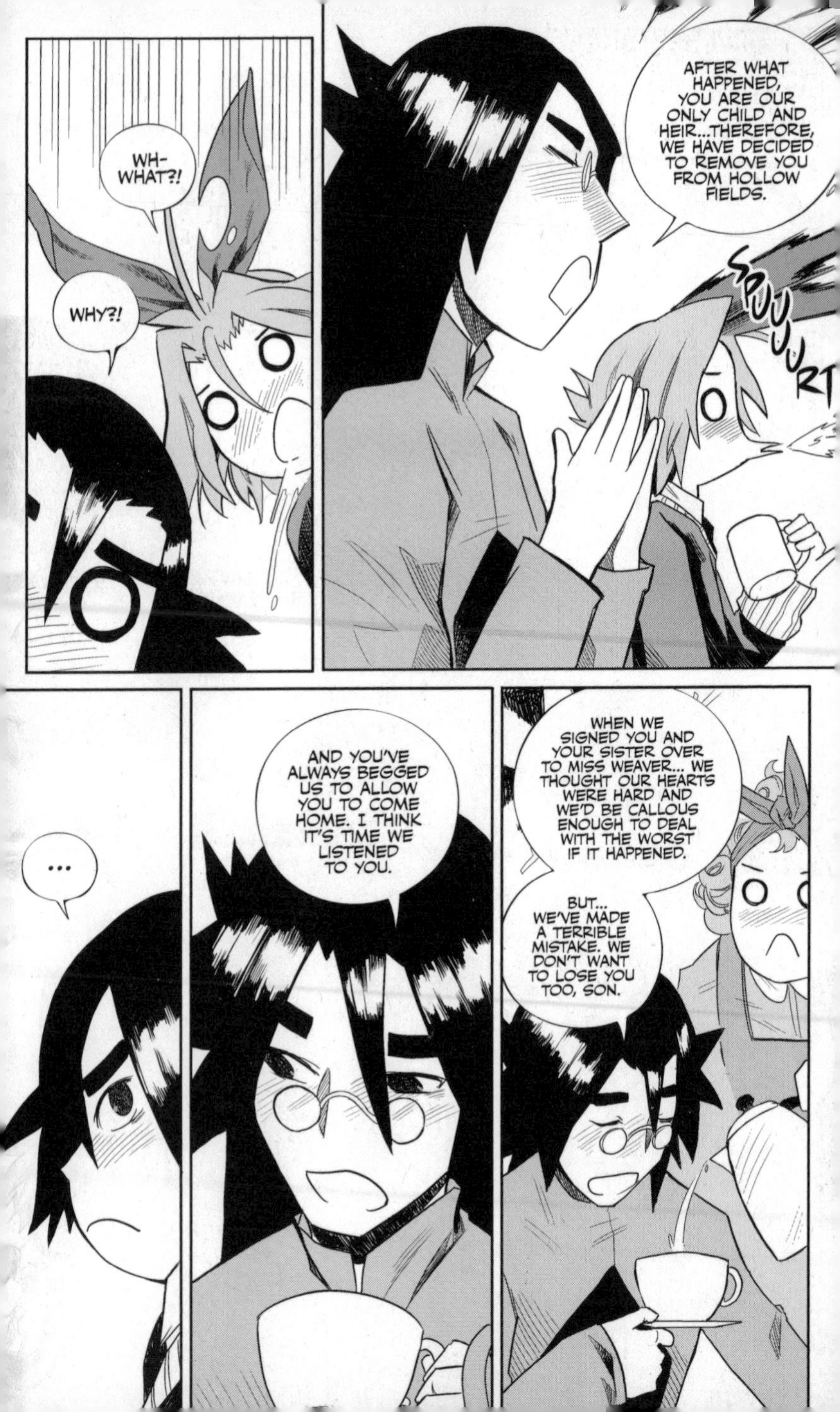
AFTER WHAT HAPPENED, YOU ARE OUR ONLY CHILD AND HEIR...THEREFORE, WE HAVE DECIDED TO REMOVE YOU FROM HOLLOW FIELDS.
SPUUUURT
WH- WHAT?!
WHY?!
WHEN WE SIGNED YOU AND YOUR SISTER OVER TO MISS WEAVER... WE THOUGHT OUR HEARTS WERE HARD AND WE'D BE CALLOUS ENOUGH TO DEAL WITH THE WORST IF IT HAPPENED.
BUT... WE'VE MADE A TERRIBLE MISTAKE. WE DON'T WANT TO LOSE YOU TOO, SON.
AND YOU'VE ALWAYS BEGGED US TO ALLOW YOU TO COME HOME. I THINK IT'S TIME WE LISTENED TO YOU.
...

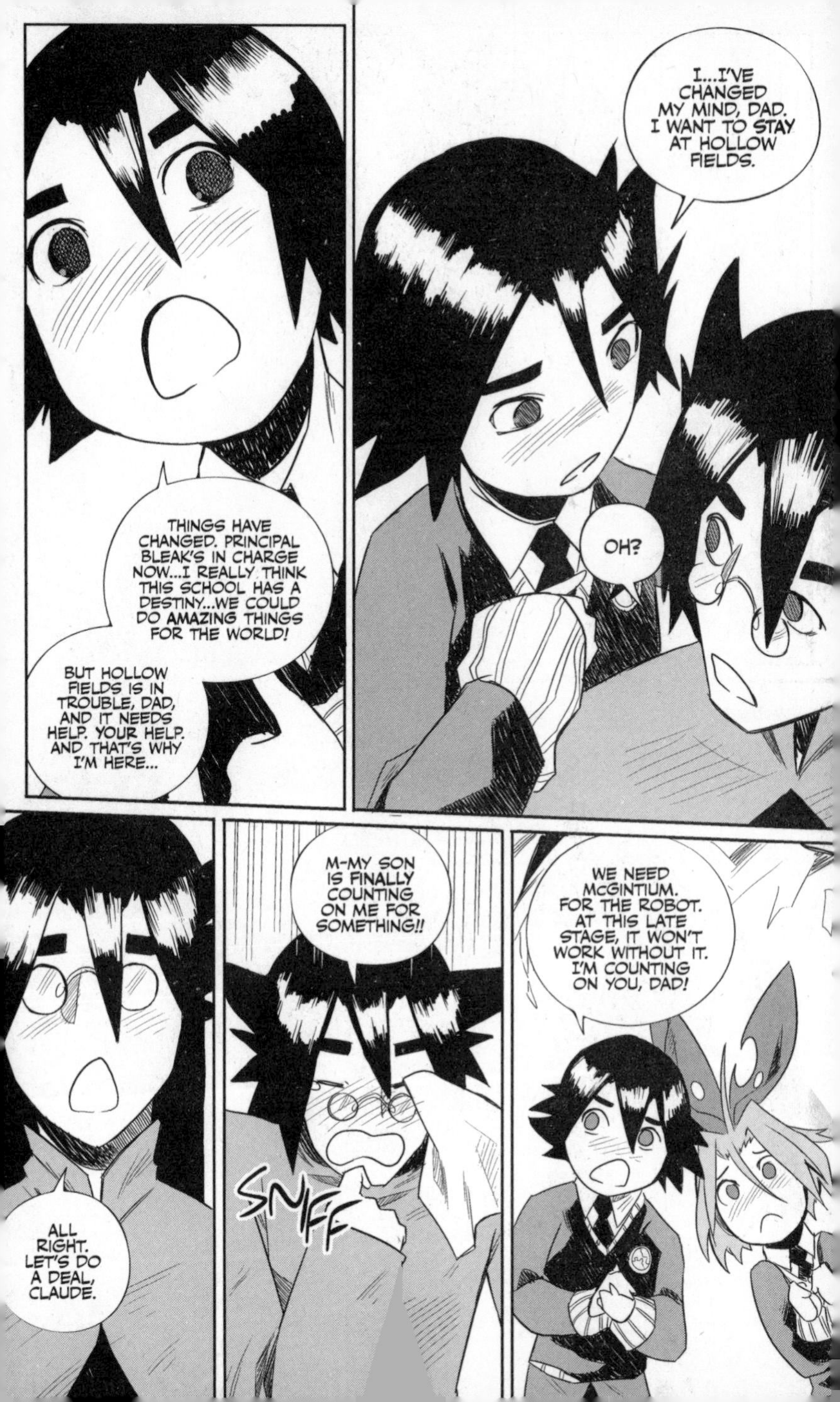
I...I'VE CHANGED MY MIND, DAD. I WANT TO STAY AT HOLLOW FIELDS.
OH?
THINGS HAVE CHANGED. PRINCIPAL BLEAK'S IN CHARGE NOW...I REALLY THINK THIS SCHOOL HAS A DESTINY...WE COULD DO AMAZING THINGS FOR THE WORLD!
BUT HOLLOW FIELDS IS IN TROUBLE, DAD, AND IT NEEDS HELP. YOUR HELP. AND THAT'S WHY I'M HERE...
WE NEED McGINTIUM. FOR THE ROBOT. AT THIS LATE STAGE, IT WON'T WORK WITHOUT IT. I'M COUNTING ON YOU, DAD!
M-MY SON IS FINALLY COUNTING ON ME FOR SOMETHING!!
SNIFF
ALL RIGHT. LET'S DO A DEAL, CLAUDE.

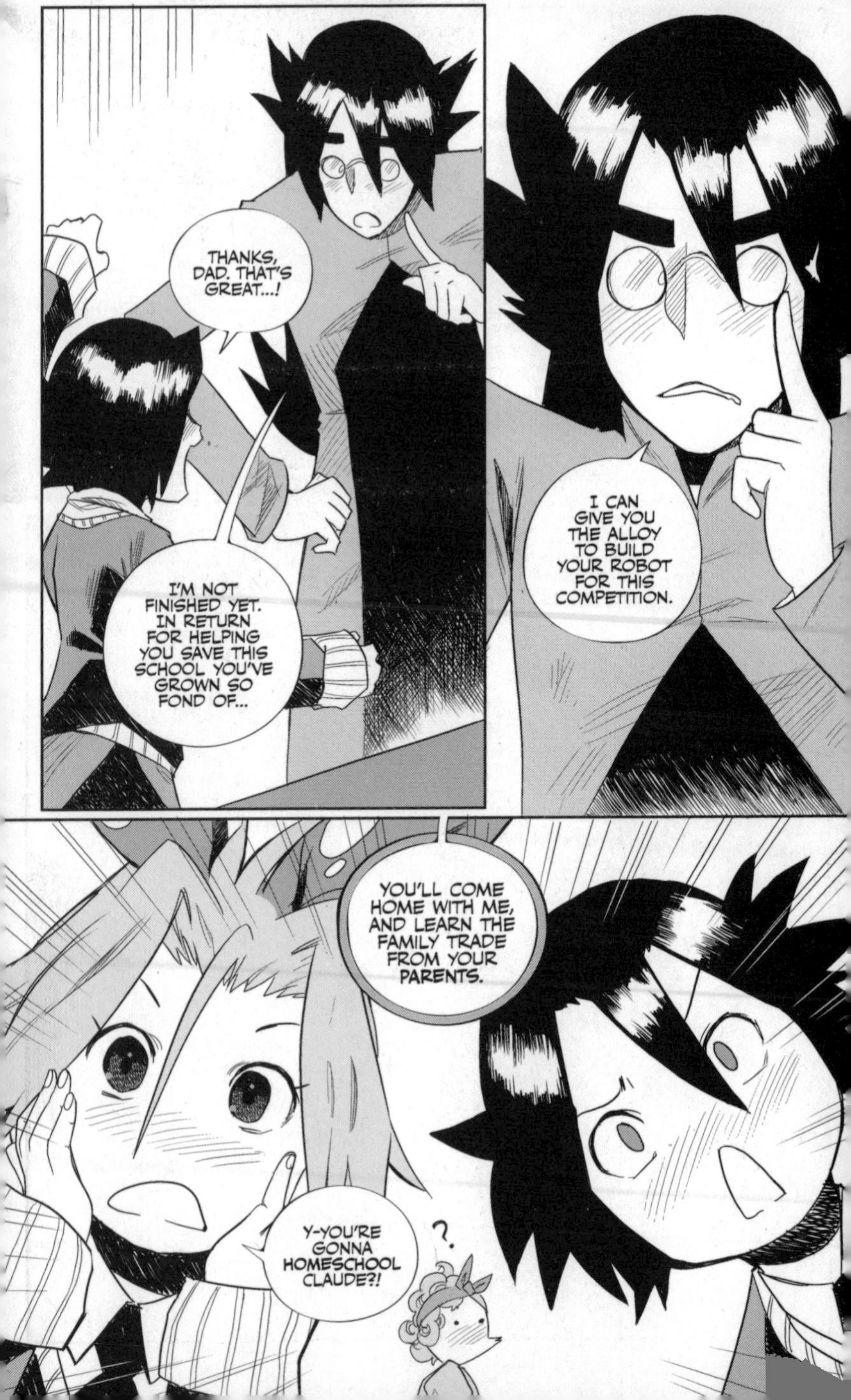
I CAN GIVE YOU THE ALLOY TO BUILD YOUR ROBOT FOR THIS COMPETITION.
THANKS, DAD. THAT'S GREAT...!
I'M NOT FINISHED YET. IN RETURN FOR HELPING YOU SAVE THIS SCHOOL YOU'VE GROWN SO FOND OF...
YOU'LL COME HOME WITH ME, AND LEARN THE FAMILY TRADE FROM YOUR PARENTS.
Y-YOU'RE GONNA HOMESCHOOL CLAUDE?!

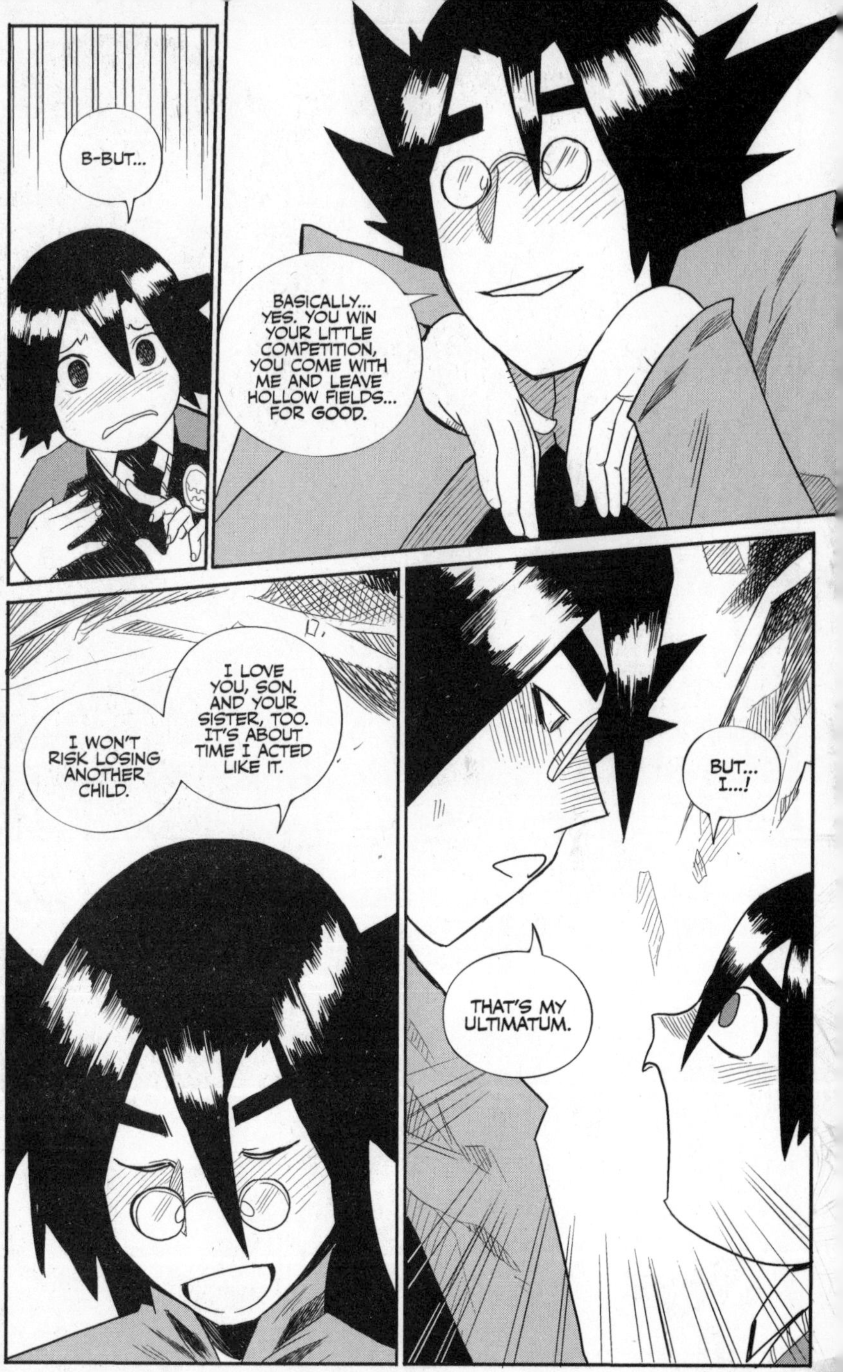
BASICALLY... YES. YOU WIN YOUR LITTLE COMPETITION, YOU COME WITH ME AND LEAVE HOLLOW FIELDS... FOR GOOD.
B-BUT...
BUT... I...!
THAT'S MY ULTIMATUM.
I LOVE YOU, SON. AND YOUR SISTER, TOO. IT'S ABOUT TIME I ACTED LIKE IT.
I WON'T RISK LOSING ANOTHER CHILD.

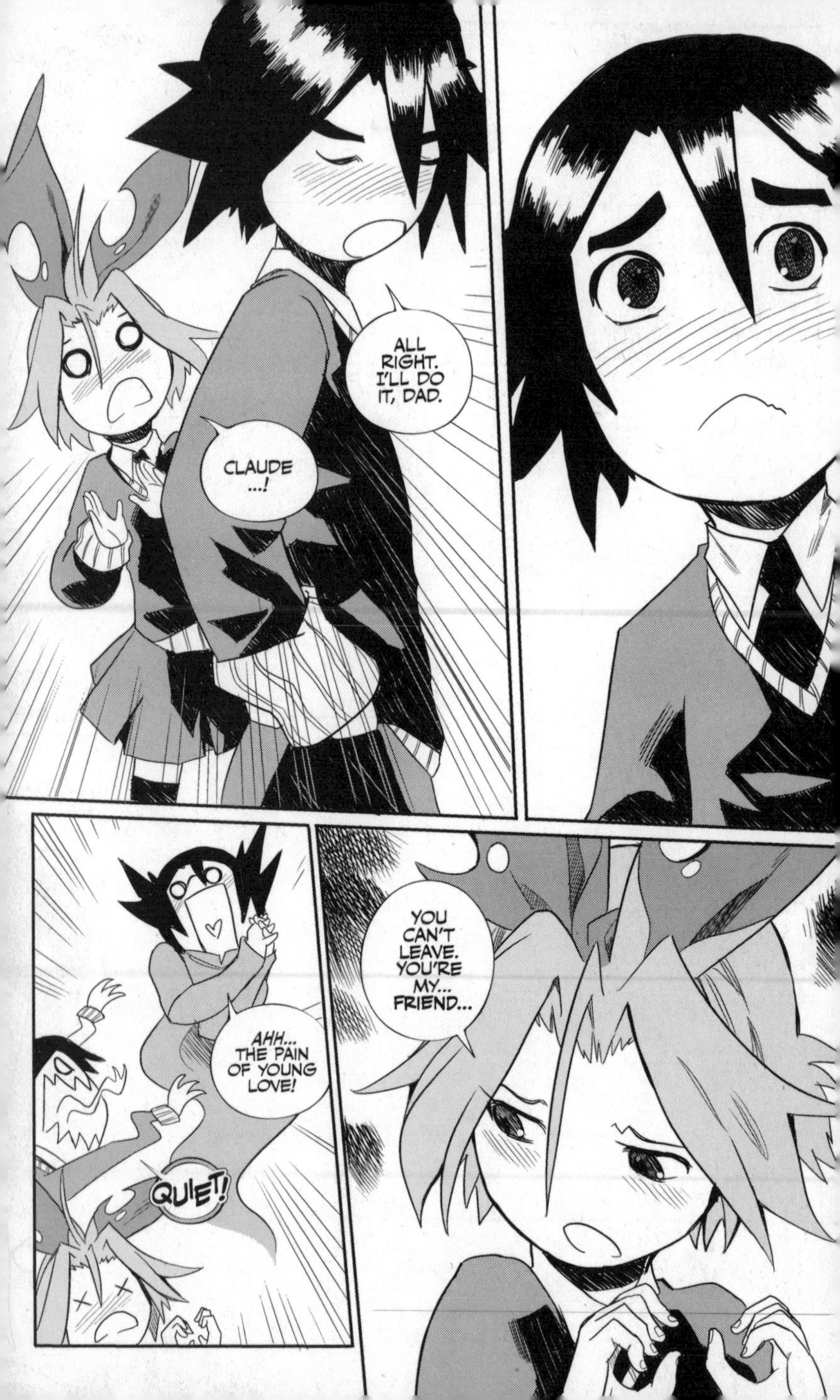
ALL RIGHT. I'LL DO IT, DAD.
CLAUDE ...!
YOU CAN'T LEAVE. YOU'RE MY... FRIEND...
AHH... THE PAIN OF YOUNG LOVE!
QUIET!

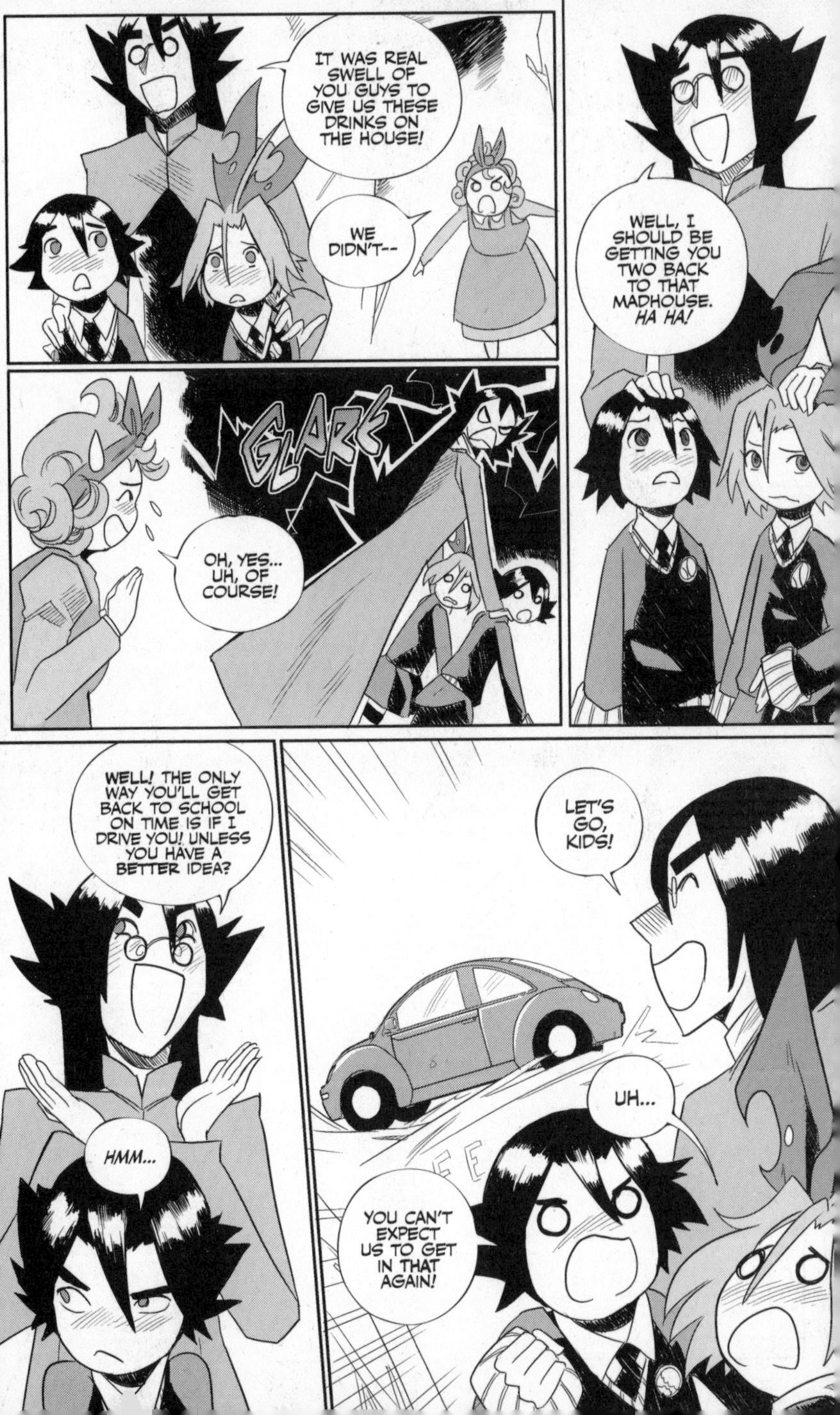
WELL, I SHOULD BE GETTING YOU TWO BACK TO THAT MADHOUSE. *HA HA!*
IT WAS REAL SWELL OF YOU GUYS TO GIVE US THESE DRINKS ON THE HOUSE!
WE DIDN'T--
GLARE
OH, YES... UH, OF COURSE!
LET'S GO, KIDS!
UH...
YOU CAN'T EXPECT US TO GET IN THAT AGAIN!
WELL! THE ONLY WAY YOU'LL GET BACK TO SCHOOL ON TIME IS IF I DRIVE YOU! UNLESS YOU HAVE A BETTER IDEA?
HMM...

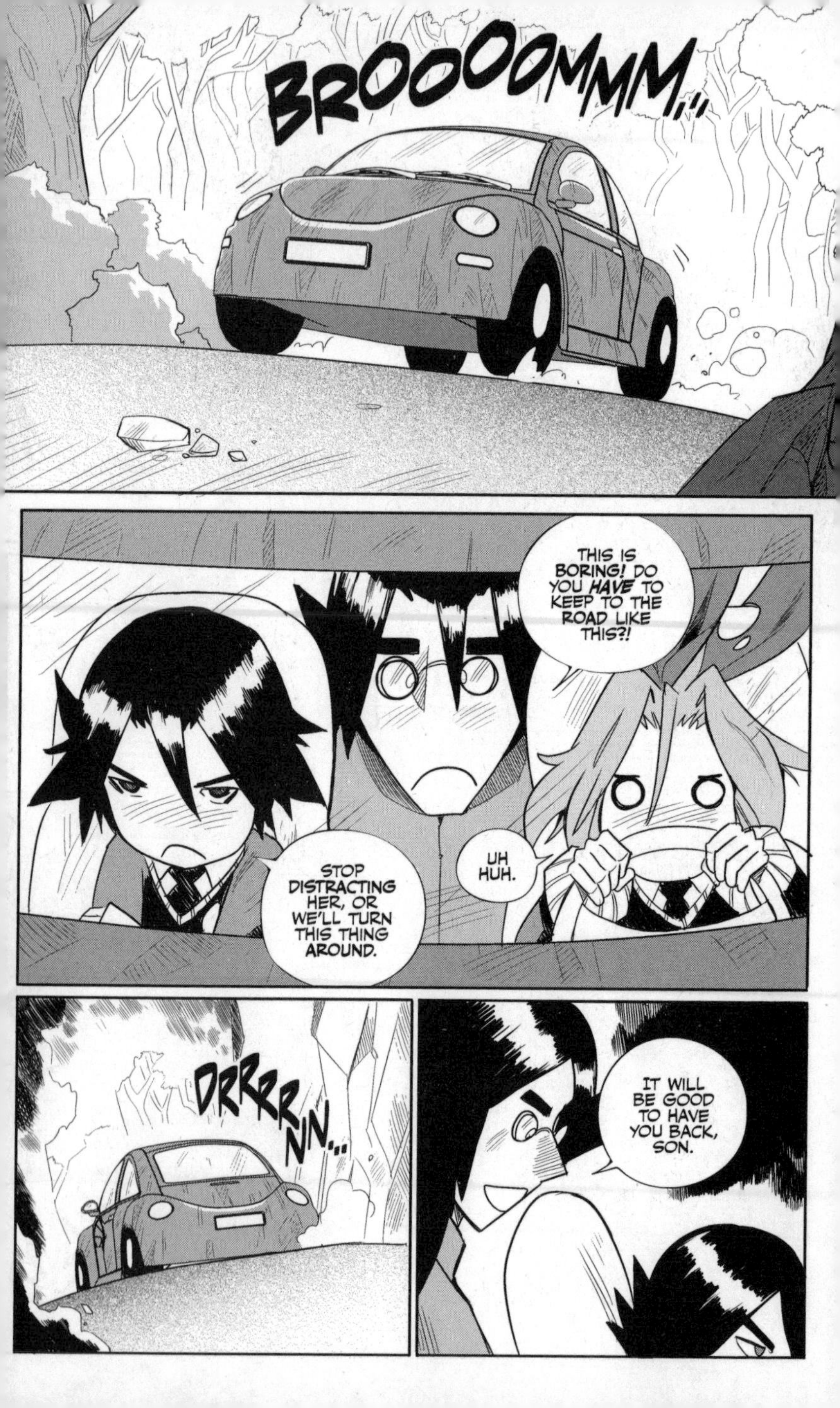
BROOOOMMM...
THIS IS BORING! DO YOU HAVE TO KEEP TO THE ROAD LIKE THIS?!
UH HUH.
STOP DISTRACTING HER, OR WE'LL TURN THIS THING AROUND.
IT WILL BE GOOD TO HAVE YOU BACK, SON.
DRRRRNN...

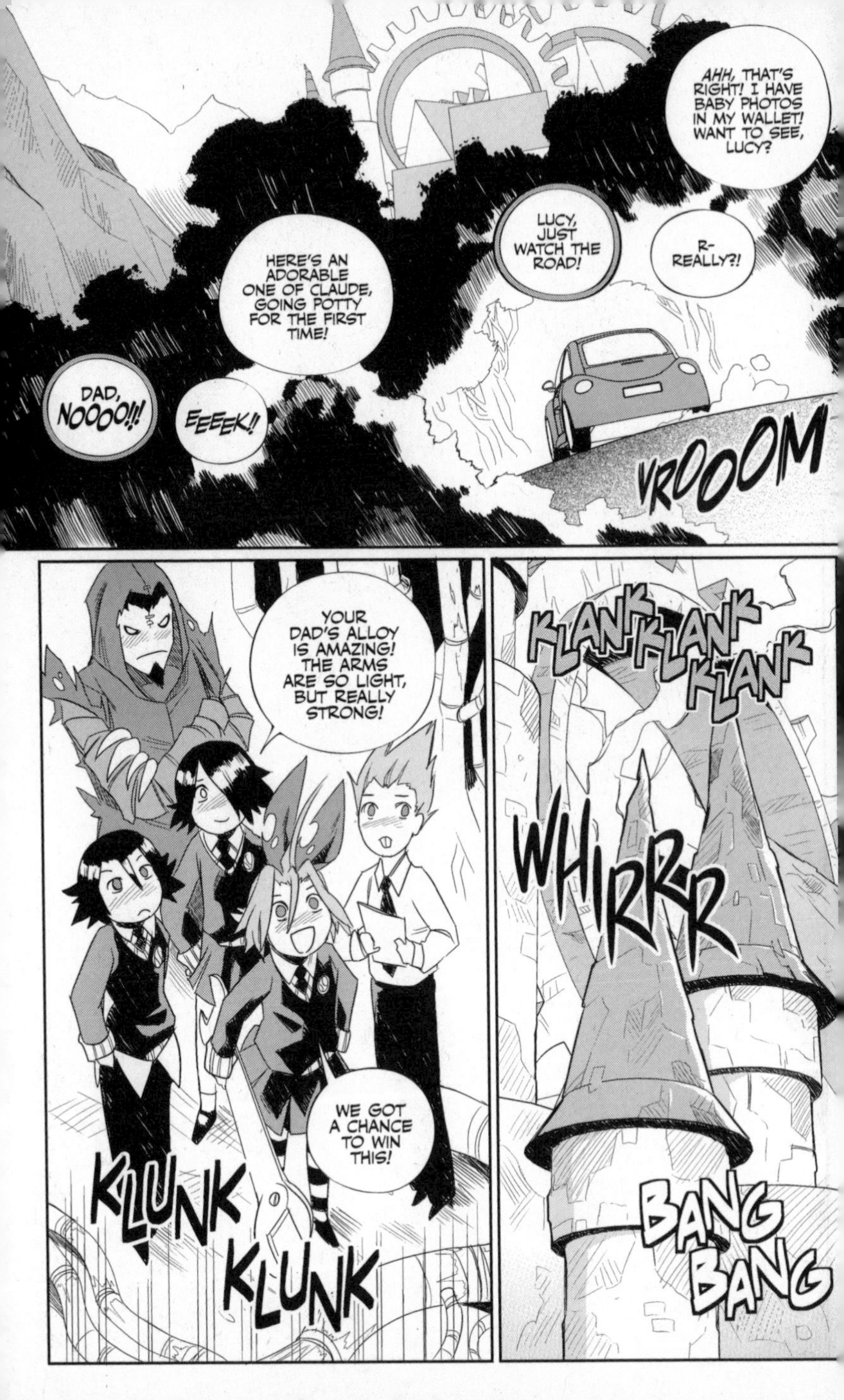
AHH, THAT'S RIGHT! I HAVE BABY PHOTOS IN MY WALLET! WANT TO SEE, LUCY?
R-REALLY?!
LUCY, JUST WATCH THE ROAD!
HERE'S AN ADORABLE ONE OF CLAUDE, GOING POTTY FOR THE FIRST TIME!
EEEEK!!
DAD, NOOOO!!!
VROOOM
KLANK KLANK KLANK KLANK
WHIRRR
BANG BANG
YOUR DAD'S ALLOY IS AMAZING! THE ARMS ARE SO LIGHT, BUT REALLY STRONG!
WE GOT A CHANCE TO WIN THIS!
KLUNK KLUNK

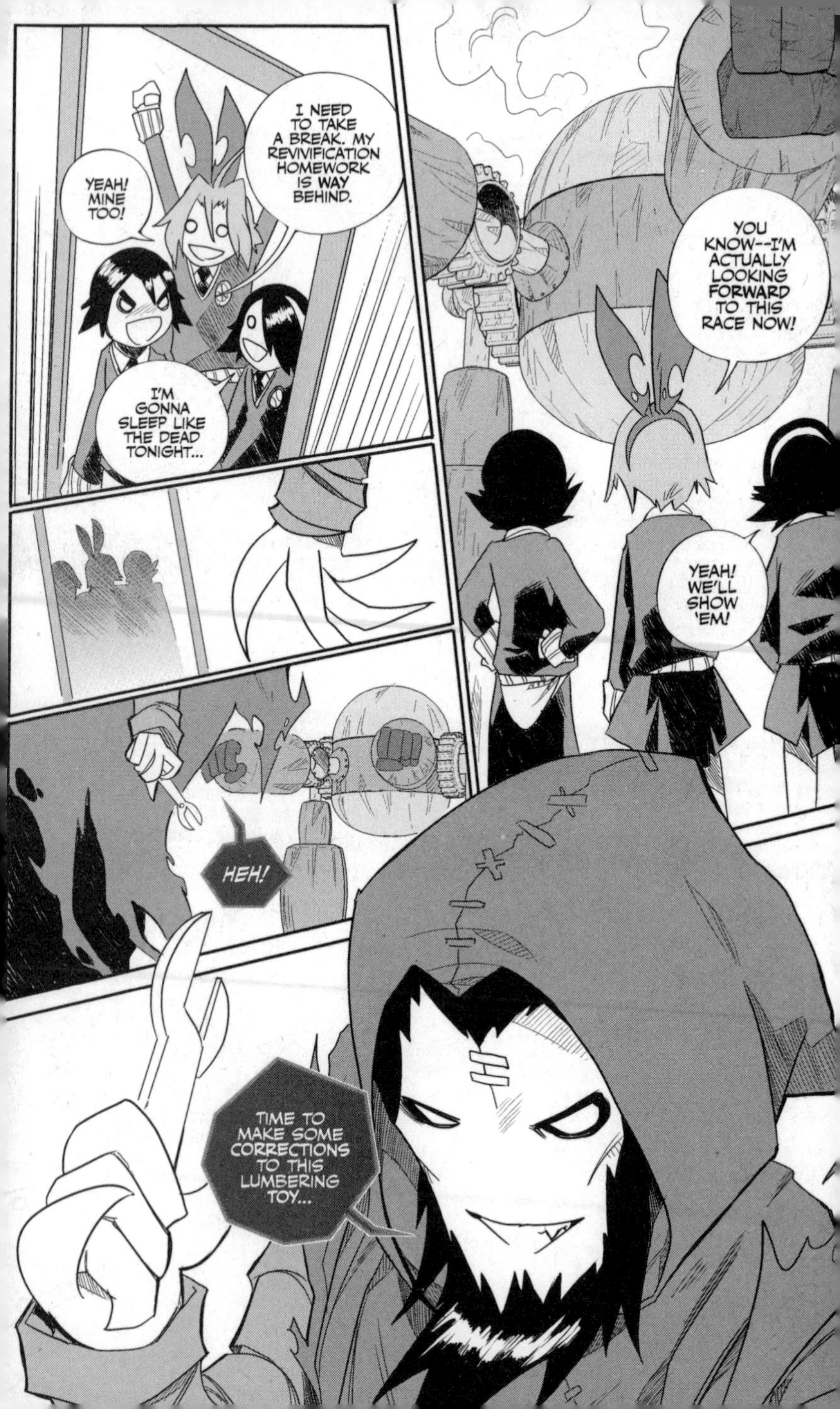
YOU KNOW--I'M ACTUALLY LOOKING FORWARD TO THIS RACE NOW!
YEAH! WE'LL SHOW 'EM!
I NEED TO TAKE A BREAK. MY REVIVIFICATION HOMEWORK IS WAY BEHIND.
YEAH! MINE TOO!
I'M GONNA SLEEP LIKE THE DEAD TONIGHT...
HEH!
TIME TO MAKE SOME CORRECTIONS TO THIS LUMBERING TOY...

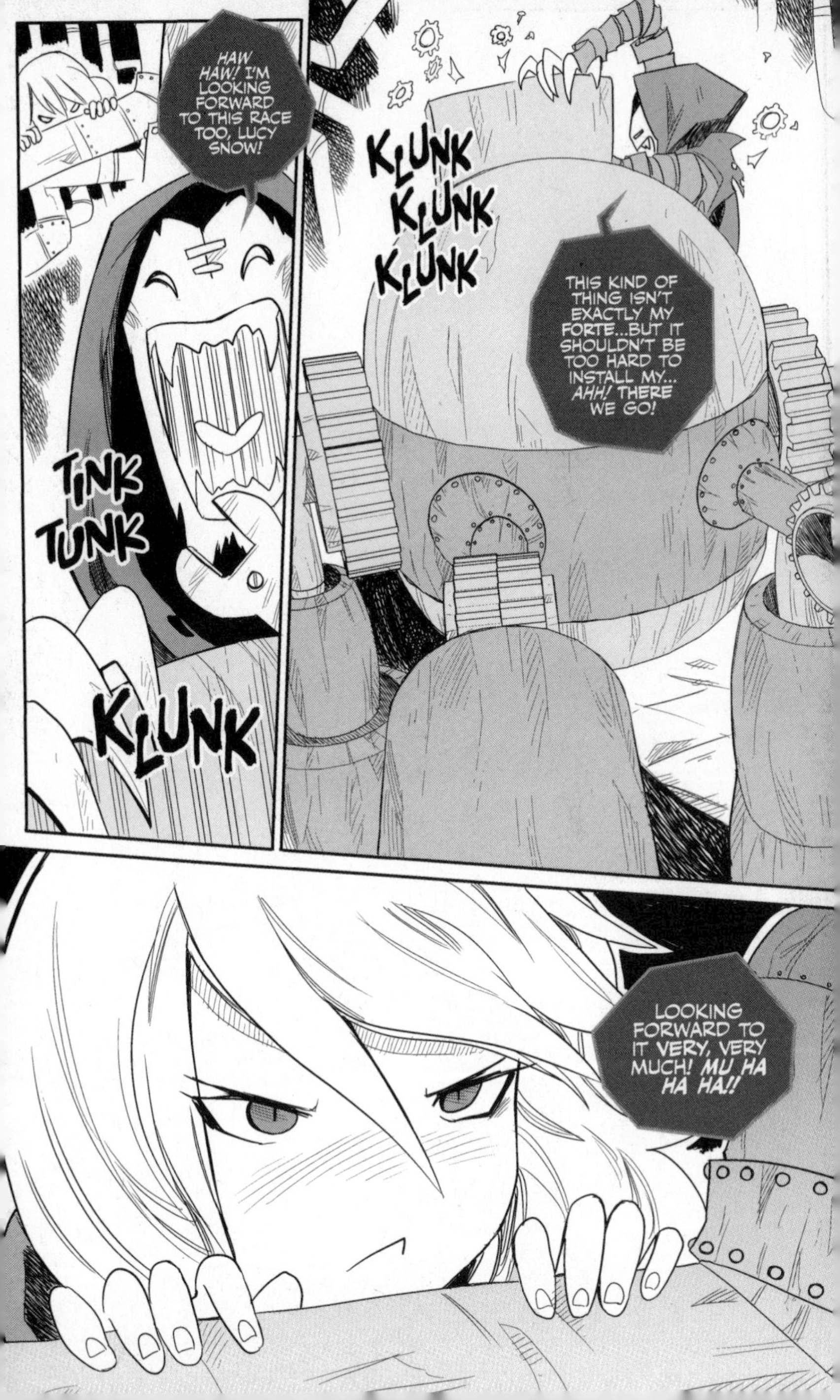
THIS KIND OF THING ISN'T EXACTLY MY FORTE...BUT IT SHOULDN'T BE TOO HARD TO INSTALL MY... AHH! THERE WE GO!
KLUNK KLUNK KLUNK
HAW HAW! I'M LOOKING FORWARD TO THIS RACE TOO, LUCY SNOW!
TINK TUNK
KLUNK
LOOKING FORWARD TO IT VERY, VERY MUCH! MU HA HA HA!!

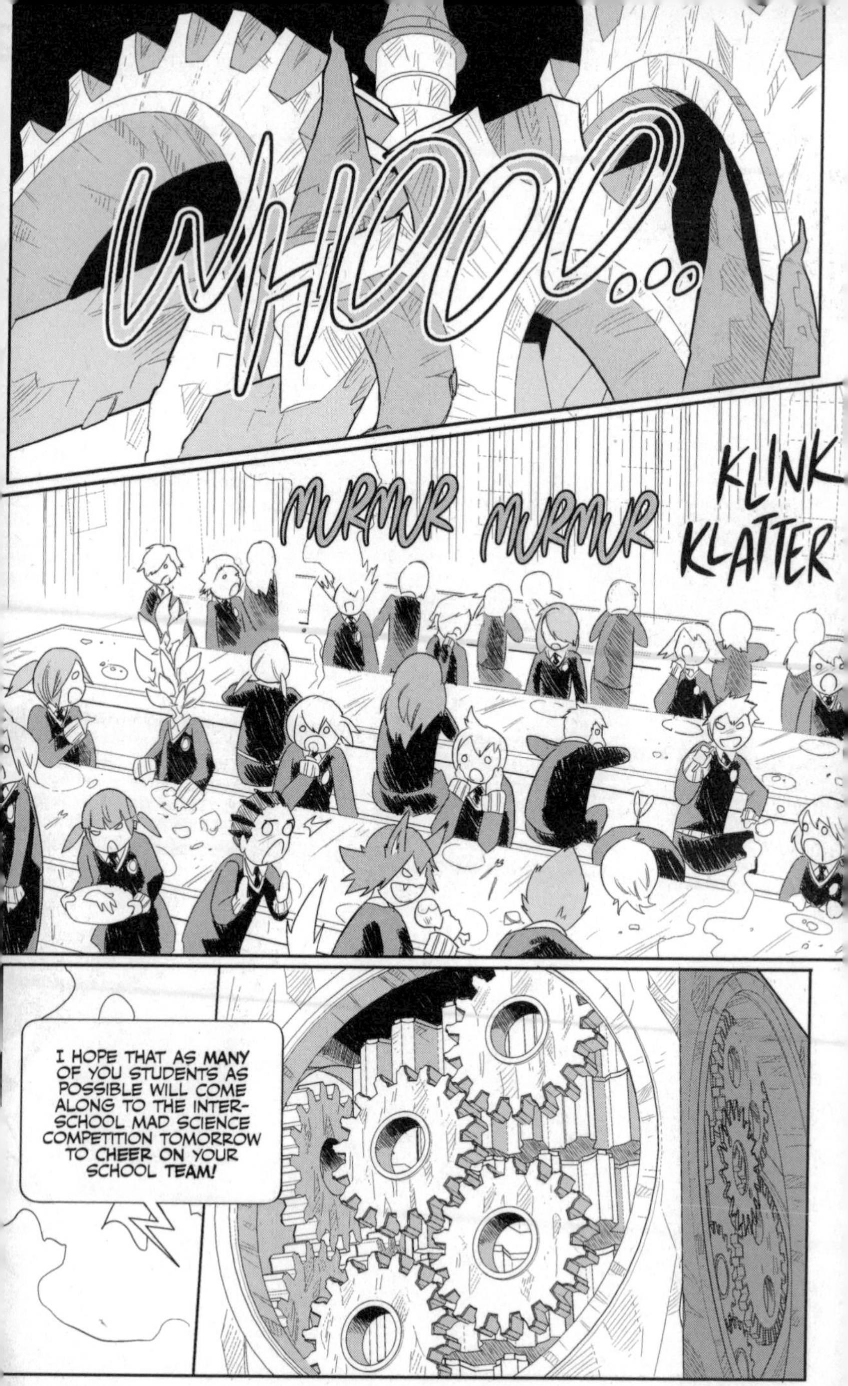
WHOOO...
KLINK KLATTER
MURMUR MURMUR
I HOPE THAT AS MANY OF YOU STUDENTS AS POSSIBLE WILL COME ALONG TO THE INTER-SCHOOL MAD SCIENCE COMPETITION TOMORROW TO CHEER ON YOUR SCHOOL TEAM!

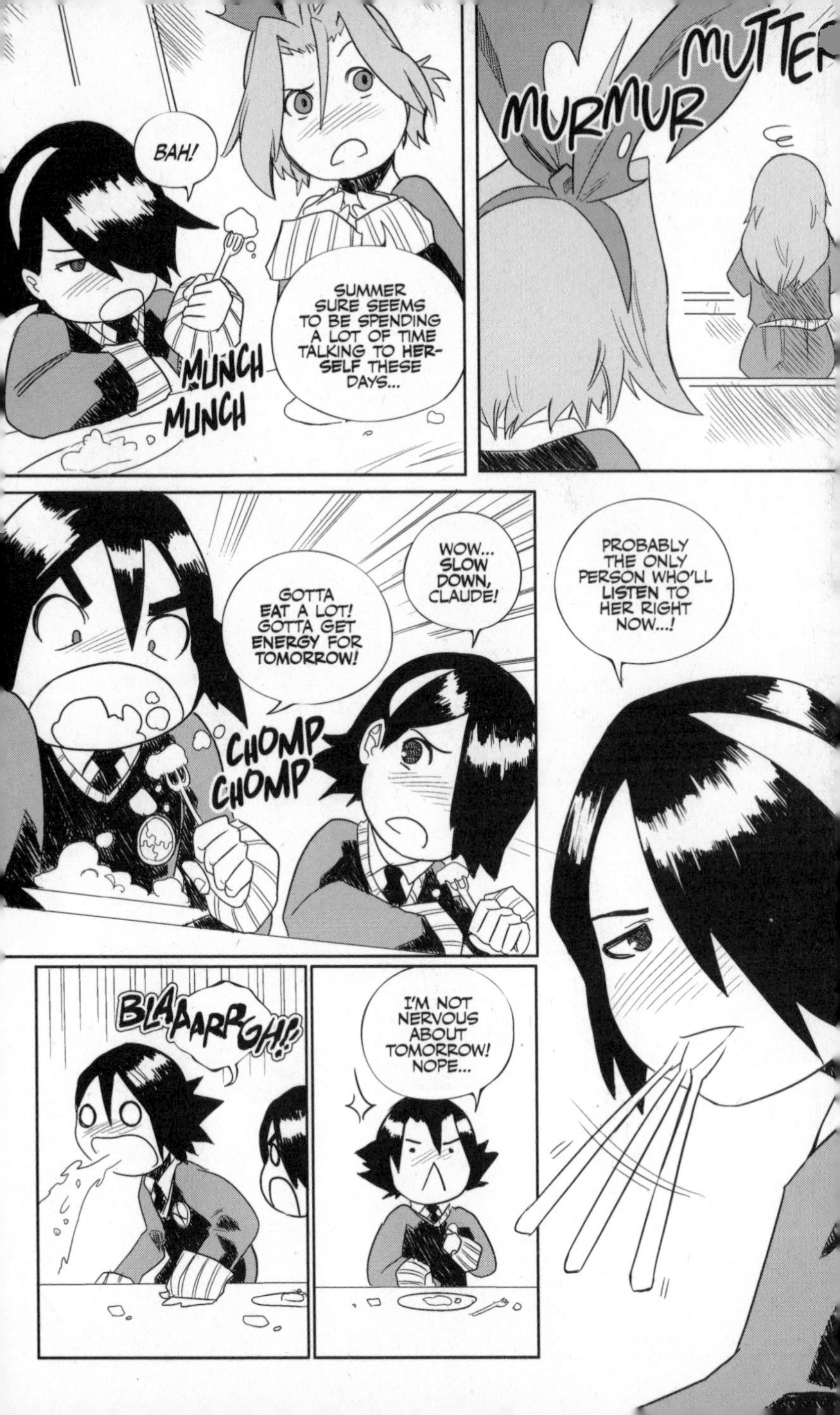
MUTTER
MURMUR
BAH!
SUMMER SURE SEEMS TO BE SPENDING A LOT OF TIME TALKING TO HER-SELF THESE DAYS...
MUNCH MUNCH
PROBABLY THE ONLY PERSON WHO'LL LISTEN TO HER RIGHT NOW...!
WOW... SLOW DOWN, CLAUDE!
GOTTA EAT A LOT! GOTTA GET ENERGY FOR TOMORROW!
CHOMP CHOMP
I'M NOT NERVOUS ABOUT TOMORROW! NOPE...
BLAAARRGH!!

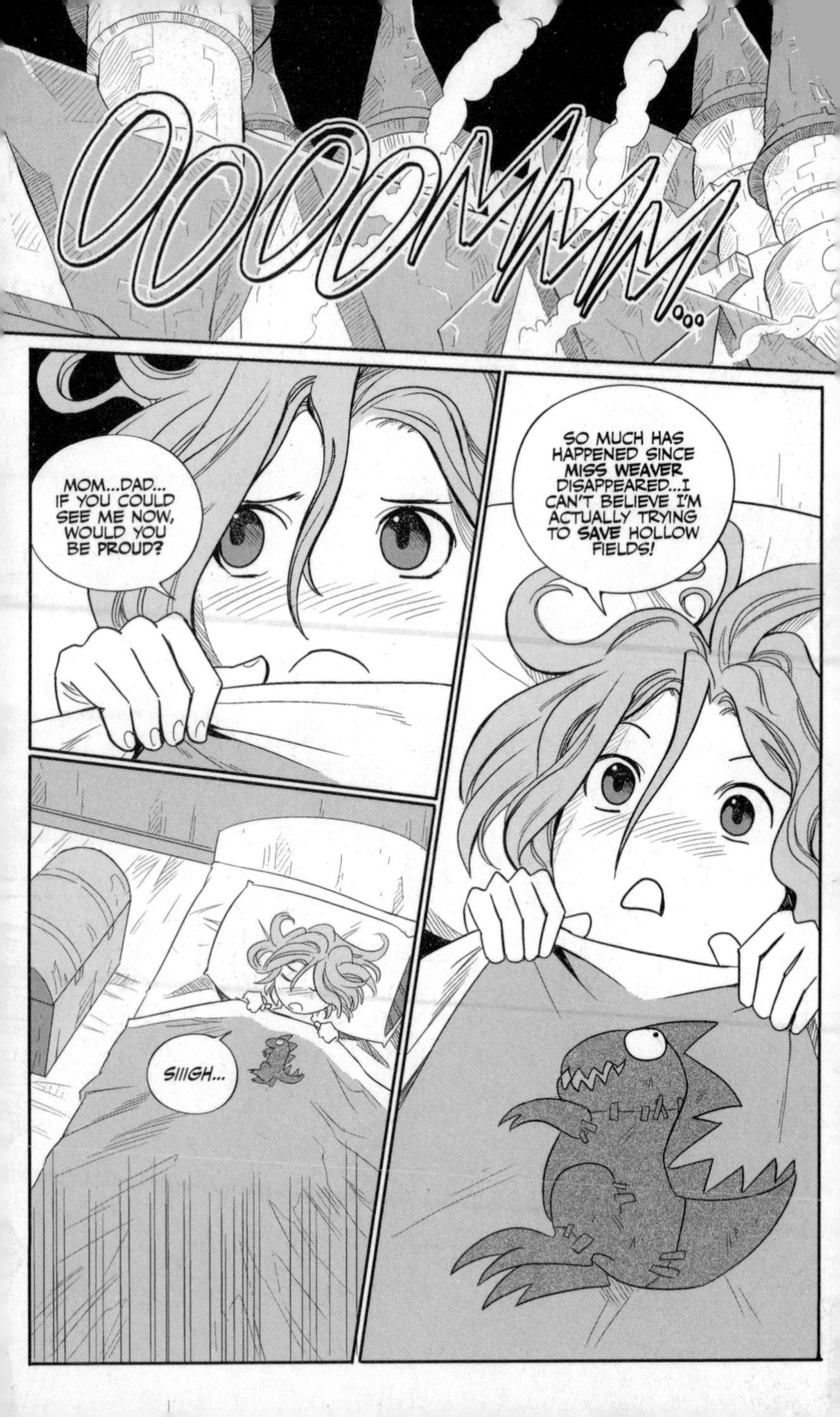
OOOOMMM
ooo
SO MUCH HAS HAPPENED SINCE MISS WEAVER DISAPPEARED...I CAN'T BELIEVE I'M ACTUALLY TRYING TO SAVE HOLLOW FIELDS!
MOM...DAD... IF YOU COULD SEE ME NOW, WOULD YOU BE PROUD?
SIIIGH...

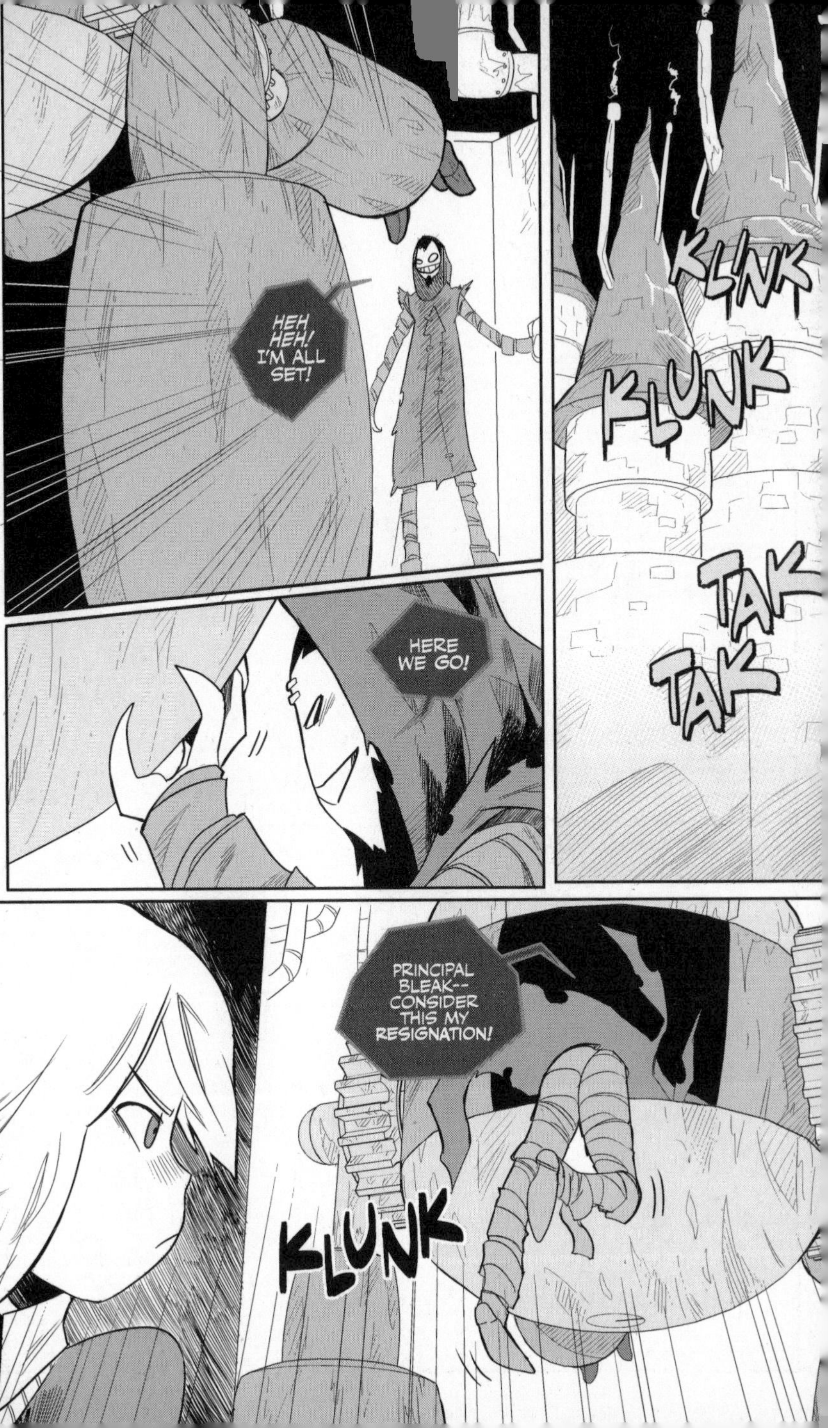
KLINK
KLUNK
TAK
TAK
HEH HEH! I'M ALL SET!
HERE WE GO!
PRINCIPAL BLEAK-- CONSIDER THIS MY RESIGNATION!
KLUNK

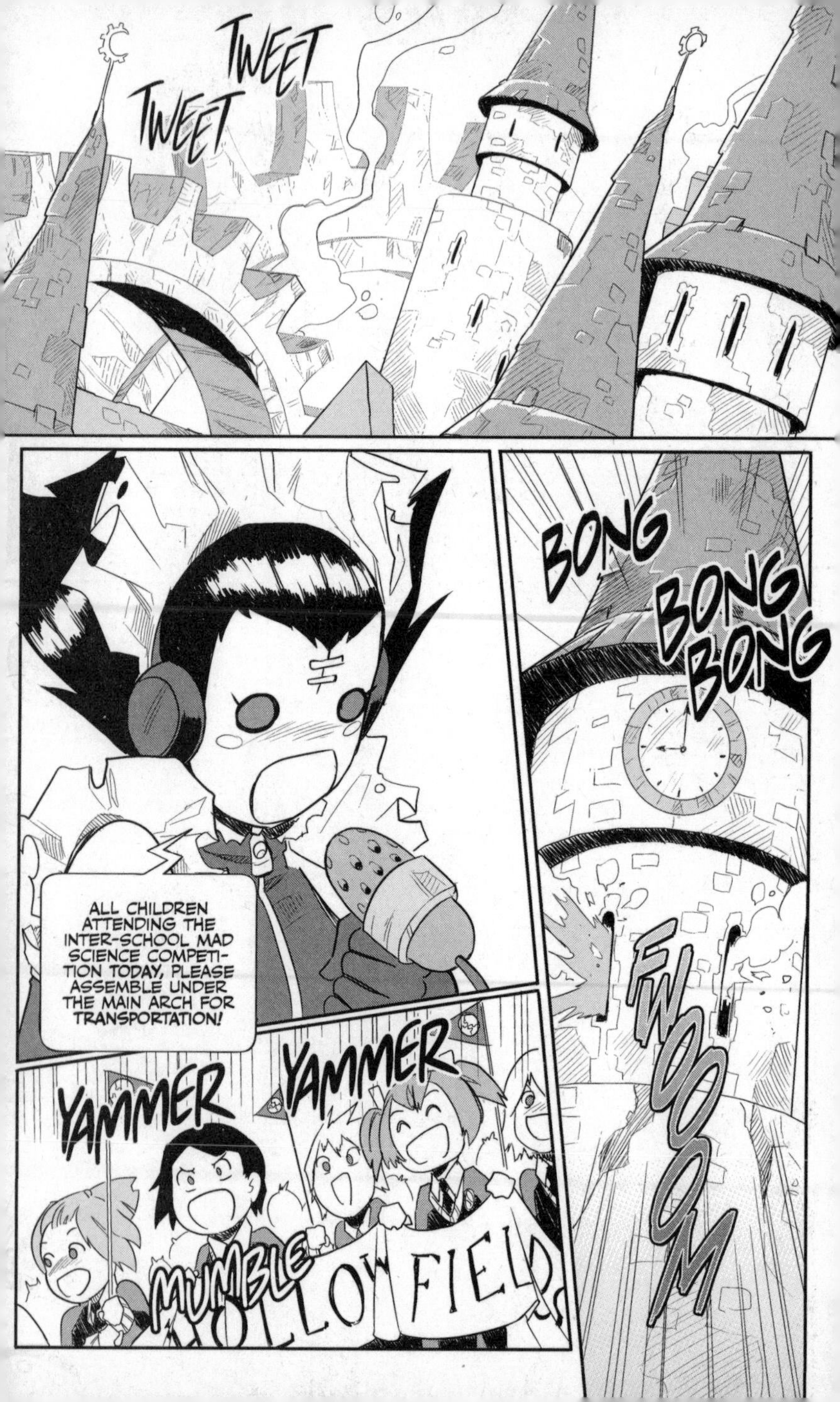
TWEET
TWEET
BONG
BONG
BONG
FWOOOOM
ALL CHILDREN ATTENDING THE INTER-SCHOOL MAD SCIENCE COMPETITION TODAY, PLEASE ASSEMBLE UNDER THE MAIN ARCH FOR TRANSPORTATION!
YAMMER
YAMMER
MUMBLE
HOLLOW FIELD

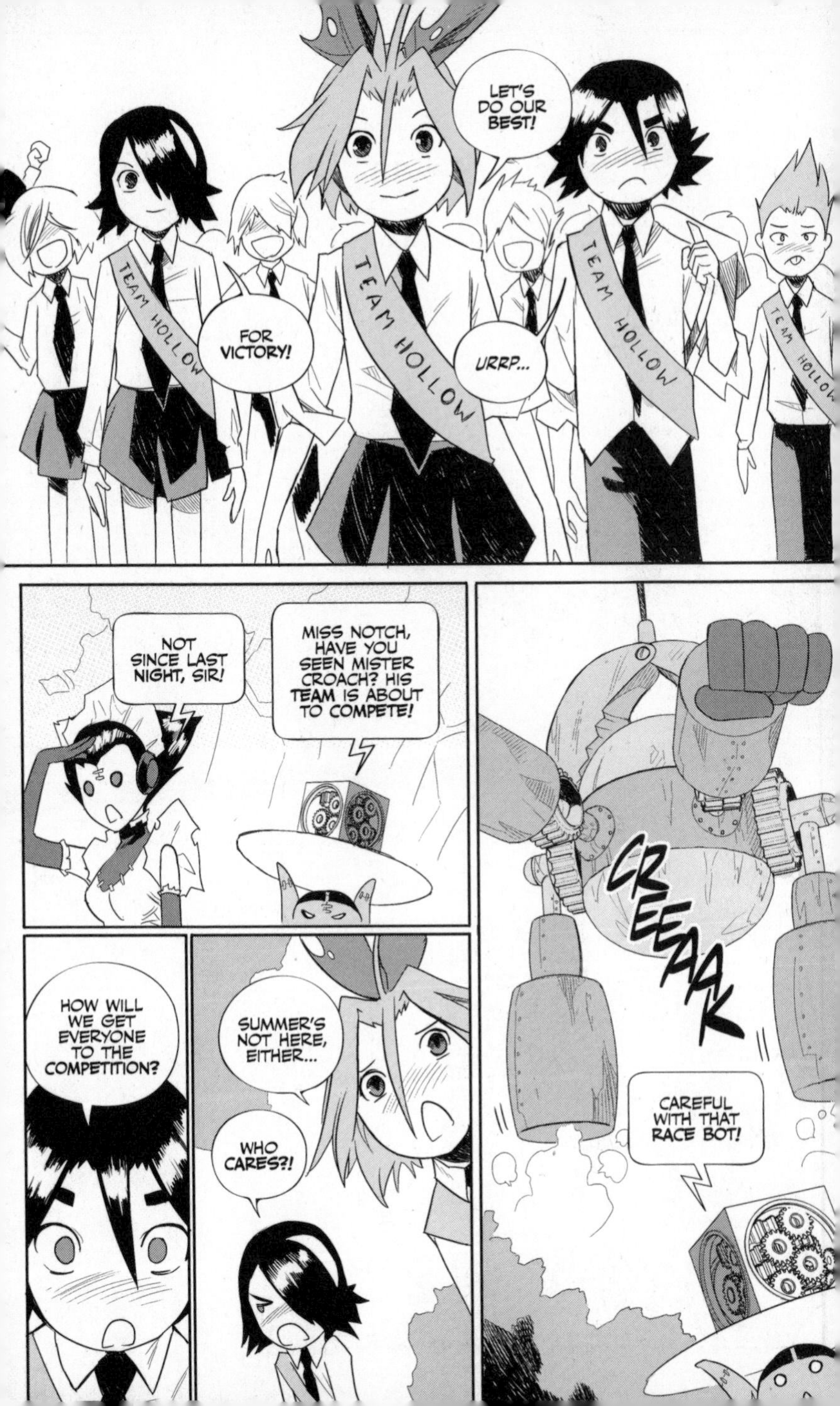
LET'S DO OUR BEST!
URRP...
FOR VICTORY!
CREEAAK
CAREFUL WITH THAT RACE BOT!
MISS NOTCH, HAVE YOU SEEN MISTER CROACH? HIS TEAM IS ABOUT TO COMPETE!
NOT SINCE LAST NIGHT, SIR!
SUMMER'S NOT HERE, EITHER...
WHO CARES?!
HOW WILL WE GET EVERYONE TO THE COMPETITION?

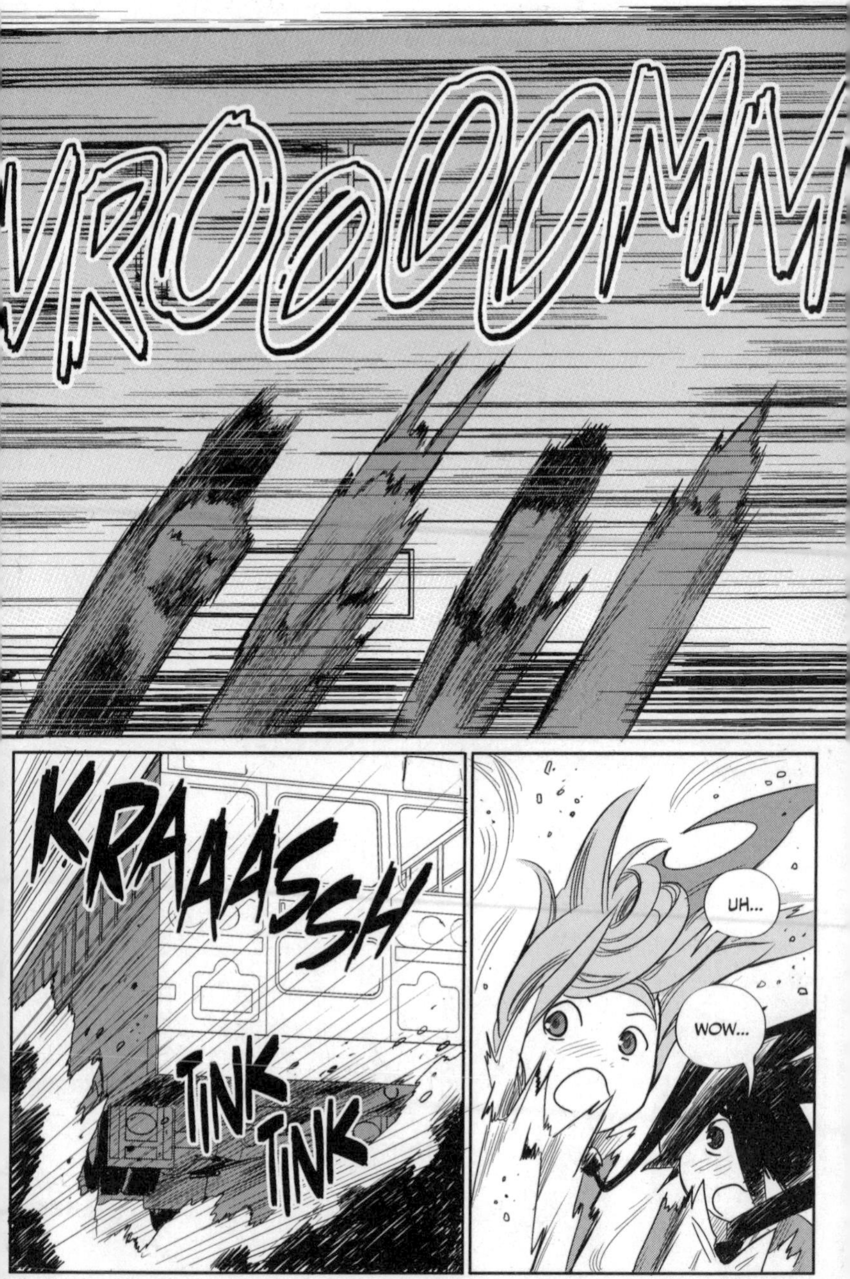
VROOOOOMM
UH...
WOW...
KRAAASSH
TINK
TINK

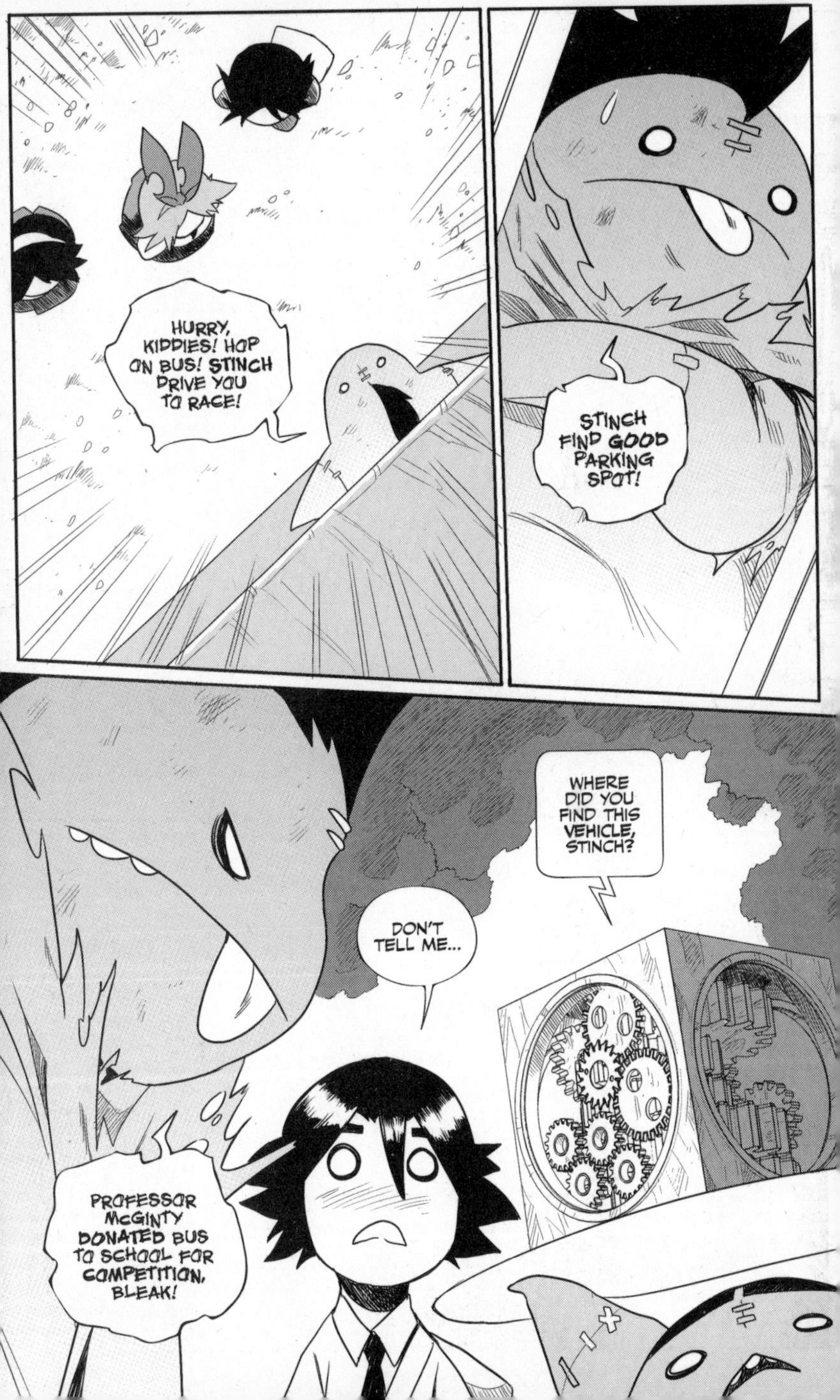
STINCH FIND GOOD PARKING SPOT!
HURRY, KIDDIES! HOP ON BUS! STINCH DRIVE YOU TO RACE!
WHERE DID YOU FIND THIS VEHICLE, STINCH?
DON'T TELL ME...
PROFESSOR McGINTY DONATED BUS TO SCHOOL FOR COMPETITION, BLEAK!

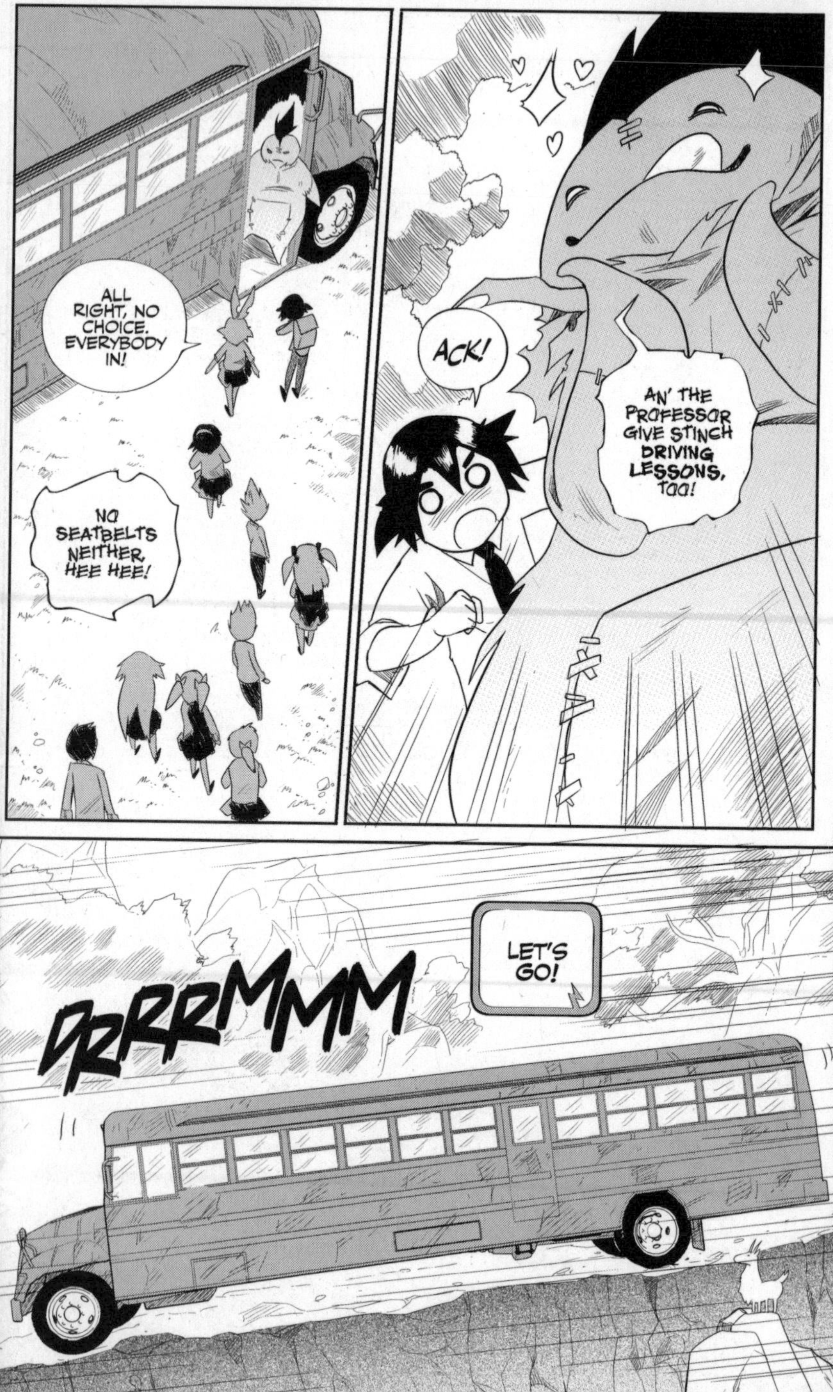
AN' THE PROFESSOR GIVE STINCH DRIVING LESSONS, TOO!
ACK!
ALL RIGHT, NO CHOICE. EVERYBODY IN!
NO SEATBELTS NEITHER, HEE HEE!
LET'S GO!
DRRRMMMM

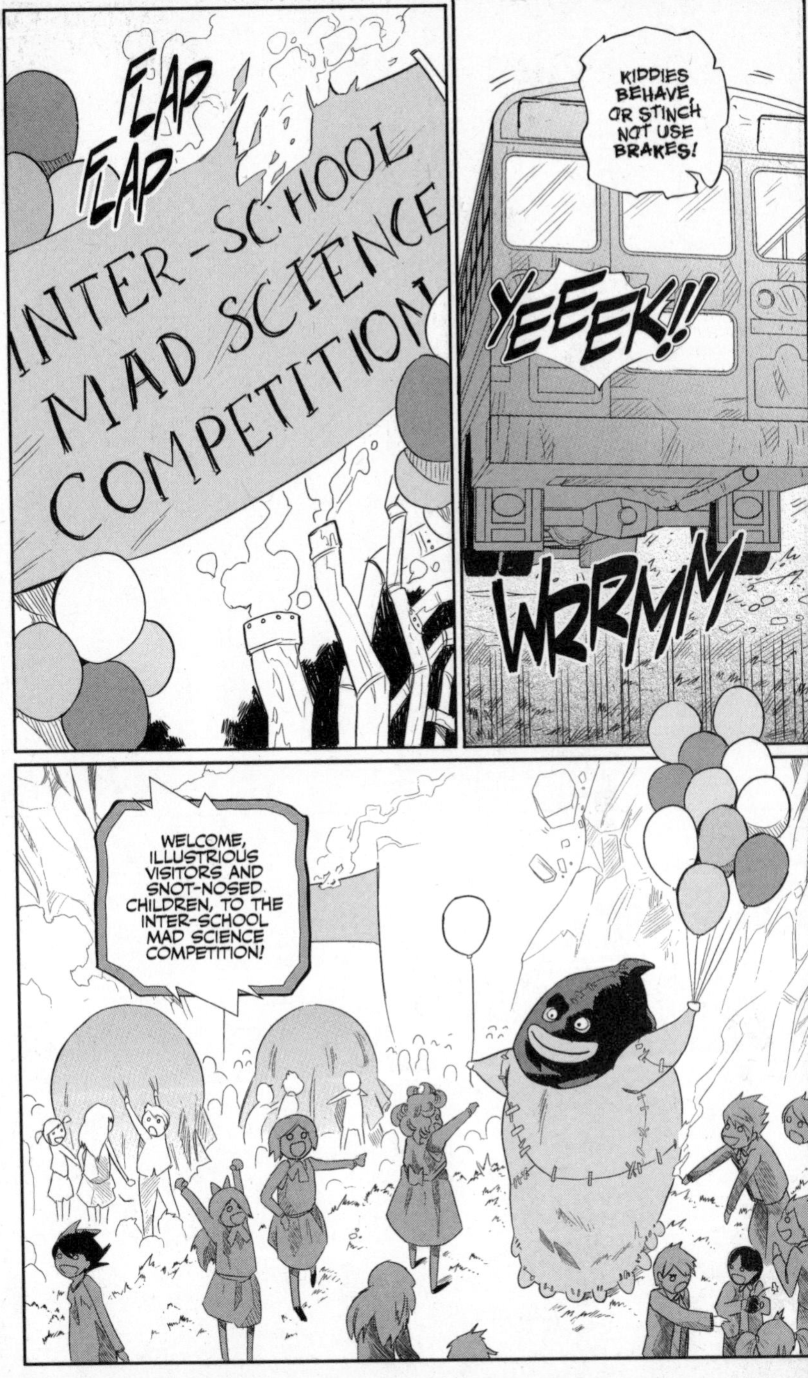
KIDDIES BEHAVE, OR STINCH NOT USE BRAKES!
YEEEK!!
WRRMM
FLAP FLAP
INTER-SCHOOL MAD SCIENCE COMPETITION
WELCOME, ILLUSTRIOUS VISITORS AND SNOT-NOSED CHILDREN, TO THE INTER-SCHOOL MAD SCIENCE COMPETITION!

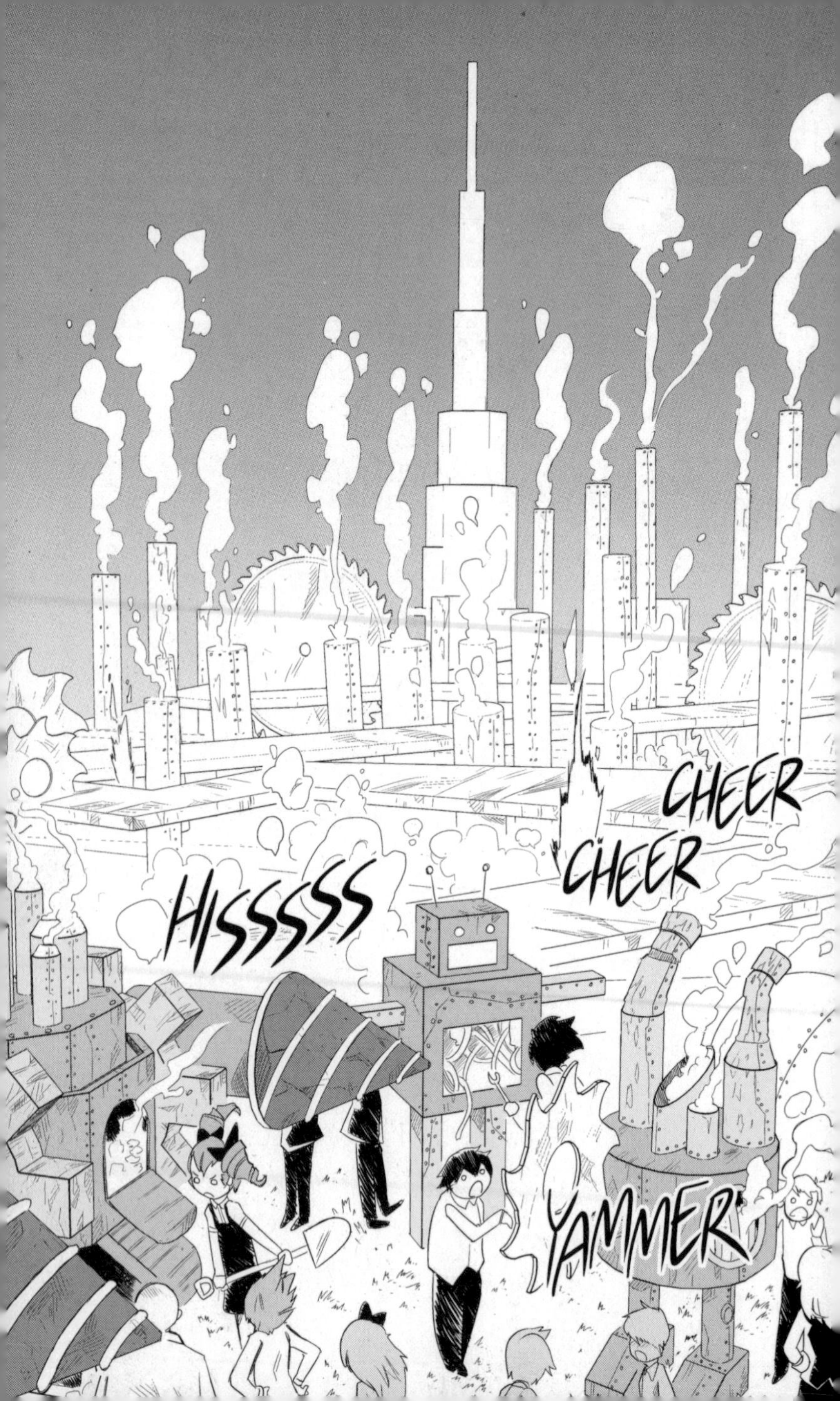
CHEER
CHEER
HISSSSS
YAMMER

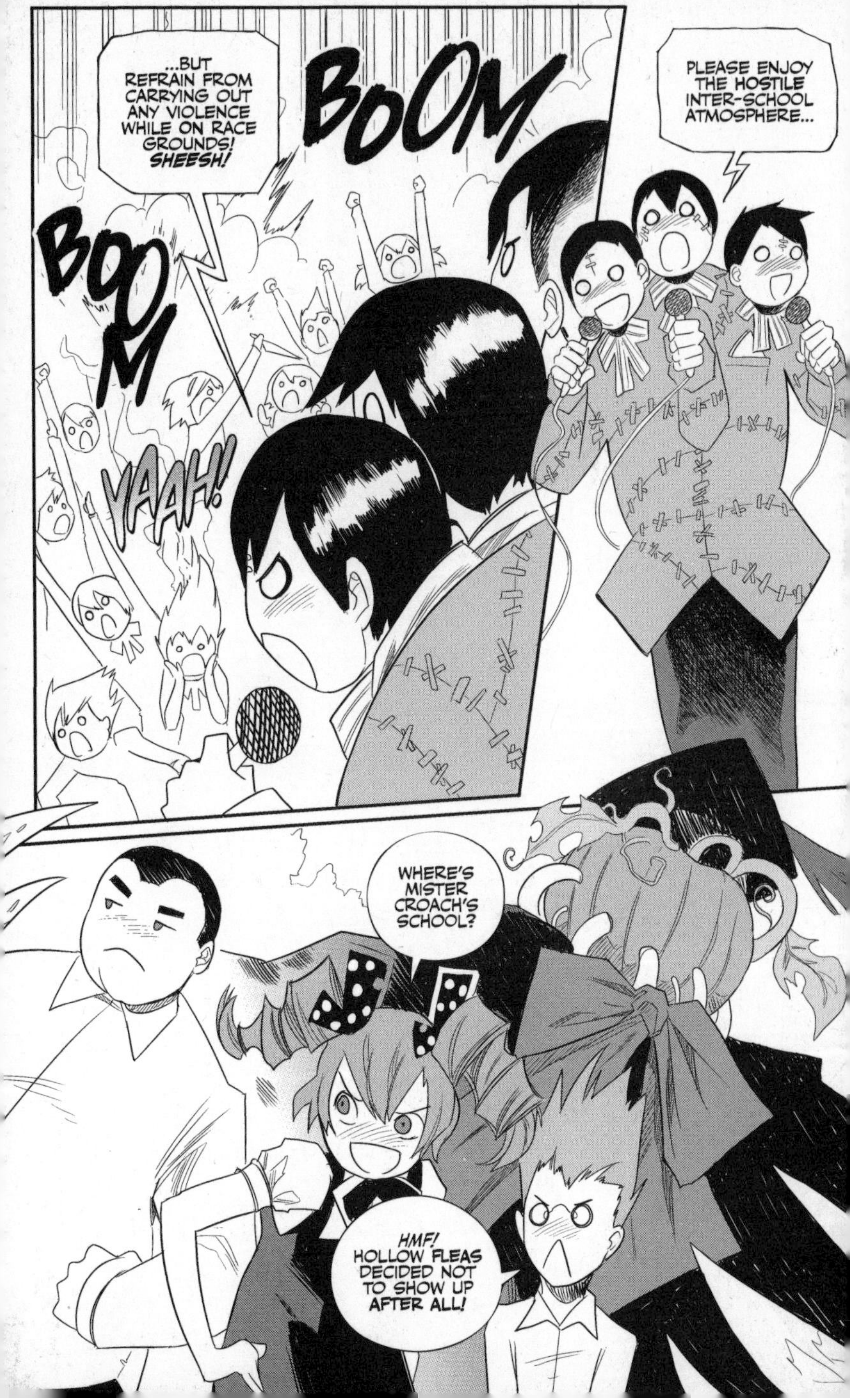
PLEASE ENJOY THE HOSTILE INTER-SCHOOL ATMOSPHERE...
BOOM
...BUT REFRAIN FROM CARRYING OUT ANY VIOLENCE WHILE ON RACE GROUNDS! SHEESH!
BOOOM
YAAH!
WHERE'S MISTER CROACH'S SCHOOL?
HMF! HOLLOW FLEAS DECIDED NOT TO SHOW UP AFTER ALL!

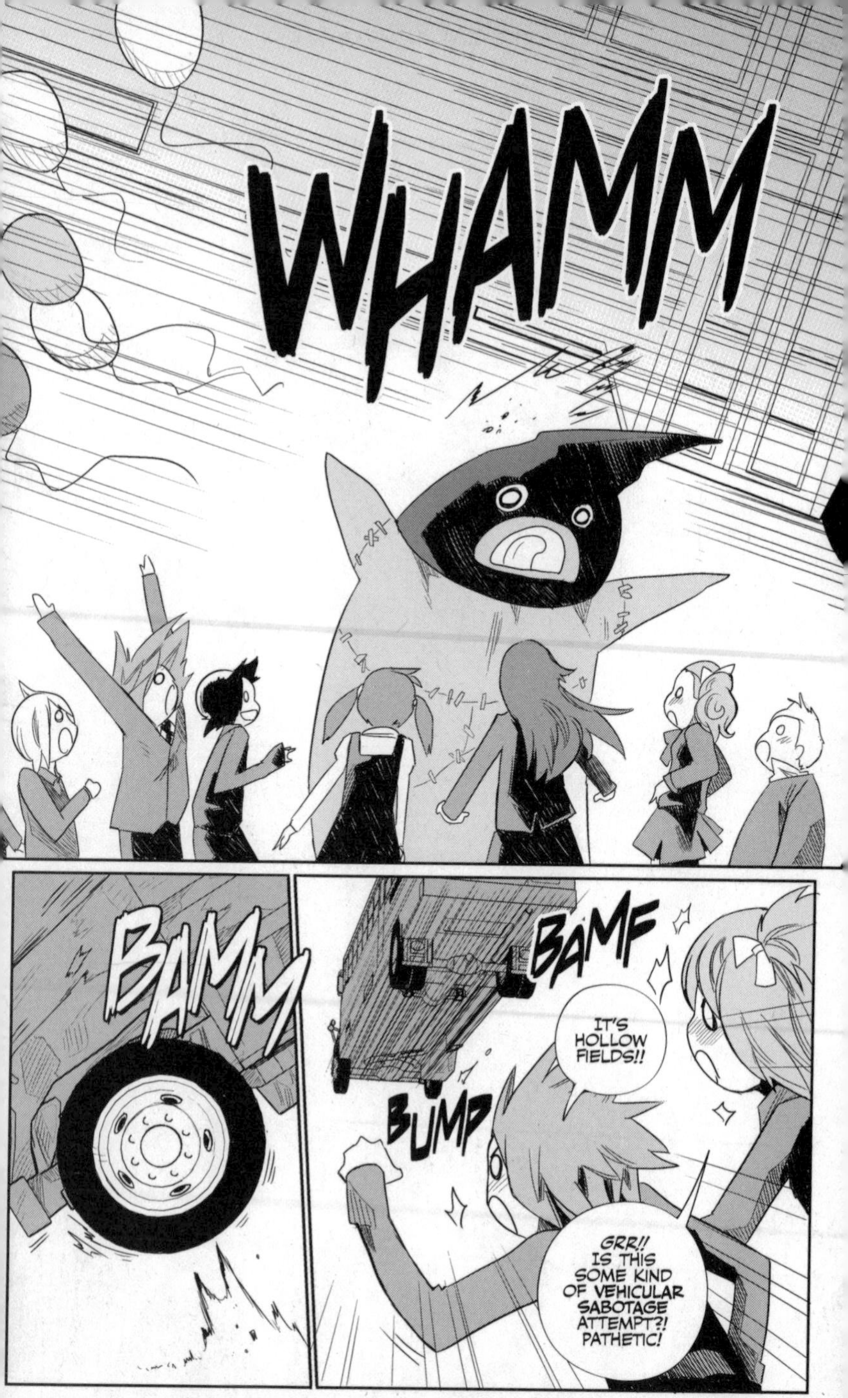
WHAMM
BAMF
IT'S HOLLOW FIELDS!!
BUMP
GRR!! IS THIS SOME KIND OF VEHICULAR SABOTAGE ATTEMPT?! PATHETIC!
BAMM

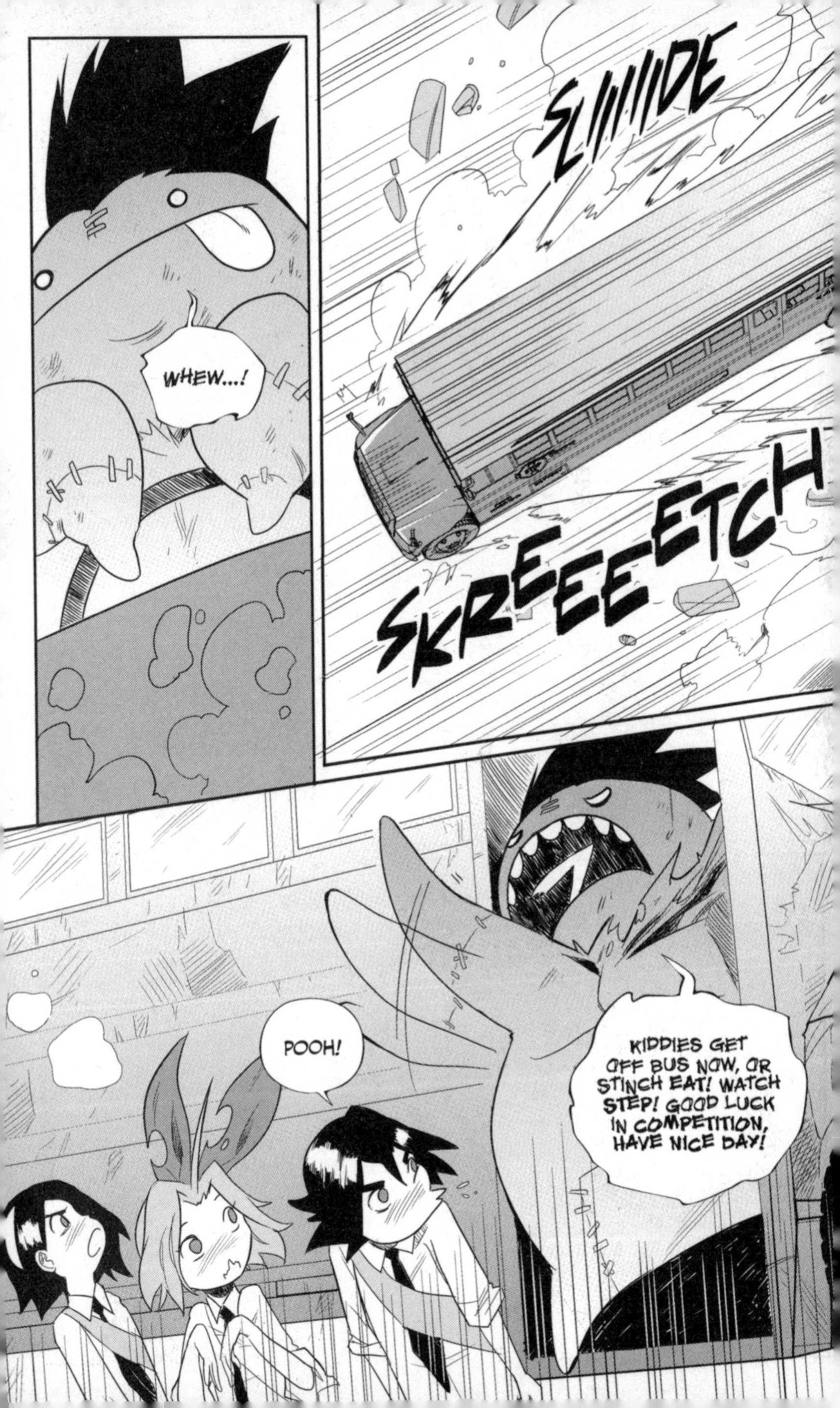
SLIIIIDE
SKREEE-ETCH
WHEW...!
KIDDIES GET OFF BUS NOW, OR STINCH EAT! WATCH STEP! GOOD LUCK IN COMPETITION, HAVE NICE DAY!
POOH!

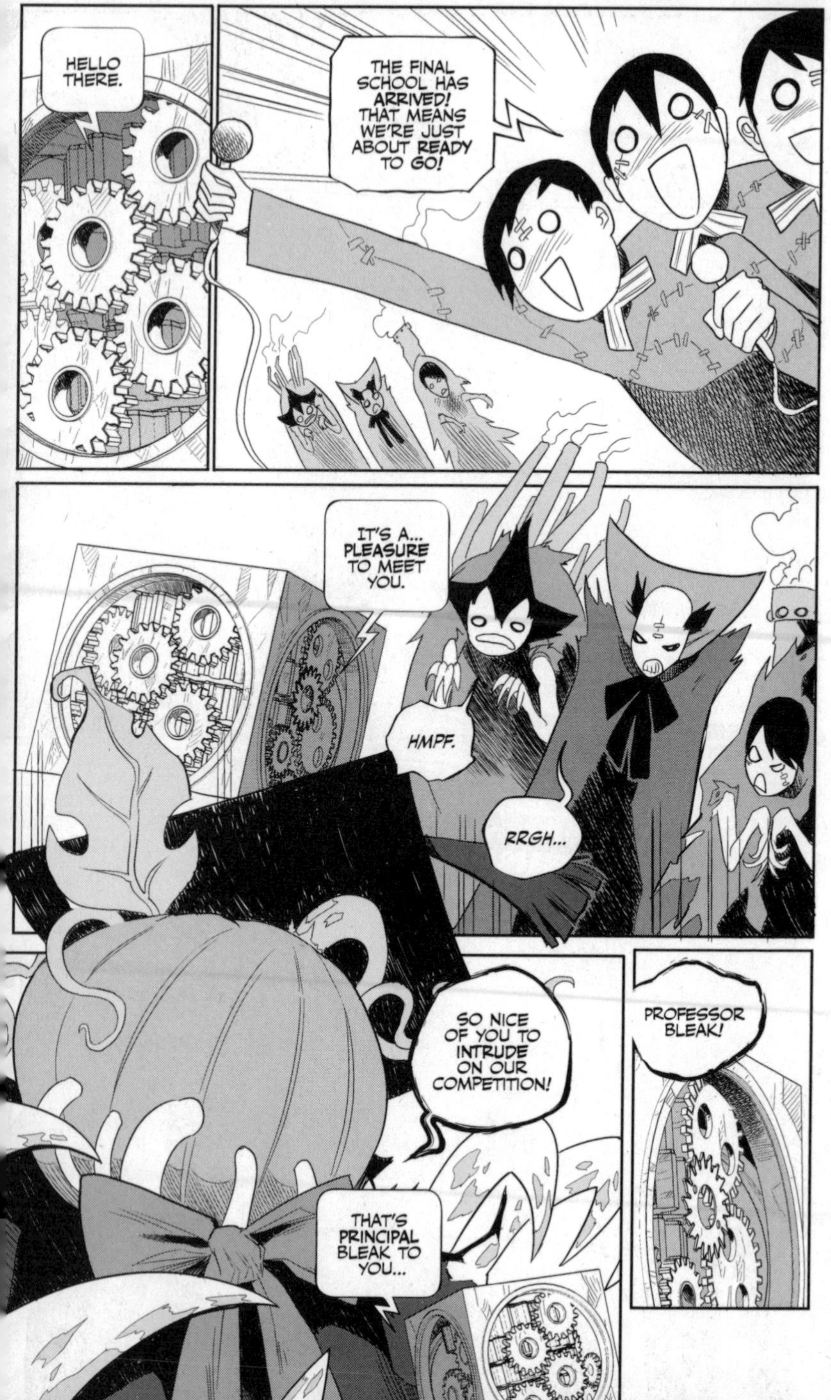
THE FINAL SCHOOL HAS ARRIVED! THAT MEANS WE'RE JUST ABOUT READY TO GO!
HELLO THERE.
IT'S A... PLEASURE TO MEET YOU.
HMPF.
RRGH...
PROFESSOR BLEAK!
SO NICE OF YOU TO INTRUDE ON OUR COMPETITION!
THAT'S PRINCIPAL BLEAK TO YOU...

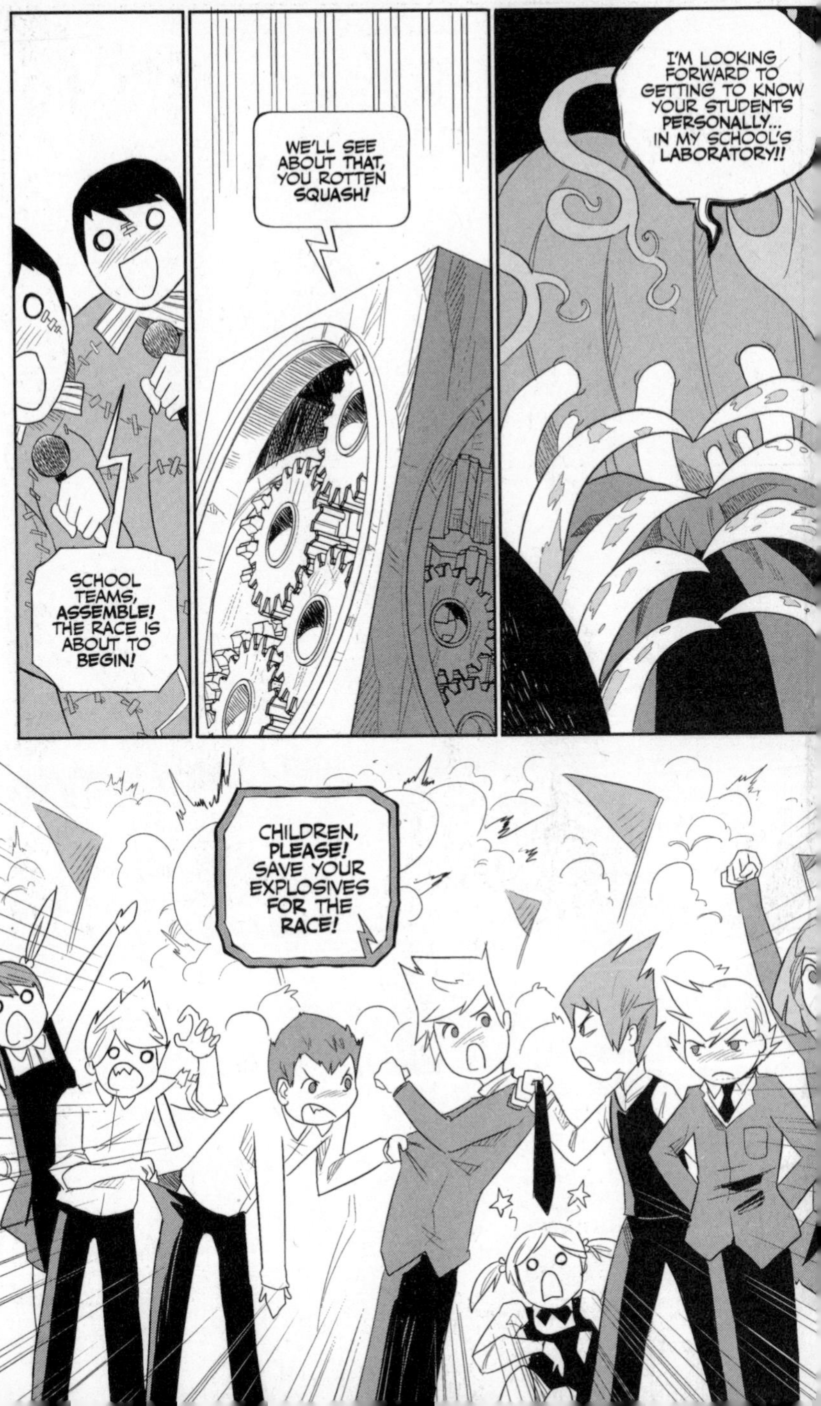

I'M LOOKING FORWARD TO GETTING TO KNOW YOUR STUDENTS PERSONALLY... IN MY SCHOOL'S LABORATORY!!
WE'LL SEE ABOUT THAT, YOU ROTTEN SQUASH!
SCHOOL TEAMS, ASSEMBLE! THE RACE IS ABOUT TO BEGIN!
CHILDREN, PLEASE! SAVE YOUR EXPLOSIVES FOR THE RACE!

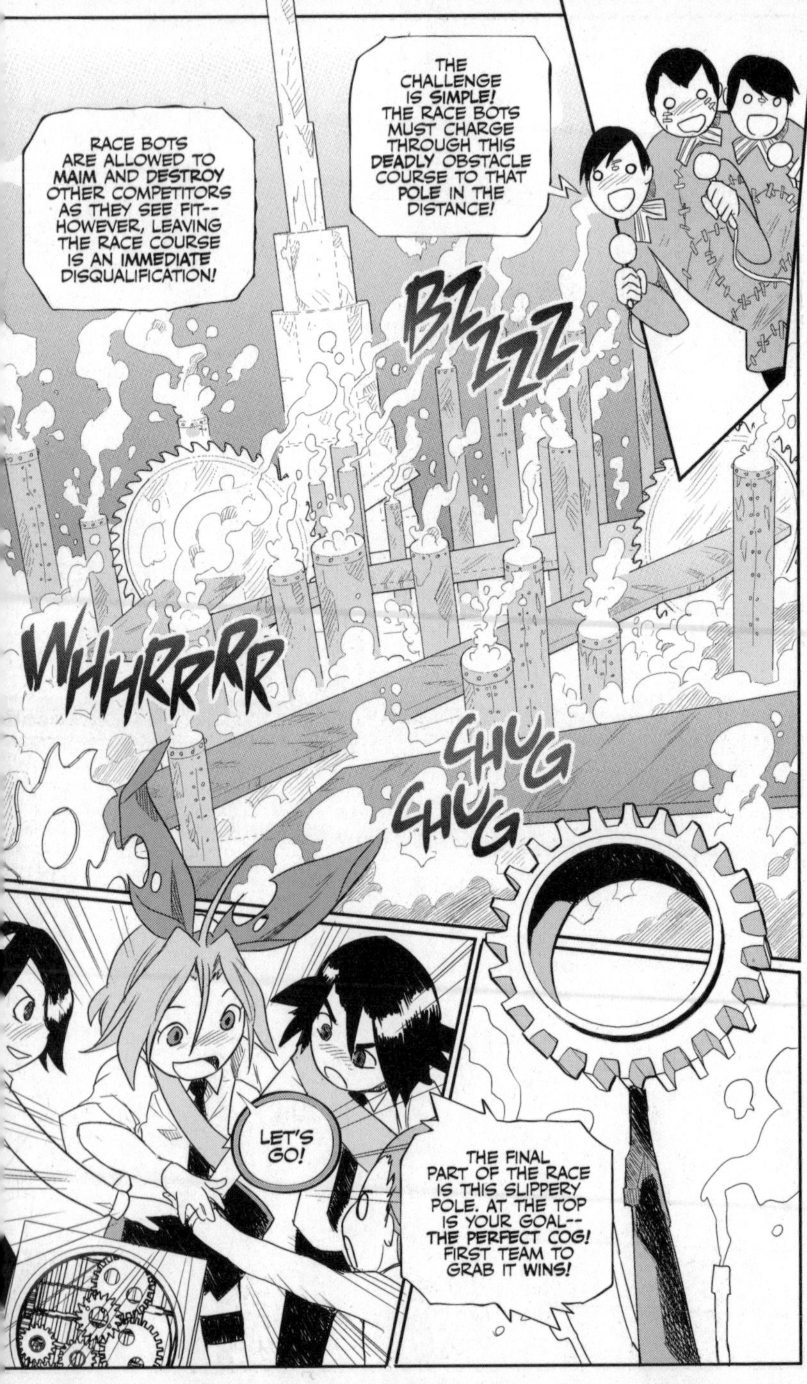
THE CHALLENGE IS SIMPLE! THE RACE BOTS MUST CHARGE THROUGH THIS DEADLY OBSTACLE COURSE TO THAT POLE IN THE DISTANCE!
RACE BOTS ARE ALLOWED TO MAIM AND DESTROY OTHER COMPETITORS AS THEY SEE FIT-- HOWEVER, LEAVING THE RACE COURSE IS AN IMMEDIATE DISQUALIFICATION!
BZZZZ
WHHRRRR
CHUG CHUG
THE FINAL PART OF THE RACE IS THIS SLIPPERY POLE. AT THE TOP IS YOUR GOAL-- THE PERFECT COG! FIRST TEAM TO GRAB IT WINS!
LET'S GO!

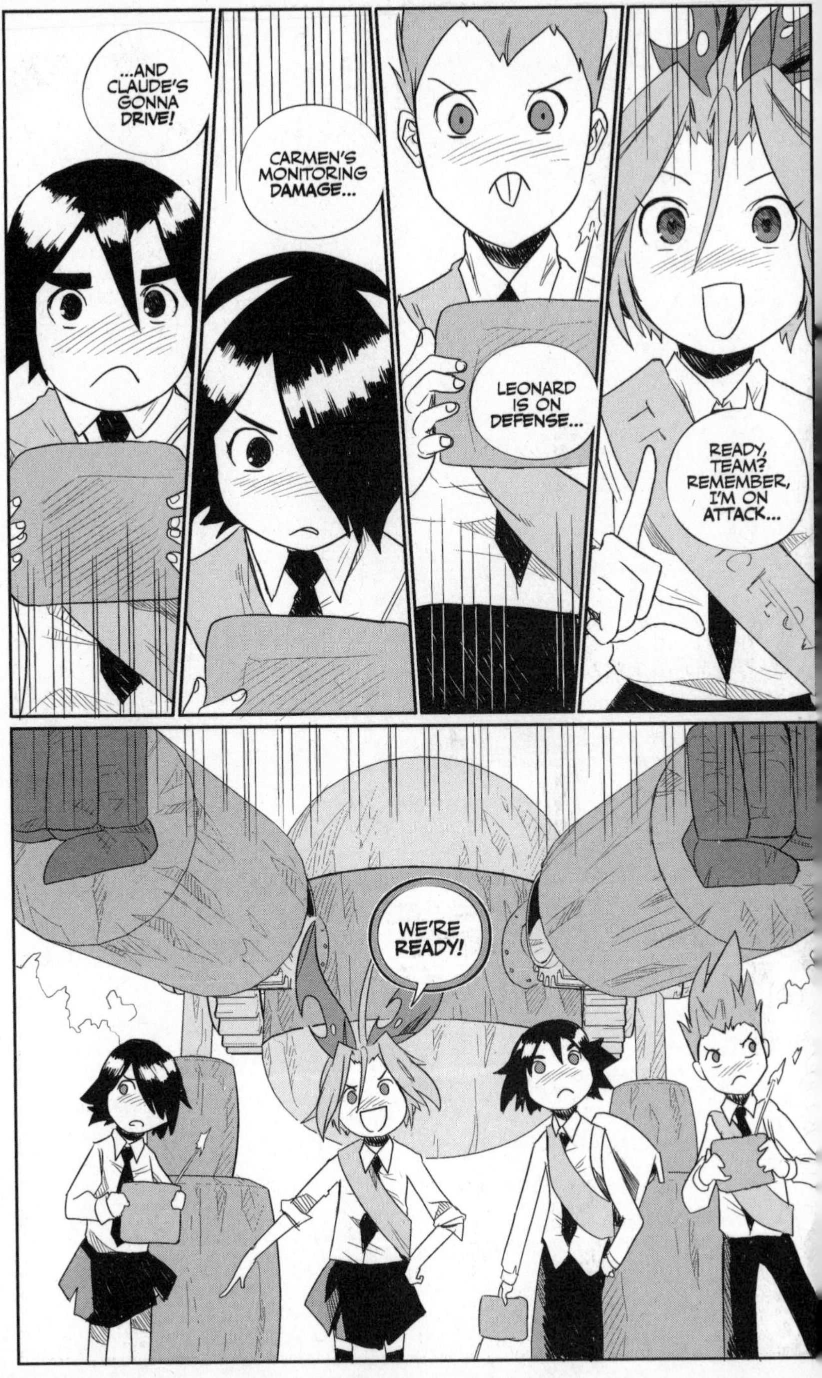
READY, TEAM? REMEMBER, I'M ON ATTACK...
LEONARD IS ON DEFENSE...
CARMEN'S MONITORING DAMAGE...
...AND CLAUDE'S GONNA DRIVE!
WE'RE READY!

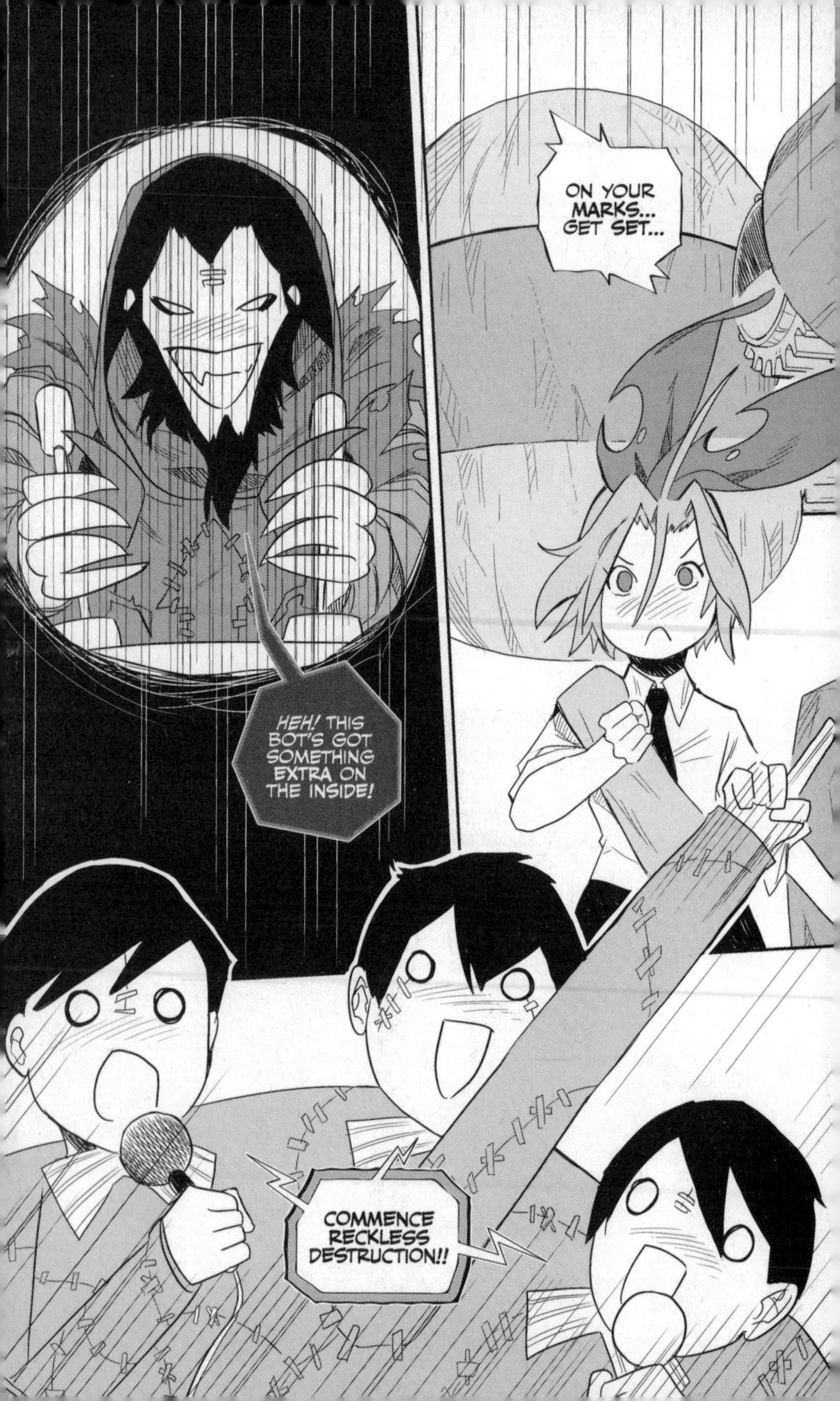
ON YOUR MARKS... GET SET...
HEH! THIS BOT'S GOT SOMETHING EXTRA ON THE INSIDE!
COMMENCE RECKLESS DESTRUCTION!!

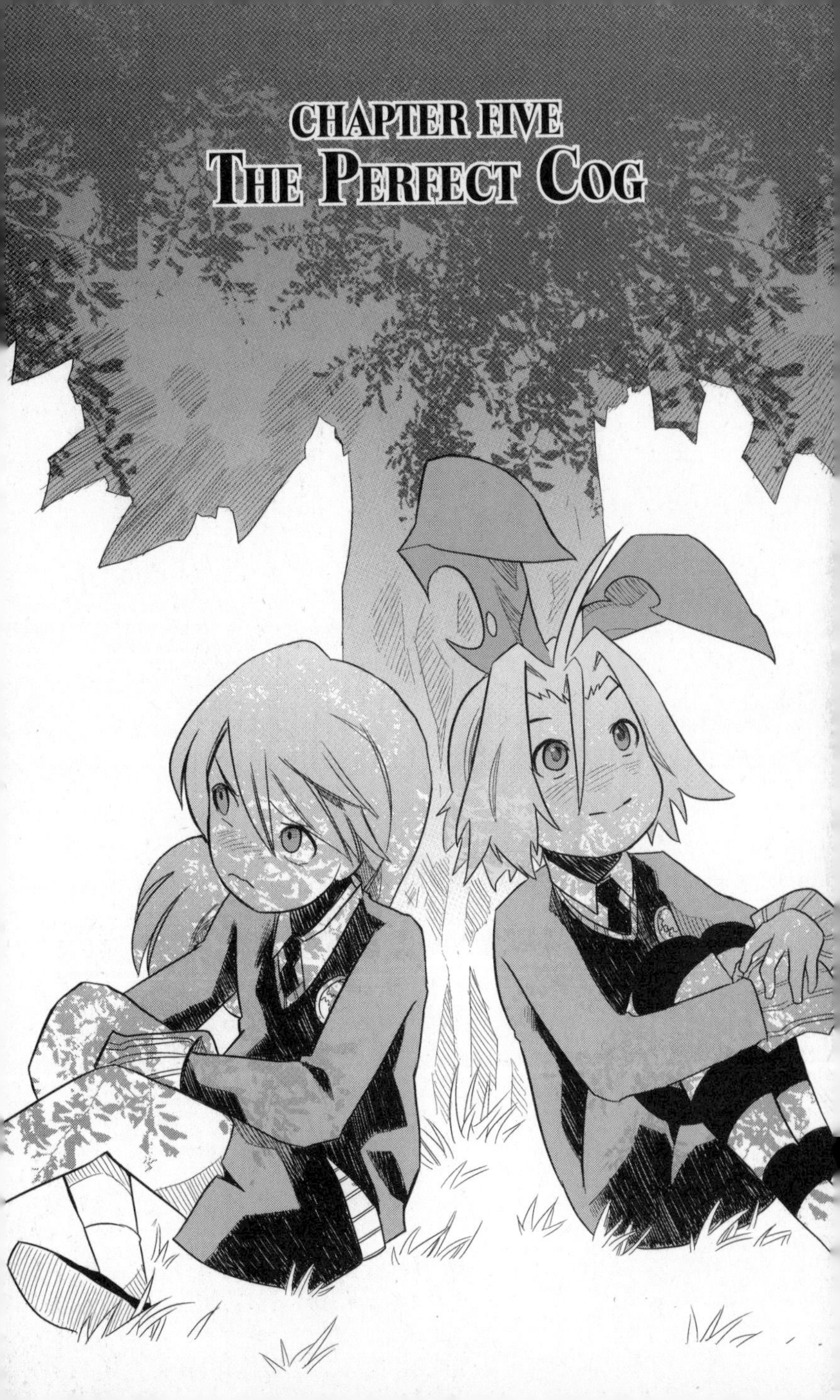
CHAPTER FIVE
THE PERFECT COG

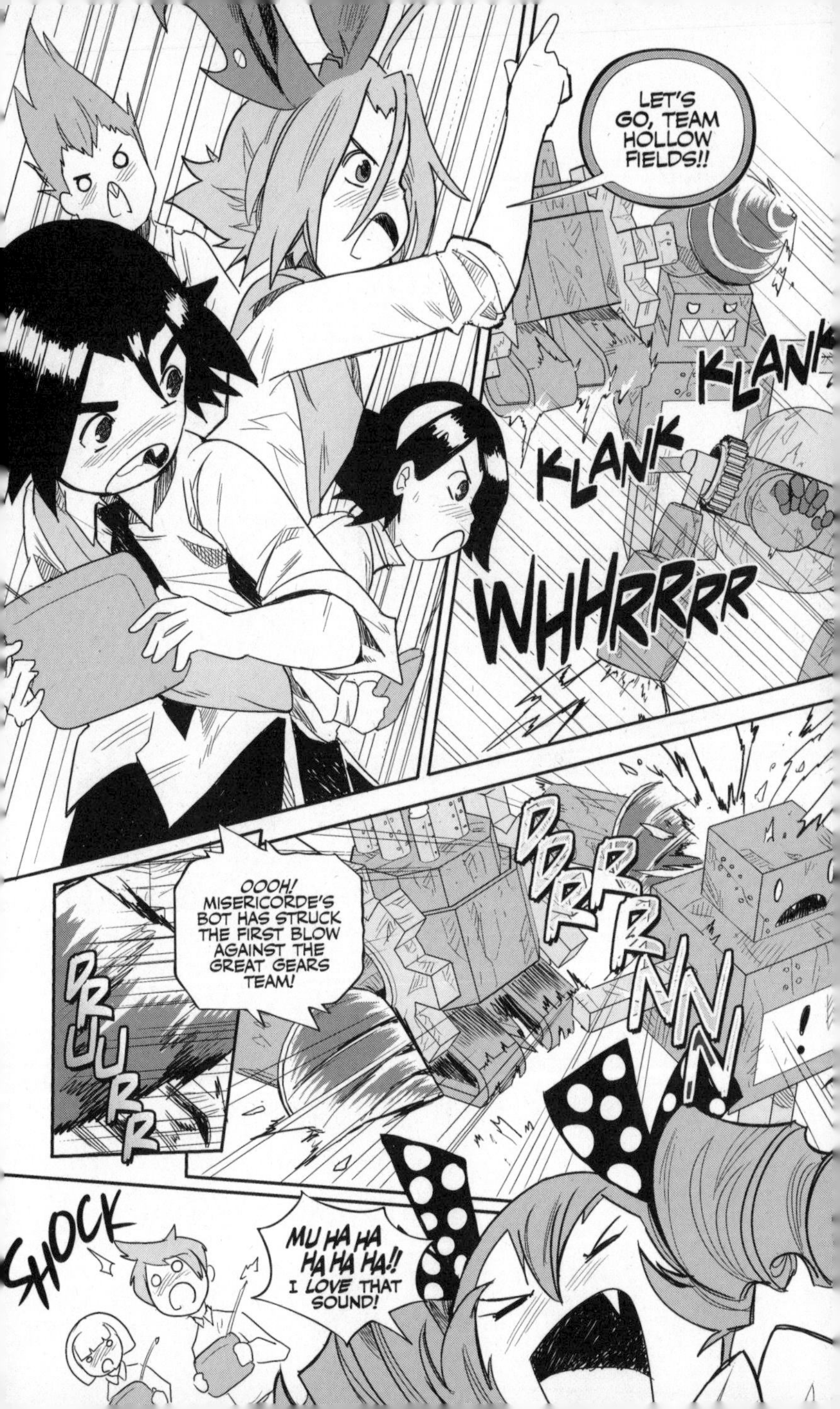
LET'S GO, TEAM HOLLOW FIELDS!!
KLANK
KLANK
WHHRRRR
DDRRRRNNN
OOOH! MISERICORDE'S BOT HAS STRUCK THE FIRST BLOW AGAINST THE GREAT GEARS TEAM!
DRUURRR
MU HA HA HA HA HA!! I LOVE THAT SOUND!
SHOCK

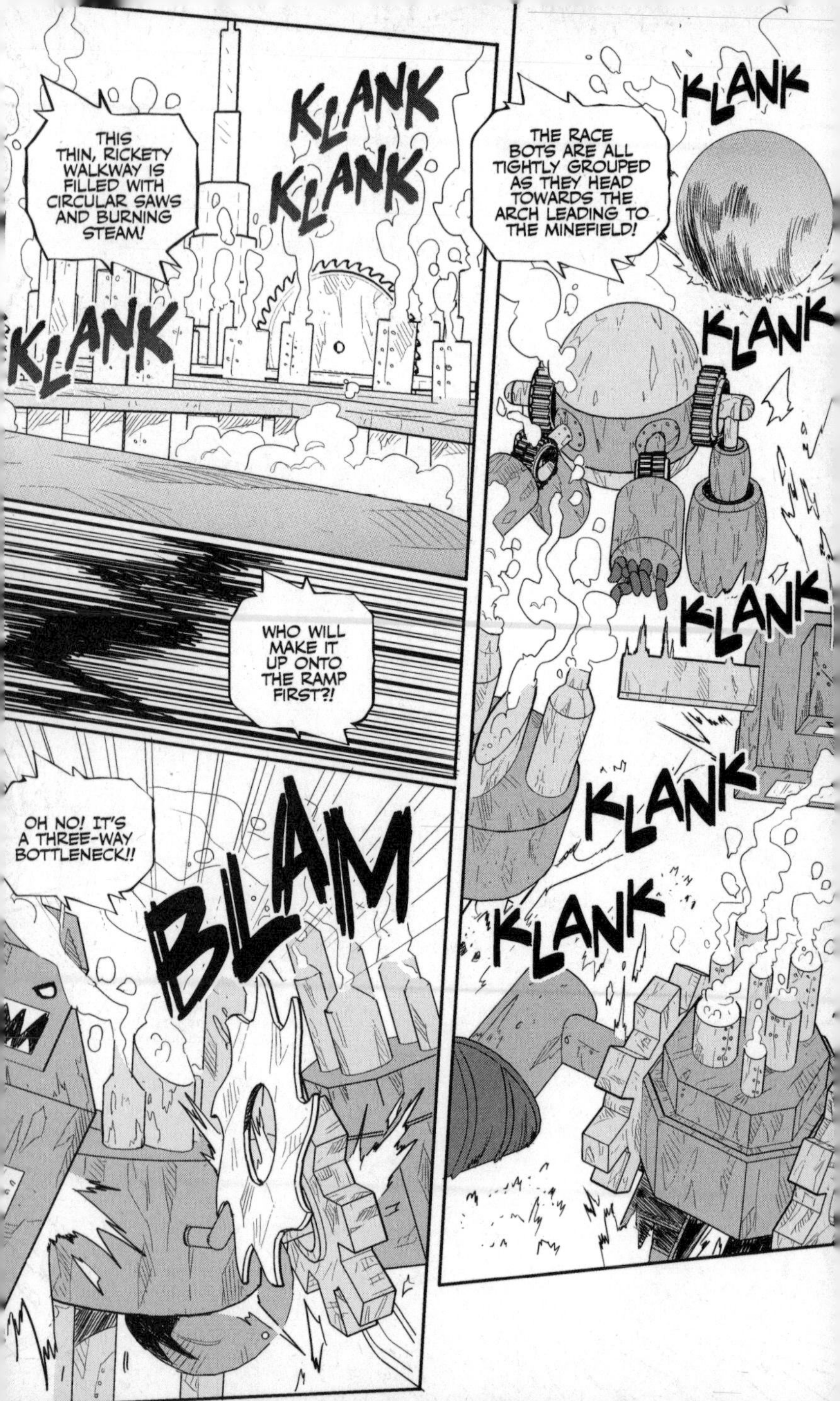
THE RACE BOTS ARE ALL TIGHTLY GROUPED AS THEY HEAD TOWARDS THE ARCH LEADING TO THE MINEFIELD!
KLANK
KLANK
KLANK
KLANK
KLANK
THIS THIN, RICKETY WALKWAY IS FILLED WITH CIRCULAR SAWS AND BURNING STEAM!
KLANK
KLANK
KLANK
WHO WILL MAKE IT UP ONTO THE RAMP FIRST?!
OH NO! IT'S A THREE-WAY BOTTLENECK!!
BLAM

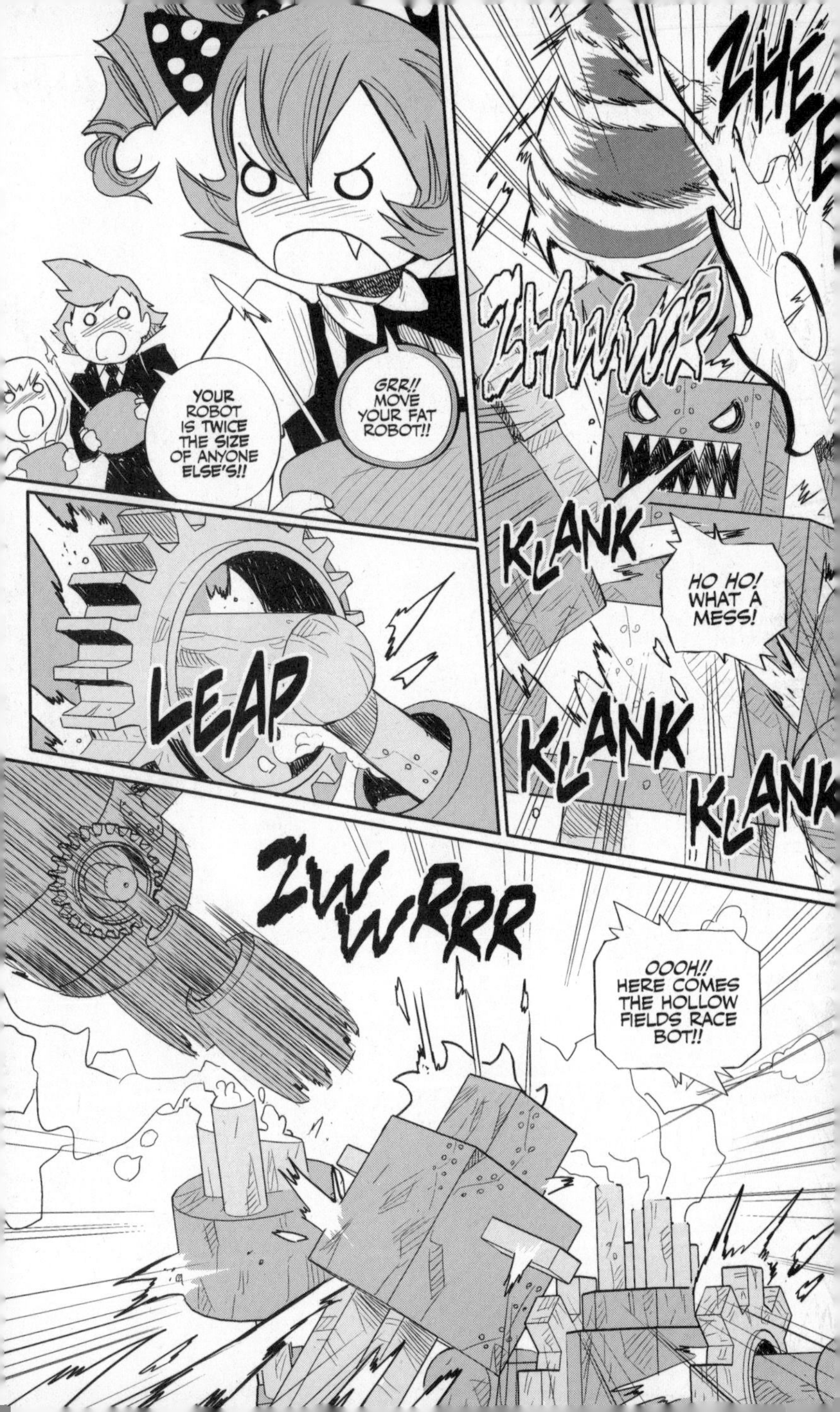
ZHEE
ZHWWP
KLANK
HO HO! WHAT A MESS!
KLANK
KLANK
GRR!! MOVE YOUR FAT ROBOT!!
YOUR ROBOT IS TWICE THE SIZE OF ANYONE ELSE'S!!
LEAP
ZW WRRR
OOOH!! HERE COMES THE HOLLOW FIELDS RACE BOT!!

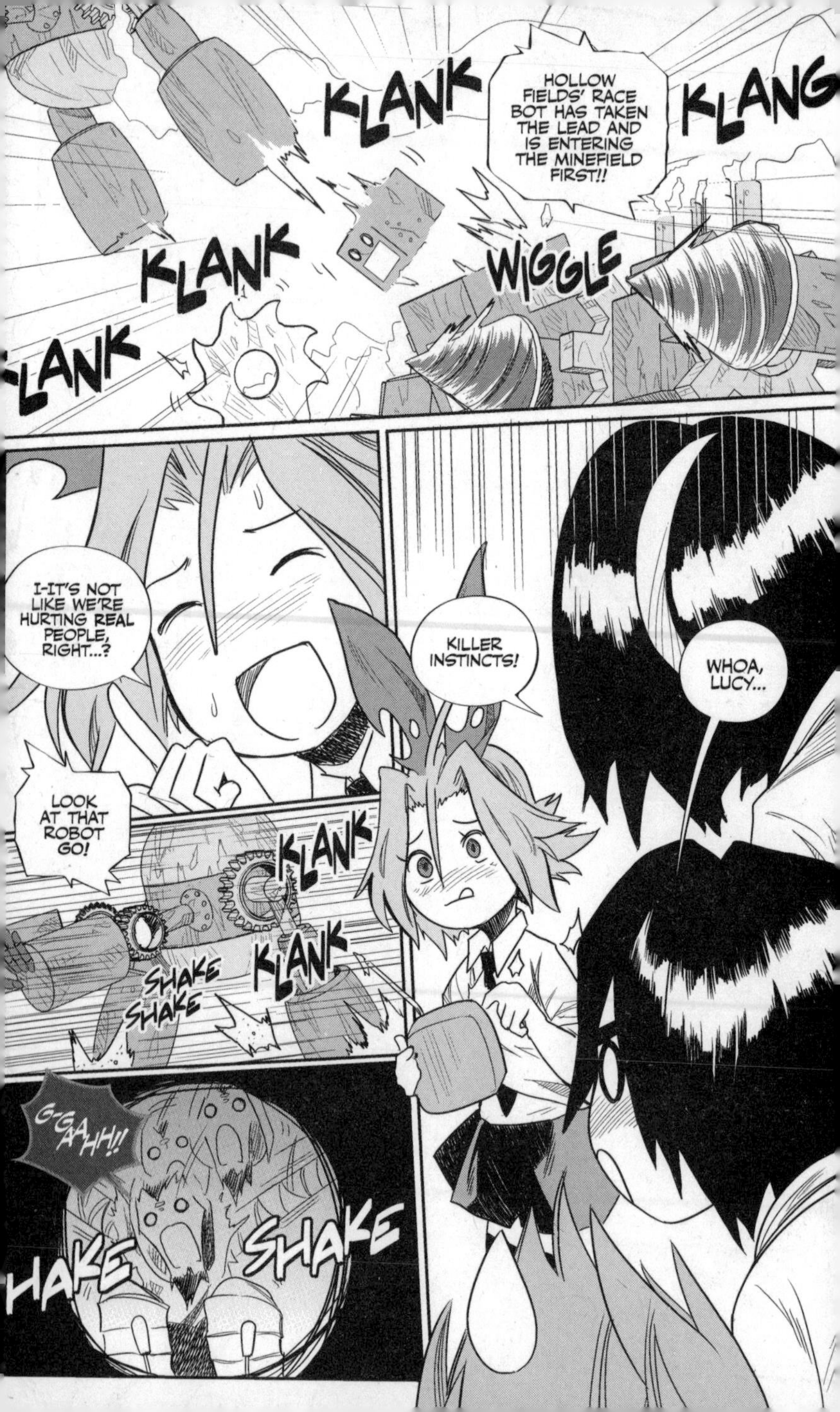
KLANG
HOLLOW FIELDS' RACE BOT HAS TAKEN THE LEAD AND IS ENTERING THE MINEFIELD FIRST!!
KLANK
WIGGLE
KLANK
LANK
KILLER INSTINCTS!
WHOA, LUCY...
I-IT'S NOT LIKE WE'RE HURTING REAL PEOPLE, RIGHT...?
LOOK AT THAT ROBOT GO!
KLANK
KLANK
SHAKE SHAKE
G-GAAHH!!
SHAKE
HAKE

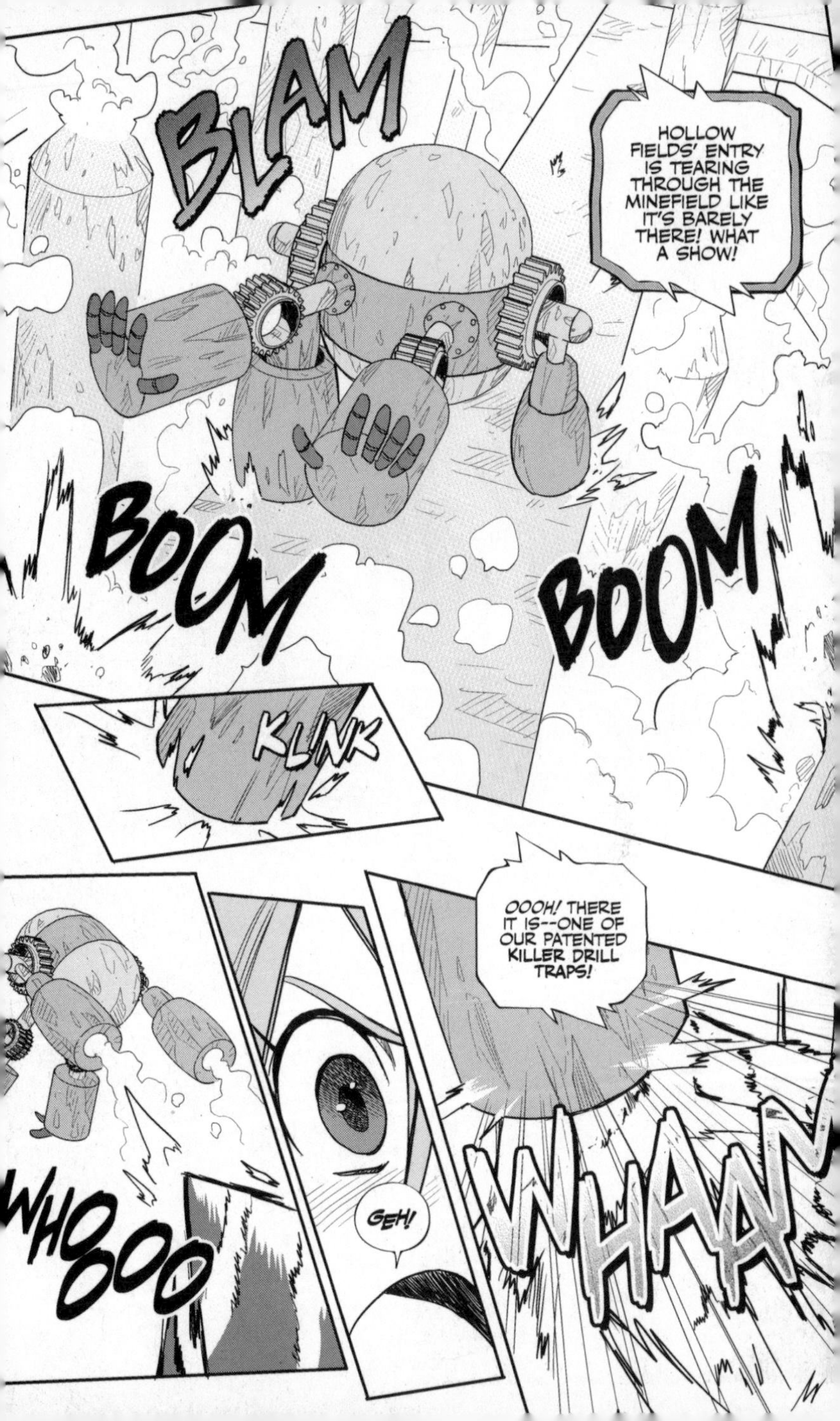
HOLLOW FIELDS' ENTRY IS TEARING THROUGH THE MINEFIELD LIKE IT'S BARELY THERE! WHAT A SHOW!
BLAM
BOOM
BOOM
KLINK
OOOH! THERE IT IS--ONE OF OUR PATENTED KILLER DRILL TRAPS!
WHAA
GEH!
WHOOOO

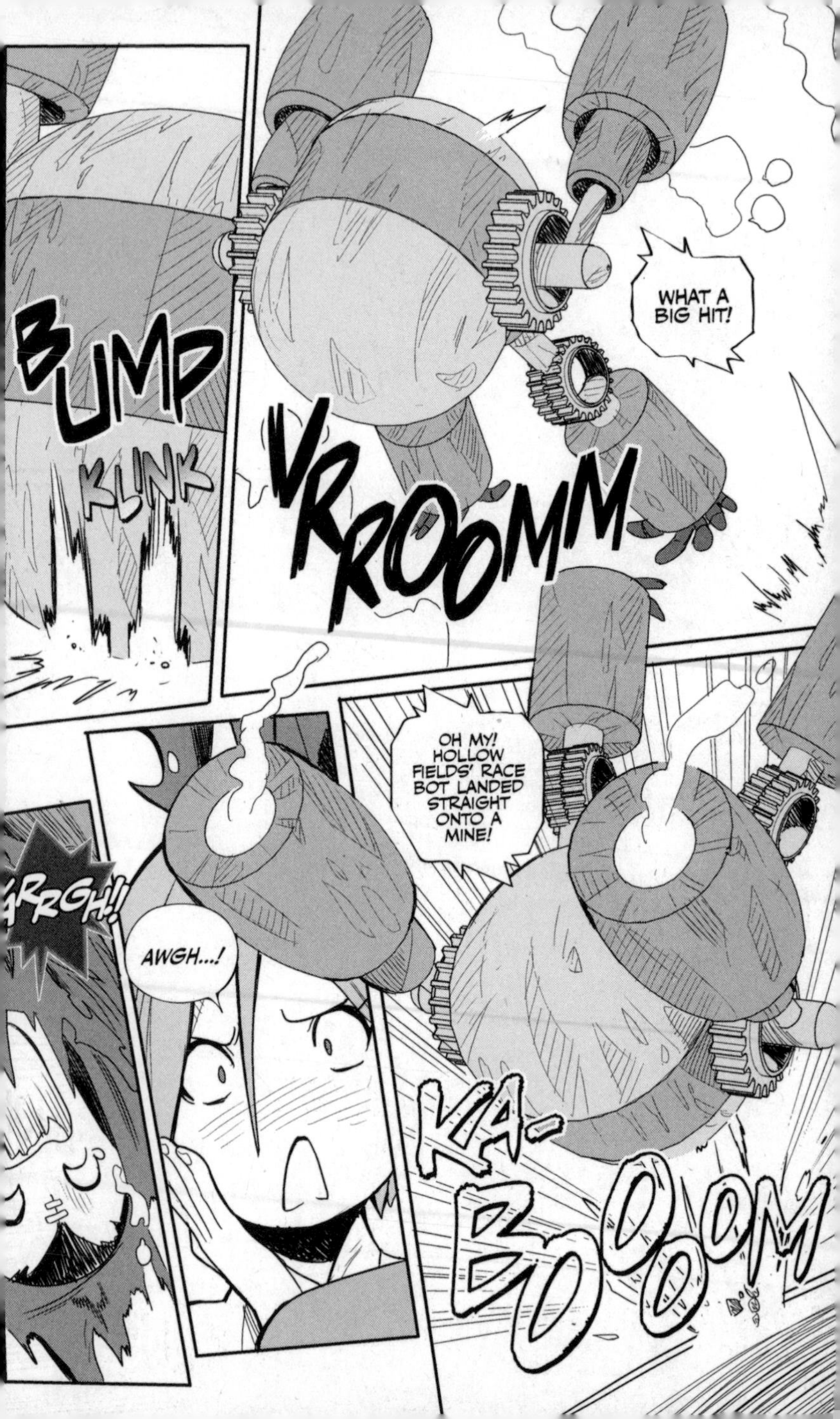
WHAT A BIG HIT!
VROOMM
BUMP
KLINK
OH MY! HOLLOW FIELDS' RACE BOT LANDED STRAIGHT ONTO A MINE!
KA-BOOOOM
RRGH!!
AWGH...!

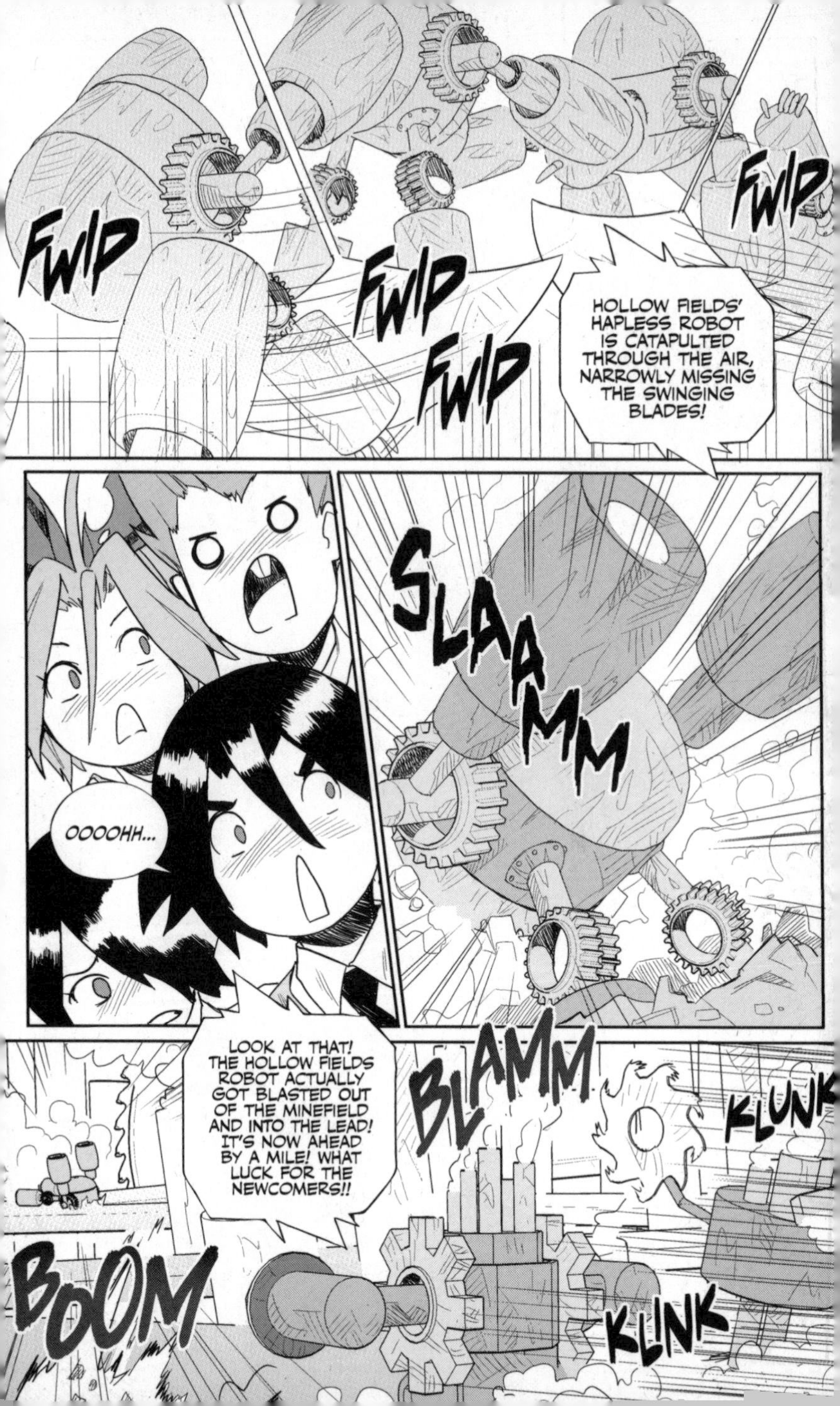
FWIP
HOLLOW FIELDS' HAPLESS ROBOT IS CATAPULTED THROUGH THE AIR, NARROWLY MISSING THE SWINGING BLADES!
FWIP
FWIP
FWIP
SLAAMM
OOOOHH...
KLUNK
BLAMM
LOOK AT THAT! THE HOLLOW FIELDS ROBOT ACTUALLY GOT BLASTED OUT OF THE MINEFIELD AND INTO THE LEAD! IT'S NOW AHEAD BY A MILE! WHAT LUCK FOR THE NEWCOMERS!!
KLINK
BOOM

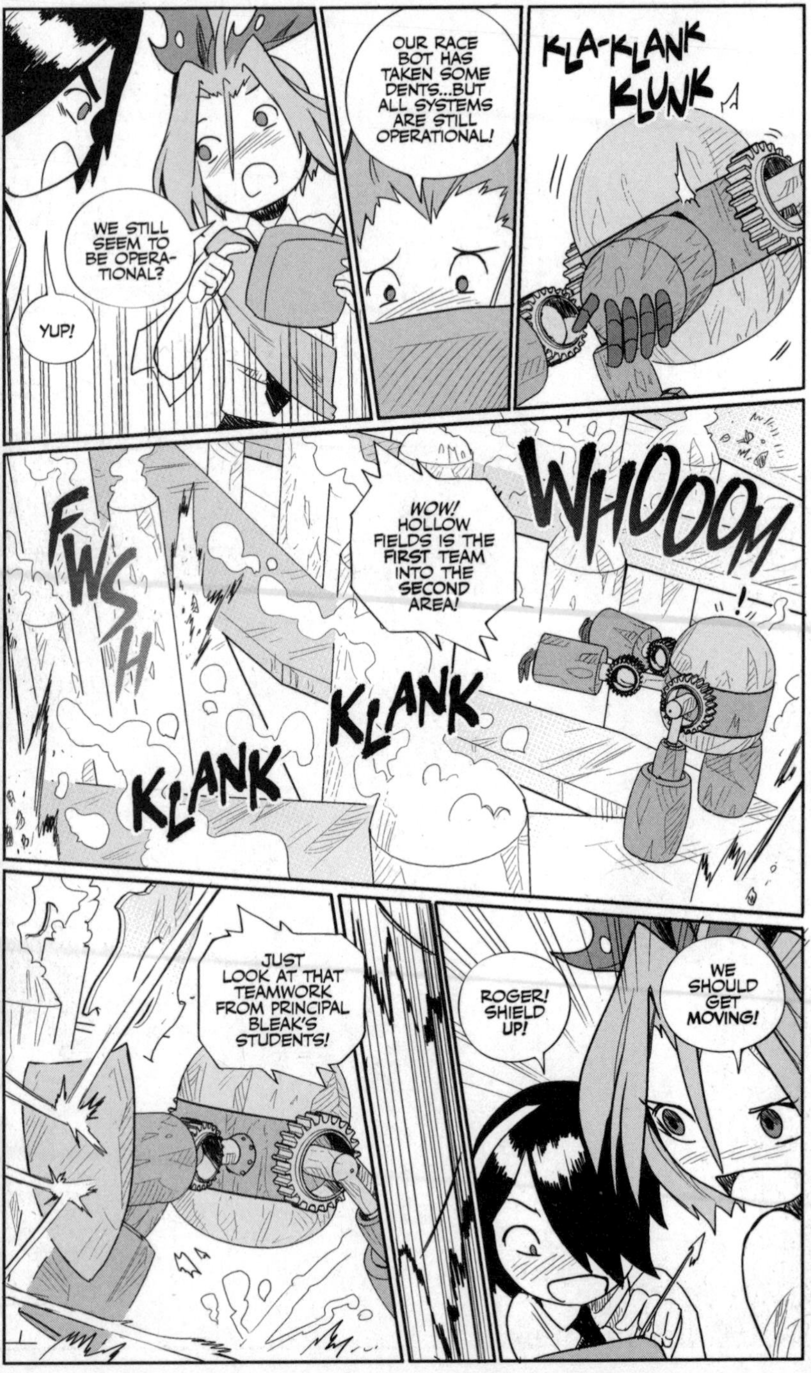
KLA-KLANK
KLUNK
OUR RACE BOT HAS TAKEN SOME DENTS...BUT ALL SYSTEMS ARE STILL OPERATIONAL!
WE STILL SEEM TO BE OPERA-TIONAL?
YUP!
WHOOOM
WOW! HOLLOW FIELDS IS THE FIRST TEAM INTO THE SECOND AREA!
FWSH
KLANK
KLANK
WE SHOULD GET MOVING!
ROGER! SHIELD UP!
JUST LOOK AT THAT TEAMWORK FROM PRINCIPAL BLEAK'S STUDENTS!

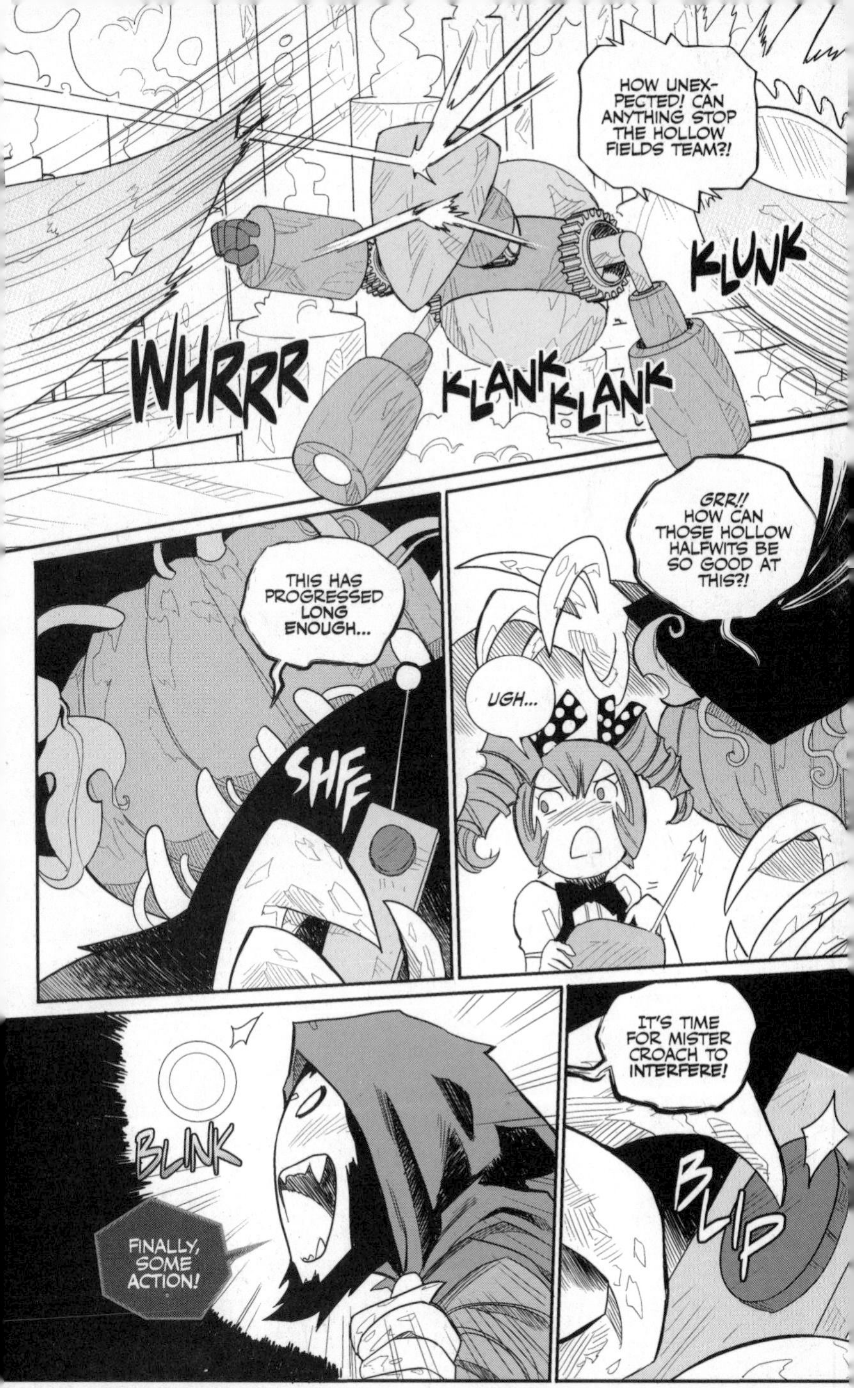
HOW UNEX-PECTED! CAN ANYTHING STOP THE HOLLOW FIELDS TEAM?!
KLUNK
KLANK KLANK
WHRRR
GRR!! HOW CAN THOSE HOLLOW HALFWITS BE SO GOOD AT THIS?!
UGH...
THIS HAS PROGRESSED LONG ENOUGH...
SHFF
IT'S TIME FOR MISTER CROACH TO INTERFERE!
BLIP
BLINK
FINALLY, SOME ACTION!

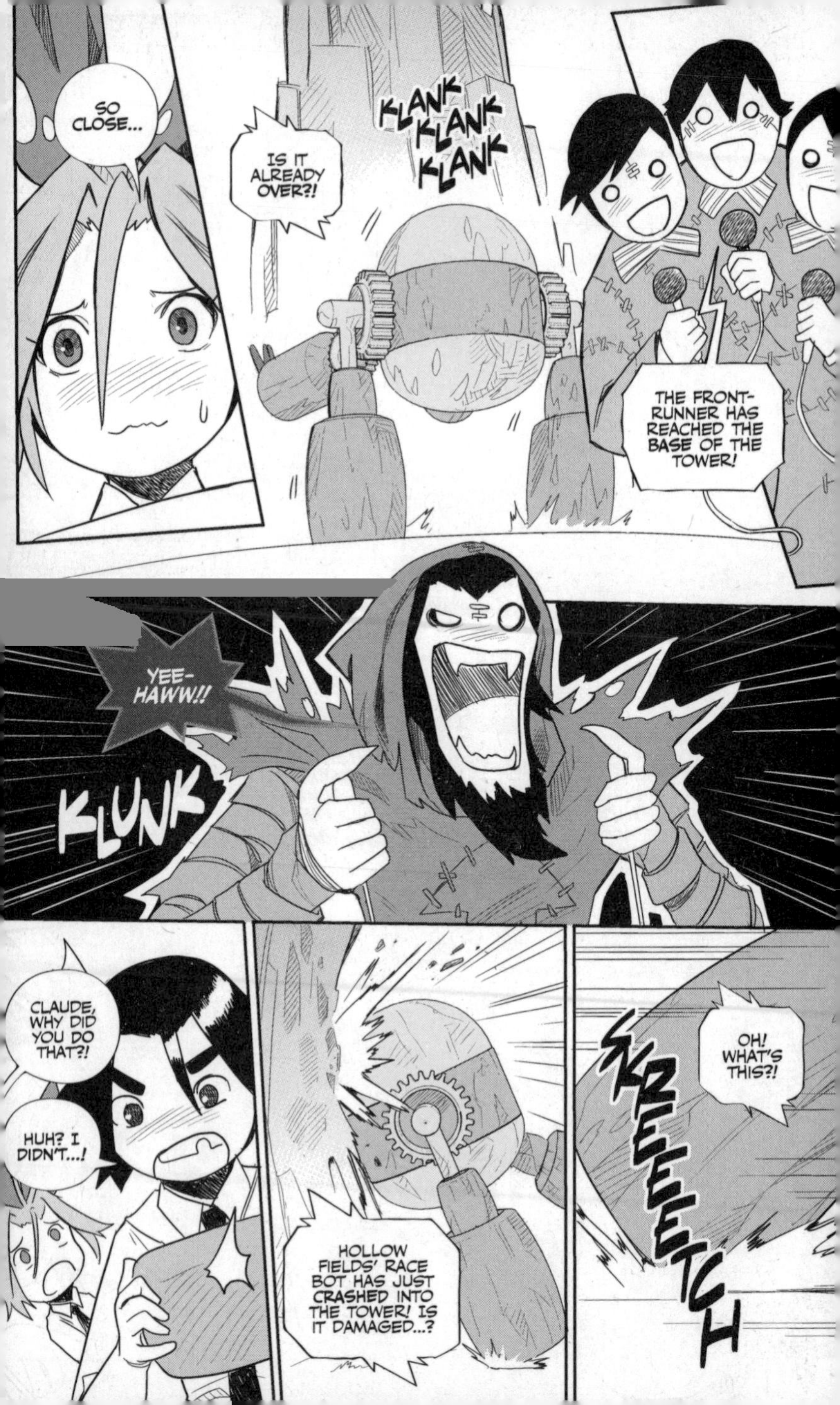
THE FRONT-RUNNER HAS REACHED THE BASE OF THE TOWER!
KLANK KLANK KLANK
IS IT ALREADY OVER?!
SO CLOSE...
YEE-HAWW!!
KLUNK
OH! WHAT'S THIS?!
SKREEETCH
HOLLOW FIELDS' RACE BOT HAS JUST CRASHED INTO THE TOWER! IS IT DAMAGED...?
CLAUDE, WHY DID YOU DO THAT?!
HUH? I DIDN'T...!

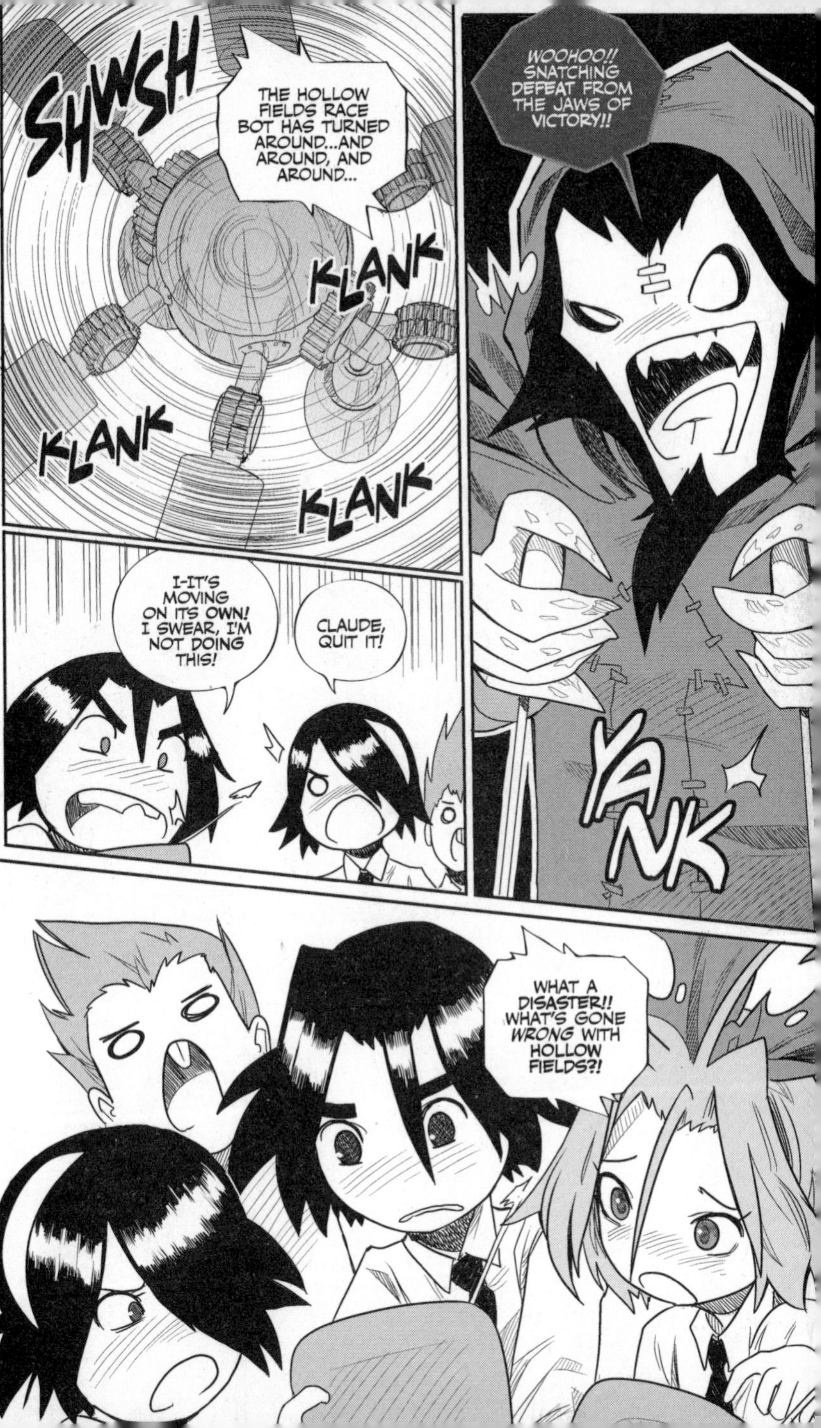
WOOHOO!! SNATCHING DEFEAT FROM THE JAWS OF VICTORY!!
YANK
THE HOLLOW FIELDS RACE BOT HAS TURNED AROUND...AND AROUND, AND AROUND...
SHWSH
KLANK
KLANK
KLANK
CLAUDE, QUIT IT!
I-IT'S MOVING ON ITS OWN! I SWEAR, I'M NOT DOING THIS!
WHAT A DISASTER!! WHAT'S GONE *WRONG* WITH HOLLOW FIELDS?!

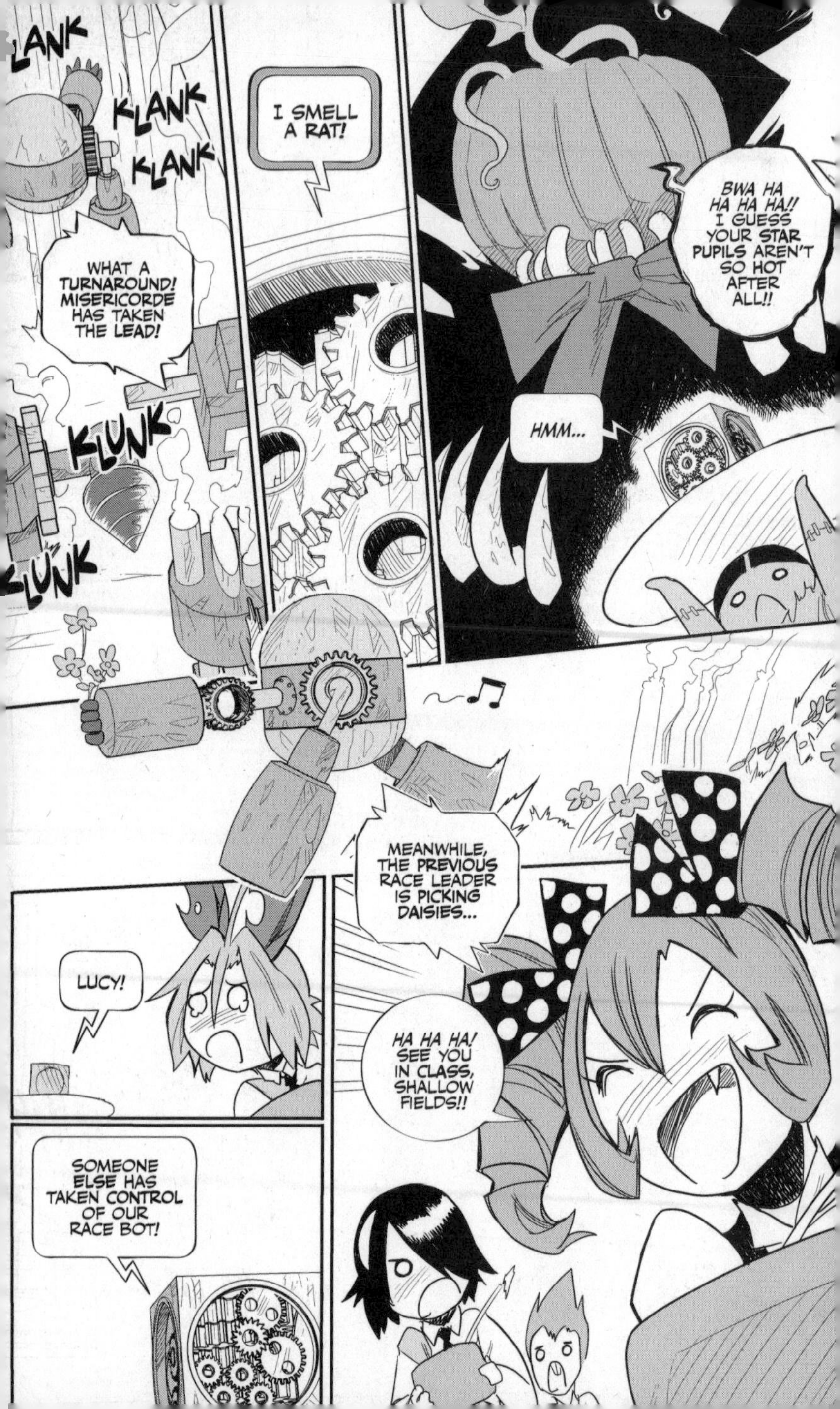
BWA HA HA HA HA!! I GUESS YOUR STAR PUPILS AREN'T SO HOT AFTER ALL!!
HMM...
I SMELL A RAT!
KLANK
KLANK
KLANK
WHAT A TURNAROUND! MISERICORDE HAS TAKEN THE LEAD!
KLUNK
KLUNK
MEANWHILE, THE PREVIOUS RACE LEADER IS PICKING DAISIES...
HA HA HA! SEE YOU IN CLASS, SHALLOW FIELDS!!
LUCY!
SOMEONE ELSE HAS TAKEN CONTROL OF OUR RACE BOT!

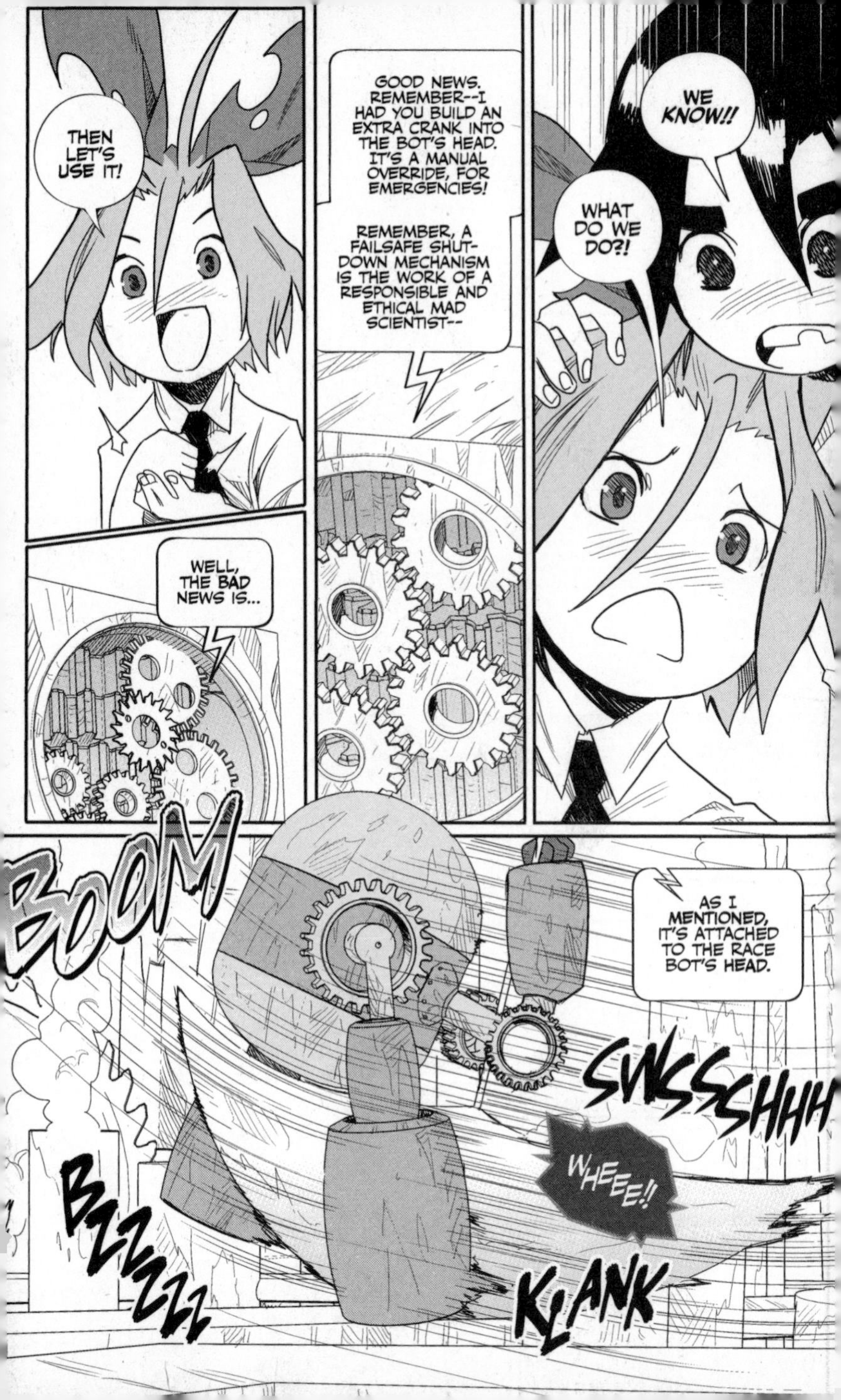

WE KNOW!!
WHAT DO WE DO?!
GOOD NEWS. REMEMBER--I HAD YOU BUILD AN EXTRA CRANK INTO THE BOT'S HEAD. IT'S A MANUAL OVERRIDE, FOR EMERGENCIES!
REMEMBER, A FAILSAFE SHUT-DOWN MECHANISM IS THE WORK OF A RESPONSIBLE AND ETHICAL MAD SCIENTIST--
THEN LET'S USE IT!
WELL, THE BAD NEWS IS...
AS I MENTIONED, IT'S ATTACHED TO THE RACE BOT'S HEAD.
SVISSSHHH
WHEEE!!
BOOM
KLANK
BZZZZZZ

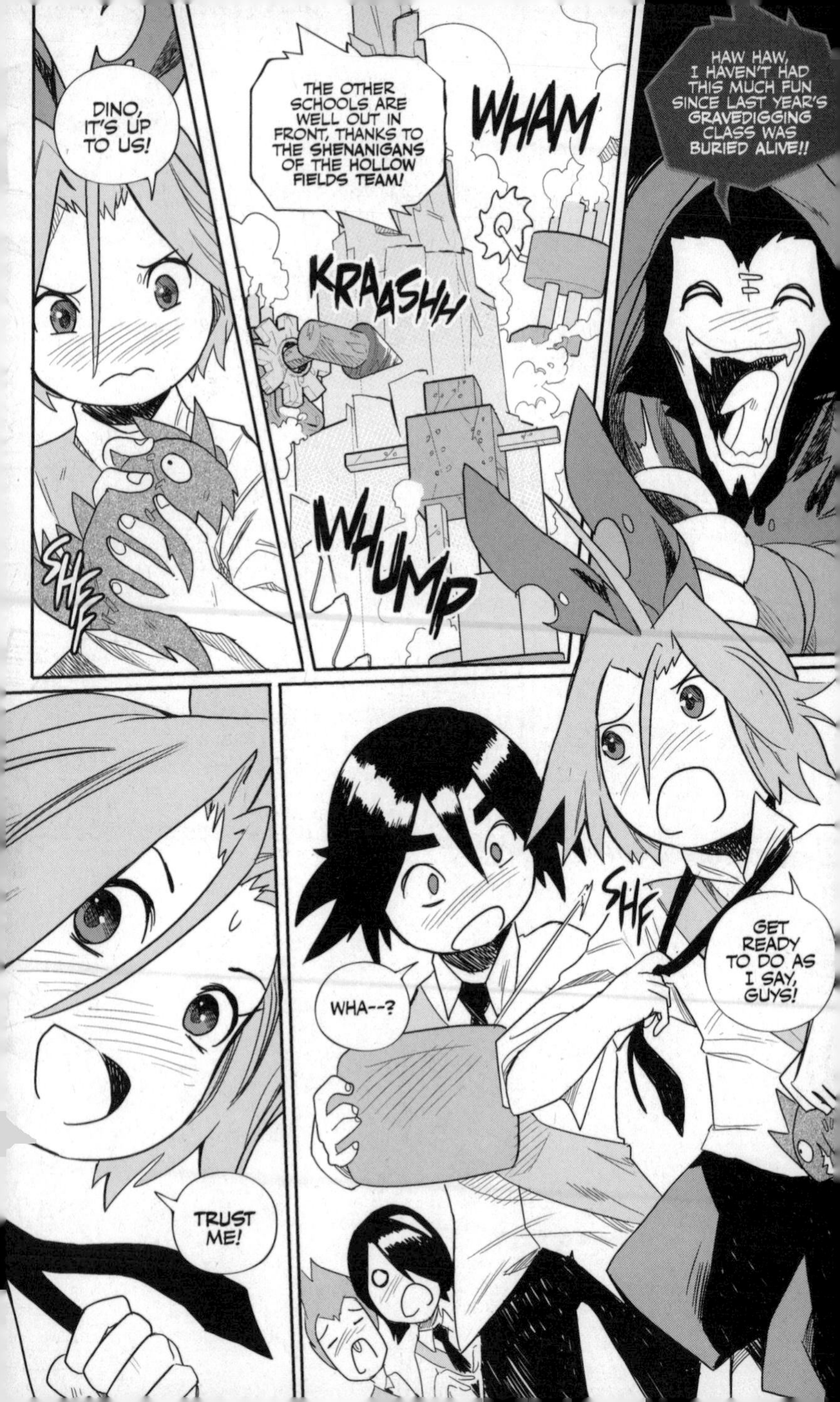
HAW HAW, I HAVEN'T HAD THIS MUCH FUN SINCE LAST YEAR'S GRAVEDIGGING CLASS WAS BURIED ALIVE!!
THE OTHER SCHOOLS ARE WELL OUT IN FRONT, THANKS TO THE SHENANIGANS OF THE HOLLOW FIELDS TEAM!
WHAM
KRAASHH
WHUMP
DINO, IT'S UP TO US!
SHF
SHF
GET READY TO DO AS I SAY, GUYS!
WHA--?
TRUST ME!

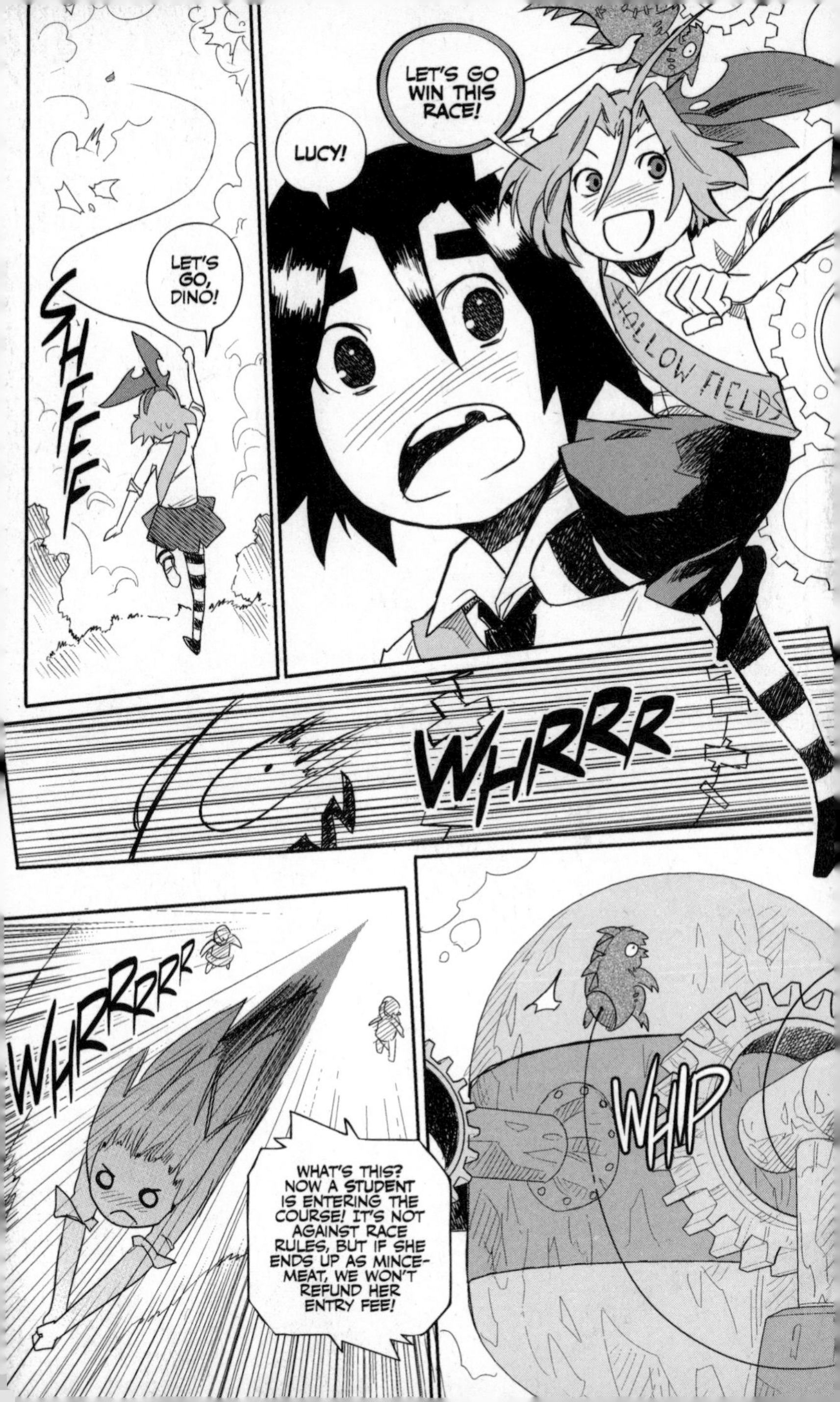
LET'S GO WIN THIS RACE!
LUCY!
HOLLOW FIELDS
LET'S GO, DINO!
SHFFFF
WHRRR
WHIP
WHRRRRR
WHAT'S THIS? NOW A STUDENT IS ENTERING THE COURSE! IT'S NOT AGAINST RACE RULES, BUT IF SHE ENDS UP AS MINCE-MEAT, WE WON'T REFUND HER ENTRY FEE!

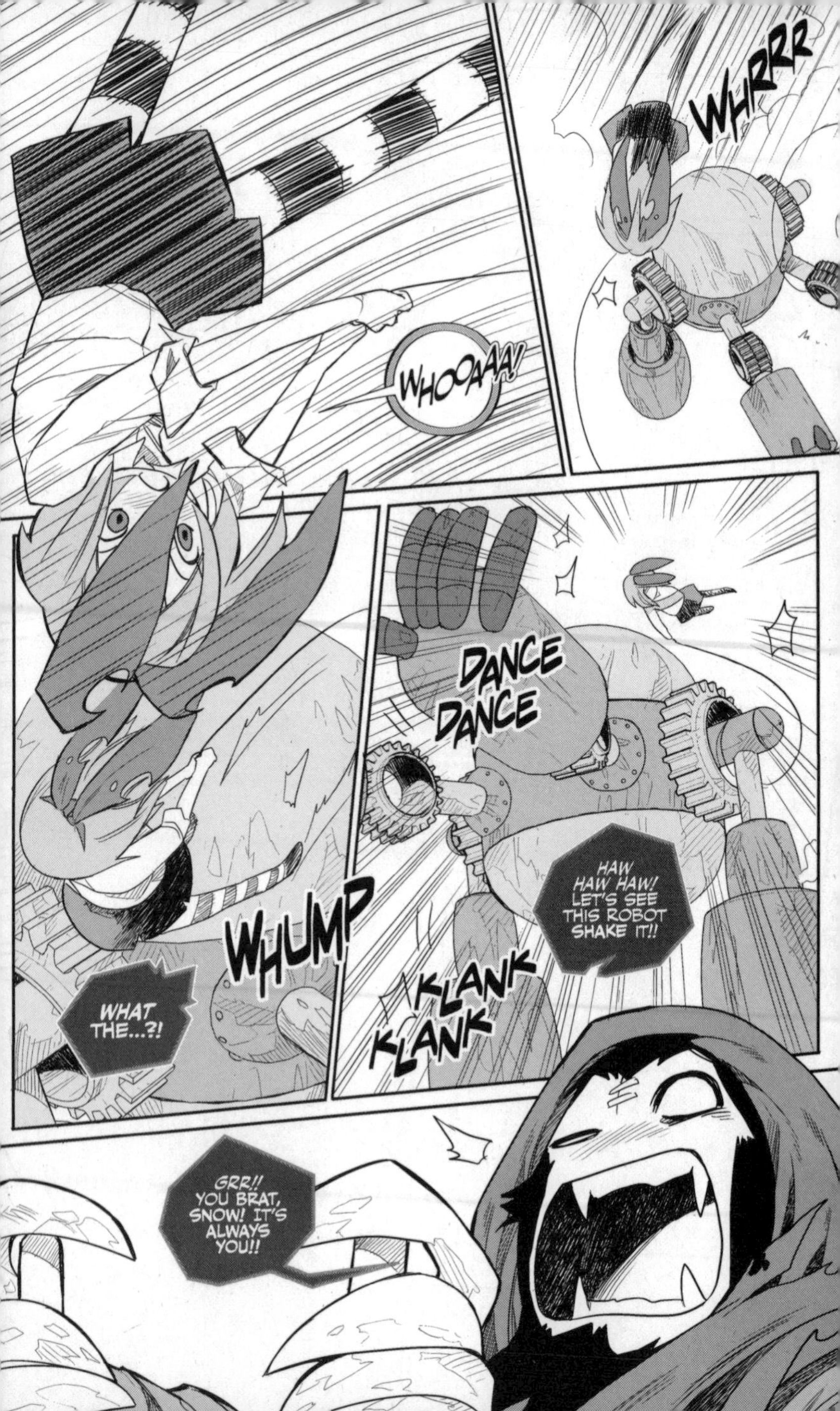
WHRRR
WHOOAAA!
DANCE DANCE
HAW HAW HAW! LET'S SEE THIS ROBOT SHAKE IT!!
KLANK KLANK
WHUMP
WHAT THE...?!
GRR!! YOU BRAT, SNOW! IT'S ALWAYS YOU!!

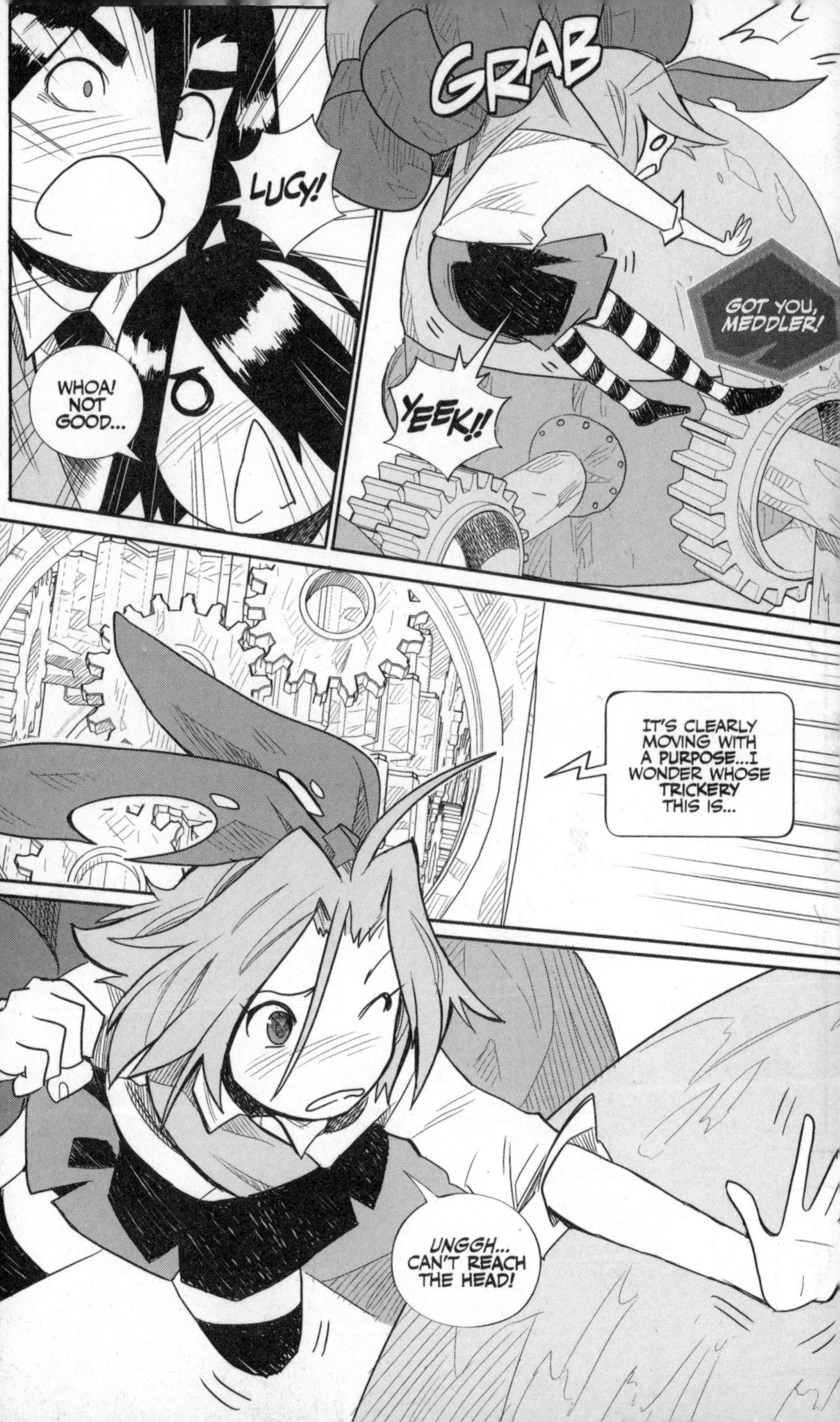
GRAB
GOT YOU, MEDDLER!
YEEK!!
LUCY!
WHOA! NOT GOOD...
IT'S CLEARLY MOVING WITH A PURPOSE...I WONDER WHOSE TRICKERY THIS IS...
UNGGH... CAN'T REACH THE HEAD!

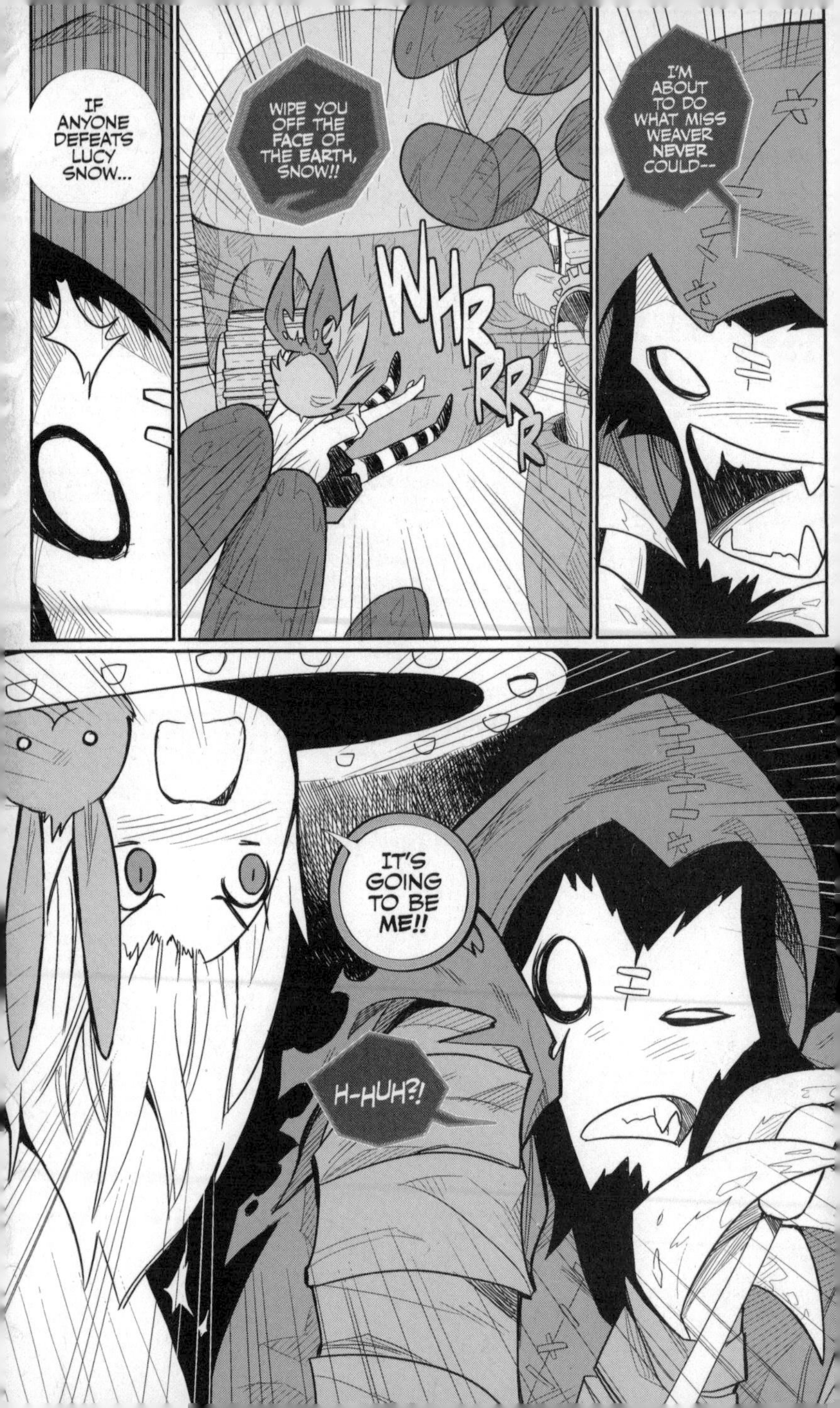
I'M ABOUT TO DO WHAT MISS WEAVER NEVER COULD--
WIPE YOU OFF THE FACE OF THE EARTH, SNOW!!
WHRRRR
IF ANYONE DEFEATS LUCY SNOW...
IT'S GOING TO BE ME!!
H-HUH?!

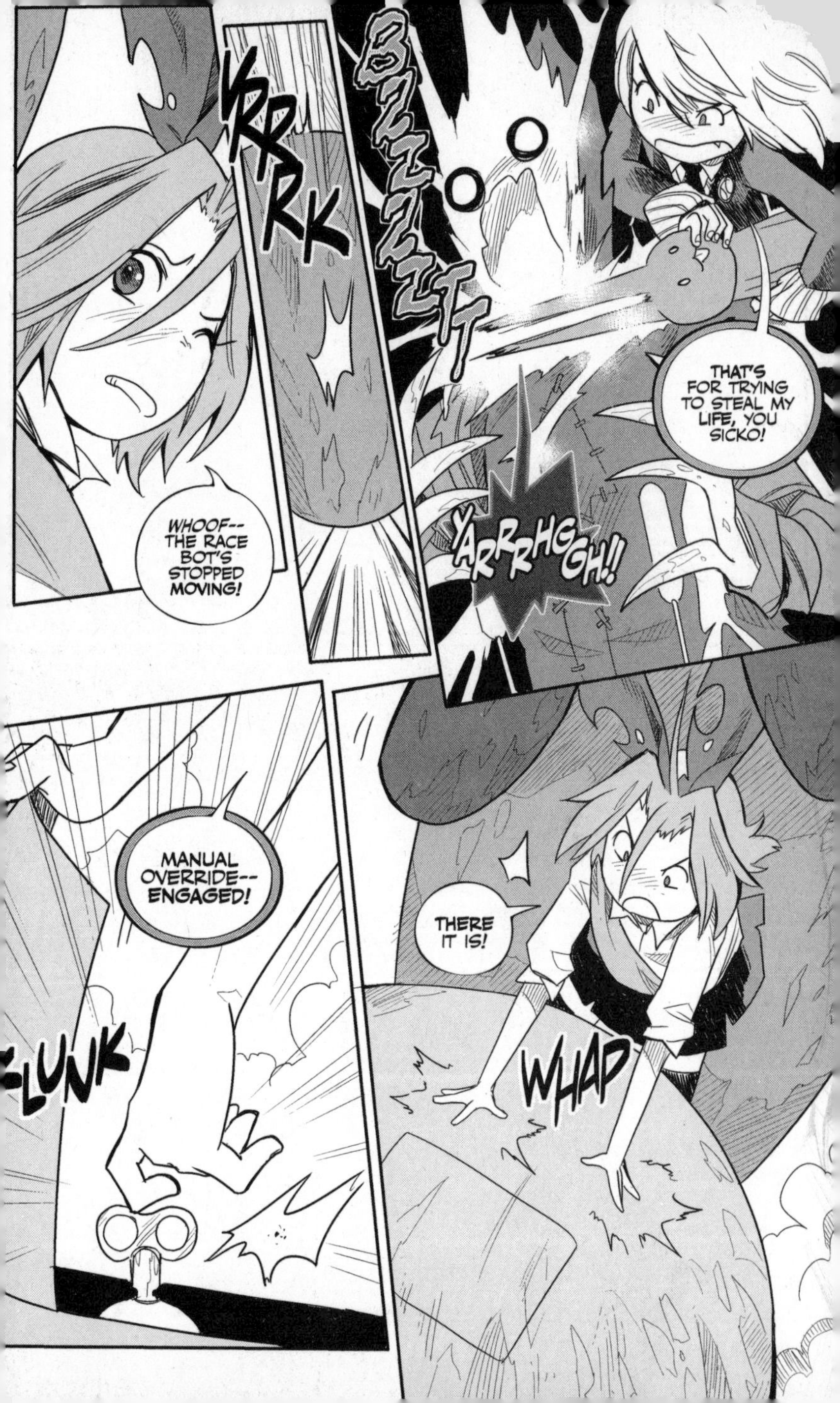
BZZZZZTTT
THAT'S FOR TRYING TO STEAL MY LIFE, YOU SICKO!
YARRRHGGH!!
VRRK
WHOOF-- THE RACE BOT'S STOPPED MOVING!
THERE IT IS!
WHAP
MANUAL OVERRIDE-- ENGAGED!
LUNK

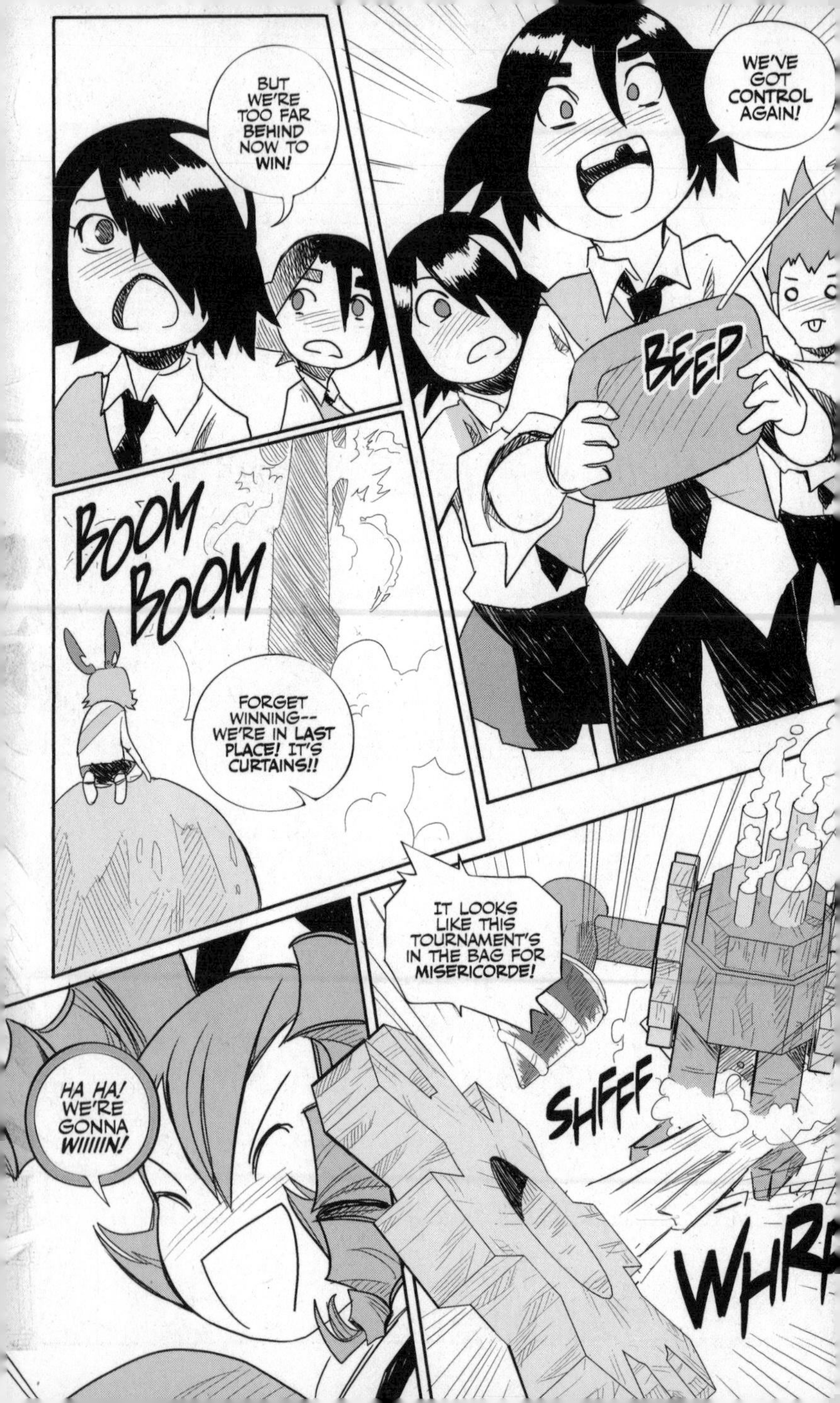
WE'VE GOT CONTROL AGAIN!
BEEP
BUT WE'RE TOO FAR BEHIND NOW TO WIN!
BOOM BOOM
FORGET WINNING-- WE'RE IN LAST PLACE! IT'S CURTAINS!!
IT LOOKS LIKE THIS TOURNAMENT'S IN THE BAG FOR MISERICORDE!
SHFFF
HA HA! WE'RE GONNA WIIIIIN!
WHR

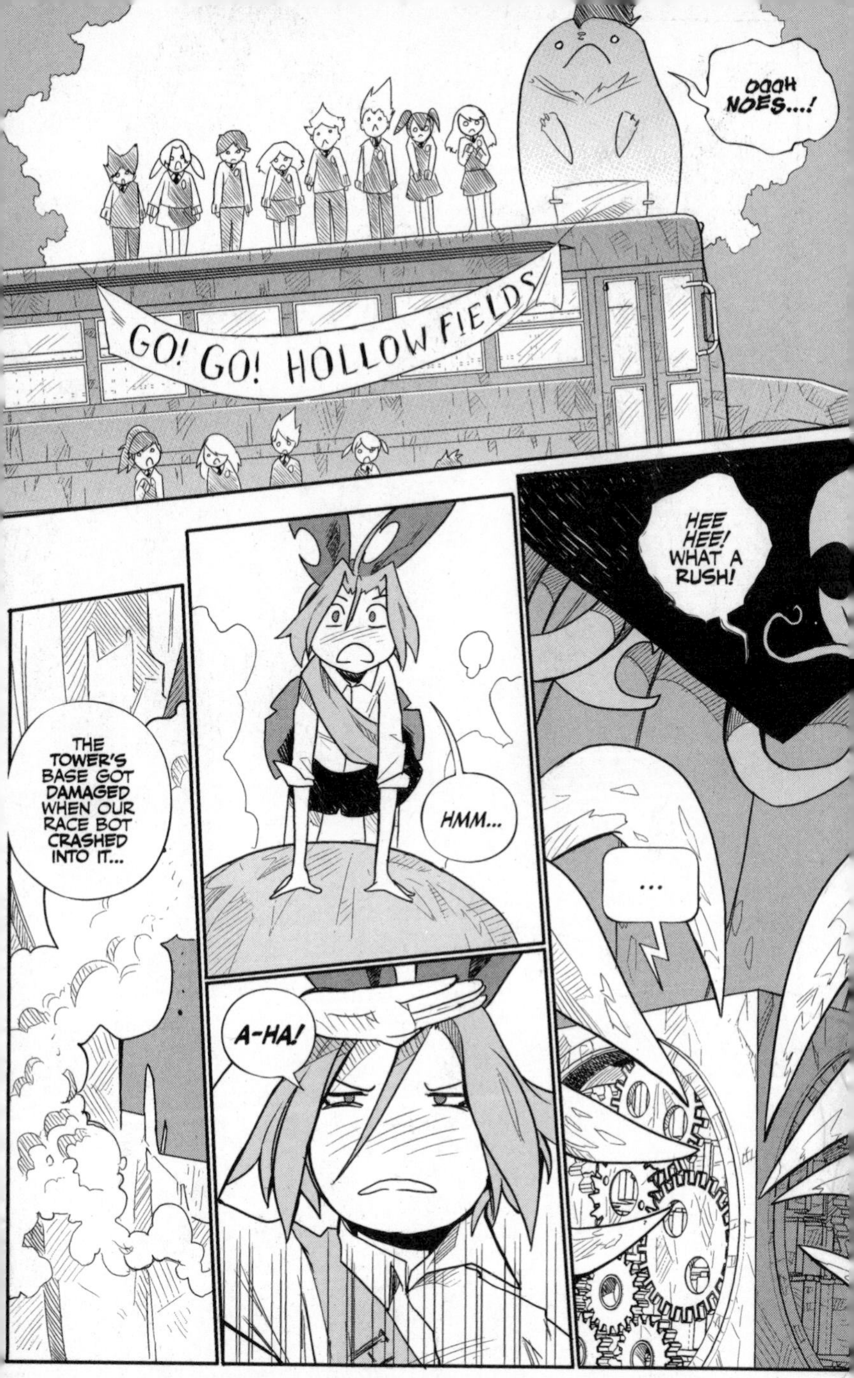
OOOH NOES...!
GO! GO! HOLLOW FIELDS
HEE HEE! WHAT A RUSH!
...
HMM...
A-HA!
THE TOWER'S BASE GOT DAMAGED WHEN OUR RACE BOT CRASHED INTO IT...

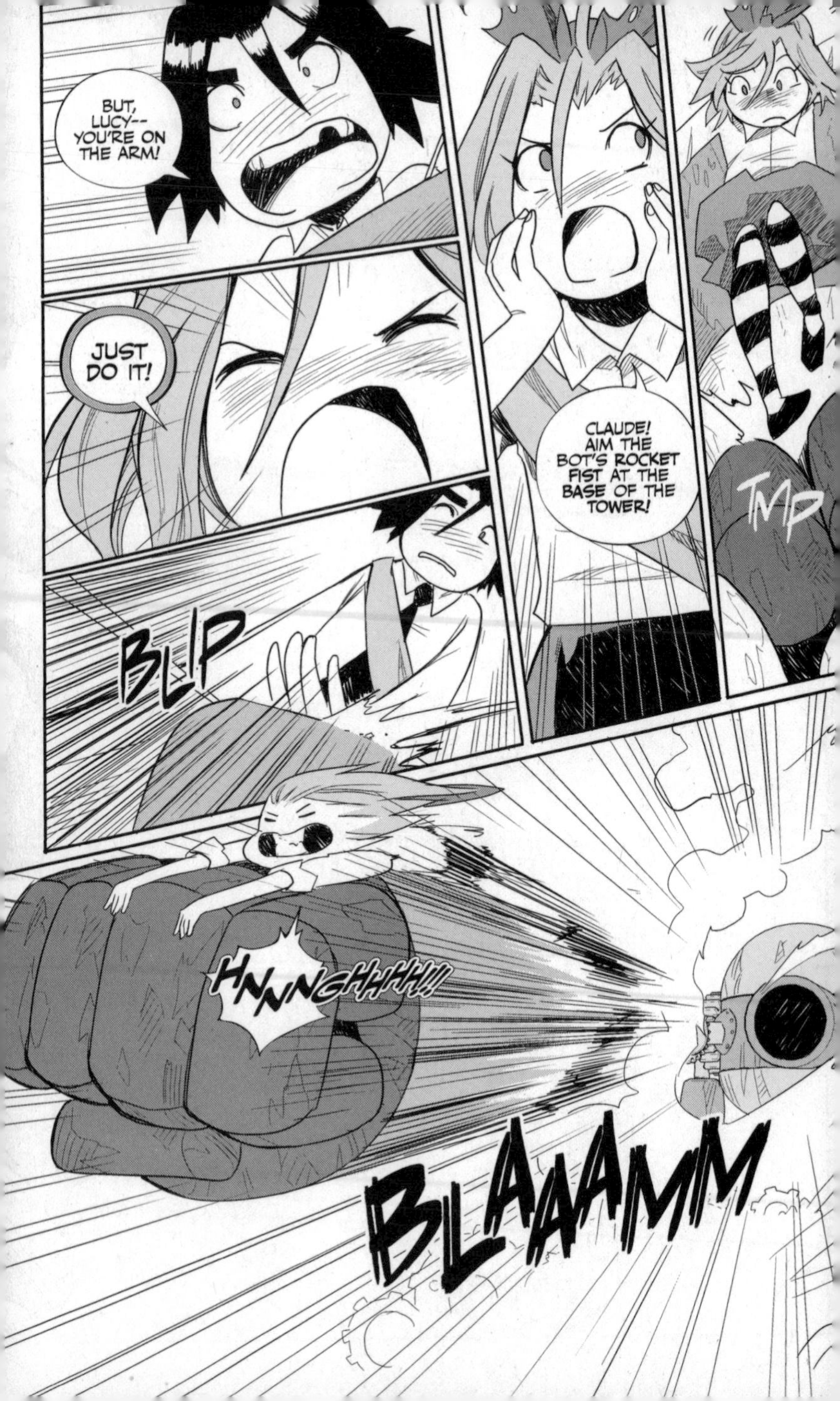

TMP
CLAUDE! AIM THE BOT'S ROCKET FIST AT THE BASE OF THE TOWER!
BUT, LUCY-- YOU'RE ON THE ARM!
JUST DO IT!
BLIP
HNNNGHHHH!!
BLAAAMM

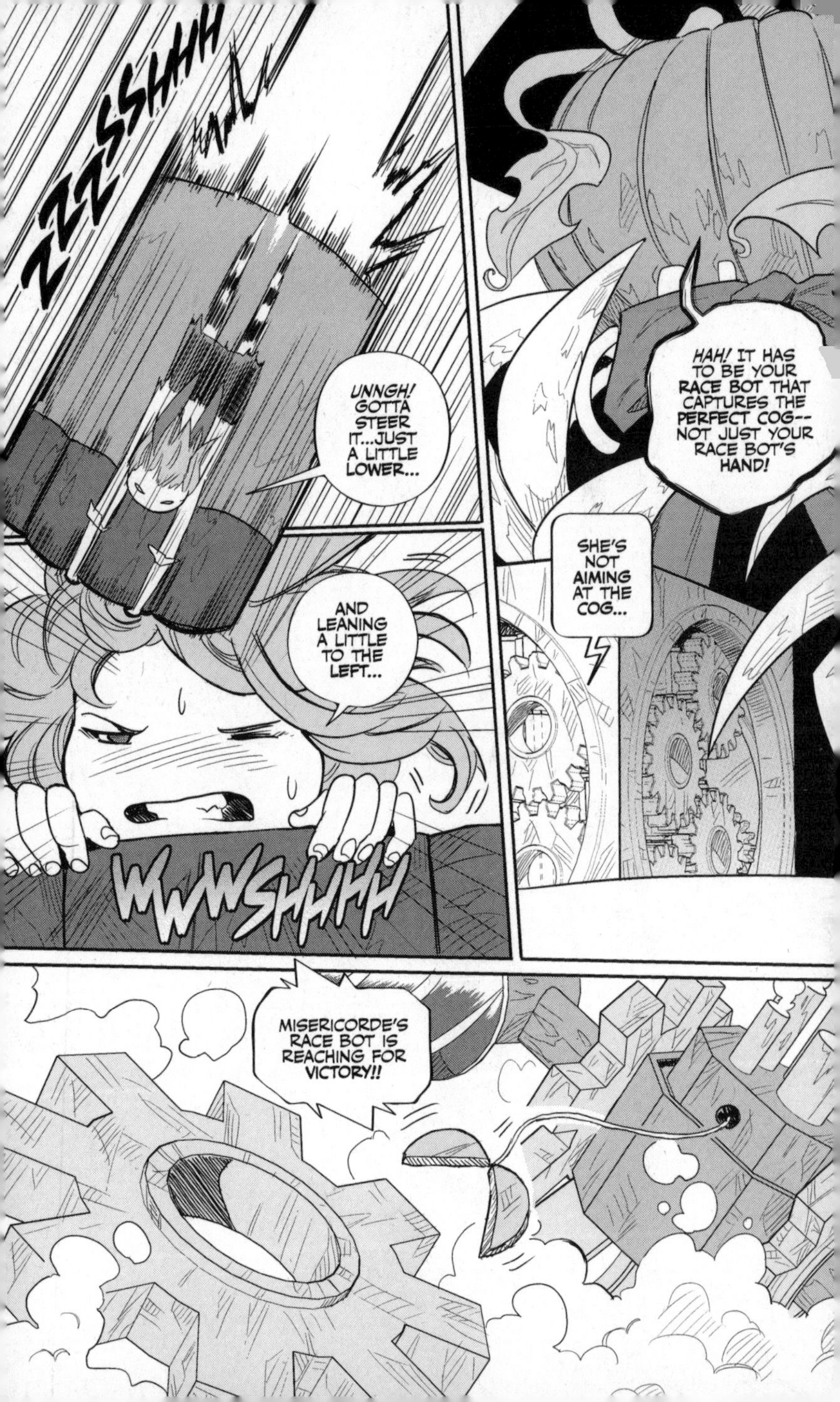
HAH! IT HAS TO BE YOUR RACE BOT THAT CAPTURES THE PERFECT COG-- NOT JUST YOUR RACE BOT'S HAND!
SHE'S NOT AIMING AT THE COG...
ZZZSSHHH
UNNGH! GOTTA STEER IT...JUST A LITTLE LOWER...
AND LEANING A LITTLE TO THE LEFT...
WWWSHHHH
MISERICORDE'S RACE BOT IS REACHING FOR VICTORY!!

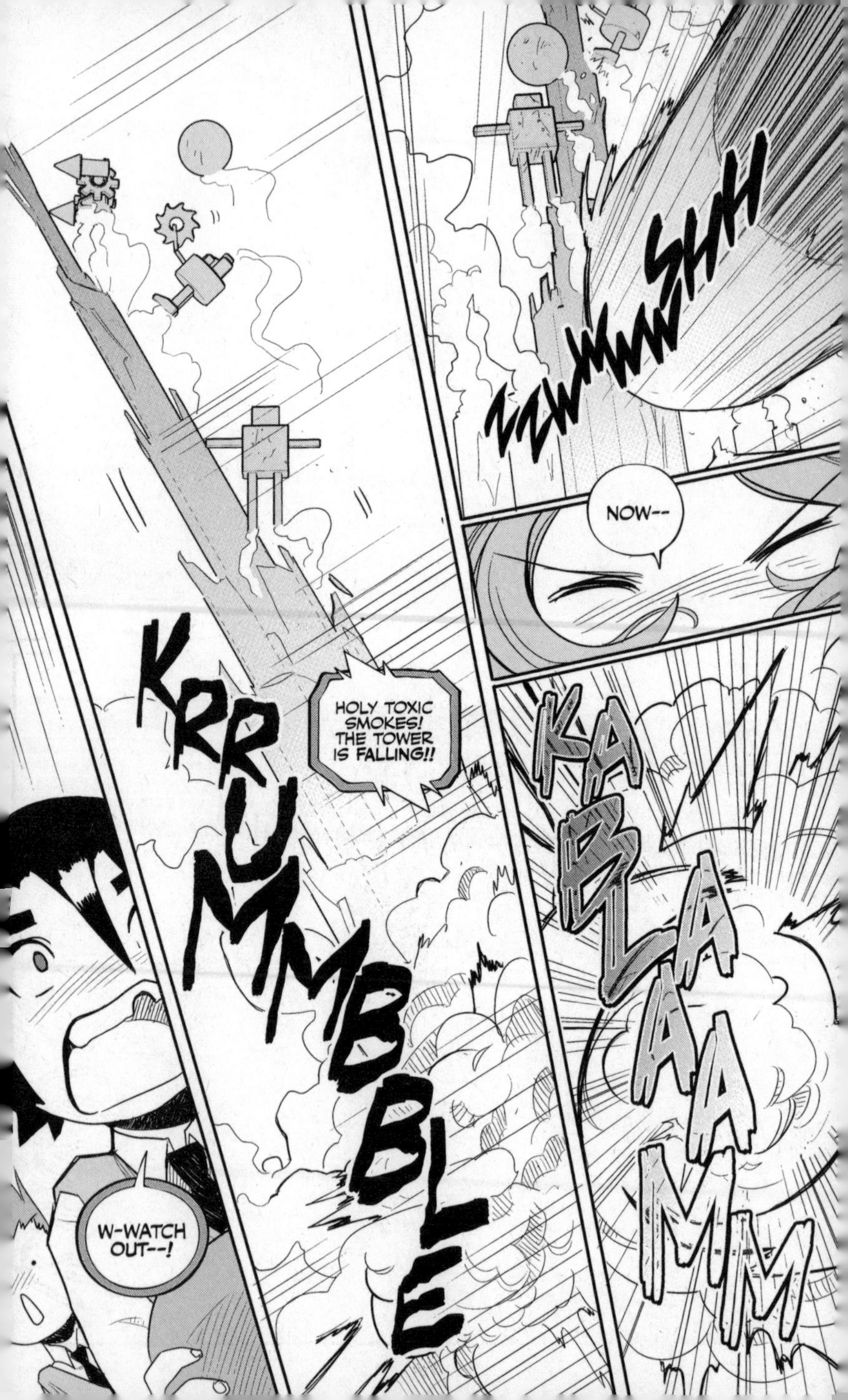
ZZWWWWSHH
NOW--
KABLAAAMM
KRRUMMBBLE
HOLY TOXIC SMOKES! THE TOWER IS FALLING!!
W-WATCH OUT--!

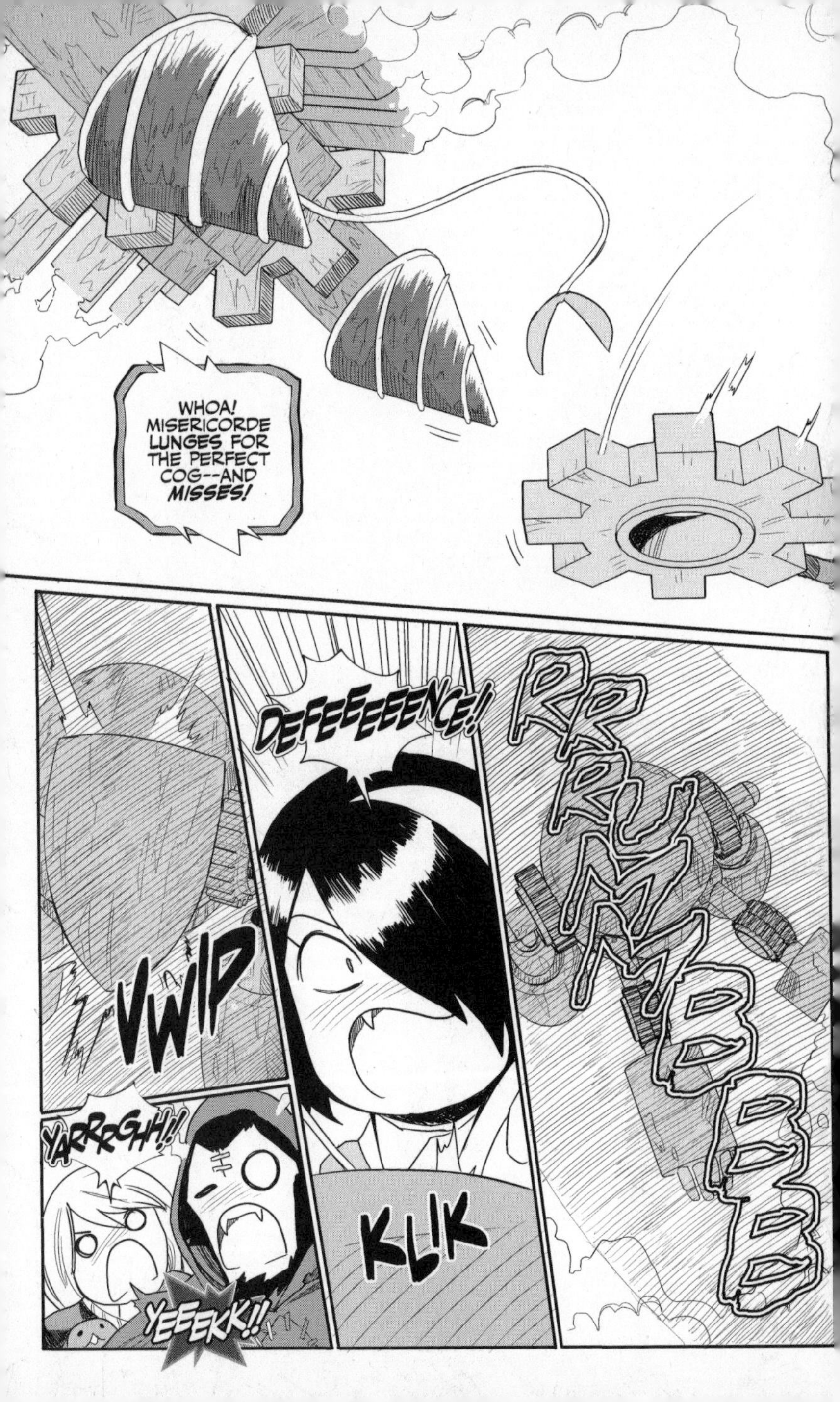
WHOA! MISERICORDE LUNGES FOR THE PERFECT COG--AND MISSES!
RRRUMMBBB
DEFEEEEEENCE!
KLIK
VWIP
YARRRGHH!!
YEEEKK!!

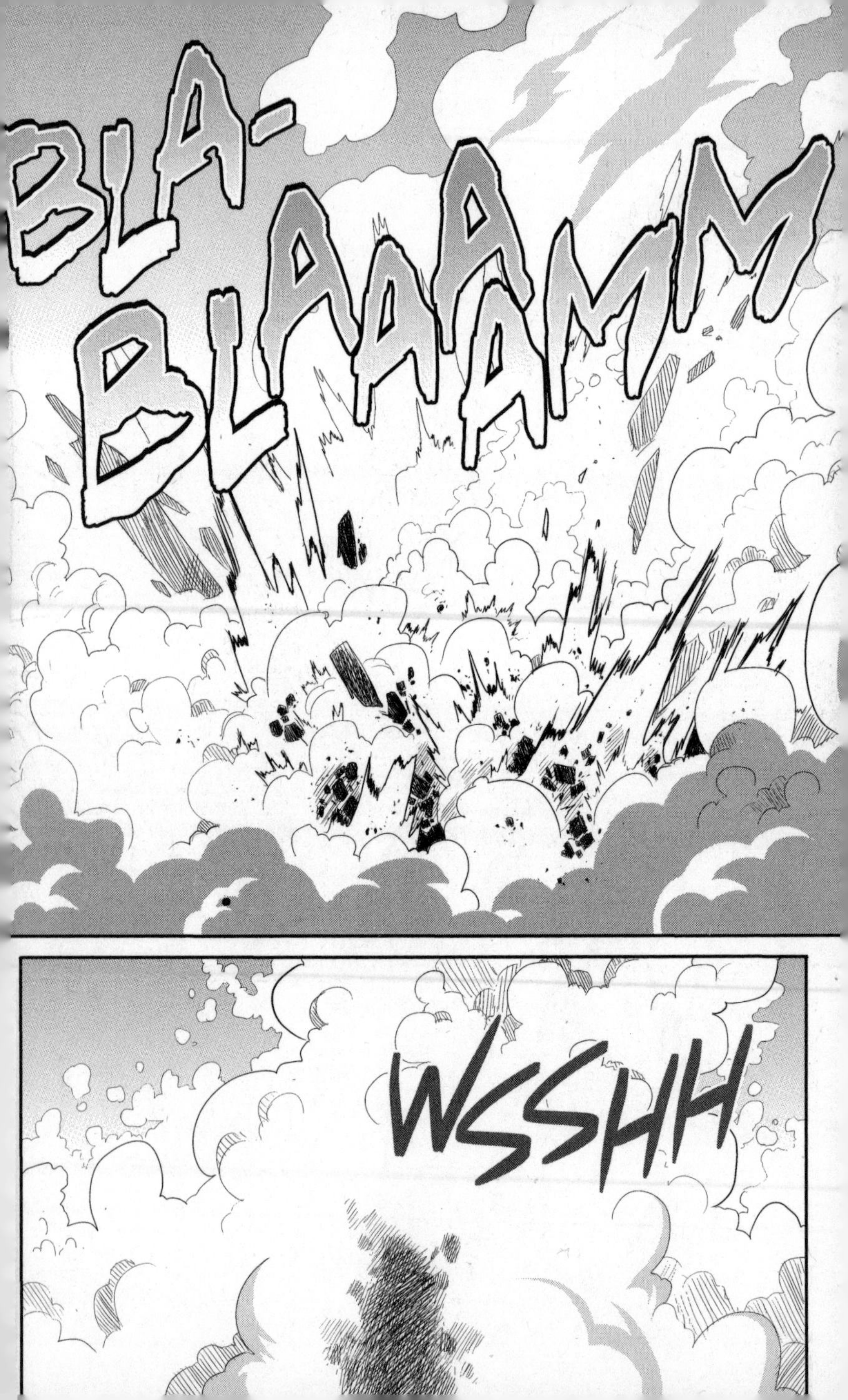
BLA-BLAAAMM
WSSHH

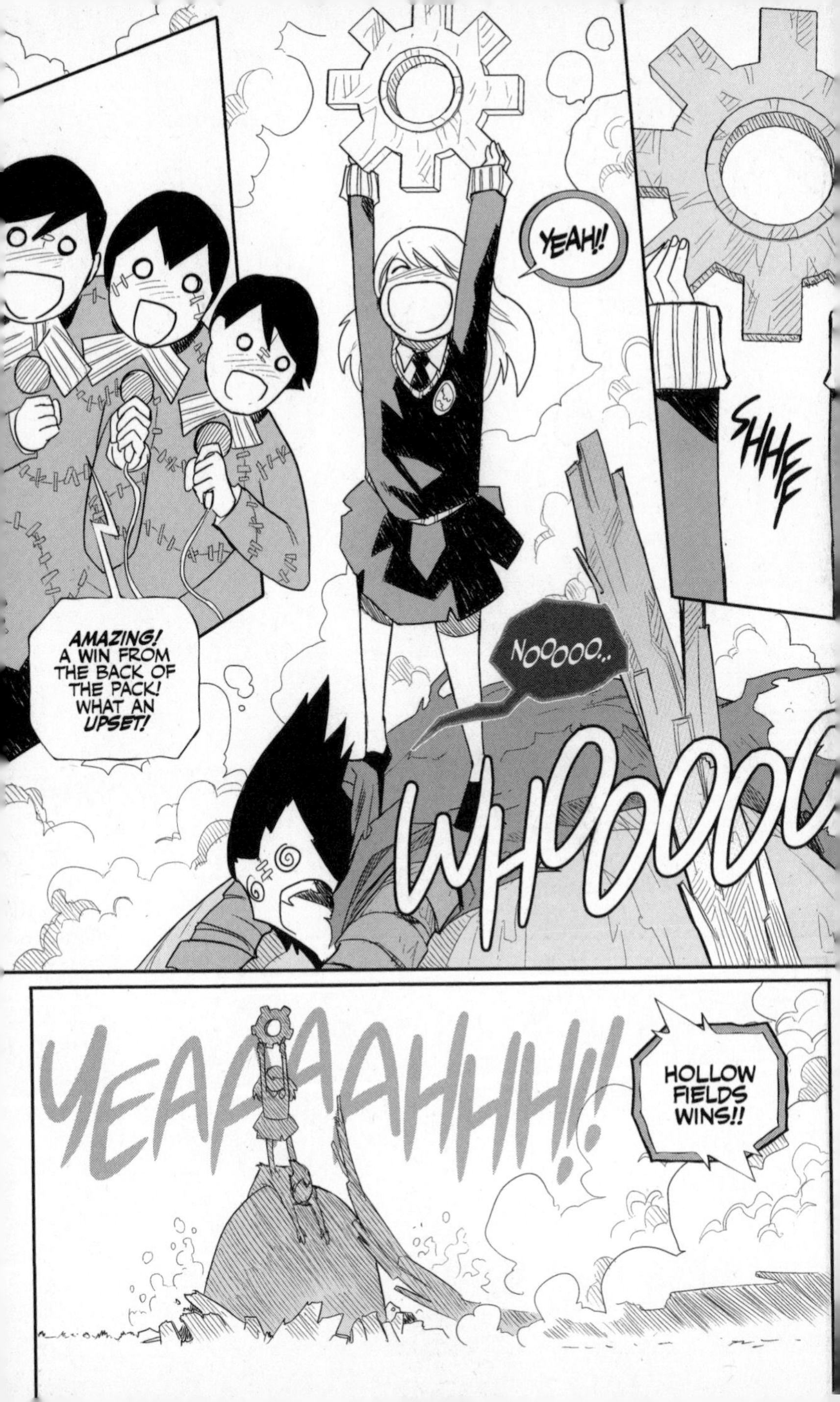
SHHEE
YEAH!!
NOOOOO...
WHOOOOO
AMAZING! A WIN FROM THE BACK OF THE PACK! WHAT AN UPSET!
HOLLOW FIELDS WINS!!
YEAAAAHHH!!

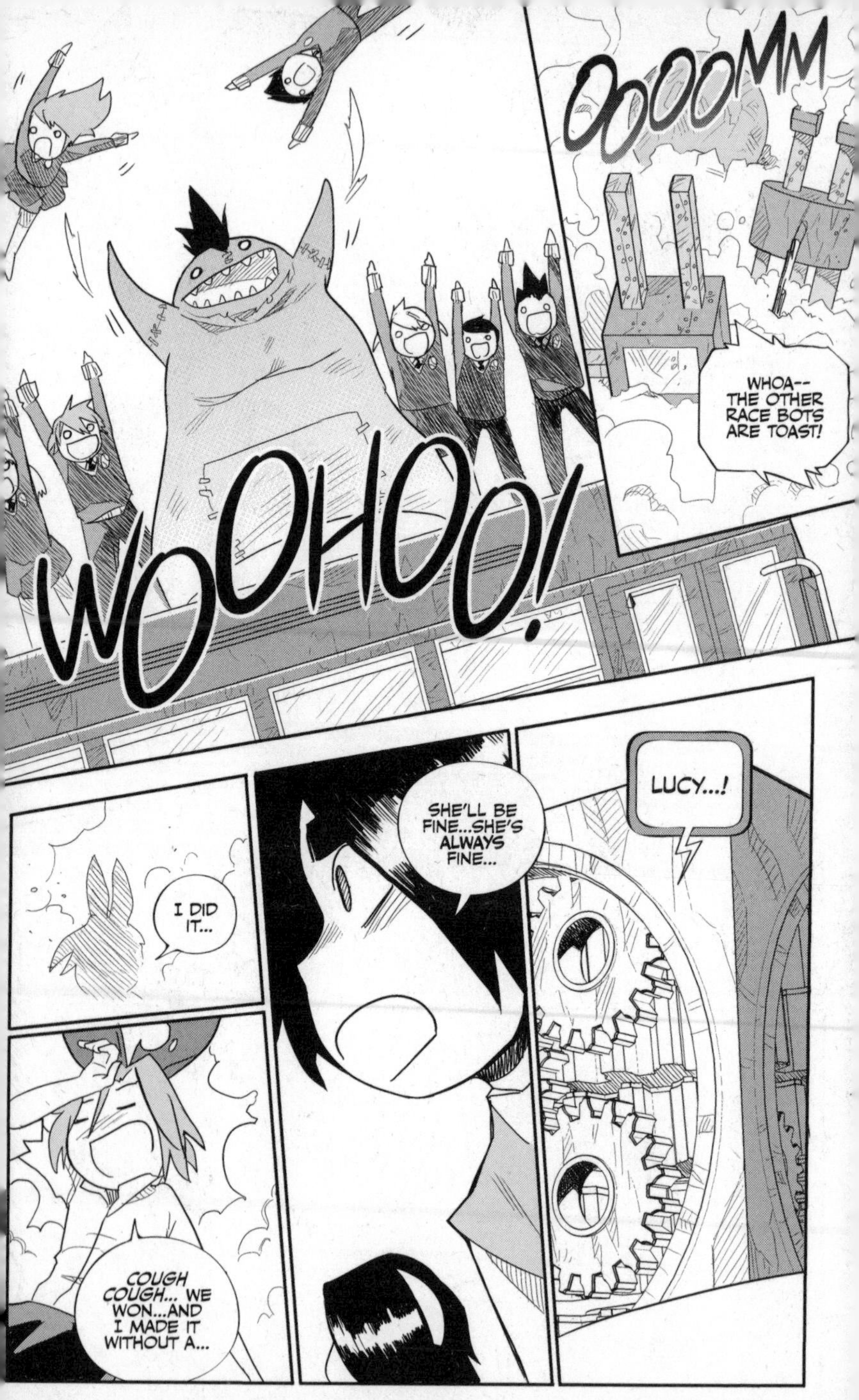
OOOOMM
WHOA-- THE OTHER RACE BOTS ARE TOAST!
WOOHOO!
LUCY...!
SHE'LL BE FINE...SHE'S ALWAYS FINE...
I DID IT...
COUGH COUGH... WE WON...AND I MADE IT WITHOUT A...

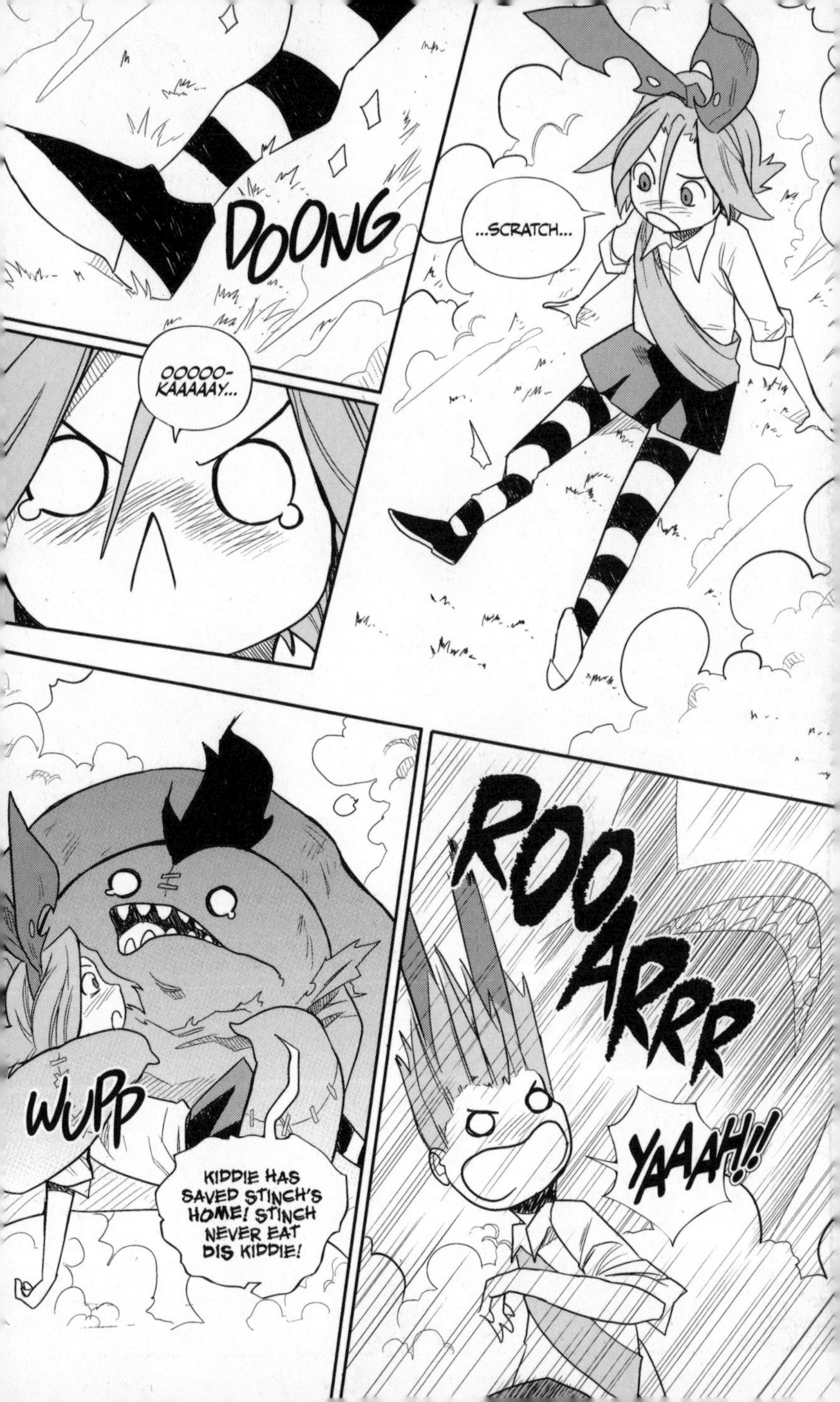
...SCRATCH...
DOONG
OOOOO-KAAAAAY...
ROOARRR
YAAAH!!
WUPP
KIDDIE HAS SAVED STINCH'S HOME! STINCH NEVER EAT DIS KIDDIE!

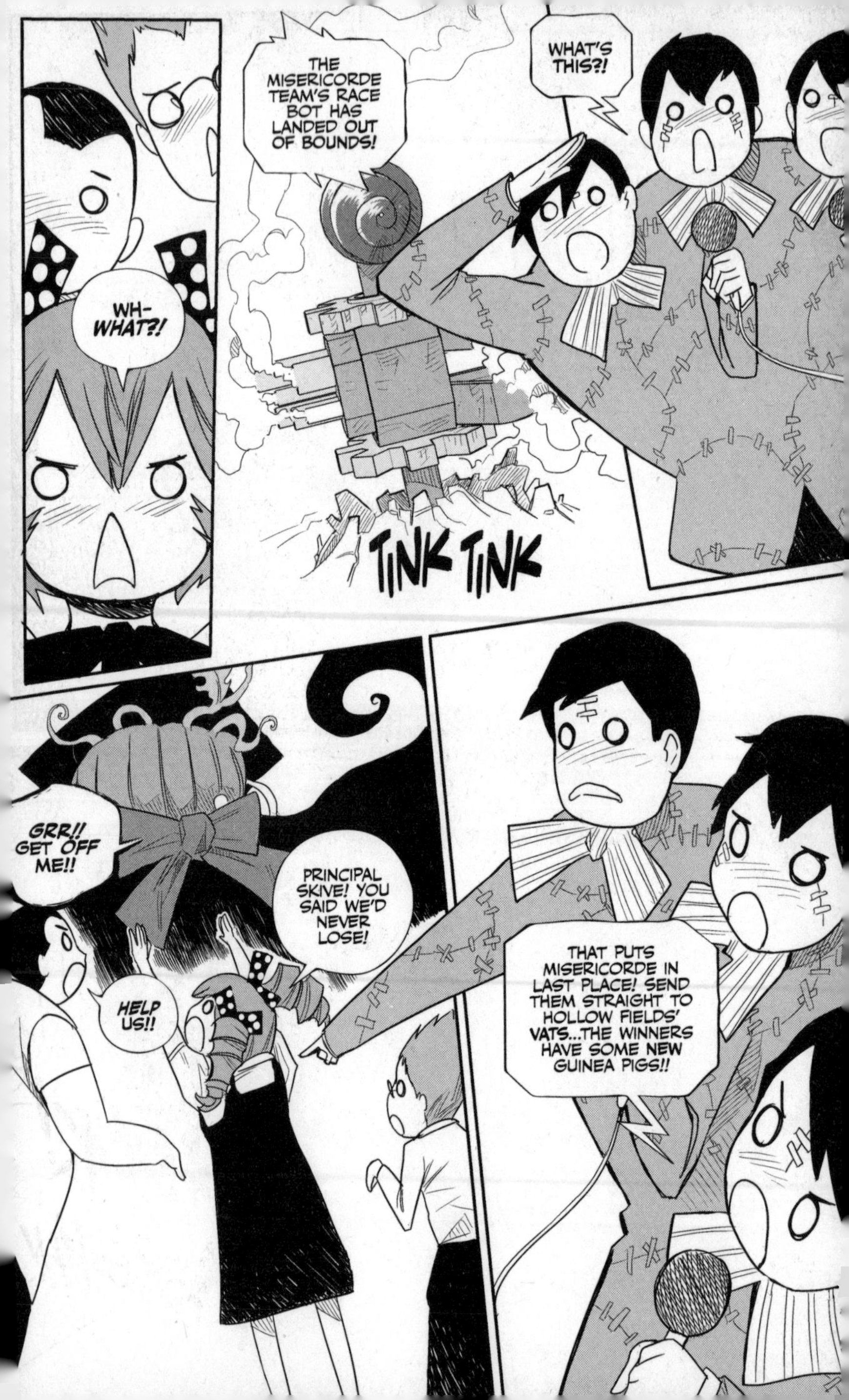
WHAT'S THIS?!
THE MISERICORDE TEAM'S RACE BOT HAS LANDED OUT OF BOUNDS!
TINK TINK
WH-WHAT?!
THAT PUTS MISERICORDE IN LAST PLACE! SEND THEM STRAIGHT TO HOLLOW FIELDS' VATS...THE WINNERS HAVE SOME NEW GUINEA PIGS!!
PRINCIPAL SKIVE! YOU SAID WE'D NEVER LOSE!
GRR!! GET OFF ME!!
HELP US!!

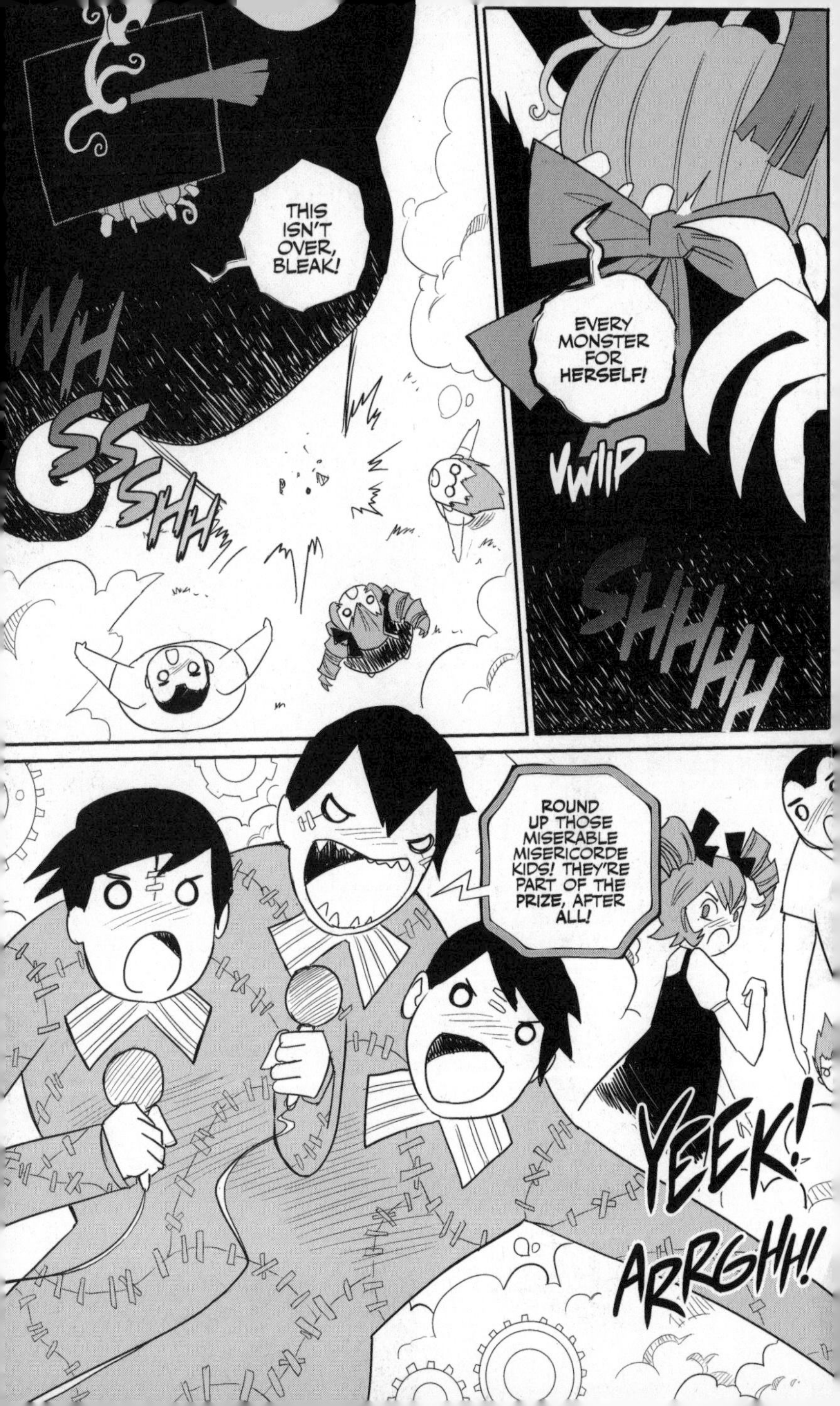

EVERY MONSTER FOR HERSELF!
VWIIP
SHHHHH
THIS ISN'T OVER, BLEAK!
WHSSSHH
ROUND UP THOSE MISERABLE MISERICORDE KIDS! THEY'RE PART OF THE PRIZE, AFTER ALL!
YEEK!
ARRGHH!

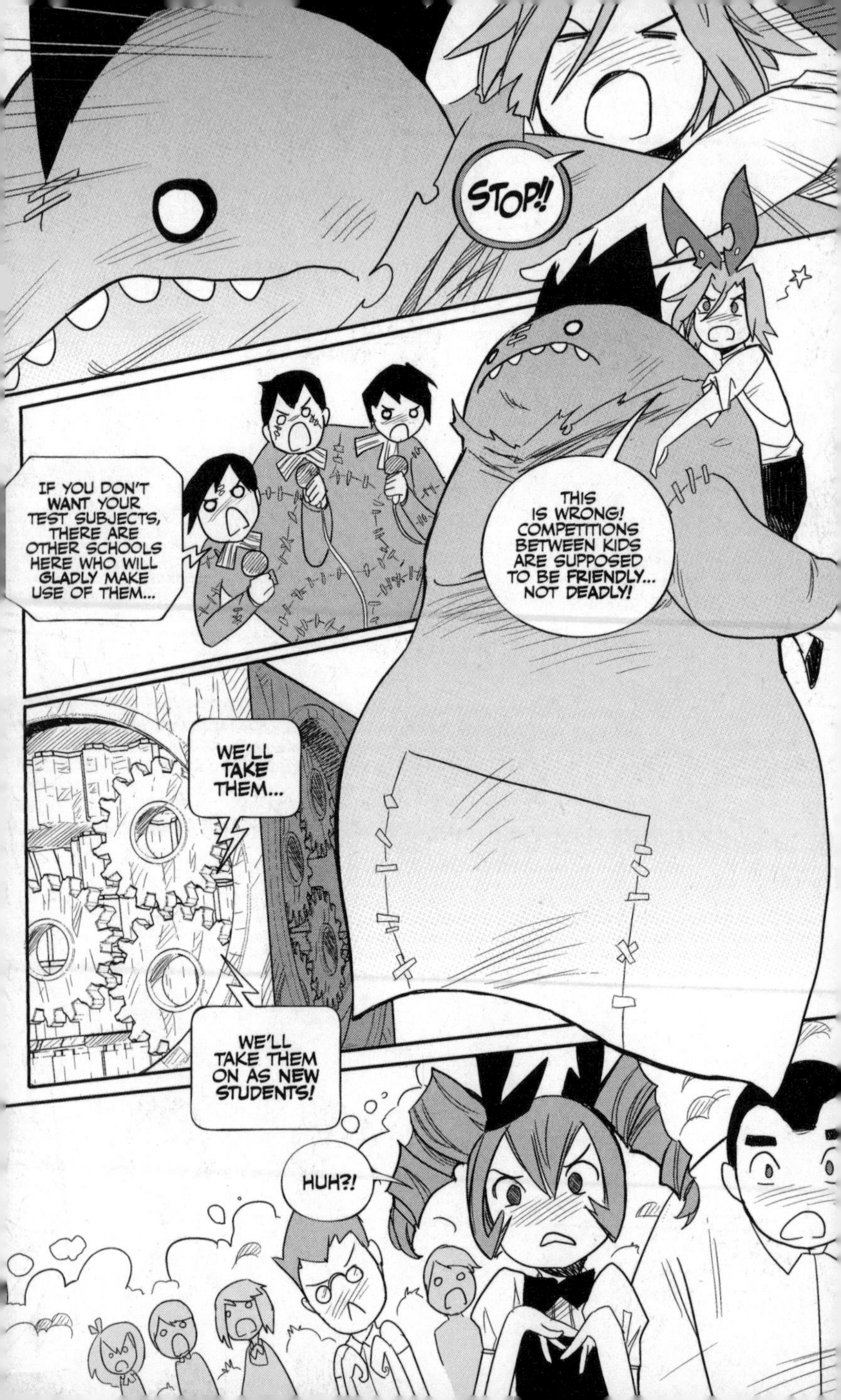
STOP!!
THIS IS WRONG! COMPETITIONS BETWEEN KIDS ARE SUPPOSED TO BE FRIENDLY... NOT DEADLY!
IF YOU DON'T WANT YOUR TEST SUBJECTS, THERE ARE OTHER SCHOOLS HERE WHO WILL GLADLY MAKE USE OF THEM...
WE'LL TAKE THEM...
WE'LL TAKE THEM ON AS NEW STUDENTS!
HUH?!

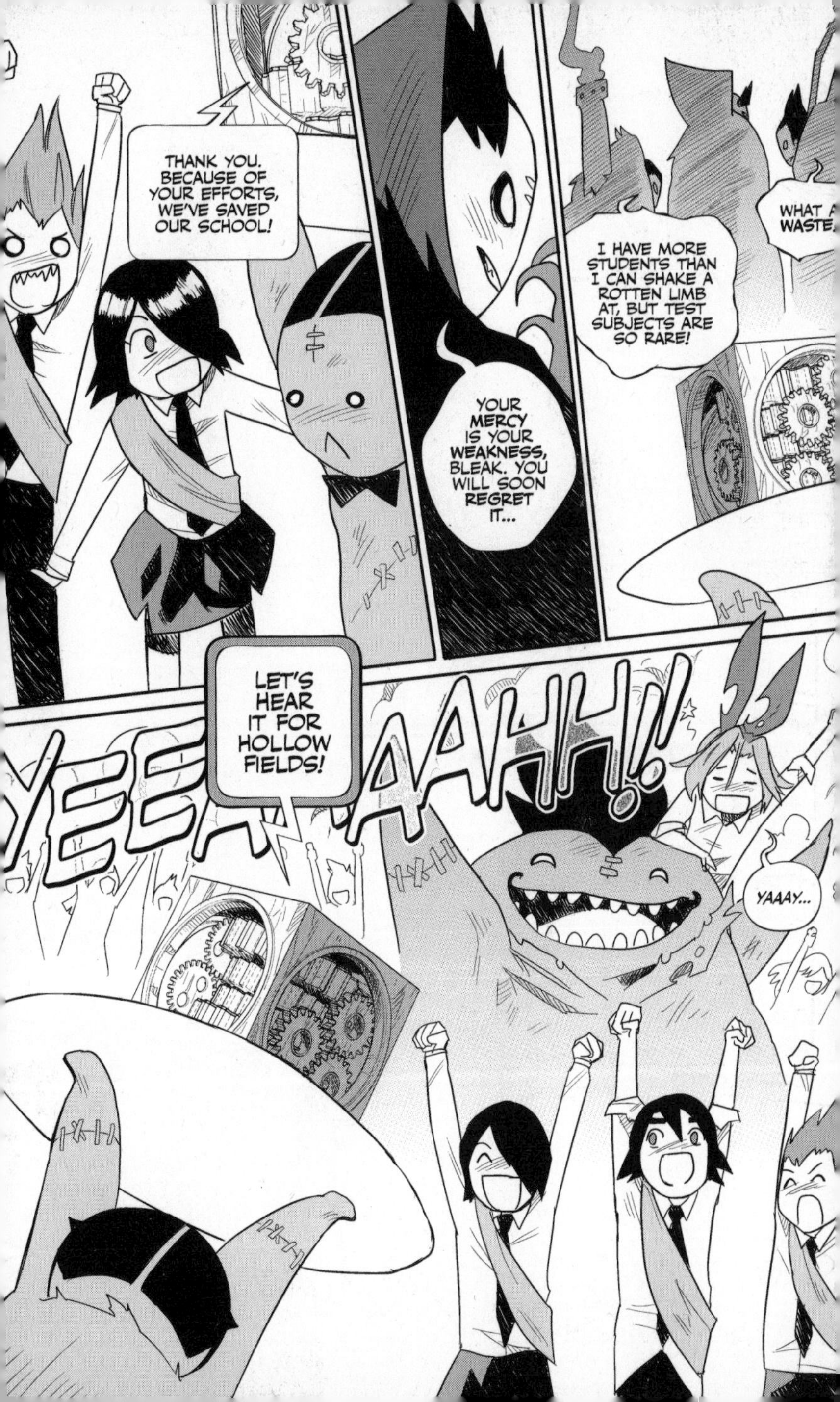
WHAT A WASTE.
I HAVE MORE STUDENTS THAN I CAN SHAKE A ROTTEN LIMB AT, BUT TEST SUBJECTS ARE SO RARE!
YOUR MERCY IS YOUR WEAKNESS, BLEAK. YOU WILL SOON REGRET IT...
THANK YOU. BECAUSE OF YOUR EFFORTS, WE'VE SAVED OUR SCHOOL!
LET'S HEAR IT FOR HOLLOW FIELDS!
YEEAAHH!!
YAAAY...

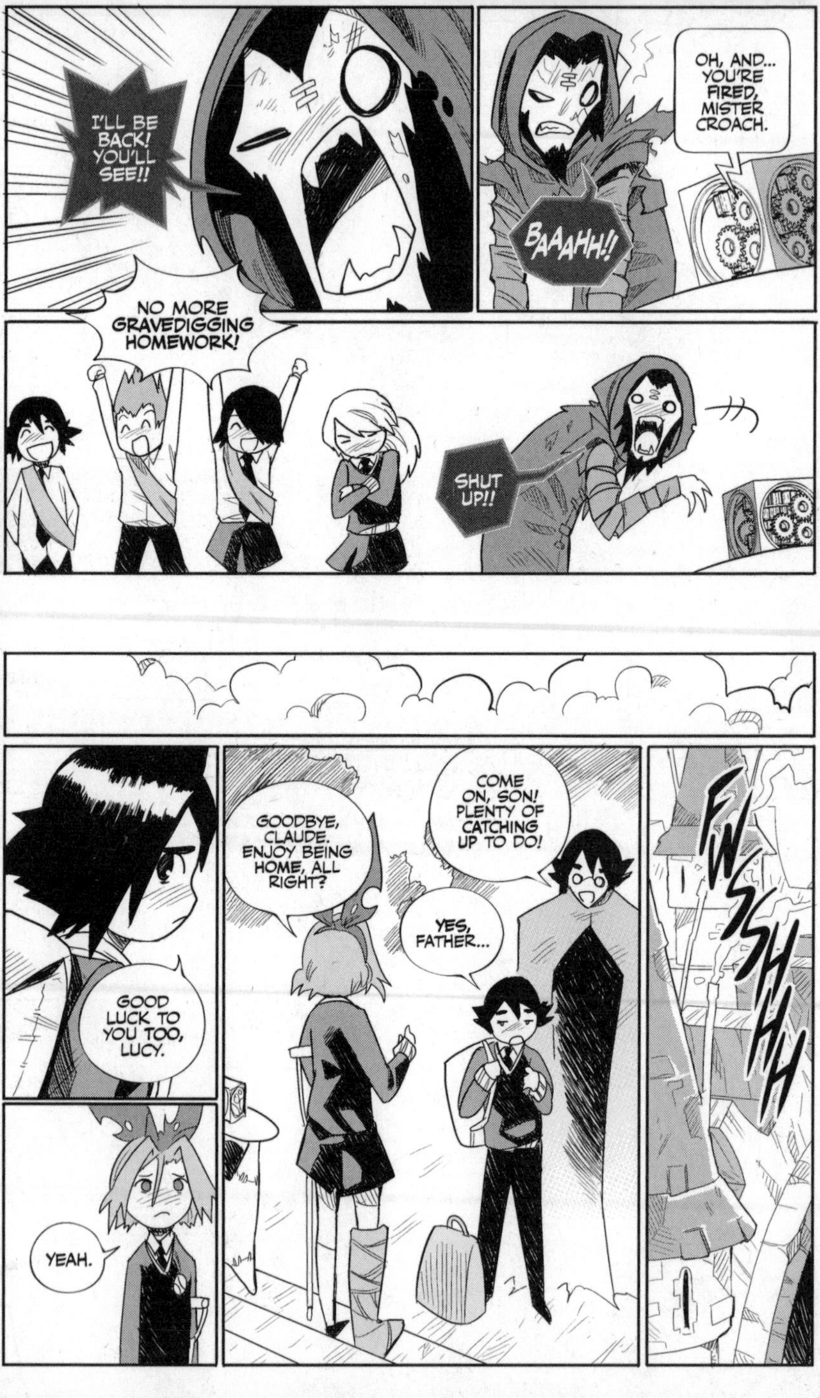
OH, AND... YOU'RE FIRED, MISTER CROACH.
BAAAHH!!
I'LL BE BACK! YOU'LL SEE!!
NO MORE GRAVEDIGGING HOMEWORK!
SHUT UP!!
FWSHHH
COME ON, SON! PLENTY OF CATCHING UP TO DO!
GOODBYE, CLAUDE. ENJOY BEING HOME, ALL RIGHT?
YES, FATHER...
GOOD LUCK TO YOU TOO, LUCY.
YEAH.

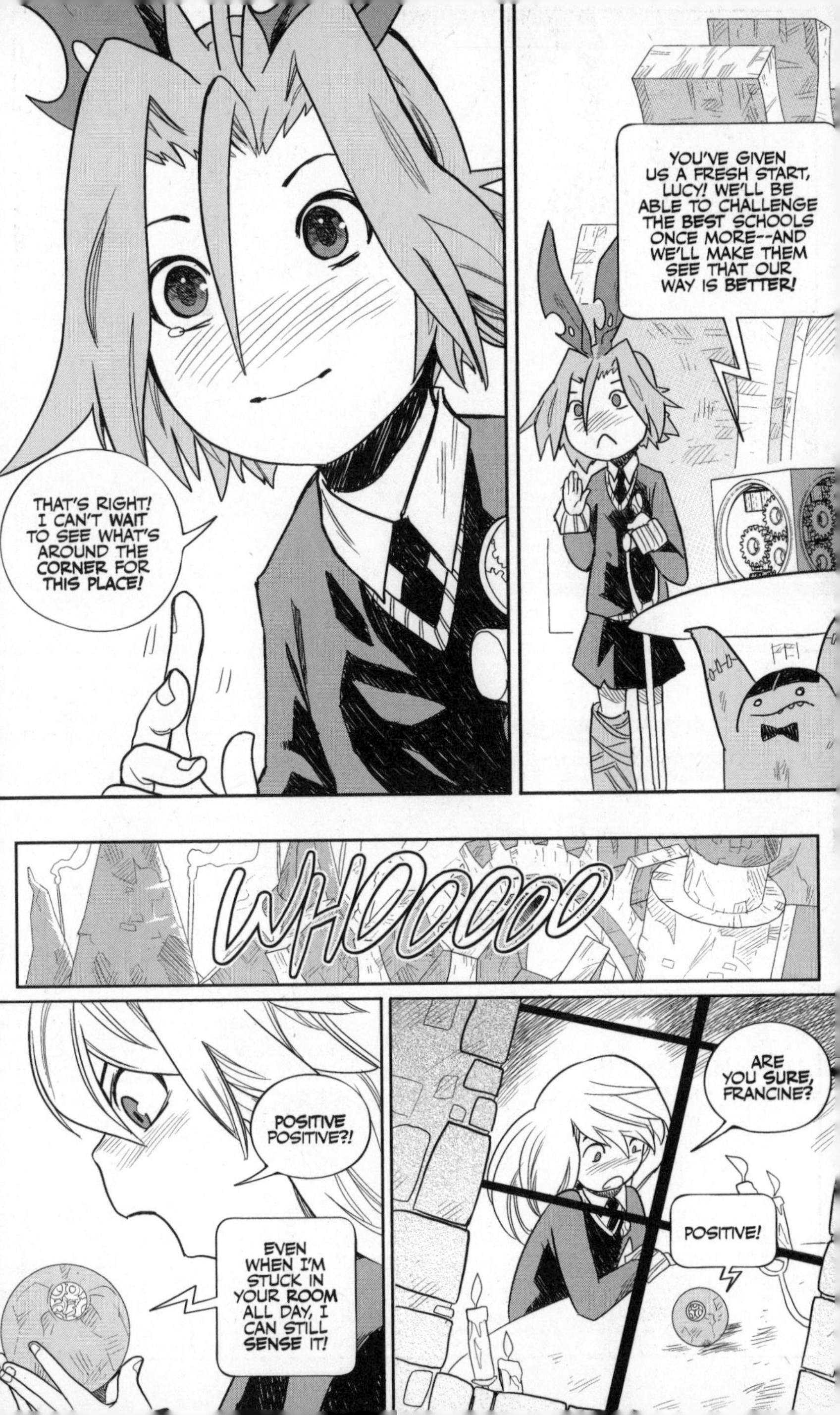
YOU'VE GIVEN US A FRESH START, LUCY! WE'LL BE ABLE TO CHALLENGE THE BEST SCHOOLS ONCE MORE--AND WE'LL MAKE THEM SEE THAT OUR WAY IS BETTER!
THAT'S RIGHT! I CAN'T WAIT TO SEE WHAT'S AROUND THE CORNER FOR THIS PLACE!
WHOOOOOO
ARE YOU SURE, FRANCINE?
POSITIVE!
POSITIVE POSITIVE?!
EVEN WHEN I'M STUCK IN YOUR ROOM ALL DAY, I CAN STILL SENSE IT!

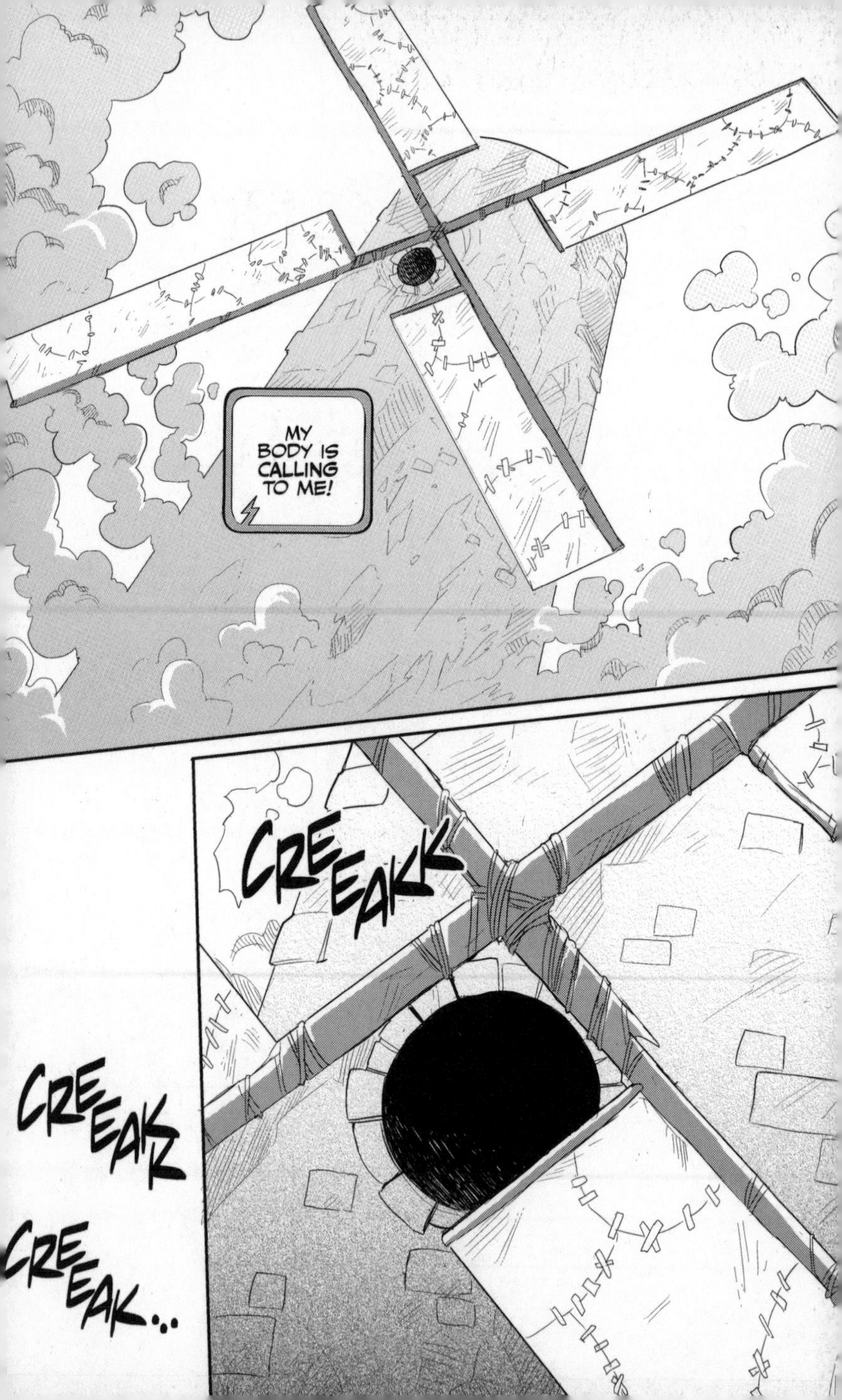
MY BODY IS CALLING TO ME!
CREEAKK
CREEAKK
CREEAK...

CHARACTER SKETCHES

• LUCY •

After the events in the third volume, Lucy has returned a little older, slightly wiser, but just as good-hearted.

• MISERICORDE •

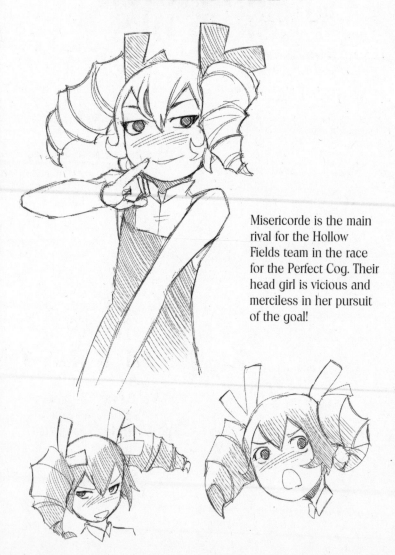

Misericorde is the main rival for the Hollow Fields team in the race for the Perfect Cog. Their head girl is vicious and merciless in her pursuit of the goal!

MISTER • CROACH •

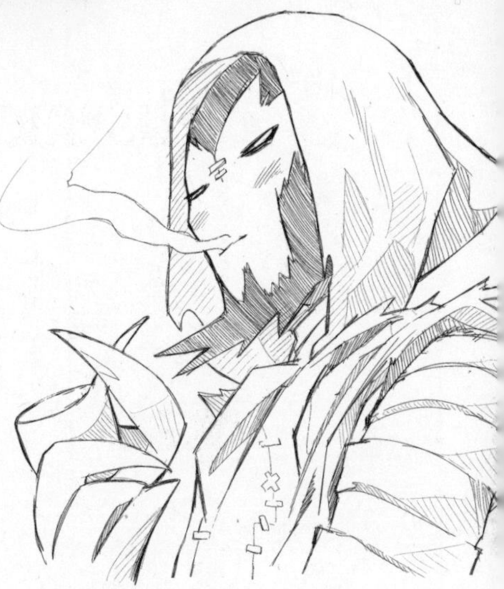

Croach comes back with a new scheme to get what he wants. He's nothing if not persistent in his pursuit of evil—and, of course, a new body...

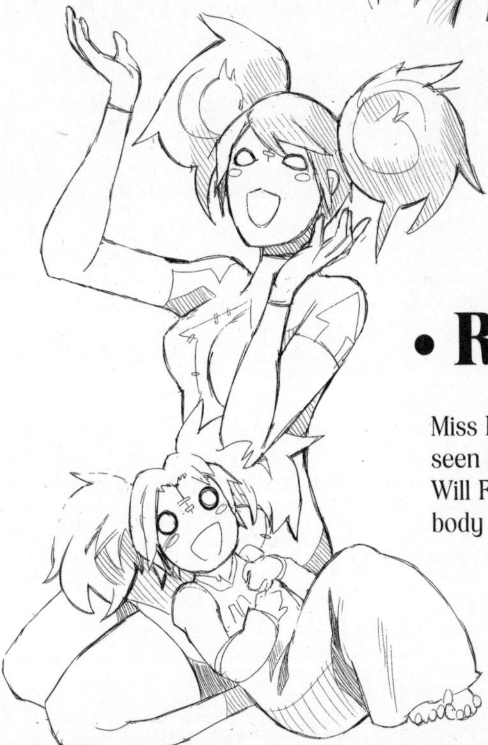

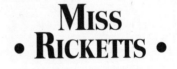

MISS • RICKETTS •

Miss Ricketts hasn't been seen since volume three. Will Francine ever get her body back?

Hollow Fields

Claude's Homework

MISTER CROACH'S GRAVE-DIGGING CLASS...
DIG FASTER, WHELPS! IN MY CLASS, YOU'RE EXPECTED TO WORK!
YOU! SNOW! WHERE IS THAT SNOTGRUB McGINTY?!
WE HAVEN'T SEEN HIM, MISTER CROACH!
I'M HERE, SIR!
HO HO!
YOUR EXCUSE FOR TARDINESS BETTER BE GOOD, McSQUINTY!
S...SOMEONE... SOMEONE'S BEEN STEALING MY GRAVEDIGGING HOMEWORK!

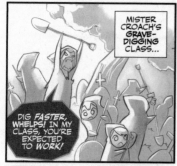

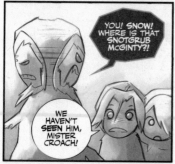

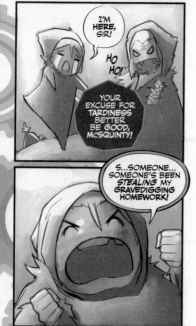

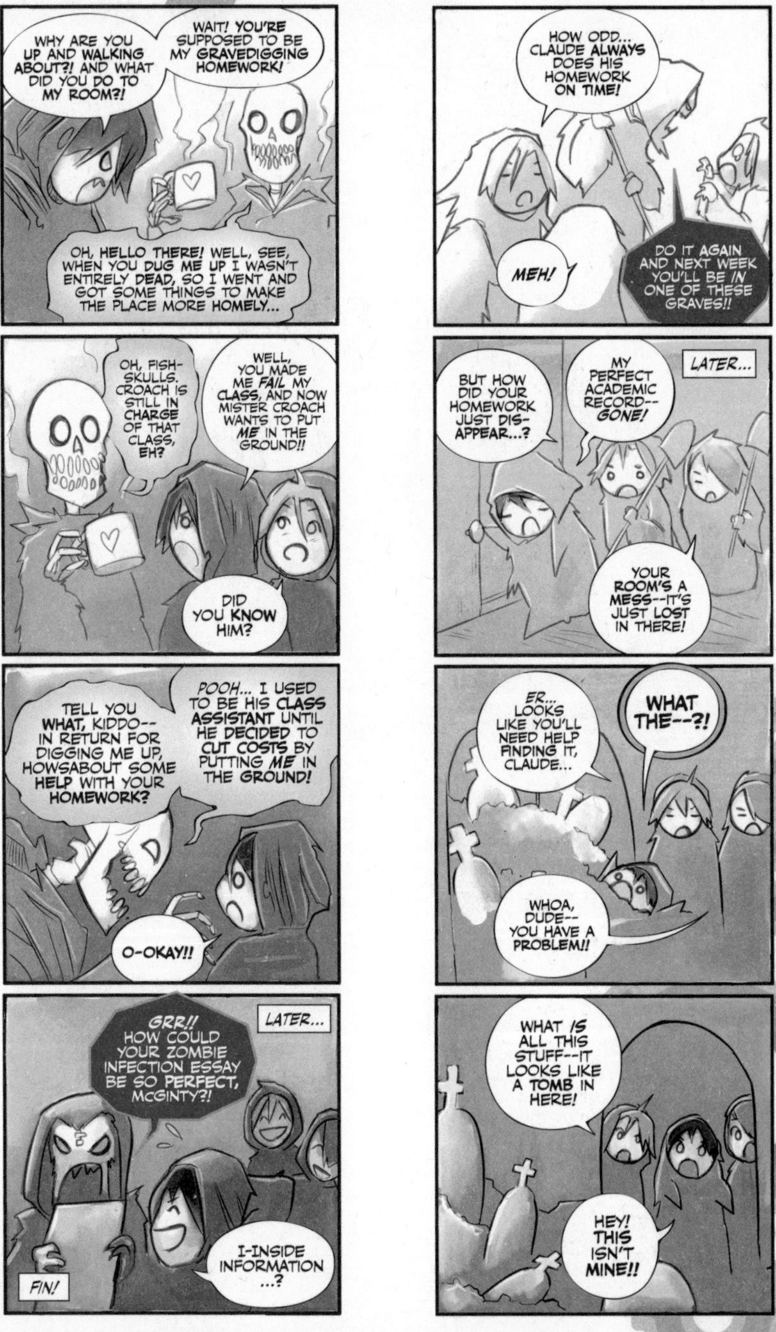
HOW ODD... CLAUDE ALWAYS DOES HIS HOMEWORK ON TIME!
DO IT AGAIN AND NEXT WEEK YOU'LL BE IN ONE OF THESE GRAVES!!
MEH!
LATER...
MY PERFECT ACADEMIC RECORD-- GONE!
BUT HOW DID YOUR HOMEWORK JUST DIS-APPEAR...?
YOUR ROOM'S A MESS--IT'S JUST LOST IN THERE!
WHAT THE--?!
ER... LOOKS LIKE YOU'LL NEED HELP FINDING IT, CLAUDE...
WHOA, DUDE-- YOU HAVE A PROBLEM!!
WHAT IS ALL THIS STUFF--IT LOOKS LIKE A TOMB IN HERE!
HEY! THIS ISN'T MINE!!
WAIT! YOU'RE SUPPOSED TO BE MY GRAVEDIGGING HOMEWORK!
WHY ARE YOU UP AND WALKING ABOUT?! AND WHAT DID YOU DO TO MY ROOM?!
OH, HELLO THERE! WELL, SEE, WHEN YOU DUG ME UP I WASN'T ENTIRELY DEAD, SO I WENT AND GOT SOME THINGS TO MAKE THE PLACE MORE HOMELY...
WELL, YOU MADE ME FAIL MY CLASS, AND NOW MISTER CROACH WANTS TO PUT ME IN THE GROUND!!
OH, FISH-SKULLS. CROACH IS STILL IN CHARGE OF THAT CLASS, EH?
DID YOU KNOW HIM?
POOH... I USED TO BE HIS CLASS ASSISTANT UNTIL HE DECIDED TO CUT COSTS BY PUTTING ME IN THE GROUND!
TELL YOU WHAT, KIDDO-- IN RETURN FOR DIGGING ME UP, HOWSABOUT SOME HELP WITH YOUR HOMEWORK?
O-OKAY!!
LATER...
GRR!! HOW COULD YOUR ZOMBIE INFECTION ESSAY BE SO PERFECT, McGINTY?!
I-INSIDE INFORMATION ...?
FIN!

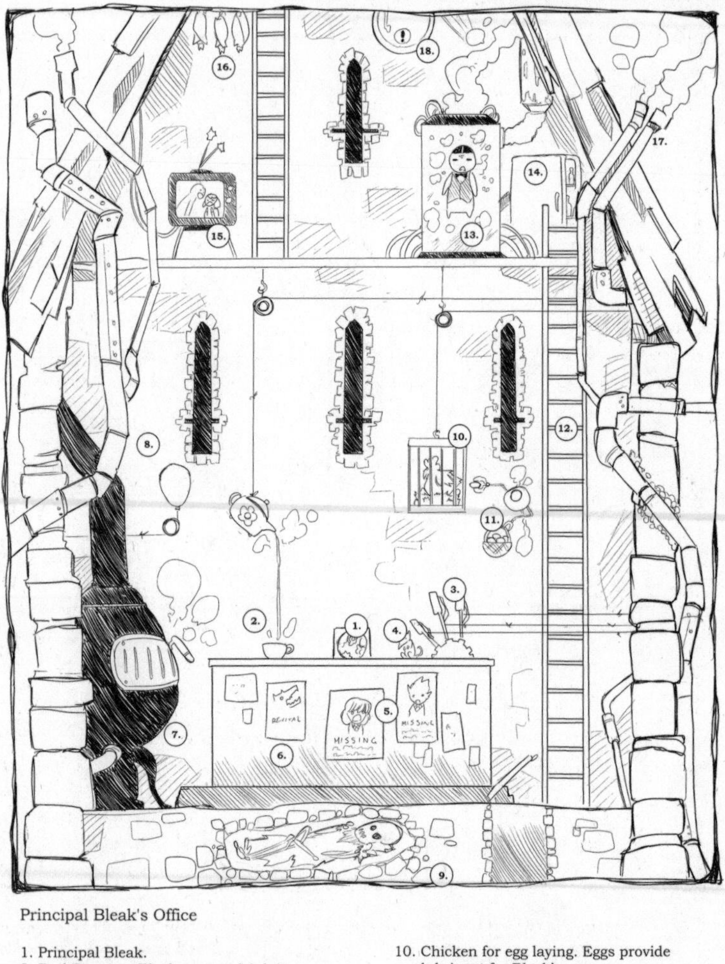
1.
2.
3.
4.
5.
6.
7.
8.
9.
10.
11.
12.
13.
14.
15.
16.
17.
18.
RECITAL
MISSING
MISSING

Principal Bleak's Office

1. Principal Bleak.
2. Earl Grey tea. Bleak cannot drink it, but the smell is invigorating.
3. Levers to work the contraptions in Bleak's office.
4. Bleak has no hands, so a trained rat does the lever-pulling grunt-work.
5. Posters of students who disappeared during experiments.
6. Werewolf howling recital poster.
7. Stove for heat. Bleak likes to make his office warm and comfy for students.
8. Simple "balloonometer" measures heat coming from stove.
9. Mummified remains of Vice Principal Hereditus, who staged a failed coup against Miss Weaver 28 years ago.
10. Chicken for egg laying. Eggs provide lubricant for Bleak's cogs.
11. Egg collection robot. Also back scratcher, can opener, and toilet brush.
12. Second floor access ladder, greased for speed of descent.
13. Mister Turtle, in his cryogenic repairator.
14. Mister Turtle's minibar, supplying him with freezing stasis and chocolate milk.
15. Soap operas. Mister Turtle won't openly admit it, but he is a hopeless romantic. He also likes films with ninjas.
16. Messenger bats. Still in the test phase.
17. Grease runoff exhaust pipes, from the kitchens below.
18. Emergency eject hatch in case of staff or student rioting.

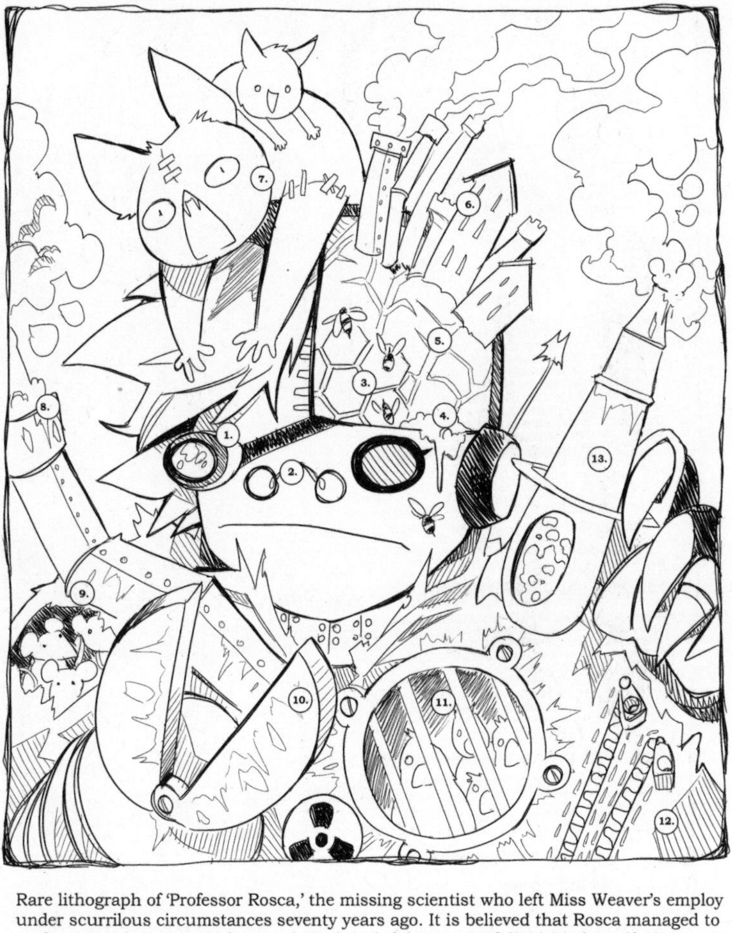
1.
2.
3.
4.
5.
6.
7.
8.
9.
10.
11.
12.
13.

Rare lithograph of 'Professor Rosca,' the missing scientist who left Miss Weaver's employ under scurrilous circumstances seventy years ago. It is believed that Rosca managed to perfect a revolutionary and excruciatingly painful process of digitizing herself. Her errant pixels are believed to be congregating around **www.clockworkhands.com.**

1. Pneumatic eye, believed to see through walls, doors, and rubber.
2. Glasses. Ironically, installation of pneumatic eye resulted in myopia.
3. Hive of beeeees.
4. Convenient honey from beeeees.
5. Assorted brainparts.
6. Small imaginary city within head. Exports include thoughts, memories, terrible ballpoint cross-sections.
7. Assorted cats.
8. Exhaust vent for artistic frustrations.
9. Mouse civilization, inhabiting robot arm, can be deployed in order to destroy enemy cheese.
10. Claw hand for pencil gripping.
11. Trapped souls which fuel super self-destruct engine in spleen.
12. Pockets which carry spare fingers.
13. Vaporizer, for rejected artwork.

FANART

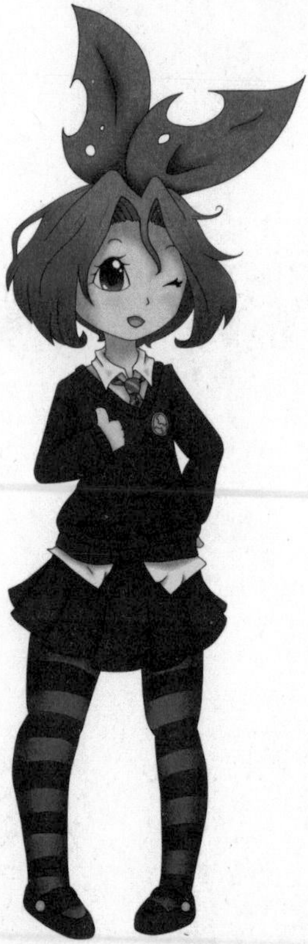

Art by Zoie K. Smith

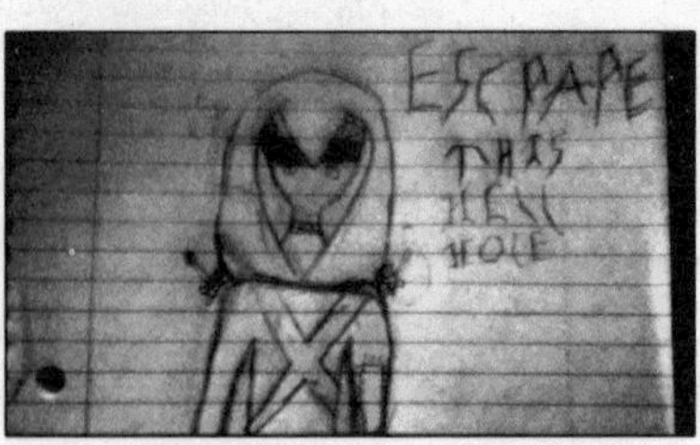
ESCAPE

Art by Paulo-Baretto-Andrade

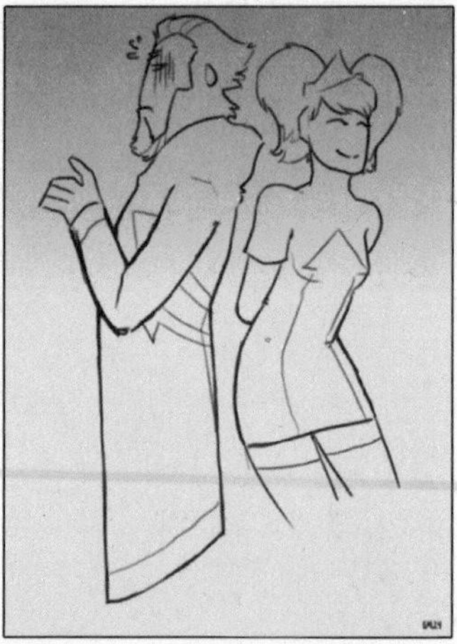

Art by masquefeir.deviantart.com

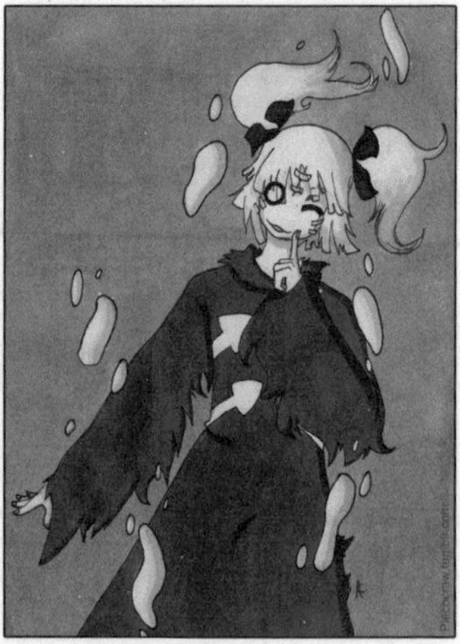

Art by Anna Cope

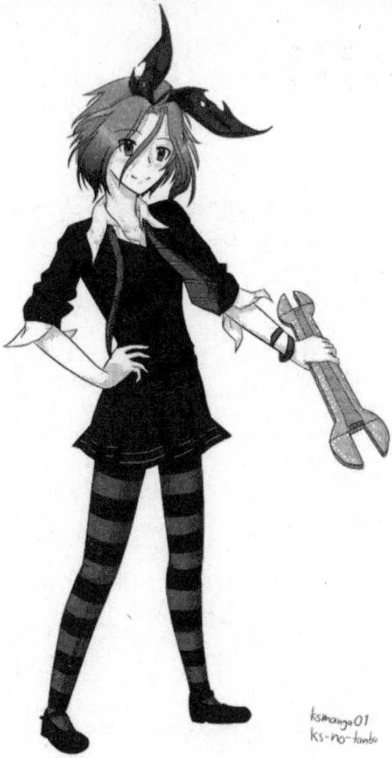
ksmanga01
ks-no-tanbu

Art by
ksmanga01.deviantart.com

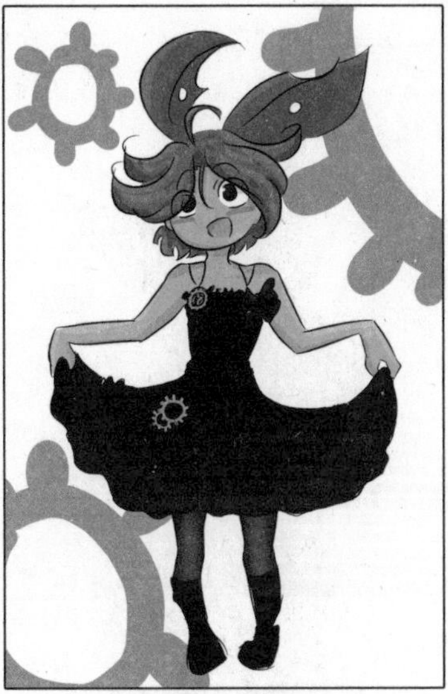

Art by Chelsea Gonzales

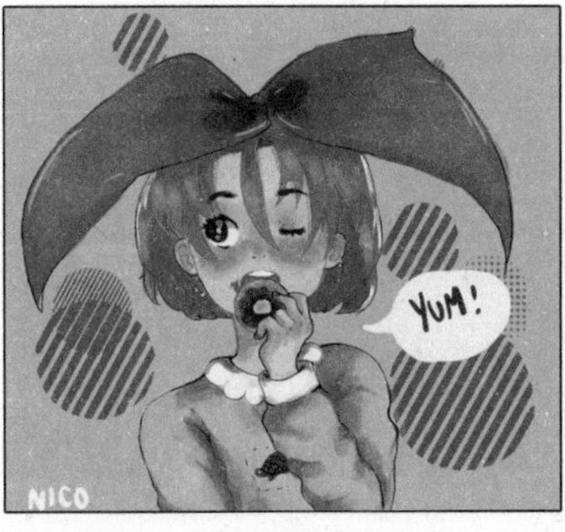
YUM!
NICO

Art by Nia Coppedge

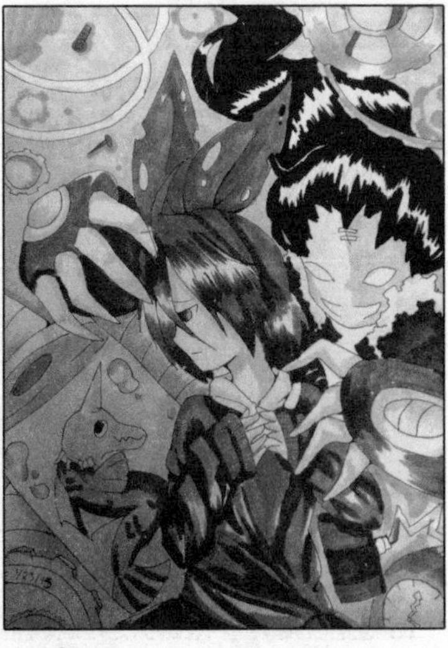

Art by
raveneevee.deviantart.com